THE LEFT AND WAR:
The British Labour Party and World War I

PROBLEMS IN EUROPEAN HISTORY:
A DOCUMENTARY COLLECTION

THE LEFT AND WAR:
The British Labour Party and World War I

EDITED BY
PETER STANSKY
Stanford University

New York
OXFORD UNIVERSITY PRESS
London   Toronto   1969

Copyright © 1969 by Oxford University Press, Inc.
Library of Congress Catalogue Card Number: 69-17241
Printed in the United States of America

FOREWORD

Problems in European History: A Documentary Collection has arisen from a collective teaching experience. The series seeks to take care of a shortcoming which the authors believe persists in college history instruction. Certainly the restricting confines of the traditional textbook have been expanded as numerous collections of "readings" have appeared. But the undergraduate still remains at a distance from the historian's workshop. A compilation of heavily edited "significant documents" does not make for the sense of contact with the past that the study of history ought to promote. And the predigested selections from contending historians, neatly arrayed on either side of "classic" controversies, do not get the student to probe the underlying evidence; in fact, these academic disputations often leave him bewildered.

The conviction that students learned little of the way in which historians actually worked prompted a group of young Harvard historians five years ago to develop a new approach. The course that resulted—Social Sciences 3: Problems in Modern European History—represented an attempt to focus intensively on a small number of problems. Each problem would involve careful analysis of a wide variety of original source material. The student could develop the skills and understanding of historical explanation. In learning to compare evidence, make and test hypotheses, and judge critically earlier accounts, he would encounter some of the problems of historical research as experienced by the working historian.

In Social Sciences 3 eight studies in historical analysis are presented in a year. Our intention here is to make these documentary collections available, not necessarily as a series except in their underlying aim, but as separate problems that can be studied individually in connection with courses in European history. Each book has been edited and introduced with that purpose in mind. Thus the student can wrestle with the problems inherent in historical writing and judgment while he studies intensively a segment of the history of the country or period being taught.

Social Sciences 3 has developed over the past four years through the efforts of our collaborators, who share in the creation of these books beyond what we can gratefully acknowledge. Individual problems were prepared or substantially recast by the respective authors, but each case study was discussed and scrutinized by the entire staff of Social Sciences 3. To all of them, to the Committee on General Education of Harvard College, which has generously given of its time and efforts, and to our students—whose criticisms and suggestions were a fundamental guideline—we extend our thanks.

Cambridge, Mass.   RICHARD BIENVENU
August 1967   JOHN F. NAYLOR

PREFACE

This book of readings first took shape as a source book for a course in Selected Topics in Modern European History, and I am extremely grateful to my colleagues in that course for the pleasure of their company and the stimulation of their ideas. I owe particular thanks for the lectures given by Abbott Gleason and Standish Meacham. I have had the considerable benefit of advice from a number of historians expert on the Labour party: A. F. Thompson, Philip Poirier, F. M. Leventhal, and John Naylor. Jane Walker has been most industrious and very cheerful in the making of this book, and for that I am most grateful. William Abrahams has given valuable editorial guidance. My greatest debt in terms of wisdom, insight, and example is to the late David Owen, and to his memory I should like to dedicate this collection.

Cambridge, Massachusetts   P.S.
July, 1968

CONTENTS

THE LEFT AND WAR:
The British Labour Party and World War I

INTRODUCTION

It is not surprising, considering the nature and the allegiances of the Liberal and Conservative parties in England in the late years of the nineteenth century, that working-class voters should have felt increasingly estranged from them. What is surprising, considering that since 1884 slightly more than half of all male workers had the vote, is not that a Labour party finally came into existence to rival the Liberal and Conservative parties, but that it should have taken as long as it did to do so. Venerating Gladstone, and by longstanding political habit, large numbers of working-class voters were drawn to the Liberal party. And many cast their lot with the party for practical reasons: they thought it closer to their interest. But as working men became more restive in the *status quo,* more conscious of their grievances and of politics as a way to rectify them, dissatisfaction with the Liberal party grew. The pattern of cooperating with the Liberals set by the so-called Lib-Lab M.P.s was not considered either a very satisfactory *pro tem* solution, or a useful strategy for future action. But what was the future to be?

It is a characteristic British irony that intellectuals of the middle class played a crucial part in the formation of the Labour party. One might begin a list of such figures with Karl Marx, who spent the last years of his life in England in the British Museum, and Frederic Engels. Marx's own involvement in the British labor movement was as an outsider, and he deplored the urge toward respectability that tended to affect English leaders on the Left.

But his daughter, Eleanor Marx, and her lover, Edward Aveling, were involved in the most radical movement of the late nineteenth century in England, the Social Democratic Federation. It is common practice to minimize the Marxist element in the British labor movement, and to point out, with a good deal of justification, that the sense of fair shares for all, of building Jerusalem in England's green and pleasant land, of restoring an older yeomen's sort of England, and the Methodist legacy of popular religion, have been significant contributing factors to the character of the labor movement. It is further pointed out that labor leaders have been practical men who shied away from anything smacking of "Continental" complications and theory. But the basic premises of the labor movement, as distinct from the trade unions, were Marxist—albeit in a very simplified way. There was a belief, shared with the Marxists, that the root causes of historical and political events were economic. There was a belief, shared with the Marxists, that the object of political power was to put into effect social and economic changes which were different from the political programs of the older parties. There was the ultimate conviction, shared with the Marxists, of the desirability of socialism and the belief that it would come about through the state taking over the means of production. Yet the most explicitly Marxist group in the labor movement, the Social Democratic Federation, established in 1881 and led by an old Etonian, H. M. Hyndman, who did not give up his top hat and frock coat, was eventually to prove to be the least successful. Patterned on the National Liberal Federation, the popular organization of the Liberals, it was intended to attract mass support, but it was too revolutionary and not reformist enough to do so. Most of the working-class radicals withdrew, leaving comparatively few middle-class socialists and Marxists in possession.

Perhaps even more than doctrine, the intellectual and emotional background for the Socialist movement had its origins in the thought of artists, critics and philosophers from the middle class. Many a future labor leader read his Ruskin, Carlyle, and William

Morris, and was influenced by them. Ruskin and Carlyle were in a number of respects reactionary and romantic in their view of the world, but they provided considerable fuel for the indignation felt at the poverty and degradation of modern industrial life; and neither was afraid of the sweeping economic and socialistic ideas that were being put forth to upset contemporary English society. Morris entered upon the political scene when he joined the Social Democratic Federation, which he quickly found uncongenial, and he went on to form a group of his own, the Socialist League. Little groups such as these seem sectarian and unimportant, yet they have been "justified by history," in that they are direct ancestors of the Labour party, and represent a crucial strand in today's England which the other, older parties failed to provide. A poet and painter, Morris called himself a communist, and believed in the thorough remaking of society. But he was more influential in making an aesthetic contribution to the socialist movement, and further developed Ruskin's idea that the enjoyment and creation of beauty were not strictly upper-class privileges. He designed wallpapers, textiles, furniture—whatever might make everyday life more agreeable and beautiful, and something of this idealism can be recognized in the thinking of the English Left. Like Ruskin and Carlyle, he has an undeniable place in the genealogy of the Labour party.

So too do Beatrice and Sidney Webb, as commanding figures in the Fabian Society. The Society originated in a rather far-out Victorian enclave, not far from the lunatic fringe, known as the Fellowship of the New Life, which had one elderly retired workman in its membership in order to demonstrate its social range. In 1884 there was a split in the Fellowship as to whether it should put ethical or economic questions first. Those who favored ethics wandered off toward the misty vale of theosophy. But those who favored economics became tough and hard-headed, became, in fact, the Fabian Society, taking their name from the Roman general Fabius, who believed in biding his time, then striking hard. But the Fabians were a good deal less revolution-minded than this might suggest, and were committed to a concept of gradualism, a program of working slowly and continuously toward their aims of improving society. They felt that, on the whole, the workers were not capable of creating a better world for themselves, and so, in the classic manner of the do-gooder, they set about creating a better world for them. George Bernard Shaw—at that time a music critic and unsuccessful novelist and not yet the successful playwright he was soon to become—was another of the Fabians, and the impatient, benevolent attitude of the Society toward the natural members and leaders of any sort of working-class party is summed up in a remark of his in the 1890's. He had gone to the effort of doing a lecture tour among the workers of Lancashire. Upon his return to London he remarked, "The men there need a thorough rousing. They are slaves through and through, standing up with a certain air of sturdiness for their rights as inferiors."

The Fabians would work with anyone whom they thought would help their program—an excess of English expediency which at times made them appear unprincipled. This was particularly so when many of them took a pro-government stand in the Boer War, contending that little countries such as the Orange Free State and the Transvaal did not make rational economic or political sense. Or again, when they co-operated with the Conservatives on the 1902 Education Bill, in full disregard of Liberal, Non-Conformist, or labor sentiment. But generally, the Fabians, like most other people then on the Left, were "natural" Liberals, and they too grew disillusioned with the party. Especially this was so during the Liberal administration of 1892–95, when the Liberals failed to forestall a labor break-away by a timely response to working-class demands. The Liberals had been held back from such a response for several reasons: they had only a precarious majority of forty in the House of Commons; the House of Lords was dominated by the Tories; Gladstone, as Prime Minister and leader of the party, was determined to push for Irish Home Rule at the expense of all other issues. The Fabians did not expect in these difficult circumstances that a great deal could be done by legislation. But as skilled "per-meators," they knew how much could be done in various adminis-trative ways, which would not need the sanction of Parliament. And this was especially true in those areas which involved the de-mands of labor. It was precisely there that the Liberals were far more slothful than they needed to be. They were held inert by Glad-stone's beady eye, and the younger leaders did next to nothing. Disgusted with the party, Sidney Webb and Shaw produced a mani-festo in 1893, "To Your Tents, O Israel," which urged progressive elements to abandon the Liberals and strike out on their own.

There were other indications of discontent. In 1885 John Burns, a working-class leader, ran for Parliament in Nottingham, not as a Liberal but as a member of the Social Democratic Federation, and received 598 votes. In February 1886 there was a workers' demon-stration in Trafalgar Square, in protest against widespread unem-ployment. It started to get out of hand, but its leaders, John Burns among them, characteristically gave their full co-operation to the police, and agreed to lead the mob out of the square to Hyde Park, where, it was thought, they would be more easily controlled and dispersed. Even so, on their way to the Park, the mob broke win-dows along Pall Mall, a show of violence that led to a notable increase of contributions to the Lord Mayor's private charity, a fund for the unemployed. But rioting was not going to be the way to significant political change, nor were the small dissident groups, no matter how much inspiration they might give. At this time the membership of the Social Democratic Federation was about a thousand; there were 500 members in Morris's Socialist League, and 150 in the Fabian Society.

. . .

But what of the workers themselves? In the mid 1880's, though union membership was about three-quarters of a million, the unions did not seem eager to do very much in the way of politics. In 1887 Keir Hardie emerged upon the scene as a potential leader. At the annual Trades Union Congress he attacked the leadership for their reluctance to play an active political role, and the next year, as a member of the newly formed Scottish Labour party, ran for Parliament. He was defeated on this first attempt, but his candidacy was a significant step in itself. Events were moving in the direction of an independent working-class party, although admittedly very slowly.

Then, two years later, there was a leap forward, spurred by the great dock strike of 1889. Thereafter new trade unions emerged, mostly for unskilled labor. Membership in the unions rose to a total well over one million, and many of the leaders of these new unions were socialists, or at least were influenced by socialist notions and contacts. In general they had a more active attitude toward politics than the earlier leaders, and higher hopes for independent, working-class political action.

In 1892 Keir Hardie and John Burns were both elected to Parliament. In January 1893, Hardie was the leading force in the founding of the Independent Labour party—another, and one of the more considerable steps toward the founding of the Labour party. At Bradford, in Yorkshire, in the heart of the Yorkshire wool and radical country, 120 delegates—workers, as well as representatives of the S.D.F. and the Fabians—met to form a party which would run candidates independent from other parties. It is typical that the great fight at the meeting should concern the naming of the party. The more conservative of the delegates won the point that it should be called the Independent Labour party, rather than the Socialist Labour party. At the same time, with an inconsistency which would become familiar, they adopted a motion in favor of the collective ownership of the means of production, distribution, and exchange.

The Independent Labour party spent much of its time debating comparatively small issues; it did not wish to allow itself to bog down in larger matters of principle. And it managed to keep its moral fervor without adding to it an air of philosophical intensity and ideological thinking that might have antagonized the British worker. One reason the Social Democratic Federation proved to be less influential, by contrast, was that it was too much like a Continental Socialist party: too doctrinaire and sectarian. As Bruce Glasier, one of the leaders of I.L.P. pointed out, "The S.D.F. has failed to touch the heart of the people. Its strange disregard of the religious, moral and esthetic sentiments of the people is an overwhelming defect."

Despite the overwhelming defeat of its first parliamentary candidates in the General Election of 1895, the I.L.P. became increasingly active on the local level, taking advantage of the Municipal Corporation Act of 1882, which had removed property qualifications for councillors, and the Corrupt Practices Act of 1883, which had made it far less expensive to run for office. By 1900 the I.L.P. had run 129 local candidates, and fifty-six of these were elected. Their attitude was aggressive toward the Liberal party. Keir Hardie declared, "The Labour and Socialist Parties will henceforth vote so as to sweep away the only obstacle in their path—the historic Liberal Party."

The new unionism after 1889 inspired the cautious and sometimes lethargic older unions to political activity as well. Employers, convinced that unions were limiting their profits, formed organizations of their own to combat them. Unions were threatened legally to an increasing degree. The T.U.C. grew worried. It began to modify its attitude of 1893, when it had said it would not run candidates who were independent of existing political parties. In the late 1890's, strikes waged by some of the oldest and most powerful of the unions, such as the Amalgamated Society of Engineers, were long, costly, and unsuccessful. Many union leaders came to believe that to secure industrial gains political action must be resorted to, and that political action would be successful only if there were members of Parliament who represented the interests of the unions. The Boer War—which started in October 1899, and which most of the leaders of the labor movement came to deplore

—made the working-class groups feel still more keenly that they should enter politics in a more formal way. In 1899, the Trades Union Congress passed a resolution that a committee should investigate the possibilities of independent action. On February 27, 1900, in London, there was a meeting of delegates, twelve from the I.L.P., the S.D.F., and the Fabians, the rest from sixty-seven unions representing half a million members, about one-third of the Trades Union Congress. Observed by nine spectators, the 129 delegates formed the Labour Representation Committee, which had the specific job of running men for Parliament. Ramsay MacDonald, a member of the I.L.P. and Keir Hardie's candidate, became the secretary of the new group, and took an important step forward in his considerable career.

The importance of the committee was underlined in July 1901, when the House of Lords handed down the famous Taff Vale decision, a decision in favor of a railway company which had brought suit for damages against a conservative union that had reluctantly backed its men in a strike. This decision was nothing less than a reversal of the laws of 1871–76 concerning unions. In the 1870's such acts had been good and reasonable politics. But now, a quarter-century later, there had been a tightening of class attitudes; the upper classes had a greater sense of being beleaguered as the working class asserted itself. It is not too surprising that the Law Lords decided that the funds of a union should now be liable for damages and losses incurred by a business during a strike. Obviously this was a severe blow, which hit not only at the new unions with their limited funds, but at the old rich unions as well. Both were now willing to give more and more support to the work of the Labour Representation Committee. No longer would the worker willingly depend on the charity of his "betters."

The evolution of the Labour party was hastened by a secret arrangement between Ramsay MacDonald, as secretary of the Labour Representation Committee, and Herbert Gladstone, the son of the former Prime Minister and, at the time, the Liberal party's Chief Whip. (However useful an arrangement, it was one that, clearly, the participants were not too proud of; there was no public knowledge of it until the 1950's when the Herbert Gladstone papers were opened to scholars.) The agreement between the two men was that, as far as they could manage it, candidates from the Labour Representation Committee would not be run against candidates of the Liberal party, and vice versa. Gladstone could not give a total guarantee, for there were limits to the power of the Liberal central organization: it could not prohibit local organizations from running a candidate. And the Labour Representation Committee had its own limitations—especially in Scotland.

The effectiveness of the arrangement became evident in the General Election of 1906. The Liberals made a triumphant return to power. The Labour Representation Committee had returned twenty-nine of its candidates as well as one labor member who immediately joined the new group. Shortly after the election, the Committee changed its name to the Labour party—the future great political party thus had its official birth. Most of the twenty-four so-called Lib-Lab members of the House of Commons, many of whom came from the mining districts and who until then had given their primary political allegiance to the Liberals, switched to the new party. It was not an insignificant beginning.

The presence of these Labour men in Parliament made a profound impression on contemporary opinion. It was felt that the Labour party had become a force to be reckoned with. Given the English prejudice for two major, opposing parties—dictated in part by the physical layout of the House of Commons—there must have been some sense, some premonition, that the existence of one of the traditional parties was being challenged.

From 1906 on, Labour became increasingly influential, though more, perhaps, as a special interest group than as a political party. In that year the Liberals passed a Trade Disputes Act, which the House of Lords did not dare to veto, and that negated the Taff Vale decision. But then, in 1909, the Labour party had to sustain another setback in the Osborne decision by the House of Lords, which ruled that a trade union could not use its funds to undertake political activity. The result was to rob the newly born Labour party of much of its financial support

Eventually the effects of this adverse decision were gotten around, in part because the financial strain upon the Labour party was decreased in 1911 when the Liberals put through a resolution which paid members £400 a year. Also, a union member had specifically to contract out of the political levy to the Labour party, if the majority of his union had agreed to support it. The result was that the party grew, if not affluent, at least solvent.

. . .

On the whole, between the election of 1906 and the end of the first World War in 1918, the Labour party played a comparatively quiet role. There was a period of extensive strikes, most particularly from 1910 to 1912, and talk of syndicalism, but the party as such was not deeply involved in these strivings of the workers. It continued its organization on the local level, and in so doing laid the foundations for a national political structure. But many of the more powerful elements that had helped to bring the party into being were not noticeably in evidence during these years. The more extreme Marxists wandered off into the British Socialist party, the ancestor of the Communist party. (The entire British labor movement—like the working-class movement all over the world—rejoiced in the Russian revolution in 1917, and there was a brief moment of romantic talk about soviets in Britain. But the fervor was never widespread, and soon cooled.)

As with those on the far left, so with the moralists. The spirit of Carlyle, Ruskin, even William Morris, was not much in evidence in these years. Presumably the Labour leaders disapproved of the plutocracy, but they did not lead a moral crusade against it. On the whole it was a time of practical politics and gains. The unions, the party's great source of strength, grew considerably in membership, and by 1918 had some four million members. (Not all would vote Labour, of course. The worker who votes Tory is an important component of the English scene.) But while this total represents a considerable gain from the approximately two million union members of 1906, for some unions, as for the party, it was a period of growth and consolidation. And while the Independent Labour party —the I.L.P.—continued to exist in alliance with the Labour party, it was increasingly overshadowed by its child.

The Labour party really recovered, or rediscovered itself, as something more than an extremely important political interest group, during the years of the first World War. It managed, in a rather schizophrenic way, to get the best of both worlds: it found again a moral stance; and it proved itself capable of playing a responsible part in governing the country.

During the tense days of August 1914, MacDonald was firm in his opposition to the war, and resigned as leader of the Parliamentary Labour party. He was succeeded by the more moderate Arthur Henderson. Thereafter a small true band, mainly of the middle-class and intellectual sort, "kept the faith" with MacDonald and continued to oppose the war. But at the same time, thanks to the effectiveness of Arthur Henderson's performance in the coalition cabinet (and that of some junior Labour ministers as well), Labour was demonstrating its ability to participate in Government. These were not the wild red men the respectable middle class had expected and feared. The Labour party had come to maturity. From the small and somewhat eccentric special groups of the 1880's, it had evolved into a full-fledged political party. Its new constitution in 1918 signified Labour's coming of age. The movement's experiences in the years before 1914 had contributed significantly to the accomplishments represented by the constitution, but it was the pressures and experiences of war-time which had the greatest effect upon the party; it is that period which is examined in the following pages.

I

BACKGROUND

ELIE HALEVY

The World Crisis of 1914–1918

LECTURE I

Allow me, before I begin, to express to you my feelings of gratitude.
That the University of Oxford should have made me, three years ago,
an honorary Doctor of Letters, that the Rhodes Trustees should have
made me their Memorial Lecturer for the year—such honours heaped
upon me make me feel, I assure you, more modest than proud; they do
not induce me to think myself a greater man than I am. My work has
been a work of patience: my patience you have meant to reward. You
will readily understand how high a value an historian of the English
people must set upon this reward, coming as it does from the very
centre of English learning. He accepts it as something more than a
reward for his past work; he accepts it as an encouragement for the
future. For his work is far from having come to its end. Whether he
will ever be able to finish it depends upon his being favoured with the
requisite strength and health and freedom from anxieties, blessings that
it is not in your power to bestow on him. But it requires also self-

The Rhodes Memorial Lectures, delivered in 1929 by Elie Halévy. Reprinted from
The World Crisis of 1914–1918, Oxford at the Clarendon Press, 1930. Reprinted
by permission.

Elie Halévy (1870–1937), a Frenchman, is probably the most distinguished
historian of nineteenth-century Britain. His five-volume *History of the English
People in the Nineteenth Century,* extended to 1914. In the lecture reprinted here,
one of three, he sets out for Europe as a whole a discussion of socialism and
nationalism which is also relevant for the English experience during the first
World War.

confidence and continued patience. These you can and do provide him with, for which he thanks you heartily.

But it is not only on my own behalf that I wish to express my gratitude to you; it is also on behalf of my native country, France. The first Rhodes Memorial Lecturer was a Canadian statesman, one of the leading figures of the British Commonwealth of nations. The second was an eminent American scientist, who belonged, if not to that Commonwealth, at all events to what might be called the Commonwealth of the English-speaking nations. But you have now remembered that this is the century of the League of Nations. You have thought that it might be well if you looked for a third lecturer outside the circle of the English-speaking world. Cecil Rhodes, who, if he was anything, was a man of imagination, would have certainly approved of the idea. And finally, having taken this decision, you have invited a Frenchman to come; for which, again, I thank you. Your purpose has been to give the Entente its true interpretation, not as a passing diplomatic contrivance, but as something more lasting, because more spiritual, not founded, let us hope, upon fear of a common enemy, but upon the more positive qualities of charity, hope, and faith. Charity towards mankind as a whole, Hope in the future welfare of the human race, Faith in the possibility of furthering, through co-operation between nations, the cause of knowledge and culture, of everything that the eighteenth century, the most Anglo-French century in history, called by a fine name, "enlightenment"—Les Lumières.

It is in this philosophical spirit that I mean to approach my difficult subject. I shall not deal with individuals. I shall not dwell upon the story of the last week before the War, dramatic as it is. I shall disregard the suggestions made retrospectively by a host of well-meaning critics, as to what such and such a Sovereign, or Prime Minister, or Foreign Secretary, should, on this particular day, at this or that particular hour, have done or not done, said or not said, in order to prevent the War. Pills to cure an earthquake! The object of my study is the earthquake itself. I shall attempt to define the collective forces, the collective feelings and movements of public opinion, which, in the early years of the twentieth century, made for strife. I say purposely "strife," not "war," because the world crisis of 1914–18 was not only a war—the war of 1914—but a revolution—the revolution of 1917. It may therefore be well for me, at the outset, to draw your attention to some aspects of those two important notions—"war" and "revolution."

My first point will be that there is a striking resemblance between the two notions. Suppose there is, at a given period, a fairly complete equilibrium between the political and the economic condition of a nation; that the distribution of political power among the several classes within the nation corresponds substantially to the distribution of economic power. Suppose, then, that, while the distribution of political power remains the same, and cannot by any normal means be readjusted to meet altered circumstances, the distribution of economic power is greatly altered. Suppose, for example, that the bourgeoisie, as in eighteenth-century France, acquires an immense increase of economic and cultural power without any corresponding increase of political power. There will come a strong temptation, almost as irresistible as a law of nature, for the class that is at a political disadvantage to resort to violence and revolution, until a new equilibrium is reached. Suppose, again, that, at a given time, the territorial distribution of the soil of Europe among the nations corresponds approximately to their respective military, economic, and cultural strength, and is in substantial harmony with the sentiments of the large majority of the subjects of each state. But suppose that, presently, one nation is found to have gained immensely in military or economic strength at the expense of one or many of the others; or that, within the limits of one or more nations, new nationalities have become self-conscious and wish to express themselves as independent States. For such a disturbance of equilibrium man has not as yet discovered any method of peaceful adjustment. It can be rectified only by an outburst of violence—called, in this instance, not a revolution, but a war—to be followed by the establishment of a new equilibrium of a more or less lasting character.

In the second place, just because the notions of war and revolution are closely allied, it is often difficult to distinguish between a revolution and a war. A nation, Ireland or Poland, which has been absorbed into an Empire, wishes to assert itself as an independent State, and rises in arms against those who are, according to the written constitution, its legitimate masters. Should this rising of a nascent nation be called a revolution, or a national war? Or again, a revolution may extend beyond the narrow limits of the country where it began. French armies, for example, in 1792 and the following years appeared in Belgium and the Rhineland, and were everywhere acclaimed by the democratic party, while their opponents fled for their lives. Was this a war, in the purely military meaning of the word, or the propagation of a revolution?

It is thus apparent why all great convulsions in the history of the world, and more particularly in modern Europe, have been at the same time wars and revolutions. The Thirty Years' War was at once a revolutionary crisis, a conflict, within Germany, between the rival parties of Protestants and Catholics, and an international war between the Holy Roman Empire, Sweden, and France. The Great War (as, until quite lately, it used to be described in England) which lasted from 1792 to 1815, having begun as a social revolution in France, became a war which spread throughout Europe, until national revolutions, or wars, recoiling against France, drove her back, after one of the most amazing successions of triumphs and disasters in history, within her former limits. The last great and greater war, which is my present subject, has similar characteristics. I shall therefore, in my first lecture, define what the forces were which, at the beginning of the century, made for revolution. I shall define, in my second lecture, what the forces were which made for war. I shall then endeavour, in my third and concluding lecture, to show how a knowledge of the two sets of forces may help us to unravel the tangled plot of the Four Years' World-Crisis.

What were the collective forces that made for revolution? One word sums them up, a word in world-wide use, "Socialism," which is the easier to define since its meaning has, so to speak, crystallized into a single doctrine. A man, who, whatever we think of his teaching, was certainly a man of genius, the most internationally minded of all internationalists, had founded his system upon his thorough knowledge of the dialectical method of Hegel and his German followers of the Left, of French Socialism, and of English economics. It may be well to recall, however briefly, the essence of Karl Marx's doctrine. The main feature of modern civilization, as he sees it, is the class-war, the war between capitalists and wage-earners. The capitalists own all the means of production; they are in a minority, and an ever-dwindling minority, it being the law of industrial competition that the smaller concerns are always defeated by, and absorbed into, the larger. Their function is a beneficent one, inasmuch as, through their power of organization, they have increased, to an almost incredible degree, the wealth-producing power of mankind. But they have not fulfilled this beneficent function for the immediate benefit of mankind, taken as a whole. They have fulfilled it through the methodical exploitation, oppression, and pauperization of the wage-earners. Mankind will only take its revenge on the day, which is bound to come, and the coming of which capitalism is unconsciously preparing, when the exploited masses will have become such a crushing majority, as compared with the constantly diminishing, and finally insignificant, number of their exploiters, that they will find it easy, at the cost of a supreme upheaval, to come at last into their inheritance, to get control of the concentrated industries, and work them henceforward, not for the profit of the few, but for the benefit of all.

The doctrine of Karl Marx has always struck me as unfair, because it directs the hatred of the multitude against that particular class of capitalists, the captains of industry, whose activity has been the most positively beneficent, to the exclusion of many more parasitic forms of capitalism. But it is easy to understand why it made a powerful appeal to the emotions of the working masses. It fitted in exactly with the conditions that prevailed in the newly industrialized districts of Western Europe. There, huge masses of suddenly congregated wage-earners faced minorities of arrogant task-masters, monopolizers of wealth, upstarts of industry. The doctrine provided them with reasons for hating those whom they hated instinctively. Little by little, it was forgotten that there had been Socialists in France and England before Karl Marx had begun to write. "Marxism" and "Socialism" became synonymous words.

This development was especially pronounced in the leading European country, Germany. There a powerful party had been expressly based upon orthodox Marxism; and Socialists in the neighbouring countries had been working, more or less successfully, to imitate the German "Social-Democratic" Party, just as soldiers, industrialists, and social reformers had done their best to imitate the methods of German militarism, German industrial organization, and German social legislation. The Social-Democratic Party had first been founded in 1875 under another name, with a still indefinite programme and imperfect organization. Then it had undergone a long ordeal, lasting over ten years, of Bismarckian persecution. But from this ordeal it had emerged triumphant, at the moment when Bismarck was dismissed by the young William the Second, and a new régime of toleration began for the Social Democrats. Already a million and a half electors voted for the Social-Democratic candidates; a figure of three millions was reached at the General Election of 1905; the fourth million in 1912. Here was a great country, the greatest country in Europe, with more than four million voters eager to send to the Reichstag members of a party whose programme was strictly revolutionary.

Now, the constant and impressive growth of the German Marxist party raises an important problem. There have never been, in any great country, four million revolutionists; there certainly were not in Germany, when the twentieth century began, four million enemies of religion, conscious antipatriots, eager for the rapid abolition of private property. What the Social-Democratic Party did, was to provide an outlet for discontents of all kinds and of all degrees of intensity; and it only succeeded in doing so, and in keeping together such a huge and mixed body of extremists and moderates of many sorts, through a clever use of the Marxian doctrine itself. For, if Marxism is in its very essence revolutionary, the leaders of German Social Democracy always reminded their followers that it was also a fatalistic doctrine. Socialism was bound to come, but only at the time when the natural process of capitalistic concentration had reached its ultimate development. Then the catastrophe would happen; but it would be dangerous and absurd to anticipate the date and mislead the masses into premature insurrection, which could result in nothing but failure. Thus did the German Social Democrats play a clever and successful game, constantly making new recruits, constantly teaching them patience at the same time as hope, pursuing a policy not so much of revolutionary action as of revolutionary expectation, a policy of waiting.

But the game was a difficult one, and after the General Election of 1912 the question had arisen how long the Party, numerically formidable as it had become, could continue to play it. It is legitimate for historians to ask, whether one of the reasons—we are far from saying the main reason—why the German military aristocracy decided, in July 1914, to run the risks of a great European war was not a growing sense of discomfort under the increasing pressure of Social Democracy, and a surmise that a bold attempt to give a set-back to Socialism, by asserting themselves once more as the party of war and victory, might prove the wisest course. There was indeed something paradoxical in the structure of the German Empire. Here was a highly industrialized country, the most highly industrialized of all the nations on the Continent, subjected to a political régime of feudalism and absolutism. Here was an Empire founded, in 1866 and 1871, upon the basis of manhood suffrage, but in which Prussia, the leading State within its boundaries, was condemned to an electoral system that was a mere travesty of democratic institutions; in which ministers were responsible not to the elective assembly but to the hereditary sovereign; in which a minister was not regarded as having even a right to resign, but must wait until it pleased the King and Emperor to dismiss him. Here was one of those cases of apparently precarious equilibrium which demand a revolution;

and, since the only party in the State that stood for democracy pure and simple was at the same time a socialistic party, it is difficult to see how the political crisis could fail to be attended by some social upheaval.

We shall see by and by how both these things happened. Nobody, however, would have been prepared to say during the years immediately preceding 1914 that Germany was the centre of the European revolutionary spirit. The revolutionary centres of Europe had to be sought elsewhere, westward and eastward, in France and in Russia.

Let us begin with France. The political and social conditions that prevailed here were very different from those which prevailed in Germany. When the twentieth century opened, manhood suffrage had been established in France for more than half a century. France had been, nominally, even under the Second Empire—since that Empire was a monarchy founded on a plebiscite—and after 1871, in reality, a country where all administrative and legislative functions depended directly or indirectly upon popular election. With what results? When they considered the results, revolutionists could not help feeling bitterly disappointed. They saw revolutionary Socialists, once admitted into a democratically elected Chamber of Deputies, become Parliamentarians instead of Revolutionists, political Radicals instead of Socialists, and, too frequently, Moderates instead of Radicals. They noticed that Bismarck's social monarchy had provided the working classes with more effective laws of protection against the risks of industrial life than had French Radicalism. They wondered whether these failures of French democracy were not inherent in the very nature of democracy. Electioneering involves catering for votes of all kinds—even bourgeois votes. Membership of Parliament entails concern in a mass of questions—national, diplomatic, military, religious—that have nothing to do with the purely economic problem of the welfare of the working classes. Hence the rise of a new doctrine, called Syndicalism, which really opened a new era in the history of Socialism, and which has only lacked, in order to be appreciated at its full value, a prophet of the calibre of Karl Marx. The Syndicalists condemned as barren what they called the indirect action of the State; they forbade trade union leaders to seek admission to democratically elected Assemblies in the fond hope of acting indirectly, through State interference, upon the employers of labour. If these leaders really meant to remain in contact with labour and faithful to the militant spirit of the class-war, their duty was consistently to ignore politics and stick to the method of "direct action" against the employers. Let the workmen, by persistent pressure on the capitalists, exerted in workshop and factory, through collective bargaining, boycotts, and strikes, conquer higher wages, shorter hours, more control over the conditions of labour and the management of industry itself; let them group their trade unions, or *syndicats,* into federations coextensive with the nation, and these federations into one single federation of all trade unions, the "Confédération générale du travail," endowed with executive powers. The day would come when, after a final revolutionary general strike, the General Confederation of Labour would achieve the annihilation of capitalism and become a pure industrial democracy, a society of producers, divested of all the political functions which appertained to the military State of the past.

Our picture of French revolutionary Syndicalism is, however, not yet complete. A schoolmaster in Burgundy, by name Gustave Hervé, started another school of revolutionary tactics, which came to be more or less completely adopted by the Syndicalist extremists. His formula was the military strike, the strike of soldiers against their officers; and, so long as he confined himself to persuading soldiers that they should decline to act as strike-breakers, there was undoubtedly a close resemblance between his ideas and those of revolutionary Syndicalism. But he went further, and advised the soldiers if ever war came to be declared not to act the part of conscientious objectors and, in a Tolstoian spirit, merely decline to fight: he wanted them to retain the weapons that circumstances placed in their hands, and, instead of making war, turn them against the government of their own country, against militarism, patriotism, and capitalism. This was a notion that had very little resemblance to the Syndicalist notion of a strike; it reminds us rather of the old formula of the "Jacobin" or "Blanquist" *coup de main* upon the central organs of government, in order to force a revolution upon a nation through the political action of the State. But the fact was that both notions appealed to extremists, and also that the word "strike" was used in both connexions; so that it often became difficult to distinguish "Hervéism" from "Syndicalism." The double programme of a general strike of workmen and soldiers was indeed to be applied, and succeed, as we shall see, in another country than France. But it was in France, during the last ten years of the nineteenth century and the first ten years of the twentieth century, that the scheme was conceived.

It was no sooner conceived than it spread like wildfire to many countries outside France. It spread to Spain and Italy, where orthodox Marxism had always found it difficult to hold its own against more revolutionary forms of Socialism, and had often been compelled to come to terms with them. It became particularly vehement in Italy at the time of the Tripoli War, towards the end of 1911. A brilliant agitator successfully organized a general strike of the whole body of workmen in the town of Forlì, which lasted several days, as a protest against the war. He thus came to the front, and was soon afterwards promoted to the post of editor of the important Roman Socialist paper, the *Avanti;* he gave it a distinctly revolutionary tone, and largely increased its sale. His name was Benito Mussolini.

Syndicalism spread also to the Anglo-Saxon world. It spread to the United States, where the so-called "Industrial Workers of the World" propagated, among the masses of the unskilled proletarians, the idea of the revolutionary strike, as against the ultra-moderate methods of the "American Federation of Labour." The "Industrial Workers of the World" in their turn found imitators in Australia, where Labour Governments were getting into trouble with their workmen, and where the discontented workmen were glad to find in Syndicalism a useful weapon with which to fight their Governments. Here two Englishmen, Ben Tillett and Tom Mann, came into contact with the Syndicalist agitators. They had been, twenty years before, active revolutionists in London, had failed to accomplish their designs, and had left their country in disgust. They now became converts to the new doctrine, and brought it back to England, which it had already begun to permeate more directly from across the Channel. In the critical summer of 1911, when the "Die-Hards" were fighting in the last ditch against the Parliament Bill, when the *Panther* was at anchor before the Moroccan harbour of Agadir, and the British Government really believed in the possibility of an immediate war with Germany, Ben Tillett and Tom Mann became the leaders of a series of big strikes among transport workers and railwaymen, strikes that contained an element of violence quite new in England and bore the mark of a foreign influence. Then came, in the following winter, the general strike of the miners, and in 1913 the general strikes in South Africa and Dublin, which so strangely and unexpectedly cut across the feud between English and Dutch overseas, between Protestant and Catholic in Ireland. Then followed, during the first months of 1914, the new move among transport workers, railwaymen, and miners towards the formation of what was called the "Triple Industrial Alliance," designed to exert a joint pressure upon the associations of their respective employers and eventually to organize the General Strike. Of course, their aspirations were not the same as those of the continental extremists and utopians. Their very definite objects were their immediate interests—higher wages, shorter hours, and recognition of the trade unions. The situation was nevertheless alarming: the nation was facing a situation approaching in gravity the crisis that was not reached until 1926, after years of trouble and suspense.

Still more serious was the position in the east of Europe, if Russia may be really considered as part of Europe. But you must not expect me to dwell, in this connexion, on the history of the beginnings of Bolshevism before the War. Suffice it to say that there was, from 1903 onwards, a Bolshevist Party; but it was a small party—one-half of the Social-Democratic Party; and the Russian Social-Democratic Party was very far from forming the whole of the Russian Socialist movement. I compare the influence of the Social Democrats (Bolsheviks and Mensheviks combined) in the revolutionary movement to that of the Baltic Barons in the reactionary circles. The Baltic Barons were a German, an exotic element: their aim and function was to introduce the orderly, if brutal, methods of German bureaucracy into a semi-Asiatic, inefficient, anarchical, and corrupt society. The Russian Social Democrats were likewise an exotic element: they were adepts of Marxist Socialism and admirers of German science, conscious enemies, as the Baltic Barons were, of eastern nonchalance and inefficiency. They understood, and explained, that the time had not yet come for a Socialist revolution in Russia. The country, according to Marx's philosophy of progress, had first to go through a long and painful process of westernization and industrialization. Not so the really powerful, and authentically Russian, Social-Revolutionary Party. They despised the west and thought it the legitimate pride of Russia that the evils of industrialism and competitive civilization were unknown to her. Their Socialism was agrarian. They believed that whereas western Socialists were inventing complicated and pedantic systems in order to escape the horrors of factory life without abolishing the factory, the Russian Moujik, in the simplicity of his primitive mind, had hit upon the true formula of unadulterated communism. The Mir, the village community, had only to be maintained, or restored where it was in risk of being destroyed by the impact of western individualism, for the social question to be solved. As to the methods to be used, the Social Revolutionaries condoned, if they did not actually encourage, the anarchist method of terrorism and wholesale assassination. Not the murder of this or that particular statesman, in order to put another more popular man in his place, but the murder of official after official, indiscriminately, so as to throw the whole of society into a state of constant panic, dislocate the machinery of government, and prepare the advent of universal liberty through universal anarchy.

In fact a revolution had already occurred in Russia, a most formidable revolution, in 1905–6, at the end of the disastrous war with Japan. It had looked for a time as if Tsarism would be unable to weather the storm. But the storm had been weathered after all. And it is a legitimate question whether the revolutionary movement in Russia did not reach its climax about 1905 and subside afterwards. Perhaps also the Syndicalist agitation, which raged in France between 1906 and 1910, was only the aftermath of the Russian Revolution, just as the English agitation of 1911 was only the aftermath of the French upheaval. No definite statement on such points is possible; but certainly no responsible statesman would have said, at the beginning of 1914, that he felt safe against the perils of some kind of revolutionary outburst. In Russia the recent assassination of Stolypin was a dangerous symptom; so was the big strike that broke out in the streets of St. Petersburg, just as President Poincaré was paying a State visit to the Tsar, in July 1914. Hervéism was still rampant in the rank and file of the French army: in England, the Industrial Triple Alliance was openly preparing to blackmail the community into submitting to its claims. "Beware," Sir Edward Grey, warns Count Mensdorf on the 23rd July 1914; "a war would be accompanied or followed by a complete collapse of European credit and industry. In these days, in great industrial States, this would mean a state of things worse than that of 1848." [1] "Beware," Lord Morley a few days later warns his colleagues, "in the present temper of Labour, this tremendous dislocation of industrial life must be fraught with public danger. The atmosphere of war cannot be friendly to order, in a democratic system that is verging on the humour of '48." [2] In 1848 a revolution had begun in Paris that spread through the whole west of the Continent and was altogether republican and socialistic in character. But what now happened was not a revolution but a war; not even, as in 1789, a revolution followed by wars, but a war that, for a time at least, threw the revolutionary peril into the background. Hence we are entitled to conclude that, powerful as were the forces which, in pre-war Europe, made for revolution, the forces that made for war were still more powerful.

1. *British Documents on the Origins of the War*, vol. xi, p. 70.
2. Viscount Morley, *Memorandum on Resignation, August 1914*, p. 5.

JOHN MORLEY

Memorandum on Resignation

I

On or about July 24–27 Grey took a very important line in the Cabinet.
He informed us of the contents of Buchanan's [British Ambassador to
Russia] telegram of July 24 from Petersburg: describing Sazonoff's
[Russian Minister for Foreign Affairs] hopes that England would not
fail to proclaim her solidarity with France and Russia; his warnings to
us that the general European question was involved and England could
not afford to efface herself from the problems now at issue; that she
would sooner or later be dragged into war if it did break out; and, as
Buchanan thought, even if England declined to join, France and
Russia were determined to make a strong stand, *i.e.* in plain language,
to fight Austria and Germany.

Then Grey in his own quiet way, which is none the less impressive
for being so simple, and so free from the *cassant* and over-emphatic
tone that is Asquith's vice on such occasions, made a memorable pronouncement. The time had come, he said, when the Cabinet was bound
to make up its mind plainly whether we were to take an active part
with the two other Powers of the Entente, or to stand aside in the
general European question, and preserve an absolute neutrality.

We could no longer defer decision. Things were moving very rapidly.
We could no longer wait on accident, and postpone. If the Cabinet was
for Neutrality, he did not think that he was the man to carry out such
a policy. Here he ended in accents of unaffected calm and candour.
The Cabinet seemed to heave a sort of sigh, and a moment or two of
breathless silence fell upon us. I followed him, expressing my intense
satisfaction that he had brought the inexorable position, to which circumstances had now brought us, plainly and definitely before us. It was
fairer to France and everybody else, ourselves included. Though he had
at least once, talking to an ambassador, drawn a distinction between

From *Memorandum on Resignation, August 1914* by John Viscount Morley,
London, Macmillan and Company, Ltd., 1928. Reprinted by permission.

John Morley (1838–1923), the trusted lieutenant and biographer of William
Gladstone, was in 1914 the Lord President of the Council in Asquith's Liberal
cabinet. An intellectual historian, he is one of the most eminent examples of late
Victorian liberalism. Yet he could not cope with the coming of the first World
War, and his incomprehension is reflected in what might be regarded as one of
the final documents of a world that was ending.

diplomatic and military intervention, it was henceforth assumed that intervention meant active resort to arms. We rambled, as even the best Cabinets are apt to do, from the cogent points and secondary aspects. I could not, on the instant, gather with any certainty in which direction opinion was inclining. No wonder. Everybody had suddenly awakened to the startling fact that nothing less than the continued existence of the Ministry was this time—the first time—in sharp peril from differences within, and not from the House of Commons.

Later, we were pressed by the Prime Minister and Grey to examine the neutrality of Belgium and our obligations under the Treaty of 1839. But it was thrown back day after day as less urgent than France. I took down to the Cabinet the words of Lord Derby about the Luxemburg guarantee of 1867; mentioning the opposition to his language from the Duke of Argyll and others. But, perhaps quite as much my fault as that of anybody else, the discussion was thin and perfunctory. Simon contributed scarcely anything and the Lord Chancellor [Haldane] even less. A Cabinet usually thinks of one thing at once, and the question of Belgium was up to this date, and in truth up to the morning of August 3rd, when Grey had to set out his whole case in the House of Commons, secondary to the pre-eminent controversy of the Anglo-French Entente. One of these days Grey rather suddenly let fall his view, in the pregnant words that German policy was that of a great "European aggressor, as bad as Napoleon." "I have no German partialities," I observed, "but you do not give us evidence." Perhaps he might have cited the series of Naval Laws.

Meanwhile Harcourt [Colonial Secretary] had been busy in organising opinion among his Cabinet colleagues in favour of neutrality. This was meant for a counter-move that was being openly worked with his best daemonic energy by Winston [Churchill], with strenuous simplicity by Grey, and *sourdement* by the Lord Chancellor—the Prime Minister seeing and waiting. There was no intrigue about it either way. All was above-board. Harcourt got me to his room in the House of Commons one night as I was passing along the corridor and I found Beauchamp, M'Kinnon Wood, Hobhouse, Pease [leading Liberals], very zealous against extension of entente to alliance. They calculated to a tune of eight or nine men in the Cabinet likely to agree with us. I think I attended one other meeting of this Peace Group in the same place, and under the same auspices. Harcourt this week two or three times threw me little slips at the Cabinet table, "That I must resign is more and more evident." One of these days I tapped Winston on the shoulder, as he took his seat next me. "Winston, we have beaten you after all." He smiled cheerfully. Well he might. *O pectora caeca!* [O blind hearts]

Lloyd George [Chancellor of the Exchequer], not by design, furthered the good cause by a very remarkable piece of intelligence communicated to the Cabinet, acquired I think at the suggestion of the Prime Minister. He informed us that he had been consulting the Governor and Deputy Governor of the Bank of England, other men of light and leading in the City, also cotton men, and steel and coal men, etc., in the North of England, in Glasgow, etc., and they were all aghast at the bare idea of our plunging into the European conflict; how it would break down the whole system of credit with London as its centre, how it would cut up commerce and manufacture—they told him—how it would hit labour and wages and prices, and, when the winter came, would inevitably produce violence and tumult. When I pressed this all-important prospect in a later debate, the Chancellor of the Exchequer said rather tartly that he had never said he believed it all. "In the present temper of labour," said I, "this tremendous dislocation of industrial life must be fraught with public danger. The atmosphere of war cannot be friendly to order, in a democratic system that is verging on the humour of [18]48." But then the wisest saws, as I have many a time found before now, count for little in the hour of practical emergency. This first-class and vital element in settling our policy received little of the attention that it well deserved; it vanished in the diplomatic hurry.

Then they were rather surprised at the stress I laid upon the Russian side of things. "Have you ever thought," I put to them, "what will happen if Russia wins? If Germany is beaten and Austria is beaten, it is not England and France who will emerge pre-eminent in Europe. It will be Russia. Will that be good for Western civilisation? I at least don't think so. If she says she will go to Constantinople, or boldly annex both northern and neutral zone in Persia, or insist on railways up to the Indian and Afghan frontier, who will prevent her? Germany is unpopular in England, but Russia is more unpopular still. And people will rub their eyes when they realise that Cossacks are their victorious fellow-champions for Freedom, Justice, Equality of man (especially Jew man), and respect for treaties (in Persia for instance)." They listened rather intently, and Lloyd George told me after that he had never thought of all this.

I think it was to-day [July 26] I put a really strong point. Grey has more than once congratulated Europe on the existence of two great confederacies, Triple Alliance and Triple Entente, as healthily preserving the balance of power. Balance! What a beautiful euphemism for the picture of two giant groups armed to the teeth, each in mortal terror of the other, both of them passing year after year in an incurable fever of jealousy and suspicion!

The Cabinet for the first time became seriously uneasy about the danger of these foreign affairs to our own cohesion. For the very first time something of the old cleavage between the Liberal League and the faithful Campbell-Bannerman [Liberal Prime Minister before Asquith], Harcourt [Liberal Chancellor of the Exchequer in the 1890's, father of Lewis Harcourt], and myself began to be very sensibly felt. Hitherto not a whisper of the old schism of the Boer war. As I walked away with Burns [John Burns, president of the Local Government Board, first working class Cabinet member] after the Cabinet of the 29th, he pressed my arm and said with vehement emphasis, *"Now mind, we look to you to stand firm."* He repeated it on Friday. I was not keen in response, as to my taking any lead. We were all first alarmed on the Saturday evening. Burns himself took the lead, to good purpose, and intimated in his most downright tones that the warning to Germany not to try it on against French coasts or ships in the Channel, was more than he could stand, not only because it was practically a declaration of war on sea leading inevitably to a war on land, but mainly because it was the symbol of an alliance with France with whom no such understanding had hitherto existed. This was a great improvement upon groups in private conclave. Somebody has said that egotism is sometimes furtive, sometimes frank. Burns is never furtive, whatever else may be said of him. This proceeding to-night was admirably frank, and took full effect. Runciman [president of the Board of Education] with an anxious face, speaking of the Cabinet that was appointed for Sunday morning, muttered to me as we left the room, "I'm very much afraid this is going to break us up tomorrow."

Curiously enough—by way of irrelevant parenthesis—as it soon fell out, on the 29th I happened to have a party for Lord Kitchener at the United Services Club. Present, besides him, Jellicoe, Winston, Crewe, Haldane, Bryce, [Liberal leaders] Knollys [formally private secretary to Edward VII and George V], Guy. Bryce was shocked at Haldane's war talk. I told him afterwards he must no longer think us a Peace Cabinet. Within ten days Kitchener was installed in my chair in the Cabinet! The only case, I should think, of an active military com-

mander in the Cabinet since Wellington joined the Liverpool Ministry
in 1819 as Master General of the Ordnance.

II

Sunday, August 2.—Cabinet. Main question resumed was the language to be held by Grey to Cambon [French Ambassador to Britain]
in the afternoon. Neutrality of Belgium, though Asquith pressed for
attention to that topic, was secondary to the question of our neutrality
in the struggle between Germany and France; and to our liability to
France under the Entente. The situation now was this: Grey admitted
that we were not bound by the same obligation of honour to France as
bound France to Russia. He professed to stand by what he had told
Cambon in his letter of 1912, that we were left perfectly free to decide
whether we would assist France by armed force. We were not committed, he always said, to action in a contingency that had not yet
arisen and might never arise. No immediate aggressive action was entailed upon us, unless there was action against France in the Channel
or the North Sea. So much then for the point of honour arising on the
French Entente.

On August 3rd Grey received news that Germany would be prepared,
if we would pledge ourselves to neutrality, to agree that its fleet would
not attack the North Coast of France. Grey replied that this was far too
narrow an engagement for us. Why? And if it was too narrow, why not
at least take it as a basis for widening and enlargement? Pure precipitancy! At any rate there had as yet been no word said in the Cabinet
about an Expeditionary Force. But I had been too virtuous an attendant
at the C.I.D.[1] for several years, not to know that this was a settled aim
in the minds of many, if not most, of its members.

Harcourt assured me before discussion began, that he believed he
could count on ten or eleven men against Grey's view that we had both
moral obligations of honour and substantial obligations of policy in
taking sides with France. After a very fair discussion Grey was authorised to give an assurance to Cambon that "if the German Fleet comes
into the Channel or through the North Sea to undertake hostile operations against French coasts or shipping, the British fleet will give all
the protection in its power. This assurance of course subject to the
policy of His Majesty's Government receiving the support of Parliament, and must not be taken as binding His Majesty's Government to

1. Committee of Imperial Defence.

take any action until the above contingency of action by the German
fleet takes place." There were two lines of argument for this warning
to Germany. (1) We owed it to France, in view of the Entente, and
also of her value to us in the Mediterranean. (2) We could not acquiesce in Franco-German naval conflict in the narrow seas, on our door-
step so to say. This authorisation, however, was not unanimous. Burns,
with remarkable energy, force, and grasp, insisted that this was neither
more nor less than a challenge to Germany, tantamount to a declaration of war against her. He wound up with a refusal to be a party to it.
Asquith took the blow a trifle too coolly, and, with a little trouble,
eventually persuaded Burns to postpone his resignation until the Cabinet to be held at 6.30 in the evening. I said to Burns as we broke up at
luncheon time, "I think you are mistaken in going on this particular
proposal. The door-step argument makes a warning to Germany de-
fensible, apart from French Entente. I expect that I am certain to go
out with you, but on the general policy of armed intervention, as against
diplomatic energy and armed neutrality, to which Grey has *step by step*
been drawing the Cabinet on." I made just as much impression on John
Burns as I expected—that is, not the slightest.

The Belgian question took its place in to-day's discussion, but even
now only a secondary place. Grey very properly asked leave to warn
the German Ambassador that, unless Germany was prepared to give us
a reply in the sense of the reply we had from France, it would be hard
to restrain English feeling on any violation of Belgian neutrality by
either combatant. This leave of course we gave him. There was a general, but vague, assent to our liabilities under the Treaty of 1839, but
there was no assent to the employment of a land force, and, I think, no
mention of it.

I do not recall whether it was at the morning or the afternoon
Cabinet that Grey told us of his talk with Lichnowsky [German Ambassador to Britain]; I remember noting that it seemed a great pity,
while "keeping our hands free," not to take advantage of the occasion
for more talk and negotiation. It was worth trying at any rate, instead
of this wooden *non possumus,* even though Lichnowsky's ideas or suggestions were merely personal and unauthorised by instructions.

The plain truth, as I conceive the truth to be, is this. The German
line on Belgian neutrality might be met in two ways. One, we might at
once make it a *casus belli;* the other, we might protest with direct
energy, as the British Government protested on the Russian repudiation
in 1870 of the Black Sea articles of the Treaty of Paris, and push on by

diplomatising. What was the difficulty of the second course? Why, our supposed entanglement with France, and nothing else. The precipitate and peremptory blaze about Belgium was due less to indignation at the violation of a Treaty than to natural perception of the plea that it would furnish for intervention on behalf of France, for expeditionary force, and all the rest of it. Belgium was to take the place that had been taken before, as pleas for war, by Morocco and Agadir.

Now for personal movements. Simon and Lloyd George drove me to lunch at Beauchamp's and our talk was on the footing that we were all three for resignation. Simon said to me privately that he felt pretty sure of decisive influence over Lloyd George, and that he (Simon) looked to resignation as quite inevitable. Present: Lord Beauchamp, Simon, Lloyd George, Harcourt, Samuel, Pease, M'Kinnon Wood (not sure about Runciman). It wore all the look of an important gathering, but was in truth a very shallow affair. On the surface they were pretty stalwart against allowing a mistaken interpretation of entente to force us into a Russian or Central European quarrel. The general voice was loud that "Burns was right," and that we should not have passed Grey's proposed language to Cambon. They all pressed the point that the Cabinet was being rather artfully drawn on step by step to war for the benefit of France and Russia. If I, or anybody else, could only have brought home to them that the compound and mixed argument of French liability and Belgian liability must end in expeditionary force, and active part in vast and long-continued European war, the Cabinet would undoubtedly have perished that very evening, Lloyd George and Simon heading the schism. I held that the door-step point was awkward, if we stopped there. I said that as for myself, I felt bound to go, on wider grounds. Personally my days were dwindling, I was a notorious peace-man and little-Englander, etc., my disappearance would be totally different from theirs; the future responsibilities to Asquith, to the party, to the constituencies, were quite different in their charge. They made a loud, prompt protest of course. Lloyd George and Simon were energetically decided at the end, as they had been at the beginning, to resist at all costs the bellicose inferences from the entente. Pease told us that he had been lunching with the Prime Minister, who begged him to keep the *conciliabule* to which he was going, "out of mischief," or some such good-natured phrase. Pease also argued that Grey was never quite so stiff as he seemed. His tone convinced me that the Quaker President of the Peace Society would not be over squeamish about having a hand in Armageddon. What exactly brought Lloyd

George among us, and what the passing computations for the hour inside his lively brain, I could not make out.

Two hours' rumination at the Club. Felt acutely what Mr. Gladstone had often told me, that a public man can have no graver responsibility than quitting a Cabinet on public grounds. No act for which he may be more justly called to full account. Anybody can hold and advocate unpopular opinions; but withdrawal from a Cabinet is a definite act, involving relations for good or ill with other people, and possibly affecting besides all else the whole machinery of domestic government. It concerns a man's principle and creed; it affects intimate and confidential relations with fellow-workers; it concerns his party, its strength and weakness, the balance of power in its ranks and its organisation. No fugitive Sabbath musing was it, either then or since, that filled my mind.

The dissolution of the Ministry was that afternoon in full view. Would even the break-up of the Ministry be less of an evil both for Liberal principles, and the prospects and power of the Liberal party, than their wholesale identification with a Cabinet committed to intervention in arms by sea and land in Central Europe and all the meshes of the Continental system? It is easy to get a question into a false position. Never easier than now. The significance of the French Entente had been rather disingenuously played with, before both the Cabinet and Parliament. An entente was evidently something even more dangerous for us than an alliance. An alliance has definite covenants. An entente is vague, rests on point of honour, to be construed by accident and convenience. The Prime Minister and Grey had both of them assured the House of Commons that we had no engagements unknown to the country. Yet here we were confronted by engagements that were vast indeed, because indefinite and undefinable. The same two Ministers and others had deliberately and frequently, in reply to anxious protests from Harcourt and myself, minimised the significance of the systematic conferences constantly going on between the military and naval officers of the two countries. Then the famous letter to Cambon of November 1912, which we had extorted from Grey—what a singularly thin and deceptive document it was turning out!

No political rumination of mine, again, could ever leave out the effect of a war upon Home Rule [of Ireland]. What more certain to impair the chances of a good settlement of Home Rule than the bottomless agitations of a great war? I travelled in my mind over all the well-trodden ground of the diplomacies of the last fortnight. I recalled a conversation, recorded in some blue print, between Grey and Lich-nowsky, in which there was almost a glow and fervour not common in such affairs, over the blessed improvement in the relations of England and Germany during the last three or four years. Why was not this great new fact, instead of the Entente, made the centre, the pivot, the starting-point of new negotiations? Grey's fine character had achieved an influence in Europe that was the noblest asset for the fame of England and the glory of peace. In a few hours it would be gone. I could not but be penetrated by the precipitancy of it all. What grounds for expecting that the ruinous waste and havoc of war would be repaid by peace on better terms than were already within reach of reason and persistent patience. When we counted our gains, what would they amount to, when reckoned against the ferocious hatred that would burn with inextinguishable fire, for a whole generation at least, between two great communities better fitted to understand one another than any other pair in Europe? This moral devastation is a worse incident of war even than human carnage, and all the other curses with which war lashes its victims and its dupes. With a fleet of overwhelming power, a disinterestedness beyond suspicion, a Foreign Minister of proved abil-ity, truthfulness and self-control, when the smoke of battle-fields had cleared from the European sky, England might have exerted an influ-ence not to be acquired by a hundred of her little Expeditionary Forces. Grey, after too long delay, had wisely and manfully posed the issue of the hour for his colleagues when he declared that we must now decide between intervention and neutrality, and that for neutrality he was not the man. Nor am I the man, said I to myself, to sit in the Council of War into which Campbell-Bannerman's Cabinet is to be transformed. It is, after all, not to be endured that not even two men in it should be found to "testify" for convictions. Nor were these con-victions merely abstract or general. They were supported by my full and accurate knowledge of the facts of the particular situation. I could not be sure that the fervid tone of the colleagues whom I had just left, sincere though it was, would last. I saw no standard-bearer. The power of Asquith and Grey, and the natural "cohesion of office," would prove too hard for an isolated group to resist. The motives of Lloyd George were a riddle. He knew that his "stock" had sunk dangerously low; peace might be the popular card against the adventurous energy of Winston; war would make mince-meat of the Land Question. And the break-up of Government and Party might well make any man pause quite apart from demagogic calculations. In plain truth the Liberal party was already shattered and could not win the approaching election, mainly owing to Lloyd George himself. He was on the eve of the mistake of his life. Let him and others do what they would, and with a balance of motives in their minds as legitimate as my own. For me at any rate—*the future being what it must inevitably be*—no choice was open.

So I wrestled all the afternoon, and in this vein I made my way through the crowds in Whitehall to Downing Street. My decision was due to no one particular conversation, telegram, despatch; to none of the private correspondence from abroad, which Grey used to confide to me as representing the Foreign Office in the House of Lords. It was the result of a whole train of circumstance and reflection.

Cabinet at 6.30. Grey reported his conversation with Cambon. Burns said he must go. The Prime Minister still bespoke him for a talk at the close of the Cabinet. As we got up from our chairs, I said quietly to Asquith that I feared I, too, must go. He looked at me with his clear open eye. "One favour at any rate," he said, "I would ask you. Sleep on it." "Of course I will," I answered. I left him trying to deal with Burns—in vain.

III

Monday, August 3.—After breakfast, composed my letter to Asquith, copied it fair at the Privy Council Office, and sent it in to him.

J. M. to Asquith

August 3, 1914

My Dear Asquith,

I have, as you wished, taken a night to think over my retirement. I have given earnest pains to reach a sensible conclusion.

The thing is clear. Nothing can be so fatal in present circumstances as a Cabinet with divided counsels. Grey has pointed out the essential difference between two views of Neutrality in the present case. Well, I deplore to think that I incline one way, and three or four of my leading colleagues incline the other way. This being so, I could contribute nothing useful to your deliberations, and my presence could only hamper the concentrated energy, the zealous and convinced accord, that are indispensable. You remember the Peelites entering Palmerston's Cabinet in the Crimean War: they entered it, and resigned in two or three days. If we abandon Neutrality, I fear that within two or three days, vital points might arise that would make my presence a tiresome nuisance.

I press you, therefore, to release me. I propose to come to the Cabinet to-day after the P.C. at the Palace. But I don't expect to be affected by what will pass there. (Cabinet.)

You will believe that I write this with heartfelt pain.

Ever yours,

M.

Privy Council at the Palace and talked with the King. Nothing particular passed, though he seemed to scent what was afoot. Then to Cabinet. Saw Lloyd George, and told him that I had sent in my resignation. He seemed astonished. *"But if you go, it will put us who don't go, in a great hole."* I made the obvious reply to this truly singular remark. He asked if I had considered the news of Germany bullying Belgium, etc. "Yes," said I, "and it is bad enough, but, in my view, war is not the only reply, and it does not alter my aversion to the French entente policy and its extended application." He told me that it changed Runciman's line and his own. My impression is that he must have begun the day with one of his customary morning talks with the splendid *condottiere* at the Admiralty, had revised his calculations, as he had a perfect right to do; had made up his mind to swing round, as he had done about the *Panther* in 1911, to the politics of adventure; and found in the German ultimatum to Belgium a sufficiently plausible excuse. I should be ashamed of this want of charity, in the case of any other of my colleagues except Churchill, and possibly the Lord Chancellor. Yet if there is a war, Winston will beat Lloyd George hollow, in spite of ingenious computation.

Then the Prime Minister arrived, with a grave look on his usually undisturbed face. We began with some miscellaneous business of secondary import, I forget what. The Prime Minister then drew himself together in his chair (next to mine), and opened with some severity of tone and aspect [2]—"I have to tell the Cabinet that I have this morning the resignations of four of its members in my hands. Burns you all heard last night. To-day I have heard to the same effect from the senior of us all, the one who is the greatest source of the moral authority of the Government. . . . Besides these two, we are to lose Simon and Beauchamp. I understand further that many others in the Cabinet, perhaps a majority, share their views, though not at present following

2. I afterwards read to Burns this version of what Asquith said, and he pronounced it "admirably right."

the same course. Then it is represented to me that a majority of our party in the House of Commons lean pretty strongly in the same direction. Well, if the circumstances in which the country is placed were of an ordinary kind, my course would be perfectly clear. I should go at once to the King and beg him to seek other Ministers. But the national situation is far from ordinary, and I cannot persuade myself that the other party is led by men, or contains men, capable of dealing with it. Then the idea of a Coalition naturally occurs to one. But Coalitions have hardly ever turned out well in our history. I could not look hopefully forward to that course. You [or we] might shape a partial Coalition. At any rate it is my duty to place my [or the] position plainly before the Cabinet."

They looked as if they expected me to say something. Naturally and most sincerely I expressed my regret at adding to the embarrassments of the hour, and repeated the points made in my letter of that morning. What could I look forward to but everlasting wrestles with Winston (at whom I looked with paternal benignity), without being able to contribute a single useful word. If I agreed and held on, I should be like the Peelites, who withdrew from Palmerston's Government two or three days after joining. I feared I must beg the Prime Minister to let me hold to my letter. Simon followed; briefly, but with much emotion, quivering lip and tears in his eyes. He was even firmer than I was. Beauchamp said that he felt bound to associate himself with me. Lloyd George earnestly expostulated, especially to my address. Crewe said a word about his wretched position in the House of Lords, depleted of Beauchamp and me, and he remarked that he could never imagine himself a member of any Government not predominantly and substantially Liberal—in which I thoroughly believe him. Grey, in a lowish tone of suppressed feeling, said how unhappy it made him to be the cause of such dissent and trouble among such friends. By the way, I have forgotten to put down that Asquith, almost at the beginning of his appeal, said with some emphasis that nothing would induce him to separate from Grey.

We then broke up without further ceremony, in that vague frame in which Cabinets so often disperse, it being understood that we three resigners present had in fact resigned. So ended my last Cabinet, eight and twenty years after my first. Beauchamp took me to his house to luncheon; I have seldom felt such relief, such lightness of heart—the reaction after all those days of tension. My host said he felt just the same. We gossiped about our successors. "Who will take your office?" he asked. "Well," said I with a laugh, "looking round the House of Lords, I can see nobody but my predecessor." "Oh, but how could I take your place, sharing the opinions for which you have left it?"

After luncheon, I went to the Club to rest an hour; then to House of Lords where everybody was talking of Grey's "convincing" exposition of his policy. Nothing passed in the House of Lords, and I soon found myself with the trees and fresh grass and open skies of my home.

Late in the evening Burns arrived. "Have you heard the news? Simon has been got over by the Prime Minister, with some stipulations, this afternoon, and after him, Beauchamp. So you and I are the only two!"

. . .

By partial coalition, I suppose that Asquith was thinking of Pitt in 1804. Temporary co-operation about war, and the conversations and conferences about Home Rule, Amending Bill, etc., might naturally ripen into a formal party engagement. The old Liberalism had done its work, and the time had come for openly changing imperial landmarks, and extinguishing beacons that needed new luminants.

IV

Tuesday, August 4.—Found the usual Cabinet summons on the breakfast table. Of course had no idea of going. While I was munching my dry toast as complacent as man could be, a messenger from Downing Street arrives, bringing a letter marked "Urgent" from the Prime Minister:

SECRET

3 Aug. 1914
Midnight

My Dear Morley,

This is, to me, a most afflicting moment.

You know well after nearly 30 years of close and most affectionate association, in the course of which we have not always held the same point of view in regard to accidentals, though in essentials I think we have rarely differed, that to lose you in the stress of a great crisis is a calamity which I shudder to contemplate, and which (if it should become a reality) I shall never cease to deplore.

I therefore beg you, with all my heart, to think twice and thrice, and as many times more as arithmetic can number, before you take a step which impoverishes the Government, and leaves me stranded and almost alone.

Always yours,
H. H. Asquith (signed)

No more complacency! Really nothing short of mental anguish held me by the throat. I paced my library quarter of an hour, and my garden for quarter of an hour more. Then I got into the motor to drive for a Privy Council at Palace. By the time I reached my Office at Whitehall, my concentrated thought in the motor had cleared all doubts away. My nerve had become good as usual, my temper was cool. I sat down and concocted my letter to the Prime Minister, copied the draft and sent it in to its destination.

Aug. 4, 1914

My Dear Asquith,
Your letter shakes me terribly. It goes to my very core. In spite of temporary moments of difference, my feelings for you have been cordial, deep, close, from your earliest days, and the idea of severing our affectionate association has been the most poignant element in the stress of the last four days.

But I cannot conceal from myself that we—I and the leading men of the Cabinet—do not mean the same thing in the foreign policy of the moment. To swear ourselves to France is to bind ourselves to Russia, and to whatever demands may be made by Russia on France. With this cardinal difference, how could I either decently or usefully sit in a cabinet day after day discussing military and diplomatic details in a policy which I think a mistake. Again I say divided counsels are fatal.

I am more distressed in making this reply to your generous and moving appeal that I have ever been in writing any letter of all my life.

Ever yours,

M.

At the Palace, the King, who had been aware since Monday of the prospect of my resignation, asked me for the second or third time whether I was in or out. I said out, until he had named my successor. He said in a rather sincere tone that he was very sorry. I take this to be the date of my resignation, though emoluments were paid up to August 5.

I looked to the past in this short episode without self-reproach. I parted from friends without a wound or even a scratch, I could not comprehend them all, and two of them I had no choice but to *judge*. I looked to my brief future with steady self-control, meaning to imitate Michelangelo's figure of the Penseroso in my library,[3]—with a firm mind pondering stern things.

> *Grato m'e 'l sonno, e più l' esser di sasso*. [I am grateful for sleep but even more for being of stone.]

3. Morley wrote in his *Recollections* (1917), Book I., chap. iv.: "I had a cast of Michelangelo's famous figure of the Penseroso in a library, presiding over an array of shelves well stocked with saints, sages, and some demoniacs, with

> A look that's fastened to the ground,
> A tongue chained up without a sound."

‖ THE OUTBREAK OF WAR

In the House of Commons, August 3, 1914
Sir Edward Grey, Andrew Bonar Law, John Redmond,
and Ramsay MacDonald

Last week I stated that we were working for peace not only for this country, but to preserve the peace of Europe. To-day events move so rapidly that it is exceedingly difficult to state with technical accuracy the actual state of affairs, but it is clear that the peace of Europe cannot be preserved. Russia and Germany, at any rate, have declared war upon each other.

Before I proceed to state the position of His Majesty's Government, I would like to clear the ground so that, before I come to state to the House what our attitude is with regard to the present crisis, the House may know exactly under what obligations the Government is, or the House can be said to be, in coming to a decision on the matter. First of all, let me say, very shortly, that we have consistently worked with a single mind, with all the earnestness in our power, to preserve peace. The House may be satisfied on that point. We have always done it.

Hansard, Fifth Series, Vol. 65, cols. 1809–34.

Sir Edward Grey (1862–1933), later Viscount Grey of Falloden, had been Foreign Secretary since the formation of the Liberal Government in 1905. He had pursued a policy of friendship with France and Russia, but Britain had not committed herself to any country through any formal alliance. The speech reprinted here, which in effect took Britain into war, is considered by many to be the greatest he ever delivered in Parliament. He was supported by the leader of the Conservative party, Andrew Bonar Law, by the leader of the Irish, John Redmond, but not by the then leader of the Labour parliamentary group, Ramsay MacDonald.

During these last years, as far as His Majesty's Government are concerned, we would have no difficulty in proving that we have done so. Throughout the Balkan crisis, by general admission, we worked for peace. The co-operation of the Great Powers of Europe was successful in working for peace in the Balkan crisis. It is true that some of the Powers had great difficulty in adjusting their points of view. It took much time and labour and discussion before they could settle their differences, but peace was secured, because peace was their main object, and they were willing to give time and trouble rather than accentuate differences rapidly.

In the present crisis, it has not been possible to secure the peace of Europe; because there has been little time, and there has been a disposition—at any rate in some quarters on which I will not dwell—to force things rapidly to an issue, at any rate, to the great risk of peace, and, as we now know, the result of that is that the policy of peace, as far as the Great Powers generally are concerned, is in danger. I do not want to dwell on that, and to comment on it, and to say where the blame seems to us to lie, which Powers were most in favour of peace, which were most disposed to risk or endanger peace, because I would like the House to approach this crisis in which we are now, from the point of view of British interests, British honour, and British obligations, free from all passion as to why peace has not been preserved.

We shall publish Papers as soon as we can regarding what took place last week when we were working for peace; and when those Papers are published I have no doubt that to every human being they will make it clear how strenuous and genuine and whole-hearted our efforts for peace were, and that they will enable people to form their own judgment as to what forces were at work which operated against peace.

I come first, now, to the question of British obligations. I have assured the House—and the Prime Minister has assured the House more than once—that if any crisis such as this arose, we should come before the House of Commons and be able to say to the House that it was free to decide what the British attitude should be, that we would have no secret engagement which we should spring upon the House, and tell the House that, because we had entered into that engagement, there was an obligation of honour upon the country. I will deal with that point to clear the ground first.

There have been in Europe two diplomatic groups, the Triple Alliance, and what came to be called the "Triple Entente," for some years past. The Triple Entente was not an Alliance—it was a diplomatic group. The House will remember that in 1908 there was a crisis, also a Balkan crisis, originating in the annexation of Bosnia and Herzegovina. The Russian Minister, M. Isvolsky, came to London, or happened to come to London, because his visit was planned before the crisis broke out. I told him definitely then, this being a Balkan crisis, a Balkan affair, I did not consider that public opinion in this country would justify us in promising to give anything more than diplomatic support. More was never asked from us, more was never given, and more was never promised.

In this present crisis, up till yesterday, we have also given no promise of anything more than diplomatic support—up till yesterday no promise of more than diplomatic support. Now I must make this question of obligation clear to the House. I must go back to the first Moroccan crisis of 1906. That was the time of the Algeciras Conference, and it came at a time of very great difficulty to His Majesty's Government when a General Election was in progress, and Ministers were scattered over the country, and I—spending three days a week in my constituency and three days at the Foreign Office—was asked the question whether, if that crisis developed into war between France and Germany, we would give armed support. I said then that I could promise nothing to any foreign Power unless it was subsequently to receive the whole-hearted support of public opinion here if the occasion arose. I said, in my opinion, if war was forced upon France then on the question of Morocco—a question which had just been the subject of agreement between this country and France, an agreement exceedingly popular on both sides—that if out of that agreement war was forced on France at that time, in my view public opinion in this country would have rallied to the material support of France.

I gave no promise, but I expressed that opinion during the crisis, as far as I remember, almost in the same words, to the French Ambassador and the German Ambassador at the time. I made no promise, and I used no threats; but I expressed that opinion. That position was accepted by the French Government, but they said to me at the time —and I think very reasonably—"If you think it possible that the public opinion of Great Britain might, should a sudden crisis arise, justify you in giving to France the armed support which you cannot promise in advance, you will not be able to give that support, even if you wish to give it, when the time comes, unless some conversations have already taken place between naval and military experts." There was force in that. I agreed to it, and authorized those conversations to take place, but on the distinct understanding that nothing which passed between military or naval experts should bind either Government or restrict in any way their freedom to make a decision as to whether or not they would give that support when the time arose.

As I have told the House, upon that occasion a General Election was in prospect. I had to take the responsibility of doing that without the Cabinet. It could not be summoned. An answer had to be given. I consulted Sir Henry Campbell-Bannerman, the Prime Minister; I consulted, I remember, Lord Haldane, who was then Secretary of State for War, and the present Prime Minister, who was then Chancellor of the Exchequer. That was the most I could do, and they authorized that on the distinct understanding that it left the hands of the Government free whenever the crisis arose. The fact that conversations between military and naval experts took place was later on—I think much later on, because that crisis passed, and the thing ceased to be of importance —but later on it was brought to the knowledge of the Cabinet.

The Agadir crisis came—another Morocco crisis—and throughout that I took precisely the same line that had been taken in 1906. But subsequently, in 1912, after discussion and consideration in the Cabinet, it was decided that we ought to have a definite understanding in writing, which was to be only in the form of an unofficial letter, that these conversations which took place were not binding upon the freedom of either Government; and on the 22nd of November, 1912, I wrote to the French Ambassador the letter which I will now read to the House, and I received from him a letter in similar terms in reply. The letter which I have to read to the House is this, and it will be known to the public now as the record that, whatever took place between military and naval experts, they were not binding engagements upon the Government:

> My dear Ambassador,—From time to time in recent years the French and British naval and military experts have consulted together. It has always been understood that such consultation does not restrict the freedom of either Government to decide at any future time whether or not to assist the other by armed force. We have agreed that consultation between experts is not and ought not to be regarded as an engagement that commits either Government to action in a contingency that has not yet arisen and may never arise. The disposition, for instance, of the French and British Fleets respectively at the present moment is not based upon an engagement to co-operate in war.

You have, however, pointed out that, if either Government had grave reason to expect an unprovoked attack by a third Power, it might become essential to know whether it could in that event depend upon the armed assistance of the other.

I agree that, if either Government had grave reason to expect an unprovoked attack by a third Power, or something that threatened the general peace, it should immediately discuss with the other whether both Governments should act together to prevent aggression and to preserve peace, and, if so, what measures they would be prepared to take in common.

LORD CHARLES BERESFORD: What is the date of that?

SIR E. GREY: The 22nd November, 1912. That is the starting point for the Government with regard to the present crisis. I think it makes it clear that what the Prime Minister and I said to the House of Commons was perfectly justified, and that, as regards our freedom to decide in a crisis what our line should be, whether we should intervene or whether we should abstain, the Government remained perfectly free, and, *a fortiori,* the House of Commons remains perfectly free. That I say to clear the ground from the point of view of obligation. I think it was due to prove our good faith to the House of Commons that I should give that full information to the House now, and say what I think is obvious, from the letter I have just read, that we do not construe anything which has previously taken place in our diplomatic relations with other Powers in this matter as restricting the freedom of the Government to decide what attitude they should take now, or restrict the freedom of the House of Commons to decide what their attitude should be.

Well, Sir, I will go further, and I will say this: The situation in the present crisis is not precisely the same as it was in the Morocco question. In the Morocco question it was primarily a dispute which concerned France—a dispute which concerned France and France primarily—a dispute, as it seemed to us, affecting France, out of an agreement subsisting between us and France, and published to the whole world, in which we engaged to give France diplomatic support. No doubt we were pledged to give nothing but diplomatic support; we were, at any rate, pledged by a definite public agreement to stand with France diplomatically in that question.

The present crisis has originated differently. It has not originated with regard to Morocco. It has not originated as regards anything with which we had a special agreement with France; it has not originated with anything which primarily concerned France. It has originated in a dispute between Austria and Serbia. I can say this with the most absolute confidence—no Government and no country has less desire to be involved in war over a dispute with Austria and Serbia than the Government and the country of France. They are involved in it because of their obligation of honour under a definite alliance with Russia. Well, it is only fair to say to the House that that obligation of honour cannot apply in the same way to us. We are not parties to the Franco-Russian Alliance. We do not even know the terms of that Alliance. So far I have, I think, faithfully and completely cleared the ground with regard to the question of obligation.

I now come to what we think the situation requires of us. For many years we have had a long-standing friendship with France. [An HON. MEMBER: "And with Germany!"] I remember well the feeling in the House—and my own feeling—for I spoke on the subject, I think, when the late Government made their agreement with France—the warm and cordial feeling resulting from the fact that these two nations, who had had perpetual differences in the past, had cleared these differences away. I remember saying, I think, that it seemed to me that some benign influence had been at work to produce the cordial atmosphere that had made that possible. But how far that friendship entails obligation—it has been a friendship between the nations and ratified by the nations—how far that entails an obligation let every man look into his own heart, and his own feelings, and construe the extent of the obligation for himself. I construe it myself as I feel it, but I do not wish to urge upon anyone else more than their feelings dictate as to what they should feel about the obligation. The House, individually and collectively, may judge for itself. I speak my personal view, and I have given the House my own feeling in the matter.

The French Fleet is now in the Mediterranean, and the Northern and Western coasts of France are absolutely undefended. The French Fleet being concentrated in the Mediterranean, the situation is very different from what it used to be, because the friendship which has grown up between the two countries has given them a sense of security that there was nothing to be feared from us. The French coasts are absolutely undefended. The French fleet is in the Mediterranean, and has for some years been concentrated there because of the feeling of confidence and friendship which has existed between the two countries. My own feeling is that if a foreign fleet engaged in a war which France had not sought, and in which she had not been the aggressor, came

down the English Channel and bombarded and battered the undefended coasts of France, we could not stand aside and see this going on
practically within sight of our eyes, with our arms folded, looking on
dispassionately, doing nothing! I believe that would be the feeling of
this country. There are times when one feels that, if these circumstances actually did arise, it would be a feeling which would spread
with irresistible force throughout the land.

But I also want to look at the matter without sentiment, and from
the point of view of British interests, and it is on that that I am going
to base and justify what I am presently going to say to the House.
If we say nothing at this moment, what is France to do with her Fleet
in the Mediterranean? If she leaves it there, with no statement from us
as to what we will do, she leaves her Northern and Western coasts
absolutely undefended, at the mercy of a German fleet coming down
the Channel, to do as it pleases in a war which is a war of life and
death between them. If we say nothing, it may be that the French Fleet
is withdrawn from the Mediterranean. We are in the presence of a
European conflagration; can anybody set limits to the consequences
that may arise out of it? Let us assume that to-day we stand aside in an
attitude of neutrality, saying, "No, we cannot undertake and engage to
help either party in this conflict." Let us suppose the French Fleet is
withdrawn from the Mediterranean; and let us assume that the consequences—which are already tremendous in what has happened in
Europe even to countries which are at peace—in fact, equally whether
countries are at peace or at war—let us assume that out of that come
consequences unforeseen, which make it necessary at a sudden moment that, in defence of vital British interests, we should go to war:
and let us assume—which is quite possible—that Italy, who is now
neutral—[HON. MEMBER: "Hear, Hear!"]—because, as I understand,
she considers that this war is an aggressive war, and the Triple Alliance
being a defensive alliance her obligation did not arise—let us assume
that consequences which are not yet foreseen—and which perfectly
legitimately, consulting her own interests—make Italy depart from her
attitude of neutrality at a time when we are forced in defence of vital
British interests ourselves to fight, what then will be the position in
the Mediterranean? It might be that at some critical moment those
consequences would be forced upon us because our trade routes in the
Mediterranean might be vital to this country.

Nobody can say that in the course of the next few weeks there is any
particular trade route the keeping open of which may not be vital to

this country. What will be our position then? We have not kept a fleet in the Mediterranean which is equal to dealing alone with a combination of other fleets in the Mediterranean. It would be the very moment when we could not detach more ships to the Mediterranean, and we might have exposed this country from our negative attitude at the present moment to the most appalling risk. I say that from the point of view of British interests. We feel strongly that France was entitled to know—and to know at once!—whether or not, in the event of attack upon her unprotected Northern and Western Coasts she could depend upon British support. In that emergency, and in these compelling circumstances, yesterday afternoon I gave to the French Ambassador the following statement:

> I am authorized to give an assurance that if the German Fleet comes into the Channel or through the North Sea to undertake hostile operations against the French coasts or shipping, the British Fleet will give all the protection in its power. This assurance is, of course, subject to the policy of His Majesty's Government receiving the support of Parliament, and must not be taken as binding his Majesty's Government to take any action until the above contingency of action by the German Fleet takes place.

I read that to the House, not as a declaration of war on our part, not as entailing immediate aggressive action on our part, but as binding us to take aggressive action should that contingency arise. Things move very hurriedly from hour to hour. Fresh news comes in, and I cannot give this in any very formal way; but I understand that the German Government would be prepared, if we would pledge ourselves to neutrality, to agree that its fleet would not attack the Northern Coast of France. I have only heard that shortly before I came to the House, but it is far too narrow an engagement for us. And, Sir, there is the more serious consideration—becoming more serious every hour—there is the question of the neutrality of Belgium.

I shall have to put before the House at some length what is our position in regard to Belgium. The governing factor is the treaty of 1839, but this is a treaty with a history—a history accumulated since. In 1870, when there was war between France and Germany, the question of the neutrality of Belgium arose, and various things were said. Amongst other things, Prince Bismarck gave an assurance to Belgium that, confirming his verbal assurance, he gave in writing a declaration which he said was superfluous in reference to the treaty in existence—that the German Confederation and its allies would respect the neutrality of Belgium, it being always understood that that neutrality would be respected by the other belligerent Powers. That is valuable as a recognition in 1870 on the part of Germany of the sacredness of these treaty rights.

What was our own attitude? The people who laid down the attitude of the British Government were Lord Granville in the House of Lords, and Mr. Gladstone in the House of Commons. Lord Granville, on August 8, 1870, used these words. He said:

> We might have explained to the country and to foreign nations that we did not think this country was bound either morally or internationally or that its interests were concerned in the maintenance of the neutrality of Belgium; though this course might have had some conveniences, though it might have been easy to adhere to it, though it might have saved us from some immediate danger, it is a course which Her Majesty's Government thought it impossible to adopt in the name of the country with any due regard to the country's honour or to the country's interests.

Mr. Gladstone spoke as follows two days later:

> There is, I admit, the obligation of the treaty. It is not necessary, nor would time permit me, to enter into the complicated question of the nature of the obligations of that treaty; but I am not able to subscribe to the doctrine of those who have held in this House what plainly amounts to an assertion, that the simple fact of the existence of a guarantee is binding on every party to it, irrespectively altogether of the particular position in which it may find itself at the time when the occasion for acting on the guarantee arises. The great authorities upon foreign policy to whom I have been accustomed to listen, such as Lord Aberdeen and Lord Palmerston, never to my knowledge took that rigid and, if I may venture to say so, that impracticable view of the guarantee. The circumstance that there is already an existing guarantee in force is of necessity an important fact, and a weighty element in the case to which we are bound to give full and ample consideration. There is also this further consideration, the force of which we must all feel most deeply, and that is, the common interests against the unmeasured aggrandisement of any Power whatever.

The treaty is an old treaty—1839—and that was the view taken of it in 1870. It is one of those treaties which are founded, not only on consideration for Belgium, which benefits under the treaty, but in the interests of those who guarantee the neutrality of Belgium. The honour and interests are, at least, as strong to-day as in 1870, and we cannot take a more narrow view or a less serious view of our obligations, and of the importance of those obligations, than was taken by Mr. Gladstone's Government in 1870.

I will read to the House what took place last week on this subject. When mobilization was beginning, I knew that this question must be a most important element in our policy—a most important subject for the House of Commons. I telegraphed at the same time in similar terms to both Paris and Berlin to say that it was essential for us to know whether the French and German Governments respectively were prepared to undertake an engagement to respect the neutrality of Belgium. These are the replies. I got from the French Government this reply:

> The French Government are resolved to respect the neutrality of Belgium, and it would only be in the event of some other Power violating that neutrality that France might find herself under the necessity, in order to assure the defence of her security, to act otherwise. This assurance has been given several times. The President of the Republic spoke of it to the King of the Belgians, and the French Minister at Brussels has spontaneously renewed the assurance to the Belgian Minister of Foreign Affairs to-day.

From the German Government the reply was:

> The Secretary of State for Foreign Affairs could not possibly give an answer before consulting the Emperor and the Imperial Chancellor.

Sir Edward Goschen, to whom I had said it was important to have an answer soon, said he hoped the answer would not be too long delayed. The German Minister for Foreign Affairs then gave Sir Edward Goschen to understand that he rather doubted whether they could answer at all, as any reply they might give could not fail, in the event of war, to have the undesirable effect of disclosing, to a certain extent, part of their plan of campaign. I telegraphed at the same time to Brussels to the Belgian Government, and I got the following reply, from Sir Francis Villiers:

The Minister for Foreign Affairs thanks me for the communication, and replies that Belgium will, to the utmost of her power, maintain neutrality, and expects and desires other Powers to observe and uphold it. He begged me to add that the relations between Belgium and the neighbouring Powers were excellent, and there was no reason to suspect their intentions, but that the Belgian Government believe, in the case of violation, they were in a position to defend the neutrality of their country.

It now appears, from the news I have received to-day—which has come quite recently, and I am not yet quite sure how far it has reached me in an accurate form—that an ultimatum has been given to Belgium by Germany, the object of which was to offer Belgium friendly relations with Germany on condition that she would facilitate the passage of German troops through Belgium. Well, Sir, until one has these things absolutely definitely, up to the last moment, I do not wish to say all that one would say if one were in a position to give the House full, complete, and absolute information upon the point. We were sounded in the course of last week as to whether, if a guarantee were given that, after the war, Belgian integrity would be preserved that would content us. We replied that we could not bargain away whatever interests or obligations we had in Belgian neutrality.

Shortly before I reached the House I was informed that the following telegram had been received from the King of the Belgians by our King—King George:

> Remembering the numerous proofs of your Majesty's friendship and that of your predecessors, and the friendly attitude of England in 1870, and the proof of friendship she had just given us I make a supreme appeal to the diplomatic intervention of your Majesty's Government to safeguard the integrity of Belgium.

Diplomatic intervention took place last week on our part. What can diplomatic intervention do now? We have great and vital interests in the independence—and integrity is the least part—of Belgium. If Belgium is compelled to submit to allow her neutrality to be violated, of course the situation is clear. Even if by agreement she admitted the violation of her neutrality, it is clear she could only do so under duress. The smaller States in that region of Europe ask but one thing. Their one desire is that they should be left alone and independent. The one thing they fear is, I think, not so much that their integrity but that their independence should be interfered with. If in this war which is before Europe the neutrality of one of those countries is violated, if the troops of one of the combatants violate its neutrality and no action be taken to resent it, at the end of the war, whatever the integrity may be, the independence will be gone.

I have one further quotation from Mr. Gladstone as to what he thought about the independence of Belgium. It will be found in *Hansard*, Volume 203, Page 1787. I have not had time to read the whole speech and verify the context, but the thing seems to me so clear that no context could make any difference to the meaning of it. Mr. Gladstone said:

> We have an interest in the independence of Belgium which is wider than that which we may have in the literal operation of the guarantee. It is found in the answer to the question whether, under the circumstances of the case, this country, endowed as it is with influence and power, would quietly stand by and witness the perpetration of the direst crime that ever stained the pages of history, and thus become participators in the sin.

No, Sir, if it be the case that there has been anything in the nature of an ultimatum to Belgium, asking her to compromise or violate her neutrality, whatever may have been offered to her in return, her independence is gone if that holds. If her independence goes, the independence of Holland will follow. I ask the House, from the point of view of British interests, to consider what may be at stake. If France is beaten in a struggle of life and death, beaten to her knees, loses her position as a great Power, becomes subordinate to the will and power of one greater than herself—consequences which I do not anticipate, because I am sure that France has the power to defend herself with all the energy and ability and patriotism which she has shown so often—still, if that were to happen, and if Belgium fell under the same dominating influence, and then Holland, and then Denmark, then would not Mr. Gladstone's words come true, that just opposite to us there would be a common interest against the unmeasured aggrandisement of any Power?

It may be said, I suppose, that we might stand aside, husband our strength, and that, whatever happened in the course of this war, at the end of it intervene with effect to put things right, and to adjust them to our own point of view. If, in a crisis like this, we run away from those obligations of honour and interest as regards the Belgian Treaty, I doubt whether, whatever material force we might have at the end, it would be of very much value in face of the respect that we should have lost. And do not believe, whether a great Power stands outside this war or not, it is going to be in a position at the end of it to exert its superior strength. For us, with a powerful fleet, which we believe able to protect our commerce, to protect our shores, and to protect our interests, if we are engaged in war, we shall suffer but little more than we shall suffer even if we stand aside.

We are going to suffer, I am afraid, terribly in this war whether we are in it or whether we stand aside. Foreign trade is going to stop, not because the trade routes are closed, but because there is no trade at the other end. Continental nations engaged in war—all their populations, all their energies, all their wealth, engaged in a desperate struggle— they cannot carry on the trade with us that they are carrying on in times of peace, whether we are parties to the war or whether we are not. I do not believe, for a moment, that at the end of this war, even if we stood aside and remained aside, we should be in a position, a material position, to use our force decisively to undo what had happened in the course of the war, to prevent the whole of the West of Europe opposite to us—if that had been the result of the war—falling under the domination of a single Power, and I am quite sure that our moral position would be such as to have lost us all respect. I can only say that I have put the question of Belgium somewhat hypothetically, because I am not yet sure of all the facts, but, if the facts turn out to be as they have reached us at present, it is quite clear that there is an obligation on this country to do its utmost to prevent the consequences to which those facts will lead if they are undisputed.

I have read to the House the only engagements that we have yet taken definitely with regard to the use of force. I think it is due to the House to say that we have taken no engagement yet with regard to sending an expeditionary armed force out of the country. Mobilization of the Fleet has taken place; mobilization of the Army is taking place; but we have as yet taken no engagement, because I do feel that, in the case of a European conflagration such as this, unprecedented, with our enormous responsibilities in India and other parts of the Empire, or in countries in British occupation, with all the unknown factors, we must take very carefully into consideration the use which we make of sending an Expeditionary Force out of the country until we know how we stand. One thing I would say.

The one bright spot in the whole of this terrible situation is Ireland. The general feeling throughout Ireland—and I would like this to be clearly understood abroad—does not make the Irish question a consideration which we feel we have now to take into account. I have told the House how far we have at present gone in commitments and the conditions which influence our policy, and I have put to the House and dwelt at length upon how vital is the condition of the neutrality of Belgium.

What other policy is there before the House? There is but one way in which the Government could make certain at the present moment of keeping outside this war, and that would be that it should immediately issue a proclamation of unconditional neutrality. We cannot do that. We have made the commitment to France that I have read to the House which prevents us from doing that. We have got the consideration of Belgium which prevents us also from an unconditional neutrality, and, without those conditions absolutely satisfied and satisfactory, we are bound not to shrink from proceeding to the use of all the forces in our power. If we did take that line by saying, "We will have nothing whatever to do with this matter" under no conditions—the Belgian Treaty obligations, the possible position in the Mediterranean, with damage to British interests, and what may happen to France from our failure to support France—if we were to say that all those things mattered nothing, were as nothing, and to say we would stand aside, we should, I believe, sacrifice our respect and good name and reputation before the world, and should not escape the most serious and grave economic consequences.

My object has been to explain the view of the Government, and to place before the House the issue and the choice. I do not for a moment conceal, after what I have said, and after the information, incomplete as it is, that I have given to the House with regard to Belgium, that we must be prepared, and we are prepared, for the consequences of having to use all the strength we have at any moment—we know not how soon —to defend ourselves and to take our part. We know, if the facts all be as I have stated them, though I have announced no intending aggressive action on our part, no final decision to resort to force at a moment's notice, until we know the whole of the case, that the use of it may be forced upon us. As far as the forces of the Crown are concerned, we are ready. I believe the Prime Minister and my right hon. Friend the First Lord of the Admiralty have no doubt whatever that the readiness and the efficiency of those Forces were never at a higher mark than they are to-day, and never was there a time when confidence was more justified in the power of the Navy to protect our commerce and to protect our shores. The thought is with us always of the suffering and misery entailed from which no country in Europe will escape and from which no abdication or neutrality will save us. The amount of harm that can be done by an enemy ship to our trade is infinitesimal, compared with the amount of harm that must be done by the economic condition that is caused on the Continent.

The most awful responsibility is resting upon the Government in deciding what to advise the House of Commons to do. We have disclosed our mind to the House of Commons. We have disclosed the issue, the information which we have, and made clear to the House, I trust, that we are prepared to face that situation, and that, should it develop, as probably it may develop, we will face it. We worked for peace up to the last moment, and beyond the last moment. How hard, how persistently, and how earnestly we strove for peace last week, the House will see from the Papers that will be before it.

But that is over, as far as the peace of Europe is concerned. We are now face to face with a situation and all the consequences which it may yet have to unfold. We believe we shall have the support of the House at large in proceeding to whatever the consequences may be and whatever measures may be forced upon us by the development of facts or action taken by others. I believe the country, so quickly has the situation been forced upon it, has not had time to realize the issue. It perhaps is still thinking of the quarrel between Austria and Servia, and not the complications of this matter which have grown out of the quarrel between Austria and Servia. Russia and Germany we know are at war. We do not yet know officially that Austria, the Ally whom Germany is to support, is yet at war with Russia. We know that a good deal has been happening on the French frontier. We do not know that the German Ambassador has left Paris.

The situation has developed so rapidly that technically, as regards the condition of the war, it is most difficult to describe what has actually happened. I wanted to bring out the underlying issues which would affect our own conduct, and our own policy, and to put them clearly. I have put the vital facts before the House, and if, as seems not improbable, we are forced, and rapidly forced, to take our stand upon those issues, then I believe, when the country realizes what is at stake, what the real issues are, the magnitude of the impending dangers in the West of Europe, which I have endeavoured to describe to the

House, we shall be supported throughout, not only by the House of Commons, but by the determination, the resolution, the courage, and the endurance of the whole country. . . .

MR. BONAR LAW: The right hon. Gentleman has made an appeal for support, and it is necessary I should say a word or two. They shall be very few. I wish to say, in the first place, that I do not believe there is a single Member of this House who doubts that, not only the right hon. Gentleman himself, but the Government which he represents, have done everything in their power up to the last moment to preserve peace, and I think we may be sure that, if any other course is taken, it is because it is forced upon them, and that they have absolutely no alternative. One thing only, further, I would like to say. The right hon. Gentleman spoke of the bright spot in the picture which only a day or two ago was a black spot on the political horizon. Everything he has said I am sure is true. I should like to say, further, that if the contingencies, which he has not put into words, but which are all in our minds as possible, arise then we have already had indications that there is another bright spot, and that every one of His Majesty's Dominions beyond the Seas will be behind us in whatever action it is necessary to take. This only I shall add: The Government already know, but I give them now the assurance on behalf of the party of which I am Leader in this House, that in whatever steps they think it necessary to take for the honour and security of this country, they can rely on the unhesitating support of the Opposition.

MR. JOHN REDMOND: I hope the House will not consider it improper on my part, in the grave circumstances in which we are assembled, if I intervene for a very few moments. I was moved a great deal by that sentence in the speech of the Secretary of State for Foreign Affairs in which he said that the one bright spot in the situation was the changed feeling in Ireland. In past times when this Empire has been engaged in these terrible enterprises, it is true—it would be the utmost affectation and folly on my part to deny it—the sympathy of the Nationalists of Ireland, for reasons to be found deep down in the centuries of history, have been estranged from this country. Allow me to say that what has occurred in recent years has altered the situation completely. I must not touch on any controversial topic. By this I may be allowed to say, that a wider knowledge of the real facts of Irish history have, I think, altered the views of the democracy of this country towards the Irish question, and to-day I honestly believe that the democracy of Ireland will turn with the utmost anxiety and sympathy to this country in every trial and every danger that may overtake it. There is a possibility, at any rate, of history repeating itself. The House will remember that in 1778, at the end of the disastrous American War, when it might, I think, truly be said that the military power of this country was almost at its lowest ebb, and when the shores of Ireland were threatened with foreign invasion, a body of 100,000 Irish Volunteers sprang into existence for the purpose of defending her shores. At first no Catholic—ah, how sad the reading of the history of those days is!—was allowed to be enrolled in that body of Volunteers, and yet, from the very first day the Catholics of the South and West subscribed money and sent it towards the arming of their Protestant fellow countrymen. Ideas widened as time went on, and finally the Catholics in the South were armed and enrolled as brothers in arms with their fellow countrymen of a different creed in the North. May history repeat itself. To-day there are in Ireland two large bodies of Volunteers. One of them sprang into existence in the North. Another has sprung into existence in the South. I say to the Government that they may to-morrow withdraw every one of their troops from Ireland. I say that the coast of Ireland will be defended from foreign invasion by her armed sons, and for this purpose armed Nationalist Catholics in the South will be only too glad to join arms with the armed Protestant Ulstermen in the North. Is it too much to hope that out of this situation there may spring a result which will be good not merely for the Empire, but good for the future welfare and integrity of the Irish nation? I ought to apologise for having intervened, but while Irishmen generally are in favour of peace, and would desire to save the democracy of this country from all the horrors of war, while we would make every possible sacrifice for that purpose, still if the dire necessity is forced upon this country we offer to the Government of the day that they may take their troops away, and that if it is allowed to us, in comradeship with our brethren in the North, we will ourselves defend the coasts of our country.

MR. RAMSAY MACDONALD: I should, had circumstances permitted, have preferred to remain silent this afternoon. But circumstances do not permit of that. I shall model what I have to say on the two speeches we have listened to, and I shall be brief. The right hon. Gentleman, to a House which in a great majority is with him, has delivered a speech the echoes of which will go down in history. The speech has been impressive, but however much we may resist the conclusion to which he has come, we have not been able to resist the moving character of his appeal. I think he is wrong. I think the Government which he represents and for which he speaks is wrong. I think the verdict of history will be that they are wrong. We shall see. The effect of the right hon. Gentleman's speech in this House is not to be its final effect. There may be opportunities, or there may not be opportunities for us to go into details, but I want to say to this House, and to say it without equivocation, if the right hon. Gentleman had come here to-day and told us that our country is in danger, I do not care what party he appealed to, or to what class he appealed, we would be with him and behind him. If this is so, we will vote him what money he wants. Yes, and we will go further. We will offer him ourselves if the country is in danger. But he has not persuaded my hon. Friends who co-operate with me that it is, and I am perfectly certain, when his speech gets into cold print to-morrow, he will not persuade a large section of the country. If the nation's honour were in danger we would be with him. There has been no crime committed by statesmen of this character without those statesmen appealing to their nation's honour. We fought the Crimean War because of our honour. We rushed to South Africa because of our honour. The right hon. Gentleman is appealing to us to-day because of our honour. There is a third point. If the right hon. Gentleman could come to us and tell us that a small European nationality like Belgium is in danger, and could assure us he is going to confine the conflict to that question, then we would support him. What is the use of talking about coming to the aid of Belgium, when, as a matter of fact, you are engaging in a whole European War which is not going to leave the map of Europe in the position it is in now. The right hon. Gentleman said nothing about Russia. We want to know about that. We want to try to find out what is going to happen, when it is all over, to the power of Russia in Europe, and we are not going to go blindly into this conflict without having some sort of a rough idea as to what is going to happen. Finally, so far as France is concerned, we say solemnly and definitely that no such friendship as the right hon. Gentleman describes between one nation and another could ever justify one of those nations entering into war on behalf of the other. If France is really in danger, if, as the result of this, we are going to have the power, civilisation, and genius of France removed from European history, then let him so say. But it is an absolutely impossible conception which we are talking about to endeavour to justify that which the right hon. Gentleman has foreshadowed.

SIR EDWARD GREY: I want to give the House some information which I have received, and which was not in my possession when I

made my statement this afternoon. It is information I have received
from the Belgian Legation in London, and is to the following effect:

> Germany sent yesterday evening at seven o'clock a Note
> proposing to Belgium friendly neutrality, covering free passage
> on Belgian territory, and promising maintenance of independ-
> ence of the kingdom and possession at the conclusion of peace,
> and threatening, in case of refusal, to treat Belgium as an enemy.
> A time limit of twelve hours was fixed for the reply. The Bel-
> gians have answered that an attack on their neutrality would be
> a flagrant violation of the rights of nations, and that to accept
> the German proposal would be to sacrifice the honour of a
> nation. Conscious of its duty, Belgium is firmly resolved to repel
> aggression by all possible means.

Of course, I can only say that the Government are prepared to take
into grave consideration the information which it has received. I make
no further comment upon it.

LORD ELTON

The Role of Ramsay MacDonald

In the afternoon of August 2, 1914, a huge crowd was wedged in
Trafalgar Square. From the plinth, Keir Hardie, Arthur Henderson,
George Lansbury, Cunninghame-Graham and other speakers were denouncing war. It was the day after Germany had declared war on
Russia. The sky over the square was dark and lowering, and at half-past
four, while Hardie was still speaking, the clouds broke suddenly in a
deluge of rain. At intervals a section of the onlookers sang the "Red
Flag" or the "International," but in general the mood of the great audience was anxiety, not excitement. A resolution was passed, protesting
against the imminent threat of war, and the secret diplomacy responsible for it, against any support for Russia and in favour of neutrality
and the international solidarity of the working classes. The meeting
ended, and the crowd dispersed through the rainy streets. Most of the

From *The Life of James Ramsay MacDonald 1866–1919* by Lord Elton. London,
Collins Publishers, 1939, pp. 242–51. Reprinted by permission.
    Ramsay MacDonald (1866–1937), chairman of the Parliamentary Labour group
at the time of the outbreak of the war, would in 1924 become Prime Minister, the
first head of a Labour Government, and again in 1929. In 1931 he was Prime
Minister of a National Government.

speakers made their way sombrely to Lincoln's Inn Fields, to MacDonald's flat. MacDonald was not there, nor had he been present at the demonstration in Trafalgar Square. He had been summoned to consultation in Downing Street. In growing anxiety, the little group in the flat at Lincoln's Inn Fields awaited his return. MacDonald meanwhile had made his way on foot towards Westminster. Shouldering his way, unnoticed, through the crowds which hung thick about Whitehall and Downing Street, he encountered Lord Morley. The old Radical stopped, and asked him what his line was going to be. MacDonald replied that he would have nothing to do with war. "Neither shall I," said Morley. But he added gloomily that the prospects were very dark. For these spokesmen of two epochs had encountered almost at the very moment when the tides of crisis turned. That morning, to Winston Churchill, it had "looked as if the majority would resign." Lloyd George himself had already taken counsel with MacDonald, and they had agreed that, if Britain went to war and Belgium had not been invaded, his only course would be to leave the Cabinet. But in the course of the day the Cabinet had decided (at the cost of John Burns's withdrawal) to promise to protect the French coasts against the German fleet; that day, too, the Conservative leaders had urged on the Prime Minister their view that any hesitation in supporting France and Russia would be fatal. That evening the German ultimatum reached Brussels. On the morrow Morley's view would be ancient history, unsupported in the Cabinet.

Meanwhile MacDonald made his way to Downing Street. It is said that he found Ministers still doubtful as to whether there would be popular support for war, and that he grimly reassured them. This, he said, would be the most popular war the country had ever fought. But there still seemed a possibility that it could be avoided. It was, however, no cheerful news that he brought back at last to the little gathering at Lincoln's Inn Fields.

That Sunday evening MacDonald was one of a party which dined at Lord Riddell's house. Three members of the Liberal Cabinet were there —Mr. Lloyd George, Sir John Simon and C. F. G. Masterman. All were oppressed by varying degrees of doubt and perplexity. Mr. Lloyd George was for neutrality, provided that Germany would give an undertaking to respect the Belgian frontier, and not to enter the Channel to attack the French coast or French shipping. Those who had already made up their minds for intervention he called Jingoes. Lord Riddell thought that MacDonald seemed to agree that peace could not be preserved if Belgium were invaded, although the Labour Party would resist war on any other grounds. After dinner, MacDonald wished to make a telephone call, and as Lord Riddell was about to get him his number, the bell of the instrument rang. It was Sir John French, then Chief of the Imperial General Staff, wanting to know whether we should send an army to the Continent, and who would command it. Riddell put his hand over the transmitter and repeated these inquiries to MacDonald, who smiled and suggested that he had better return to the dining-room and ask what to reply. Riddell did so, and came back to tell French that the odds were that we should go to war, that we should send an army, and that he would be in command. Upon which MacDonald observed, "They are all wrong. In three months there will be bread riots, and we shall come in."

Next day was August 3rd, Bank Holiday. The tempo of the tragedy quickened. The British Cabinet authorised mobilisation, Belgium rejected the German ultimatum, Britain replied with her own ultimatum to Germany, warning her to keep out of Belgium, or be at war with us; and in the afternoon Sir Edward Grey went down, through the straining crowds, to Parliament, to make his historic speech. He told the packed, intent, and at first uncertain House that, technically, we were not committed to France, but that, morally, "let every man look into his own heart." And then he turned to Belgium. Here law, sentiment and interest all pointed unequivocally in the same direction. We had guaranteed Belgian integrity in 1839 and in 1870; for more than three hundred years the foundation of all our foreign policy had been to protect the independence of the Low Countries. And if we let France be crushed now, could we save ourselves, alone, disgraced and friendless, later on? By now there could be no doubt. Virtually the whole House was with the speaker. The news "they have cheered him" flew to the anxious diplomats in the Foreign Office. It had been a triumphant speech—"I think in the circumstances . . . the greatest speech delivered in our time," wrote Lord Hugh Cecil. When MacDonald rose—after Bonar Law had briefly pledged the Conservatives, and Redmond, amidst much enthusiasm, the Irish, to the war—it was with a profound sense of isolation. The House, of course, would be overwhelmingly and resentfully against him—there was a murmur of hostility when he rose, and some Members ostentatiously left the Chamber as he began to speak. And though he was speaking with full authority for his Party—twice within the last five days the Labour Members had met and condemned Sir Edward Grey and war—he can have had little hope, as he

sensed the mounting passions inside and outside the House, that even
his Party would be with him for long. It was with an inner foreknowl-
edge of all that he would soon have to face, that he rose to make his
protest. The brief speech contained in miniature almost all the arguments—in parts apparently so hard to reconcile, and in their totality so
little understood by the mass of his fellow-countrymen—which he was
to employ throughout the war . . .

By eleven o'clock next night we were at war. The speed of the
unfolding tragedy, and in particular the invasion of Belgium, was
transforming opinion hourly. The Radical journalist, Massingham,
hastened to recant, in the mid-week *Daily News,* the opposition to war
he had expressed in the *Nation* at the previous week-end; H. G. Wells
proclaimed that the sword had been drawn for peace (and was soon
engaged in a vituperative controversy with Hardie and MacDonald in
the columns of the *Labour Leader,* in the course of which he referred
to "the spiteful, lying chatter of the shabbiest scum of Socialism").
The Labour Party itself wavered, and then bent, before the blast. On
August 5th, the Executive and the Parliamentary Party, it is true,
repeated its condemnation of Sir Edward Grey; "the Labour movement
reiterates the fact that it has opposed the policy which has produced
the war, and that its duty now is to secure peace at the earliest possible
moment on such conditions as will provide the best opportunities for
the re-establishment of amicable feelings between the workers of
Europe." Nothing perhaps more clearly illustrates how narrow, though
sundering, was the intellectual division which separated MacDonald
from the majority of his colleagues than the fact that this resolution
remained, unrescinded, theoretically, at least, the official policy of
Labour, throughout the war. "We condemn the policy which has produced the war, we do not obstruct the war effort, but our duty is to
secure peace at the earliest possible moment"—from first to last both
he and they would have claimed that they were faithfully fulfilling that
declaration. Both they and he were for winning the war, now that it
had begun. Yet from that identical point of departure, they were in due
course to become loyal members of the war coalition, Cabinet Ministers or orators on recruiting platforms, he the best-hated man in
Britain, decried and derided by the man in the street as a pacifist, a
pro-German, and even as a traitor. The Labour declaration of August
5th was not a refusal to participate in the war. But it was essentially a
moderate pronouncement. And the clue to MacDonald's attitude during
the next four years, as during the previous eight, is that, even in war-

time, he was to remain a moderate. And in a war there is no room for moderates—on either side of the controversy.

The parting of the ways came at once, on the very day of the resolution. As the Parliamentary Party itself reported, eighteen months later, "the opinion of the majority of the Party . . . crystallised into a conviction that under the circumstances it was impossible for this country to have remained neutral." And on that same evening, August 5th, a majority of Labour Members declined to accept MacDonald's proposal that, as Chairman, he should speak, in the sense of the resolution they had just passed, against the Prime Minister's demand for a war credit of one hundred millions. The resolution had in fact been a compromise, passed in a vain attempt to maintain the unity of the Party. MacDonald at once resigned his Chairmanship. A few minutes later he walked down the corridor of the House to a board meeting of the Labour newspaper, the *Daily Citizen,* of which he was also Chairman, and very calmly went through the same discussion again. Here, too, as had become inevitable, he was outvoted; but of this Board he remained Chairman until the demise of the paper, in June of the following year. The work of Chairman of the Parliamentary Party was handed over to Henderson, who at first remained Chief Whip, but was subsequently elected to the Chairmanship proper. MacDonald now found himself one of a small minority in his own Party. The I.L.P. Members, Hardie (who died in August, 1915), Richardson, Jowett, Anderson, when he was elected towards the end of 1914, and, when he returned from Australia, Snowden were also, though not for precisely the same reasons or in precisely the same sense, critics of the war. But all the other Labour Members were, first and foremost, for winning the war, and therefore for thorough co-operation with the Government. On August 29th the Labour Party agreed to a political truce in the constituencies and to co-operation in the recruiting campaign; on May 19th, 1915, it entered the Coalition Government. From both decisions, needless to say, MacDonald dissented. Almost miraculously, as we shall see, the Party did not split. MacDonald remained Treasurer, and a member therefore of its executive. On committees of various kinds majority and dissentients worked amicably together. But henceforth till the end of the war, if he was to continue, as he was determined, to put his views before the country, it could not be from the official Labour platforms. And so he found himself at once in renewed intimacy with the I.L.P., chief spokesman of the very body which had chiefly housed those "phraseologists," whose enthusiasm had sometimes in recent years so embarrassed his leadership. From being so constantly suspect, he became suddenly once again the idol of the Left wing. The association was not entirely easy for MacDonald. The realistic and rational Lowlander in him remained fundamentally a moderate all through the war, almost the last moderate left in the British Isles. Intellectually therefore he would never be altogether comfortable in the I.L.P., which was always essentially an organisation of extremists, in which passions ran as high, and thinking was as confused, as on the other side of the controversy. But the strong emotional vein in him enabled him to sympathise with his colleagues' fervour, and in a sense to share it, even while he consciously stood aloof from the mental confusions which it often bred. With all its difficulties, the association was to have the most far-reaching effects upon MacDonald, upon his later fortunes and upon the political history of his country.

The I.L.P. had no hesitations as to its attitude to war. Within a week of the outbreak, its Administrative Council was drafting a manifesto in a small hotel in Manchester. MacDonald, who was not a Member of the Council, was not present, and Hardie, as I have been told by one who was there, made a generous and foresighted plea for loyalty to him. "We must forget," he said, "the little differences we have had with MacDonald. I have had some rather serious differences with him myself, but now we must rally round him. He will need all the help and support we can give him. He it is who will have to bear most of the abuse; the Press attack has commenced, and most of it will be centred round him."

III

THE LABOUR PARTY IN 1914

The Labour Party Constitution of 1914

I.—AFFILIATION.

1.—The Labour Party is a Federation consisting of Trade Unions, Trades Councils, Socialist Societies, and Local Labour Parties.

2.—A Local Labour Party in any constituency is eligible for affiliation, provided it accepts the Constitution and policy of the Party, and that there is no affiliated Trades Council covering the constituency, or that, if there be such a Council, it has been consulted in the first instance.

3.—Co-operative Societies are also eligible.

4.—A National Organisation of Women, accepting the basis of this Constitution and the policy of the Party, and formed for the purpose of assisting the Party, shall be eligible for affiliation as though it were a Trades Council.

II.—OBJECT.

To organise and maintain in Parliament and the country a political Labour Party.

III.—CANDIDATES AND MEMBERS.

Candidates and Members must maintain this Constitution; appear before their constituencies under the title of Labour Candidates only;

abstain strictly from identifying themselves with or promoting the interests of any other Party; and accept the responsibilities established by Parliamentary practice.

IV.—CANDIDATURES.

1.—A Candidate must be promoted by one or more affiliated Societies which make themselves responsible for his election expenses.

2.—A Candidate must be selected for a constituency by a regularly convened Labour Party Conference in the constituency. [The Hull Conference accepted the following as the interpretation of what a "regularly convened Labour Party Conference" is:—All branches of affiliated organisations within a constituency or divided borough covered by a proposal to run a Labour Candidate must be invited to send delegates to the Conference, and the local organisation responsible for calling the Conference may, if it thinks fit, invite representatives from branches of organisations not affiliated but eligible for affiliation.]

3.—Before a Candidate can be regarded as adopted for a constituency, his candidature must be sanctioned by the National Executive; and where at the time of a bye-election no Candidate has been so sanctioned, the National Executive shall have power to withhold its sanction.

4.—Twenty-five per cent. of the Returning Officer's net expenses shall be paid in respect of Candidates, but no such payment shall be made to a Candidate of any Society which is in arrears in its contributions to the Party.

V.—THE NATIONAL EXECUTIVE.

The National Executive shall consist of sixteen members, eleven representing the Trade Unions, one the Trades Councils, Women's Organisations, and Local Labour Parties, and three the Socialist Societies, who shall be elected by ballot at the Annual Conference by their respective sections, and the Treasurer, who shall also be elected by the Conference.

VI.—DUTIES OF THE NATIONAL EXECUTIVE.

The National Executive Committee shall

1.—Appoint a Chairman and Vice-Chairman, and shall transact the general business of the Party;

2.—Issue a list of its Candidates from time to time, and recommend them for the support of the electors;

3.—Take all necessary steps to maintain this Constitution;

4.—All its members shall abstain strictly from identifying themselves with or promoting the interests of any other Party.

VII.—THE SECRETARY.

The Secretary shall be elected by the Annual Conference, and shall be under the direction of the National Executive.

VIII.—AFFILIATION FEES AND DELEGATES.

1.—Trade Unions and Socialist Societies shall pay 1d. per member per annum, with a minimum of 10s., and may send to the Annual Conference one delegate for each thousand members.

NOTE.—The membership of a Trade Union for the purpose of this Clause shall be those members contributing to the political fund of the Union established under the Trade Union Act 1913.

2.—Trades Councils and Local Labour Parties with 5,000 members or under shall be affiliated on an annual payment of 15s.; similar organisations with a membership of over 5,000 shall pay £1 10s., the former Councils to be entitled to send one delegate with one vote to the Annual Conference, the latter to be entitled to send two delegates and have two votes.

3.—In addition to these payments a delegate's fee to the Annual Conference may be charged.

IX.—ANNUAL CONFERENCE.

The National Executive shall convene a Conference of its affiliated Societies in the month of January each year.

Notice of resolutions for the Conference and all amendments to the Constitution shall be sent to the Secretary by November 1st, and shall be forthwith forwarded to all affiliated organisations.

Notice of amendments and nominations for National Executive, Treasurer, Secretary, two Auditors, and Annual Conference Arrangements Committee of five members, shall be sent to the Secretary by December 15th, and shall be printed on the Agenda.

X.—VOTING AT ANNUAL CONFERENCE.

There shall be issued to affiliated Societies represented at the Annual Conference voting cards as follows:—

1.—Trade Unions and Socialist Societies shall receive one voting card for each thousand members, or fraction thereof paid for.

2.—Trades Councils, Local Labour Parties and Women's Organisations shall receive one card for each delegate they are entitled to send.

Any delegate may claim to have a vote taken by card.

G. D. H. COLE

The State of the Party

In 1914, when the first World War began, the Labour Party had been in effective existence for only eight years. It had been created, as a party, in the General Election of 1906, which sent the Liberals back to power with an overwhelming majority; and the great majority of its seats had been won with the aid of Liberal votes. For the first four years, from 1906 to 1909, it had been in a position, when and if it wished, to act pretty much in independence of the Liberals, whose majority was too big to be endangered by anything it did; but in practice it had usually found itself supporting Liberal measures of social reform. Its chief success, as a party, had come right at the beginning, when it forced the Liberals, tied by their own election pledges, to accept the complete reversal of the Taff Vale Judgment by passing the Trade Disputes Act of 1906.

After 1909, the situation had been different. The General Elections of 1910, fought mainly on the issues raised by Lloyd George's Land Tax Budget of 1909 and by the Lords' rejection of it, had cost the Liberals enough seats to leave the Government dependent on Labour and Irish votes; and the Labour Party, with its very existence menaced

From *A History of the Labour Party from 1914* by G. D. H. Cole, London, Routledge & Kegan Paul, Ltd., 1948, pp. 1–21. Reprinted by permission of the publisher.

G. D. H. Cole (1889–1959) was an historian of all aspects of the labor movement in Great Britain, and an extremely influential political thinker.

by the Osborne Judgment * and in view of its agreement with the
Liberals over the Budget, the Lords, and Irish Home Rule, could not
afford to risk the Government's fall. It was thus tied, as a very junior
partner, to the fortunes of the Liberal Party; and its position was complicated by the sharp differences of opinion within its own ranks over
the social insurance legislation of 1911. A section of the party, headed
by Philip Snowden, denounced the contributory principle and regarded
the National Insurance Bill as an anti-Socialist measure designed to
make the poor pay for the poor; whereas most of the Trade Unionists
in the party saw in it a means of strengthening the bargaining position
of the Trade Unions as well as of reducing the hardships of sickness
and unemployment. There were thus divided voices inside the party at
a time when, in any event, its hands were largely tied; and in relation
to the section of the electorate to which it had to look for support—the
Trade Unionists in the main centres of industry—its influence was
waning because it seemed able to do so little to focus parliamentary
attention on working-class grievances. Rising prices, with wages lagging
behind, were leading to a growth of industrial militancy and to a
preaching of "direct action" doctrines which denied the effectiveness of
parliamentary proceedings and denounced the Labour parliamentarians
as "collaborationists" whose compromising tactics blurred the realities
of the class-war. Syndicalism and Industrial Unionism were in the air,
and owed their vogue not only to the lag in real wages but also to the
catchingness of the militancy of the women suffragists and of the
Ulster diehards and their English Conservative allies.

Between the General Election of December, 1910, and the outbreak
of war the Labour Party fought fourteen by-elections, without a single
success. Indeed, it actually lost four seats, three through the death of

---

* The Osborne Judgment, given in the House of Lords on a case brought by a
certain W. V. Osborne against his Trade Union, the Amalgamated Society of
Railway Servants, declared all political action by Trade Unions to be *ultra vires*.
It thus prevented Trade Unions from either putting forward their own candidates
at national or local elections or subscribing out of their funds to any political
party. This judgment struck away the main foundation of the Labour Party
finances, and caused it to contest the two General Elections of 1910 under a serious
handicap. The effect of the judgment was reversed in 1913, when the Trade Union
Act legalised political expenditure by Trade Unions on condition (*a*) that such
expenditure was to be met only from a separate Political Fund; (*b*) that such a
fund should be set up only after a ballot vote of the members had given a favourable decision; and (*c*) that any member of the Union concerned who objected to
contributing to the Political Fund should be allowed to sign a form "contracting-
out" of payment of the Political Levy, without thereby forfeiting any of his other
rights as a member of the Union.

ex-Liberal-Labour miners and one when George Lansbury, disagreeing
with his party's attitude on the issue of Women's Suffrage, resigned and
fought a by-election as an independent champion of the women's cause.
In addition, seven by-elections were fought by Socialist Independents,
where official Labour failed to produce a candidate; but they were all
heavily beaten. Labour's political fortunes in 1914 were on the ebb, and
the hopes aroused by the advent of the party in 1906 had suffered a
sad reverse.

No doubt, to a great extent this setback was not the Labour Party's
fault. It could not help playing second fiddle to the Liberals, first in the
struggle over the Land Tax Budget and then over Irish Home Rule.
It was badly handicapped by the Osborne Judgment, which had upset
its financial basis; and it was in a real difficulty over Women's Suffrage,
because it was not prepared to give the women's claims priority over
everything else. But, when all this has been admitted, the Labour Party's
own shortcomings still appear serious enough; for, in sober truth, it had
no clearly conceived policy of its own and was made up of elements
which were too discrepant to provide the basis for an effective fighting
party.

Right up to 1914 the Labour Party neither stood, nor professed to
stand, for Socialism. There were, of course, Socialists in its ranks and
Socialist Societies affiliated to it and playing a large part in its work:
indeed, most of its leaders were Socialists and so, probably, were a
majority of its members. But in its ranks were quite a number who
neither were, nor called themselves Socialists; and behind these men
were Trade Unions, as yet precariously attached to the Labour Party,
and by no means ready to insist that their candidates must profess the
Socialist faith. The Fabian leaders, intent on their policy of "permea-
tion" and sceptical of the Labour Party's prospects, were hardly more
than lukewarm supporters right up to 1914. The I.L.P., its largest
affiliated Socialist Society, and in effect its creator, of course stood for
Socialism, but the I.L.P. leaders inside the Labour Party were in no
mind to jeopardise its unity by pressing too hard upon the Trade Union
section. The L.R.C. had been based on a compromise whereby Trade
Unionists and Socialists had agreed to work together under the banner
of "Labour" without raising awkward questions about who were Socialists and who were not; and Ramsay MacDonald, of the I.L.P., was as
set as Arthur Henderson, of the Friendly Society of Ironfounders, who
was then barely a Socialist, or as other Trade Union leaders who were
not Socialists in any sense of the term, on keeping strictly to the terms

of the compact. The Trade Union leaders who sat in the Parliaments of 1906 to 1914 included some who had fought side by side with Keir Hardie to make the Independent Labour Party a success—men such as G. N. Barnes, John Hodge, and J. R. Clynes. It included at any rate one old stalwart of the Social Democratic Federation—Will Thorne, of the Gasworkers' Union. But it was heavily weighed down on the right by men who had changed their party at the behest of their Trade Union without therewith changing their opinions; and this right wing of the party was the stronger in influence because most of the rest were well aware that they held their seats upon Liberal sufferance, and with the support of Liberal votes.

Of the forty-two Labour M.P.s elected in December, 1910, twenty-seven had been elected in straight fights against Conservatives, and one (in Scotland) against a Liberal with no Conservative in the field. Three had been returned unopposed; and eleven had been elected in two-member constituencies in which only one Labour candidate had been put forward. All these eleven had Liberal colleagues in the representation; and among the eleven were Keir Hardie, MacDonald, Snowden, Thomas, and G. H. Roberts. Not one Labour M.P. had been elected in the eleven three-cornered contests, and only one, a Scottish miner, against a Liberal opponent. Any serious clash with the Liberal Government might have endangered every Labour seat, except perhaps a very few which were "pocket boroughs" of the Miners' Federation. Of course, a clash would also have endangered many Liberal seats, where the M.P.s were dependent upon Labour votes. The Liberals had good cause for keeping on friendly terms with the Labour Party, as well as the Labour Party for keeping in with the Liberals. Nevertheless, the effect was that the party could not easily assert itself or show a bold front; and it was in fact in continual difficulties with its own Left Wing, which denounced it for not fighting by-elections except where the Liberals could be persuaded to stand down, and in particular for refusing to allow a second Labour candidate to enter the lists in any double-barrelled constituency where there was an informal pact between Liberals and Labour to share the seats.

It needs to be emphasised that right up to 1914 the Labour Party was making no real claim to be more than a minority party, with a mission to press working-class claims in Parliament, but with no immediate prospect of challenging the predominance of the two great traditional parties. In 1906 the Labour Party fought only fifty-one seats (*plus* five fought by the separate Scottish Workers' Representation Committee).

It fought eighty-one seats in January, 1910 when it had been reinforced
by the accession of most of the miners, and had absorbed the S.W.R.C.;
but in December 1910, it fought only fifty-seven, in an election which
caught it seriously short of funds, as well as reluctant to jeopardise the
Parliament Bill by three-cornered contests. Even if all its candidates
had been elected, it would have been smaller than the Irish Nationalist
Party. In the great majority of constituencies, including almost all the
county areas outside the coalfields, there was no sort of Labour electoral organisation—not even a struggling I.L.P. branch. Except in
Woolwich and in Barnard Castle, where Will Crooks and Arthur Henderson had built up their own independent local organisations, the
Labour Party had no individual members. In most places where it was
organised, it worked through a local Trades and Labour Council or a
group of Miners' Lodges, or depended almost entirely on the local
branch of the I.L.P. Two-thirds of all the seats fought by Labour in
December, 1910, were in the North or in South Wales: over a large
part of the country not a single Labour candidate took the field. How
localised Labour political activity still was can be seen from the accom-
panying Table.

DISTRIBUTION OF LABOUR SEATS IN PARLIAMENT, 1914 AND OF SEATS
CONTESTED IN JANUARY OR DECEMBER, 1910

	M.P.s in 1914	Seats contested in either Election, 1910	Additional seats contested by Independent Socialists
Scotland	3	12	1
North-east	4	7	—
North-west	1	2	1
Lancs and Cheshire	10	21	3
Yorkshire	6	13	3
Midlands	6	11	2
Eastern Counties	1	1	—
Greater London	3	5	3
South	0	3	—
Wales and Monmouth	5	9	—
N. Ireland	0	1	—
	39	85	13

Thus, in 1914, the political Labour movement was still at a rudimentary stage of development, and, except at election times, the I.L.P. still counted for a good deal more over most of the country than the Labour Party of which it was nominally a part. The outstanding leaders of the Labour Party in Parliament, except Arthur Henderson and J. H. Thomas, were much more closely associated in their everyday work with the I.L.P. than with the Labour Party; and in effect the work of framing Labour policy and of gaining adherents was left mainly to the I.L.P., though its views were always liable to be over-ridden either at the Labour Party Conference, where the Trade Unions had the decisive voice if they chose to use it, or at party meetings, where most of the Miners' members and some of the other Trade Union representatives were still inclined to put a brake on any action that might be liable to cause a breach with the Liberals.

No doubt the Labour Party had been since 1904 affiliated to the Socialist International, to which the leading British Socialist bodies—the I.L.P., the Fabian Society, and the British Socialist Party—also independently belonged. There had been many hesitations on both sides over the admission of the Labour Party to the International, which included the "class war" among its tenets and rested on professedly Marxian foundations. The difficulty had been overcome, on Karl Kautsky's motion, by admitting the Labour Party as a party which practised the class war, even though it refused to preach it; but the Party had not in fact taken its affiliation very seriously, though it had participated in the discussions in which, during the pre-war decade, the International had been attempting to define its attitude to war and to devise means of preventing it by the united action of the working class. There had been much discussion of the project of an international general strike to stop any war between the nations; and this very question was down for consideration at the Vienna Conference which was due to meet in August, 1914. In the meantime, the action of the affiliated parties towards any threat of war, and in face of its outbreak should their efforts fail to prevent it, had been laid down at the Stuttgart Conference of 1907, and reaffirmed three years later at Copenhagen. The declaration of the International on this issue was worded as follows:—

> If war threatens to break out, it is the duty of the working class in the countries concerned and of their parliamentary representatives, with the help of the International Socialist Bureau as a means of coordinating their action, to use every

effort to prevent war by all the means which seem to them most
appropriate, having regard to the sharpness of the class war and
to the general political situation;

Should war none the less break out, their duty is to intervene
to bring it promptly to an end, and with all their energies to use
the political and economic crisis created by the war to rouse the
populace from its slumbers, and to hasten the fall of capitalist
domination.

This resolution, which was the result of a compromise unanimously
endorsed after long debate, obviously failed to face up to essential
considerations. At the back of it was the assumption, made consciously
by some of the delegates but by no means by all, that from the standpoint of the working classes in any war between the nations the question of who was in the right or wrong simply would not arise. It was
assumed that in the first instance the Socialists of all countries, including those of the prospective belligerents, would feel able to act together
in an attempt to stop the war, without being inhibited by any conflicts
of opinion concerning the responsibility for provoking it. Still larger
was the assumption that, should war actually break out, the workers of
the belligerent countries would be indifferent about its military outcome
and would be prepared to take united anti-war action and to concentrate their efforts on "hastening the fall of capitalist domination"—a
phrase which, if seriously meant, implied revolutionary action against
their own Governments. In fact, it even appeared, in 1914, that, though
nearly all the Socialist Parties in the International were prepared to
demonstrate against war prior to its outbreak, most of them were not
prepared, even at this stage, to attempt any action designed to make
war impossible by hampering the military preparations of their own
States. Even less were most of them prepared, when war had actually
broken out, to do anything that would prejudice their own country's
aims, or play into the hands of its enemies. Nor, had the leaders of the
various parties been prepared to act up to the terms of the International's resolution, would the majority of the workers in most countries
have been prepared to follow them. . . .

When war broke out in 1914, the Labour Party had approximately
1,600,000 affiliated members connected with it through Trade Unions,
and 33,000 on whom affiliation fees were paid by the two Socialist
Societies. The I.L.P. paid dues on 30,000 members, and the Fabian
Society on 3,304. In the case of the I.L.P. the actual membership was
doubtless considerably greater, as many of its branches paid dues to its

own head office on much less than their full membership, and the head office itself paid at most only in accordance with what it received. When the British Socialist Party was accepted as an additional affiliated body, it paid on 10,000 members; but its application to join, though made before the outbreak of war, was not accepted until January, 1916, no Conference being held in 1915 owing to the war situation. If we count the B.S.P., there were perhaps as many as 65,000 individual members enrolled in the three Socialist Societies.

In 1914, as we have seen, the Labour Party itself had no individual members, though in a very few constituencies—notably Woolwich and Barnard Castle—there were local Labour Parties or Associations which enrolled individuals as members. Elsewhere the local organisation was in the hands of a variety of federal bodies, which were in many cases simply the local Trades Councils formed for mainly industrial purposes, in others the Trades Councils with representatives of the local Socialist Societies added, and in yet others specially formed Local Labour Parties. In all, the local constituents of the Labour Party in 1914 were made up as follows:

LABOUR PARTY LOCAL ORGANISATION IN 1914

Mainly Industrial		Mainly Political	
Trades Councils . . .	74	Local Labour Parties . .	34
Trades and Labour Councils	11	Labour Representation	
Trades Councils and Labour		Committees . . .	25
Representation Committees		Labour Associations . .	6
or Labour Parties (com-			
bined)	5		
Labour Councils or Leagues	3		
	—		—
	93		65

Thus the Labour Party had some sort of local organisation in only 158 areas, except where it was in effect represented by a branch of the I.L.P. It had an organisation designed mainly for political, as distinct from industrial, purposes in only sixty-five places. A number of these places were big towns, where a single organisation covered more than one constituency; but even when allowance has been made for this factor, it remains true that in the great majority of constituencies the

Labour Party had, in 1914, no organisation at all of its own, and in the majority not even a Trades Council acting as its agent. As against this, the Independent Labour Party had in 1914 no fewer than 670 branches, covering a much wider field. The figures are not comparable, because in a number of large towns the I.L.P. had several branches, linked up in a Federation of their own. Moreover, many of the I.L.P.'s branches were very small: only 244 of them were actually represented at the I.L.P.'s "Coming-of-Age" Conference held at Bradford in 1914. Even so, it is plain that a very large part of the Labour Party's local organisation was still in the hands of the I.L.P., which was in effect in most places both the natural organisation for active Labour propagandists to join and the only body which kept up any sort of continuous political activity between elections. . . .

Just before 1914 the Second International had been engaged in a campaign for Socialist Unity in each country. The British Section of the International then included, besides the Labour Party, which appointed representatives of the Trades Union Congress as members of its delegation, the three leading Socialist Societies—the I.L.P., the Fabian Society, and the B.S.P. Each of these was separately affiliated to the International, had its own members in the British Section, and sent its own delegations to International Socialist Congresses. The International wanted the British Societies to come together into a united body. The I.L.P. and the Fabian Society already had a joint Committee, mainly for educational and lecturing work, but felt no need to carry unity further, as they worked along essentially different and complementary lines. The position of the British Socialist Party was another matter. It had been formed only in 1911, by the fusion of the Social Democratic Party (formerly the S.D.F.) with a number of left-wing groups, largely seceders from the I.L.P. The B.S.P. was not affiliated to the Labour Party, which indeed it was accustomed fiercely to denounce for its compromises with capitalist Liberalism and for its refusal to wage, or to preach, the class war. The B.S.P. was Marxist, and had gathered most of the left-wing malcontents into its ranks—except the still more extreme adherents of the Socialist Labour Party (in Scotland) and the Socialist Party of Great Britain (mainly in London), both of which had left the S.D.F. because it did not go far enough. These two, not being connected with the International, were not invited to the Unity negotiations. A Committee representing the other three, under pressure from the International Socialist Bureau, agreed, not to fusion, which was rejected as impracticable, but to the formation of a United Socialist Council, on condition that it should be open only to bodies affiliated to the Labour Party. When, however, the representatives met again, after reporting to their respective Societies, a fresh issue arose, out of a demand from the B.S.P. that candidates standing under Labour Party auspices should be allowed to describe themselves as not merely "Labour," but, if they wished, "Labour and Socialist." The joint committee agreed that a proposal to allow this should be laid before the next Labour Party Conference; but when the proposal was reported to the I.L.P. Conference of 1914, the delegates rejected it, mainly on the ground that it would open the door to other proposals from bodies which might wish to put forward candidates as "Labour and Progressive," or even "Labour and Liberal." Several of the County Miners' Associations had been insisting on putting forward candidates in association with the Liberals, and their exclusion had cost the Labour Party several coalfield seats. The I.L.P. was not prepared, in the interests of unity with the B.S.P., whose leaders it much disliked, to risk encouraging further "Lib-Lab" activities; and accordingly it rejected the B.S.P. plan. It did, however, agree to support the B.S.P.'s application for affiliation to the Labour Party; and this, as we have seen, was ultimately accepted in 1916, after a long delay due to the postponement of the 1915 Labour Party Conference.

Meanwhile, a Socialist Unity Demonstration Committee, formed at the end of 1913, had held a series of demonstrations in favour of unity, addressed by leading speakers from the three Socialist Societies, including Keir Hardie, H. M. Hyndman, Sidney Webb, and Bernard Shaw. But the Fabian Annual Conference of 1914, after hearing addresses by Hardie and Hyndman, voted to proceed to the next business, mainly because, like the I.L.P., it was not prepared to run the risks involved in the proposal to allow candidates to run on a "Labour and Socialist" ticket. Then came the war, and despite further attempts by the B.S.P. to stir the other bodies into action, the project of Socialist Unity was quietly shelved. Indeed, the B.S.P. itself was in process of splitting into pro-war and anti-war factions. Hyndman and Robert Blatchford were strongly in favour of the war, whereas the majority of the members took up an anti-war line. In 1916, the B.S.P. having voted down the followers of Hyndman, a number of the old stalwarts of the Social Democratic Federation seceded and set up the National Socialist Party, which joined the Labour Party, and, a few years later, resumed the old name, and became the S.D.F.

The "Unity" plan had, in fact, never stood any real chance of success.

The Fabians were throughout quite unwilling to merge their identity, as a society concerned mainly with research and education and with the conversion of the "intellectuals," in a general propagandist body, and especially in one in which they would become utterly eclipsed. The I.L.P. leaders, even when they were critical of the Labour Party, were determined to do nothing that might risk breaking their alliance with the Trade Unions—the more so because most of them were bitterly opposed to Hyndman's doctrinaire Marxism, and scornful of the mixed assembly of malcontents that had joined forces under the B.S.P. banner. The B.S.P., for its part, wanted Unity, but only on terms which would preserve its full freedom to attack the Labour Party from within and to denounce the compromising policies of MacDonald and other I.L.P. leaders as well as of Henderson and the Labour Party head office. The conditions of acute labour unrest of the years just before 1914 had put the Socialist rank and file into a mood to wish for unity; and the I.L.P. leaders did not venture to attack it openly. But most of them were glad when the outbreak of war, by creating a new situation, enabled them to drop negotiations for which they had never felt any enthusiasm. Even a common opposition to the war did not suffice to unite the I.L.P. and the B.S.P., though, as we shall see, it did presently lead to a renewal of negotiations on a somewhat different basis.

Austria-Hungary declared war on Serbia on July 25, 1914: British mobilisation began officially on August 3, and Great Britain declared war on Germany on August 4. Into the ten days between the first of these events and the British mobilisation were crowded the attempts of the British Labour movement and of the International Socialist Bureau to act on the policy laid down at Stuttgart in 1907. The Austrian declaration of war was met by prompt protests from the various Socialist bodies, and on July 29 the International Socialist Bureau met at Brussels and agreed that the Socialist bodies in every country should organise demonstrations and take every possible action for the preservation of peace in Europe. On the same day, at an international demonstration held in Brussels, Keir Hardie for Great Britain, Haase for Germany, Jaurès for France, Vandervelde for Belgium, Morgari for Italy, and Rabinovitch for Russia, joined in the demand that the war should be stopped. On July 30, the British Labour Members of Parliament met and passed a resolution in favour of Great Britain staying out of the war, even if it could not be prevented altogether. On August 1, the British Section of the International, including the Labour Party as well as the Socialist bodies, drew up a manifesto against war; and on the following day the British Section held a great meeting in Trafalgar Square, at which Keir Hardie and Arthur Henderson joined in the demand for peace. On that same day Germany declared war on France and Russia and delivered its ultimatum to Belgium. The next day Sir Edward Grey made his famous speech in the House of Commons, in effect bringing Great Britain into the war. Ramsay MacDonald, speaking on behalf of the Labour Party and with its authority, urged that every possible step should be taken to keep Great Britain out of the war; but on August 4, the British Government declared war on Germany, and the Labour Party, after several meetings, decided to give its support. Thereupon, Ramsay MacDonald resigned from the leadership of the Labour Party, and Arthur Henderson was elected in his place. Meanwhile, the German Social Democratic Party had decided to vote for the war credits demanded by the German Government, and in France the Socialist Party had rallied by a majority to the support of the war.

The Labour Party's support of the war was not unqualified. In a circular issued on August 7 it attributed the outbreak to the action of "Foreign Ministers pursuing diplomatic politics for the purpose of maintaining a balance of power," and argued that the British "national policy of understandings with France and Russia only was bound to increase the power of Russia both in Europe and Asia, and to endanger good relations with Germany." It went on to argue that Sir Edward Grey "committed, without the knowledge of the people, the honour of the country to supporting France in the event of any war in which she was seriously involved, and gave definite assurances of support before the House of Commons had any chance of considering the matter." The circular went on to say that "the Labour movement reiterates the fact that it has opposed the policy which has produced the war, and that its duty is now to secure peace at the earliest possible moment on such conditions as will provide the best opportunities for the re-establishment of amicable feelings between the workers of Europe." Then it was added that the Labour Party Executive, "without in any way receding from the position that the Labour movement has taken up in opposition to our engaging in a European War, advises that, while watching for the earliest opportunity of taking effective action in the interests of peace . . . all Labour and Socialist organisations should concentrate their energies meantime upon the task of carrying out the resolutions passed at the Conference of Labour organisations held at the House of Commons on August 5, detailing measures to mitigate the destitution which will inevitably overtake our working people while the state of war lasts."

The reference here made is to an emergency conference, to which all important Labour and Socialist bodies were summoned while war and peace were still in the balance. This Conference actually met after war had broken out and, instead of discussing the peace issue, decided to set up an all-inclusive Labour body—called the "War Emergency Workers' National Committee"—to deal with the serious problems of economic dislocation and distress that were expected to arise. On this body, which continued in active existence throughout the war, pro-war and anti-war Socialists acted for the most part amicably together on economic and social issues, carefully keeping off the political questions which divided them. The emphasis soon shifted from unemployment and distress to rising prices and rents, profiteering, and the problems arising out of a shortage, instead of a surplus, of man-power; but throughout the war the War Emergency Workers' Committee was able to do a great deal of useful work, and was an important factor in preventing a serious split in the British Labour movement such as occurred in most other countries.

At the stage when the W.E.W.N.C. was formed and when the Labour Party Executive sent out the circular from which I have quoted, the Labour movement's attitude to the war was still equivocal. The Parliamentary Labour Party had voted for war credits, and had changed its leader, and the Trades Union Congress's Parliamentary Committee had also given its support to the war; but the Labour Party Executive, on which the I.L.P. was influential, was moving more cautiously. Its Chairman, W. C. Anderson, was a leading member of the I.L.P.; and the I.L.P. was already making clear its determination to take a line of its own. On August 13, it issued a manifesto in the cause of International Socialism, in the course of which it declared:

> Out of the darkness and the depth we hail our working-class comrades of every land. Across the roar of guns, we send sympathy and greeting to the German Socialists. They have laboured unceasingly to promote good relations with Britain, as we with Germany. They are no enemies of ours, but faithful friends.
>
> In forcing this appalling crime upon the nations, it is the rulers, the diplomats, the militarists who have sealed their doom. In tears of blood and bitterness the greater democracy will be born. . . . Long live Freedom and Fraternity! Long live International Socialism!

Despite this manifesto, the differences inside the Labour Party did not come to a head until August 29, 1914, when the Labour Party Executive was called upon to pronounce upon the question of the Labour movement taking part in a recruiting campaign for voluntary enlistment in the armed forces. The Parliamentary Labour Party had already voted in favour of this course, and the Executive by a majority endorsed its decision and agreed to place the party machinery at the service of the campaign. At the same time, the political parties agreed upon an Electoral Truce for the duration of the war, an Industrial Truce having been already declared on August 24.

In the meantime the International Socialist Conference originally due to meet in Vienna towards the end of August, 1914, had been definitely abandoned, after an attempt on July 29 to summon it to Paris instead for August 9. The British Trades Union Congress, due to meet early in September, was also called off, the Congress's Parliamentary Committee issuing instead a Manifesto in which it gave strong support to the war, and endorsed participation in the recruiting campaign. By September 11, even Ramsay MacDonald, responding to an invitation to take part in a recruiting effort in his own constituency, Leicester, expressed the view that "we are in it: it will work itself out now . . . Victory, therefore, must be ours . . . We cannot go back, nor can we turn to the right or to the left. We must go straight through." Even Keir Hardie, who was heart-broken by the collapse of International Socialism, and died in 1915, largely because he no longer felt the will to live, was of much the same opinion, and felt it impossible to refuse support to the workers who had responded to the call for war service.

Nevertheless, the rift was wide. The majority of the British Socialist Party was uncompromisingly anti-war, and hardly less so was the rank and file of the I.L.P. Of the seven M.P.s who sat in the House of Commons under I.L.P. auspices, five were against the war, or at any rate in favour of the earliest possible peace by negotiation. These were Hardie, MacDonald, Snowden, Jowett, and Thomas Richardson, who were soon joined by W. C. Anderson, returned unopposed for Attercliffe under the Electoral Truce. Only two, J. R. Clynes and James Parker, went with the majority of the Labour Party. But most of the Members of Parliament who belonged to the I.L.P., but had been elected under Trade Union auspices, took the pro-war view, or soon rallied to it: so that the I.L.P. group in the House of Commons was reduced to a very few.

On October 15, 1914, the majority of the Labour M.P.s, in conjunction with the Parliamentary Committee of the Trades Union Congress and with other Labour leaders, came out with a Manifesto that was plainly meant as a counterblast to the I.L.P.'s Manifesto of August 15. Putting the entire blame for the outbreak of war on the German Government, it in effect repudiated not only the I.L.P. view, but also that which had been stated on August 7 by the Executive of the Labour Party itself. The Manifesto was in part a defence of the fullest participation of Labour in the recruiting campaign and in any other national effort that might be needed for winning the war, which it represented simply as a struggle of democracy against military despotism. The change of tone from the earlier Manifesto of the Labour Party was striking: those who signed were no longer in a mood to consider any pre-war faults in British diplomacy, or to take account of any pre-war struggle for power: they had caught the war mood, and did not stop to argue. All that remained of the earlier attitude was an insistence that "when the time comes to discuss the terms of peace the Labour Party will stand, as it has always stood, for an international agreement among all civilised nations that disputes and misunderstandings in the future shall be settled not by machine guns but by arbitration."

MARY AGNES HAMILTON

The Role of Arthur Henderson

Too often it is forgotten how much British workmen, through their Unions, actually did to bring the Internationale into being. But it was, in fact, born in London. Robert Owen sowed the seed; first among the early Socialists to think in terms of the working class, he was also the first to foresee their organisation on a basis broader than that of their own single nation. George Odger, Secretary of the London Trades Council, was convener of the Conference which founded the first International Working Men's Association; for it, Karl Marx, then living in London, drafted a constitution and a set of rules. In the latter, he laid it down that "to conquer political power has become the great duty of the working classes." This earliest International soon died, since it was

From *Arthur Henderson* by Mary Agnes Hamilton, London, William Heinemann, Ltd., 1938, pp. 92–98. Reprinted by permission of the publisher.

Arthur Henderson (1863–1935) came from a working-class background. He had been a member of Parliament since 1903. He was Home Secretary in MacDonald's government of 1924, and Foreign Secretary in his government of 1929.

deserted by the Mazzinians, who went their own way, and torn by dissensions between Bakunists and Marxians; but in 1889, it was born
again, as the Second International, with a clear Socialist basis, of pure
Marxian brand. Because of this, the application for affiliation of the
British Labour Party was opposed by H. M. Hyndman and the Social
Democratic Federation, alert to defend the purity of their own Marx-
ism. The ingenuity of Karl Kautsky, however, devised a formula on
which the Labour Party was formally admitted to membership in 1907:
"The English Labour Party is to be admitted to the International
Socialist Congress because, although it does not recognise the class
struggle, it carries it on; and because the organisation of the Labour
Party, being independent of the bourgeois parties, is based upon the
class struggle." From this time on there was a British member of the
Bureau, or executive body of the International; and Henderson, as
Party secretary, was secretary to the British Section, with Hardie as
chairman.

On July 29th, 1914, there was a meeting of the Bureau, in Brussels.
Keir Hardie was there for Great Britain. On the 23rd the Austrian
ultimatum had been delivered to Serbia; on the 25th the Austrian
declaration of war followed. The Foreign Offices of Europe were in a
state of feverish activity; notes and telegrams were flying hither and
thither, in last-minute efforts to stop the slide into catastrophe. In
Russia and in Austria, mobilisation was preparing. But in Brussels,
though all might fear, nobody believed in war. The Bureau had met to
organise an International Conference; there was no talk of abandoning
it. Its place was changed from Vienna to Paris, and its date advanced
from August 23rd to August 5th; that was all. It was still hoped that
such a meeting would serve to keep the Socialists of the world firm in
resistance to any threat to world peace on the part of their individual
national Governments, in accordance with the solemn undertakings to
which they were collectively committed. On the evening of July 29th,
at great public meetings in Brussels, passionate speeches against war
were delivered in common terms and tones by Emile Vandervelde, on
behalf of the Belgians; by Hugo Haase, on behalf of the Germans; by
Jean Jaurès, on behalf of the French; and by Keir Hardie on behalf of
the British. Next morning the delegates parted to travel to their various
homes.

They did not know and could not believe that they stood on the
crater of a volcano about to burst into ruinous flames. They still hoped,
as W. C. Anderson wrote in *The Labour Leader,* organ of the I.L.P.,

which came out on the 30th, that "There will be no war." On the 31st, came the terrible news that Jaurès had fallen by the hand of an insane assassin. This frightful event acted on taut nerves like a pistol shot. It gave a new and awful actuality to reports of fighting in Serbia and general mobilisation in Austria and Russia. There were tense and hurried consultations in Party offices. A major European war now seemed almost certain. But the view taken by everyone was that Britain need not, must not, be involved in that war. Over the names of Keir Hardie as president, and Arthur Henderson as secretary of the British section of the International, a manifesto was hastily drafted. Meetings were summoned by telegram to take place all over the country on the Sunday. At these meetings, including the monster one in Trafalgar Square, a resolution was put from the platform and carried by acclamation, of which the essential sentence was:

> We protest against any step being taken by the Government of this country to support Russia, either directly or in consequence of an undertaking with France, as being not only offensive to the political traditions of the country but disastrous to Europe, and declare that as we have no interest, direct or indirect, in the threatened quarrels which may result from the action of Servia, the Government of Great Britain should rigidly decline to engage in war, but should confine itself to efforts to bring about peace as speedily as possible.

Trafalgar Square was packed with dense and anxious crowds, as from the steps round the plinth, Keir Hardie, Arthur Henderson, Mary Macarthur, Margaret Bondfield, Will Thorne, George Lansbury, Mrs. Despard, R. B. Cunninghame-Graham and others spoke. They denounced war as a horror and as needless; they dwelt on its price in unemployment and innocent suffering; they protested with passion against being dragged in an alliance with the Russia of the Tsars. There was a moment of almost sinister drama when, just as Keir Hardie was speaking, the livid clouds that had been massing overhead burst in torrential downpour. The people stood; the rain passed as suddenly as it had come; the sentimental hoped that the clearing of the sky was of happy augury. There was a great speech—by all accounts the finest delivered—from Cunninghame-Graham; the resolution was carried amid thunderous cheers. The people dispersed to wander, unhappy and for the most part silent, about the streets. They watched ministers hurrying to Downing Street; they exchanged fantastic rumours; they hoped still; but fear grew as they waited for news that did not come. The speakers at the demonstration had meantime gathered in MacDonald's flat in Lincoln's Inn, where they waited for him to come back from consultation with Mr. Lloyd George.

When he came he had no good news to give them. By Sunday evening the balance of opinion within the Cabinet had begun to shift. In the morning, Lord Morley was still counting on there being a majority of eight or nine, including Lloyd George and Simon, against British participation in war. By the afternoon, his friends had begun to waver. MacDonald had to report to those who so anxiously awaited him that it was going to be war.

By Monday morning, Morley had on his side only one Cabinet colleague, John Burns, and outside the Cabinet only one junior minister, Charles Trevelyan. By then, ministers knew that Belgium was to be invaded: outside, this was, of course, not yet known. Henderson went home and told his sons. On Monday, Bank Holiday, the House of Commons met. Grey made his historic speech. MacDonald, in refusing to follow Grey—"We think he is wrong"—was, of course, speaking on the lines agreed to at the Party meeting held earlier that day. Inside the House, as outside it, the machinery of the Party was entirely democratic: what MacDonald said was what his colleagues had settled. But on Monday morning members did not know of Germany's entry into Belgium. This action—entirely expected by the military experts—came as a profound shock to general opinion: it swung it, *en masse,* over to the view that Britain must come to the aid of France and Belgium. It converted the Cabinet. It converted the great majority of the members of the Labour Party. It converted Arthur Henderson. By Monday evening MacDonald and Hardie were isolated; part of a small minority in their own party, as in the nation.

When the Party met again, on August 6th, England had declared war on Germany. The meeting was face to face with grim, accomplished fact. For arguments as to how and why—how it might have been prevented, why it was there—members had, for the most part, little patience now. They were British citizens, first: only in second line members of a party. There was, of course, a minority, and to that minority belonged the outstanding leaders, who were also the men who had, hitherto, taken the keenest interest in foreign affairs. Keir Hardie and MacDonald felt that the very soul of the nation would perish if this crime of war were not denounced. They wanted to attack the foreign policy of Grey, since they held that policy to be largely responsible for a catastrophe that might have been prevented and ought, therefore, to be denounced; the other I.L.P. members—Tom Richardson and F. W. Jowett—were of the same mind, as Philip Snowden was to be, when he got home from Australia. But this line did not commend itself to the feelings of the main body. They agreed with Henderson: the time for that was past. It might have its interest in the future; for the moment, faced as they were with an immense and terrible actuality of life-and-death significance, it was irrelevant. War was, now, fact. It was a horrible, atrocious fact; but a fact that put talking on one side. It was there; it was upon them; it was with it they had to deal. For its being there, he believed that responsibility rested on other shoulders than those of Britain. Grey's speech had impressed him deeply: the attack on Belgium stirred him to the soul: the obligation of honour to defend an invaded small country he accepted to the full. His strong practical nature turned from the past, which could not, now, be affected or altered, to the present, with its urgent call of duty and of service. He, like the majority of his colleagues, was, from now on, primarily an Englishman.

MacDonald, finding that the line he proposed to take was not one on which the Party was prepared to follow him, resigned his leadership. Henderson was at once elected leader in his place.

With few illusions as to its difficulties, he took up a heavy task. There were two things he wanted to do in it: to keep the Party united, as a party; and to have it play a worthy part in the national effort. Since war was there, Labour must help to win it. That, he saw, just as his three sons did, as a simple duty. He would have gone, had he been in the twenties instead of the forties. His reactions were the normal reactions of the plain man; his attitude to the war was that of the great majority of workmen, whom he truly represented. He felt—as they felt—that the subtle analysis of MacDonald and even the heart-broken resistance of Keir Hardie were, somehow, out of place. With the force of a catastrophe of nature the storm had burst; action, not understanding, was called for from men.

But while he felt this, and threw himself and the machine, with the full consent of nine-tenths of the rank and file, into the nation's effort, he never let go of the other half of the task he saw imposed on him by temporary leadership. Even before the national executive met on August 29th, it was plain that the division in the Parliamentary Party was going to be reflected there; there was a section that was already, and was going to go on being, in opposition to any co-operation with the Government, any participation in "winning the war." It was critical both of the Government and of those who did so co-operate. The then chairman, W. C. Anderson, was a leading member of the I.L.P.; on August 13th, the I.L.P. had issued a manifesto in which "across the roar of the guns, we send greeting and sympathy to the German Socialists." They took the line that the only legitimate and useful form of co-operation was with Socialists. This meant, in effect, co-operation with German and Austrian Socialists, since the French and Belgian Socialist parties had ranged themselves solidly behind their governments. To the majority inside the British Labour Party, the salutation, with the suggested co-operation, was simple treachery. They felt strongly. They were for hounding out the pacifists. Henderson firmly threw the whole of his great influence on the side of toleration and the avoidance of a breach. He disagreed with MacDonald and his friends: he hated their attitude; but he set his face like granite, now and from this time on, against any kind of heresy hunt or any movement for turning out the I.L.P. MacDonald, Anderson, Snowden, Jowett and Smillie remained throughout the war in the inner counsels of the Party. Their criticism was immensely salutary in keeping Labour alert, both on economic problems and, later, on peace aims, although it was prickly enough and many resented it intensely. But there was no moving Henderson on this. There were angry hours at conferences, and difficult clashes on the executive; but inside Party ranks there was no ostracism and no breach. There was never a moment when the minority was denied a hearing. MacDonald and Snowden and the other pacifists had to put up with harsh attack inside and the most bitter vilification outside. Outside, indeed, they were denounced as mere cowards and traitors; so violently denounced, indeed, that the Party was continually attacked for permitting them to remain in its counsels. Remain they did, however. They were never denied a hearing. There was bitterness, but never any kind of formal split.

IV
THE BEGINNING OF PROTEST

E. D. MOREL

The Morrow of the War

OUR PURPOSE

This country is at war, and has for the moment one overwhelming preoccupation: to render safe our national inheritance.

The Union of Democratic Control has been founded for the purpose of trying to secure for ourselves and the generations that succeed us a new course of policy which will prevent a similar peril ever again befalling our Empire. Many men and women have already joined us holding varying shades of opinion as to the origins of the war. Some think it was inevitable, some that it could and should have been avoided. *But we believe that all are in general agreement about two things: First, it is imperative that the war, once begun, should be prosecuted to a victory for our country. Secondly, it is equally imperative, while we carry on the war, to prepare for peace. Hard thinking, free discussion, the open exchange of opinion and information are the duty of all citizens to-day, if we are to have any hope that this war will not be what most wars of the past have been—merely the prelude to other wars.*

The Morrow of the War was the first pamphlet issued by the Union of Democratic Control. It was written in 1914.

E. D. Morel (1873–1924) had become well known through his campaign exposing the cruelties in the treatment of natives in the Congo. He was secretary and presiding figure of the Union of Democratic Control; he was imprisoned for six months in 1917 for a violation of the Defence of the Realm Act.

Our contribution to this necessary discussion are the principles put forward for consideration by the Union of Democratic Control.

The Union of Democratic Control has been created to insist that the following policy shall inspire the actual conditions of peace, and shall dominate the situation after peace has been declared:—

1. No Province shall be transferred from one Government to another without consent by plebiscite or otherwise of the population of such Province.

2. No Treaty, Arrangement, or Undertaking shall be entered upon in the name of Great Britain without the sanction of Parliament. Adequate machinery for ensuring democratic control of foreign policy shall be created.

3. The Foreign Policy of Great Britain shall not be aimed at creating Alliances for the purpose of maintaining the "Balance of Power"; but shall be directed to the establishment of a Concert of the Powers and the setting up of an International Council whose deliberations and decisions shall be public, part of the labour of such Council to be the creation of definite Treaties of Arbitration and the establishment of Courts for their interpretation and enforcement.

4. Great Britain shall propose as part of the Peace settlement a plan for the drastic reduction by consent of the armaments of all the belligerent Powers, and to facilitate that policy shall attempt to secure the general nationalisation of the manufacture of armaments, and the control of the export of armaments by one country to another.

It is the purpose of this pamphlet to elaborate and explain the considerations which underlie the policy outlined above.

I

No Province shall be transferred from one Government to another without the consent by plébiscite of the population of such province.

This condition has been placed first because if adhered to practically and in spirit, and if recognised by the European Powers as a principle that must guide all frontier rearrangements, it would help to put an end to European war.

If no province were retained under a Government's power against the will of its inhabitants, the policy of conquest and the imposition of political power would lose its *raison d'être*.

The subject as a whole is wrapped up, of course, with the principle of democratic government and is not merely a problem of international but of internal politics, and could not be treated briefly in a mere out-

line like the present. But anyone who reflects carefully on the subject
will see that the peace in Europe ultimately depends upon the acceptance of this idea.

It is obvious that there are many difficulties of detail in its application; that a plébiscite may be a mere form and not reflect the real wishes
of the population concerned, and under military control it can be used
as an instrument for obtaining an apparent sanction for oppression,
and that in populations of mixed race it is very difficult of application.
But it should not be impossible to guard against the defeat of the
principle through defects in the working machinery. Plébiscites, where
used at the end of the war, might be carried out under international
supervision. The essential is that the principle involved should be
clearly enunciated.

Fortunately the Government have already given the country a valuable lead in this matter. For Mr. Churchill, speaking on September 11,
said:

> Now the war has come, and when it is over let us be careful
> not to make the same mistake or the same sort of mistake as
> Germany made when she had France prostrate at her feet in
> 1870. (Cheers.) Let us, whatever we do, fight for and work
> towards great and sound principles for the European system,
> and the first of those principles which we should keep before us
> is the principle of nationality—that is to say, not the conquest
> or subjugation of any great community, or of any strong race of
> men, but the setting free of those races which have been subju-
> gated and conquered; and if doubt arises about disputed areas
> of country we should try to settle their ultimate destination in
> the reconstruction of Europe which must follow from this war
> with a fair regard to the wishes and feelings of the people who
> live in them.

We agree with Mr. Churchill that the terms of peace should secure
that there shall in the future be no more Alsace Lorraines to create
during half a century resentment, unrest, and intrigues for a *revanche*.
The power of the victorious parties must not be used for vindictive
oppression and dismemberment of beaten nationalities, but for the creation, by co-operation with all the belligerents, victors and vanquished
alike, of a true society of nations, banded together for mutual security.
The future relationship of the States of Europe must be not that of
victor and vanquished, domination or subserviency, but of partnership.

The struggle of one nation for domination over another must be replaced by the association of the people for their common good.

II

No Treaty, Arrangement, or Undertaking shall be entered upon in the name of Great Britain without the sanction of Parliament. Adequate machinery for ensuring democratic control of foreign policy shall be created.

The peoples of all constitutionally-governed countries are justified in demanding that diplomatic relations with their neighbours shall be conducted with the main object of maintaining friendly international intercourse. The increasing social and economic interdependence, the ramifications of the credit system, the facility and rapidity of intercommunication, the developing community of intellectual interest, the growth of a collective social consciousness, are combining to minimise the significance of the purely political frontiers which divide civilised States. For these reasons the world is moving towards conferences when political difficulties arise as a substitute for war. The determination to preserve national ideals and traditions offers no real obstacle. But the common interest of civilised democracies cannot be advanced by a secret diplomacy out of touch with democratic sentiment.

The anomaly of such practices in a democratic State has only to be understood to be condemned. All the domestic activities of a constitutional Government are tested in the crucible of public analysis and criticism. But the Government department charged with the supervision of the nation's intercourse with its neighbours, which if wrongly handled may react with ruinous effect upon the whole field of its domestic activities and upon the future of its entire social economy, *not only escapes efficient public control, but considers itself empowered to commit the nation to specific courses and to involve it in obligations to third parties entailing the risk of war, without the nation's knowledge or consent.*

During the past eight years particularly, the management of the Foreign department has become avowedly and frankly autocratic. Parliamentary discussion of foreign policy has become so restricted as to be perfunctory. It is confined to a few hours' roving debate on one day in each session. The eliciting of information by means of questions, never satisfactory, is rendered extremely difficult by the ingenuity employed in evading the issues it is attempted to raise. Advantage has been taken of the wholesome desire that discussion of foreign policy should

not partake of mere Party recriminations, to burke discussion altogether, and this process has received the endorsement of both Front
Benches. A claim to "continuity" has been further evolved to stifle
debate on foreign affairs, whereas in point of fact, if one feature more
than another has characterised British foreign policy of recent years,
it has been its bewildering fluctuations. Parliamentary paralysis has had
its counterpart in the country. The present Government's tenure of
office has been marked by an almost complete abstention from public
reference to foreign affairs. The public has been treated as though
foreign affairs were outside—and properly outside—its ken. And the
public has acquiesced. Every attempt to shake its apathy has been
violently assailed by spokesmen of the Foreign Office in the Press. The
country has been told that its affairs were in the wisest hands, and that
mystery and silence are the indispensable attributes to a successful
direction of foreign policy. The caste system which prevails in the
diplomatic service, and which has survived unimpaired the democratis-
ing of the majority of the public services, facilitates these outworn
political dogmatisms. Appointment is made by nomination and selection.
Candidates are required to possess an income per annum of £400.
The natural result is that the vast bulk of the national intelligence is
debarred from the diplomatic field of employment. A study of the
Foreign Office list will disclose the fact that over 95 per cent. of the
British Diplomatic Staff is composed of members of the aristocracy
and landed gentry.

Inevitable exile from their country results in our diplomatic representatives abroad losing touch with the centre of affairs and living in a
mental atmosphere remote from the popular and progressive movements of the time. Another pronounced characteristic of the system is
the indifference displayed by the Foreign Office to the business interests
of the nation. Our vast commercial interests, so intimately affected by
our relations with foreign Powers, are regarded as lying outside the
orbit of diplomatic considerations. The connection between politics and
business—and by business we mean the entire framework of peaceful
commerce upon which the prosperity of this country depends—appears
to be ignored, or, at least, treated with indifference and something like
contempt. The services of our Consuls abroad are not sufficiently utilised, and the Consular machinery requires complete overhauling. Such
questions as, for instance, the effect upon British commercial interest of British diplomacy supporting the acquisition of undeveloped
areas of the world's surface by a Power like France, which imposes

diffeerntial tariffs upon British goods, and opposing the acquisition of such areas by a Power like Germany, which admits British goods on terms of equality, does not appear to enter into Foreign Office calculations.

In the last few years also has been added another institution which modifies national policy without coming under Parliamentary control, the Committee of Imperial Defence. Its influence upon the Cabinet is nominally indirect, and its activities confined to the discussion of hypothetical events. But no one can doubt that its recommendations exercise a powerful effect on the executive decisions of the Government. No criticism of the advice given by the Committee is possible in Parliament. Momentous military and naval schemes are prepared there on which hang the issues of peace and war, as in the case of our recent relations to France. It is an intimate and powerful means of framing Government policy according to the ideas of military experts, without the knowledge and control of Parliament.

In the various ways indicated, opportunities of evincing an intelligent concern in its foreign policy has been increasingly withdrawn from the nation. The work of the Department escapes all outside control, loses all sense of contact with national life, and tends more and more to become an autocratic institution, contemptuous of the efforts of a small group of Members in the House to acquire information, and utilising a powerful section of the Press to mould public opinion in the direction it considers public opinion should travel.

The nation awoke with a shock to the evils of this state of affairs in the summer of 1911, when it suddenly found itself on the very brink of war with Germany over a Franco-German quarrel about Morocco, and became cognisant of the existence of diplomatic entanglements of which it had no previous intimation.

It is obviously impossible to attempt here a full presentment of the Moroccan crisis of 1911. But the story is inseparably intertwined with the avowals to the House of Commons on August 3rd last of the secret understanding with France which has played so capital a part in bringing about British intervention in the present war.

So long as this situation prevails it must be perfectly clear to any man of ordinary intelligence that the system of Government under which we live is not a democratic system, but its antithesis. It cannot be too often insisted upon that the domestic concerns of the nation, its constitutional liberties, its social reforms, all its internal activities in short, depend upon the preservation of peaceful relations with its neighbours. War in which this country is involved is certain to prove a serious check to social progress. Hence it is a matter of absolutely vital concern to the nation that the machinery of its Foreign Office should be thoroughly capable of performing its functions, and that the policy pursued by that Department should be pursued with the knowledge and the consent of the nation. It is imperative not only that a Treaty with a foreign Power should require endorsement by Parliament, but that no agreement or understanding possessing binding force and postulating the use of the national military and naval forces should be valid without the assent of Parliament. The nation should insist upon this essential reform, and should seriously apply itself to considering what other steps are needed to ensure some mechanical means whereby a greater national control of foreign policy can be secured; whether by the establishment of a permanent Committee of the House of Commons, by the adaptation to suit our needs of the American system under which a two-thirds majority of one branch of the Legislature is required for the validity of international agreements, or other procedure. *But real and permanent reforms will not be obtained unless the nation is determined to assert its fundamental right to participate in the formation of its own foreign policy.*

III

The Foreign Policy of Great Britain shall not be aimed at creating Alliances for the purpose of maintaining the "Balance of Power"; but shall be directed to the establishment of a Concert of Europe and the setting up of an International Council whose deliberations and decisions shall be public.

What does the "Balance of Power" mean?

It is popularly supposed to mean that no single Power or group of Powers should, in the interests of international peace, be allowed to acquire a preponderating position in Europe, and that the policy of Great Britain should be directed against such a consummation. British policy during the past few years has been based upon the assumption that Germany had attained, or was seeking to attain, that position of eminence.

It is that idea which, in the minds of masses of our people, justifies the present war.

But if this policy has been right in the past, what prospect does the future hold? The victory of the Allies—which is a vital necessity—must enormously upset the "balance" by making Russia the dominant military power of Europe, possibly the dictator both in this Continent and in Asia.

Russia can draw upon vast resources of human military material, only partly civilised. At present she is governed by a military autocracy which is largely hostile to Western ideas of political and religious freedom. There is a hope in the minds of Western Liberals that the war may bring political liberation to Russia. At present that is only a hope. For wars have as often been a prelude to tyranny as to liberty. It is only too likely that after a victorious war our national feeling may revert to its old anti-Russian channel, and we shall again have the "Balance of Power" invoked to protect Europe and India against a new Russian pre-eminence.

Speaking generally, the "Balance of Power" is little more than a diplomatic formula made use of by the mouthpieces of the interests from whose operations war comes. It signifies nothing more than that, at a given moment, in a given country, there is an effort to hold up to the public gaze the Government and the people of another country as being intent upon the destruction of its neighbours. At one moment it is Russia, at another France, and at another Germany. The "Balance of Power" was invoked for several years and down to within a few weeks of the Crimean War to inflame British public opinion against France. It was invoked against Russia to justify the Crimean War, and France was chosen as the ally with which to fight Russia! No sooner had peace been signed than France became once more the potential threat to the "Balance of Power"; and again during the period of rivalry in West and Central Africa, and in the Far East, in the late nineties.

Once the ball has been set rolling in the required direction, influences of all kinds are brought to bear for the purpose of permanently fixing this idea in the public mind. A flood of innuendo, denunciation, and distorted information is let loose. Every dishonourable motive and the most sinister of projects are attributed to the Government and the people selected for attack. The public becomes the sport of private ambitions and interests, of personal prejudices and obscure passions, which it can neither detect nor control, and, for the most part, does not even suspect. The power for mischief wielded by these forces is to-day immense, owing to a cheap Press and to the concentration of a large number of newspapers, possessing in the aggregate an enormous circulation, under one directing will. At the present moment the editorial and news columns of some fifty British newspapers echo the views of one man, who is thus able to superimpose in permanent fashion upon public thought the dead weight of his own prejudices or personal aims and intentions, and to exercise a potent influence upon the Government of the day.

For the last few years these newspapers have striven with unceasing pertinacity to create an atmosphere of ill-will and suspicion between Great Britain and Germany. The effort has been continuous, systematic, and magnificently organised, and inferential evidence is not lacking that it has been pursued with the approval and even with the assistance of certain official influences, and to the satisfaction of certain foreign Governments. This propaganda has had, needless to say, its counterpart in Germany. *The net result of the latest recrudescence of the "Balance of Power" policy with its Alliances and Ententes as the dominating factor in international relationships is now visible to all men. A quarrel (whose culminating episode was the murder in a Bosnian town of the heir to the Austrian throne last June) between Austria and Servia, to which the Russian Government determined to become a party, has already involved the peoples of France, Belgium, Britain, and Germany, the first three of whom were not even remotely concerned, in a terrible and desolating war.*

Japan and Montenegro have also become involved, and the same fate may overtake Holland, Italy, the other Balkan States, and the Scandinavian Powers. But for the policy of the "Balance of Power" the results of the quarrel would almost certainly have been confined to the parties immediately affected, and an early mediation by the neutral Powers would have been possible.

Bright's scathing denunciation of the fetish of the "Balance of Power" appeals with even greater force to us to-day:—

> You cannot comprehend at a thought what is meant by this balance of power. If the record could be brought before you— but it is not possible to the eye of humanity to scan the scroll upon which are recorded the sufferings which the theory of the balance of power has entailed upon this country. It rises up before me when I think of it as a ghastly phantom . . . which has loaded the nation with debt and with taxes, has sacrificed the lives of hundreds of thousands of Englishmen, has desolated the homes of millions of families, and has left us, as the great result of the profligate expenditure which it has caused, a doubled peerage at one end of the social scale, and far more than a doubled pauperism at the other.

For a system therefore which carries with it the implication that the interests of nations are necessarily in constant conflict and which involves the permanent division of Europe into two hostile competing groups, we must substitute machinery which will facilitate co-operation and a reasonable solution of differences between all the peoples of the world.

The objective should be a real council of the nations with at first very limited powers, rather an expansion of an alliance of three Powers against three, into a league of six Powers, designed to act against any one recalcitrant member which might threaten the peace of the whole. To this ideal, indeed, the pronouncement of Mr. Aisquith in his Dublin speech has already pointed, while it is noteworthy that Sir Edward Grey himself seems in a significant passage of one of his dispatches to admit the failure of the balance principle and to indicate that the nations must "start afresh" on the basis of a general council. This passage is as follows:

> If the peace of Europe can be preserved, and the present crisis safely passed, my own endeavour will be to promote some arrangement to which Germany could be a party, by which she could be assured that no aggressive or hostile policy would be pursued against her or her allies by France, Russia, and ourselves, jointly or separately. I have desired this and worked for it as far as I could through the last Balkan crisis; and Germany having a corresponding object, our relations sensibly improved. The idea has hitherto been too Utopian to form the subject of definite proposals, but if this present crisis, so much more acute than any Europe has gone through for generations, be safely passed, I am hopeful that the relief and reaction which will follow may make possible some more definite *rapprochement* between the Powers than has been possible hitherto.

It is from some such simple beginning, pursued with good will and perseverance by all parties, that the nations may hope to arrive at a system of co-operation to replace the system of hostile alliances, the fruits of which are the present war.

It is essential, of course, if the negotiations of such a council are to be lifted out of the atmosphere of diplomatic intrigue which the secrecy of negotiations always involves, that its deliberations be public. Publicity will at one and the same time be a guarantee of openness, of good faith, and of democratic control.

IV

*Great Britain shall propose as part of the Peace settlement a plan for
the drastic reduction by consent of the armaments of all the belligerent
Powers, and to facilitate that policy shall attempt to secure the general
nationalisation of the manufacture of armaments, and the control of
the export of armaments by one country to another.*

The theory of the "Balance of Power" and secret diplomacy are two
factors which, in combination, make for war.

Two other factors intimately connected with these ensure its certainty. They are: a constant progression in expenditure upon armaments, and the toleration of a private armament interest.

It would be labour wasted to endeavour to apportion responsibility
between the various European Governments for the insane competition
in armaments which of recent years has attained incredible proportions.
No Government can escape liability. Each Government has defended
its policy on the ground that its neighbour's action compelled it to do
so. Many of the governing statesmen of the world have alternately confessed their helplessness, attacked their rivals, appealed to public opinion, and blamed the warlike tendencies inherent in the people whose
destinies they control. Every Government, without exception, has proceeded on the assumption that in order to ensure peace it had to be
stronger than its neighbour, a philosophy which could have but one
possible outcome—war. In pursuance of this phantom, a considerable
proportion of the wealth of the European States has been wasted, and
activities have been withdrawn from the constructive work of the
world, to prepare for the world's destruction. And with every fresh
outburst of expenditure, responding to some diplomatic check or alarm-
ist propaganda, fresh faggots have been piled around Europe's powder
magazine. The disaster which has fallen upon Europe is the fitting
sequel to the bankruptcy of statesmanship which this policy embodies.

*The more extensive the armaments, the greater the temptation to
seize an opportunity for testing their efficiency; the greater the nervous-
ness and irritation of Governments when negotiating; the greater the
pressure upon those Governments of the powerful professional and
other interests concerned in armament construction.*

The policy of gigantic armaments cannot in the very nature of things
ensure any final settlement of disputes between States. It leads, and can
only lead, to an intolerable situation from which war comes to be
regarded by diplomacy as the only escape.

An all-round limitation of armaments must follow the present war if the world is to be permanently relieved of the nightmare which has weighed upon it for so long. We can no longer afford to listen to arguments as to the impracticability of such a course from those whose claims to the possession of human wisdom and experienced guidance have so utterly broken down.

The difficulty of compelling a change in the policy of European Governments has been intensified by the conditions under which armament construction is carried on in this and other countries. Everyone is familiar with the fact that the object of a commercial firm is to push its wares in every legitimate manner, to advertise them, and systematically to tout for orders both at home and abroad. Everyone is aware that there exists a powerfully-equipped industry for the manufacture of military and naval engines and instruments of offence. Disguise it as we may, that industry waxes and wanes, the profits its management derives rise and fall, the dividends earned by its shareholders increase and dwindle in the measure of the demand for the articles it produces. That demand does not emanate from members of the public. It emanates from the military and naval departments of the public services. The industry relies, therefore, for its existence and for its profits not upon a private demand, but upon a Government demand, and the extent of that Government demand will depend upon the view which the Government may take of the number and nature of these articles required to ensure the national safety. Such a condition of affairs is a permanent and terrible danger both to democratic government and to international peace. What are its implications?

There is created in every country an economic force in private hands directly interested in war and in the preparation for war; directly interested in assisting to bring about a general atmosphere advantageous to an industry which, were wars to cease or the expenditure on armaments to be substantially reduced, would suffer accordingly. What the successful prosecution of an ordinary commercial undertaking requires this industry also requires. The demand for the article must be created. That basic situation engenders effects which can only be appreciated in their cumulative significance. It is not at all necessary to attribute sinister machinations to individuals. These effects are automatic. An industry disposing, as does this one, of an enormous aggregate of capital possesses almost unlimited power of influence and suggestion. For such purposes the Press is a potent instrument ready at hand. Many of those most closely associated with this great industry are men of considerable influence. Some have been in the public service and have acquaintances in the Government Departments. Others may be on friendly and perfectly honourable terms with the proprietors or editors of newspapers or associations of newspapers. The proprietor of a newspaper may be honestly convinced, or may by arguments be persuaded, that an agitation for increased armaments is advisable. If he is acquainted with one of the directors of the armament industry that acquaintance will hardly act as a deterrent to his entertaining those views. He may be furnished with special information, accurate or otherwise, as to the projects, real or alleged, of other Governments, which will be familiar to the director through his connection with Continental branches of the same industry. The Press may be utilised in a similar manner by certain permanent officials in the nation's Foreign Department, who feel that their views of the international situation can be best served by a Press campaign of a certain kind. The influence of the industry which stands to gain from the existence of these views, and the willingness of newspaper editors and proprietors to push them on to the public, cannot be expected to intervene against their propagation. Again, an ambitious Minister, in charge of one of the fighting branches of the public service, desirous of placing his personality in the limelight and focusing public attention upon the affairs of his Department, will be from that circumstance a readier listener to representations from the industry in question. Those representations may quite legitimately take the form of pointing out that heavy expenses have been incurred in providing a certain type of machinery or special accommodation for the construction of a particular kind of offensive instrument, that the orders have not kept pace with the expenditure, and that if further orders be not forthcoming losses will ensue and future facilities for production be necessarily restricted. There would be nothing indefensible in representations of this character. And again, it is not unlikely that a Member of Parliament, convinced of certain public dangers associated with the existing system, but representing a constituency where this great industry is established and employs, perhaps, not an inconsiderable section of the local labour, may find his freedom of speech considerably curtailed lest he should be accused of taking the bread from the mouths of some of his constituents.

Endless, indeed, are the ramifications of a *private* industrial interest so wealthy and so well organised, and dependent for its profits upon *national* expenditure in instruments of warfare, and, consequently, in the ultimate resort, upon war itself. *The general influence exerted upon public life as a whole by the very fact that this industry is a private one, and possesses a large body of shareholders usually belonging to the upper strata of society, cannot be regarded otherwise than as an unhealthy and dangerous element in the nation.* Emphasis is lent to this aspect of the case when it is borne in mind that the armaments industry has of late years become internationalised to a remarkable degree. Recent disclosures, the accuracy of which has not been disputed, in Germany, France, England, and Japan have clearly shown an interconnection of the armament interest productive of repellent accompaniments. This inter-connection of interest has, for example, made it possible for a body of British shareholders, including prominent ecclesiastics, Members of Parliament, and even Cabinet Ministers, to be financially interested in enterprises engaged in the manufacture of engines of destruction impartially used in the slaughter of Englishmen, Frenchmen, Germans, and Russians.

But however revolting this may be, it is insignificant compared with the graver peril to which precedent allusion has been made. *Reflection must bring with it the conviction that the armament industry is not one which the nation can safely permit to be retained in private hands and to be the subject of private profit.*

WHAT DEMOCRACY MUST DO

What, then, is to be our policy in connection with the war? First and foremost we must be victorious. That is a prime necessity upon which the nation is unanimous. We must win not only because many British institutions of the highest value would be destroyed by our defeat, not only because Prussia, our principal enemy, is the leading exponent of that doctrine of military domination and intolerance which is incompatible with a permanently peaceful Europe; but also because we must see justice done, as far as may be, to the least powerful of our Allies. *Ample compensation must be secured for Belgium to repair her material loss and in recognition of the wrong done to her.*

What of the future? What lessons do the incompetence and secretiveness, the jealousies and vanities of that vaunted European statecraft which has plunged the world in war convey to the peoples who are its victims?

What can the people do to amend a system under which they are used as pawns in a game of chess?

They can begin to understand what that system is and that its existence is their undoing. They can begin to understand the monstrous errors and fallacies which underlie the whole teaching imposed upon their intelligence. They can begin to understand that this immunity from public control enjoyed by the small group of professional men who manipulate international relations has led to the establishment amongst the latter of a standard of conduct which would not be tolerated in the ordinary affairs of a well-ordered community. They can begin to understand that "high politics" in the diplomatic world has become a synonym for intrigue; that a code of morals is therein practised which, in other branches of the public service, would entail dismissal, and in the business world would involve disgrace.

They can force themselves to a mental effort which shall lead them to the realisation of the complete artificiality of the conditions under which they suffer, the remoteness from their real and vital needs of the issues for which they are asked to sacrifice all that they hold dear. *They can rid themselves of the paralysing belief that their relations with their neighbours are so complicated and mysterious as to be beyond their comprehension. They can bring themselves to grasp a plain and demonstrable truth, and to appreciate its full significance, which is that those to whom they have looked for guidance, those who have told them that in the preservation of the "Balance of Power," and in the multiplication of colossal armaments lay the one chance of international peace, have been utterly, hopelessly, calamitously wrong. They can put to themselves these simple issues.*

> By the terrible logic of events which now confront us we see that the methods advocated by those to whose training and wisdom we trusted to ensure peace among the nations have entirely failed. The system which we were induced reluctantly to support, far from preserving peace, has precipitated us into the greatest conflict in history, a conflict we passionately desired to avoid, and for the avoidance of which we made heavy sacrifices because, we were told, that therein lay our hope of averting it. The system was wrong. We must evolve another.

The idea of a federalised Europe, regulated by an Areopagus, involving the disappearance, or substantial reduction, of standing armies and navies, and the submission of all disputes to a Central Council, is not to be dismissed. It is the ultimate goal to aim at. But it cannot be attained until the constitutionally governed democracies of the West are brought to realise how impossible it is that their moral and spiritual development and their happiness and well-being can be secured under a system of government which leaves them at the mercy of the intrigues and imbecilities of professional diplomatists and of the ambitions of military castes; helpless, too, in the face of an enormously powerful and internationalised private interest dependent for its profits upon the maintenance of that "armed peace" which is the inevitable prelude to the carnage and futility of war.

To awaken these sentiments among the democracies of this and other countries, to instil into them these convictions, to ensure the co-operation of all forces in all countries working to that end—is the task to which we must all turn our attention.

Potentates, diplomatists, and militarists made this war. They should not be allowed to arrange unchecked and uncontrolled the terms of peace and to decide alone the conditions which will follow it. The mass of the people who suffer from their blunders and their quarrels must claim the ineradicable right of participating in the future settlement.

And, when peace has come, the democratic parties of Europe must set before themselves a new province of political effort. That peace will be permanently preserved only if our artisans and industrialists keep up with the artisans and industrialists of other countries a constant and deliberate communication through their political parties and other organisations which will prevent misunderstandings and subdue the hatreds out of which war ultimately comes.

BERTRAND RUSSELL

War—The Offspring of Fear

To all liberal-minded and humane men, this war has come as a shock and a challenge, shattering hopes, and too often uprooting life-long convictions. The horror of what is happening through Europe is so staggering that men seek to escape realisation by various means—some by such minor deeds of humanity as the time allows, nursing the

War—The Offspring of Fear was the third pamphlet published by the Union of Democratic Control.
Bertrand Russell (1872–   ), the philosopher, had established a considerable reputation by the outbreak of the first World War, most notably with the publication in 1910 of *Principia Mathematica,* written with Alfred North Whitehead.

wounded, providing for the relief of distress, or finding an asylum for stranded aliens; some by cherishing hopes of a regenerated Europe to emerge at the end of the struggle; and some by yielding to a fiery conviction in the righteousness of the nation to which they happen to belong. But in these preoccupations there is some danger that the larger humanity, which combats the passions out of which the war has arisen, may be obscured. If a better world is to emerge, if Europe is to be spared a repetition of slaughter and madness, it is necessary to know and recognise the causes, in the hopes and fears of ordinary men, that have made it hitherto impossible to substitute reason and law for force in the relations of nations. Perhaps at this moment an appeal to impartial reason may find little sympathy, and may seem to the majority ill-timed and unpatriotic. But peace, as well as war, requires preparation: if it is right in time of peace to make schemes for the destruction of possible enemies, can it be wrong in time of war to make schemes for the preservation of possible friends? War does not do away with all other duties, nor is it unpatriotic to suggest that there are higher goals than victory and nobler ideals than the destruction of hostile armies.

Before we can hope to find any road to the future preservation of peace, we must understand the causes of war. In every war it appears to each side that it is fighting to resist unprovoked aggression, and that in spite of almost criminal forbearance it has been at last reluctantly compelled to draw the sword in defence of home and country. The exactly similar assertions made by the other side sound like wanton hypocrisy, and inflame the passion of moral reprobation which enables men to forget humanity and mercy. From the *Times* of August 25 I see that Professor Ernst Haeckel, one of the foremost intellectual forces in Germany, and Professor Rudolf Eucken, a world-famous leader of religious thought, have published a protest against England's action in which they say:

> What is happening to-day will be inscribed in the annals of history as an indelible shame to England. England fights to please a half-Asiatic Power against Germanism. She fights not only on the side of barbarism, but also of moral injustice, for it is not to be forgotten that Russia began the War because it was not willing that there should be a thorough expiation of a wretched murder. It is the fault of England that the present War is extended to a world-war, and that all culture is thereby endangered. And why all this? Because she was envious of Ger-

many's greatness, because she wished at all costs to hinder a further extension of this greatness. She was only waiting for a favourable opportunity to break out to the detriment of Germany, and therefore she seized most promptly on the necessary German advance through Belgium as a pretext in order to cloak her brutal national selfishness with a mantle of respectability.

These statements must seem to Englishmen an utterly grotesque travesty of the facts, and they illustrate the spirit of censure which blinds nations to the folly and cruelty of their actions. But do not the views of most Englishmen seem to their enemies equally grotesque, equally one-sided, equally filled with paltry self-righteousness? Europe at this moment is like a house on fire, where the inmates instead of trying to escape and to extinguish the flames are engaged in accusing each other of having caused the conflagration, and are willing to be burned themselves provided the others can thereby meet the just punishment of their crimes. This state of mind is barbarous, contrary to reason, contrary to humanity, utterly contrary to self-interest, a return to the savage beneath the miserable rags of a tawdry morality. Let us try for a moment to forget praise and blame, to forget that we are members of one of the belligerent nations, and to view the whole tragic irony from the standpoint of impartial compassion and understanding. Let us try to view the conflict from the standpoint of each nation in turn, not through the mist of diplomatic details, but in its large outlines. In each nation men are willing to die and women are willing to starve and see their homes devastated. Such sacrifices are not incurred for merely selfish ends: each nation believes that it is defending a sacred cause. Immense forces of heroism and devotion are destroying each other through a tragedy of blindness and fear. These very same forces, by clearer insight and calmer judgment, might be used for the good of mankind, instead of for mutual death. But this can only come about through mutual understanding and respect, not through partisan accusations of perfidy and greed.

A RACE CONFLICT IN THE EAST

Essentially, this war, like the barbarian invasion of the Roman Empire, or the mediaeval wars of Christian and Musselman, is a great race-conflict, a conflict of Teuton and Slav, in which certain other nations, England, France, and Belgium, have been led into co-operation with the Slav. It has been called a diplomatists' war, and this is partially true as regards the Western nations, but it is not true as regards the

struggle between Germans and Russians. (In modern Europe diplomatists alone cannot make a war; they must have the support of public
opinion, and it is public opinion that must be changed if there is to be
any hope of secure peace hereafter.) The conflict of Germany and
Russia has been produced, not by this or that diplomatic incident, but
by primitive passions expressing themselves in the temper of the two
races. But primitive passions among civilised men clothe themselves in
an armour of what seems to be reason and political wisdom. This
armour must be pierced before we can see events truly.

Taking the nations in the order in which they became involved—
Austria, Russia, Germany, France, England—I shall attempt for each
in turn, not an impartial statement of the case, but a statement of the
case as it appears to the average citizen of the country in question, and
of the real reasons, as opposed to the diplomatic pretexts, for participation in the struggle.

THE AUSTRIAN VIEW

Austria, if we judge by the diplomatic correspondence published in
the White Paper, might seem more to blame than any other Power.
Yet the average Austrian supported enthusiastically the action of his
Government, and the average Austrian is neither better nor worse than
the average Englishman. We may be sure that Austria is as convinced
of the justice of its cause as we are of the justice of ours. It is worth
while to see how this can be.

The Austrians are a highly civilised race, half surrounded by Slavs
in a relatively backward state of culture. Within their own Empire, in
which the German race are in a minority, a large population of Slavs
forms an element of instability, and offers a plausible pretext for Russian aggression. Servia, a country so barbaric that a man can secure
the throne by instigating the assassination of his predecessor, is engaged
constantly in fermenting the racial discontent of men of the same race
who are Austrian subjects. Behind Servia stands the all-but irresistible
power of Russia, a constant menace, along many hundred miles of
frontier, to all that makes Austrian civilisation of value to Austria and
to the world. By the instigation of Servia, as all Austrians believe, the
heir-apparent to the Austrian Emperor was murdered at Serajevo. In
the despatch of Sir M. de Bunsen to Sir Edward Grey of September 1
he says, "So just was the cause of Austria held to be that it seemed to
her people inconceivable that any country should place itself in her
path, or that questions of mere policy or prestige should be regarded

anywhere as superseding the necessity which has arisen to exact summary vengeance for the crime of Serajevo." Attempts to secure the
punishment of Servian accomplices in this crime being met by evasion,
Austria, after some time, had recourse to an ultimatum, which demanded, *interalia,* that Austrian officials should take part in the trial
of suspect Servians. If the Prince of Wales had been assassinated on
the borders of Afghanistan, and we had reason to believe that the
Afghans had procured his assassination, we should probably make a
similar demand with the full support of English public opinion. But the
Servians refused to agree to this "national humiliation," and in this
refusal Russia supported them. The Servians, it is true, were willing to
submit to arbitration on this point, but the arbitration must have gone
in their favour unless they were to be treated as outside the pale of
civilised races, and Austria was persuaded that, in spite of their misdeeds, Russia would be able to prevent their being so treated. And so
"national honour" became involved, and fear and hatred of the Slavs
made it seem useless to attempt to patch up a truce, which, it was
believed, would be broken at the first moment at which Russia felt
prepared for war.

THE RUSSIAN VIEW

The position of Russia is simpler than that of Austria. By all
accounts, the consciousness of race and religion is still, in Russia, in
that primitive condition from which the Western nations have partially
emerged; moreover, the Pan-Slavist agitation has for a long time past
been fostered as a distraction from the need of internal reform.
Austria's attack on a small orthodox Slav State roused all the chivalry
and honour of Russia, which had been restrained with difficulty in the
matter of Bosnia and Herzegovina, and chivalry let loose the instinctive
racial expansiveness which produced the Russian Empire and the war
with Japan. The *Times* of July 28 reported the Tsar as saying: "We
have stood this sort of thing for seven and a half years. This is enough."
These words, which no doubt expressed the feeling of almost all the
politically conscious part of the nation, were followed by the order for
partial mobilisation—the first definite military action directed by one
great Power against another.

THE GERMAN VIEW

By Russia's action Germany was brought in. The part of Germany
is a controversial matter, as to which, since the facts are unknown,

everybody here is firmly persuaded of one view, and everybody in Germany is firmly persuaded of another quite opposite view. All parties profess knowledge, though in fact all are ignorant except the German Government. It is no use attempting to ascertain the facts, since they are not at present ascertainable. It may be worth while instead portraying what seem to be the beliefs of the average German as to the rights and wrongs of the war.

The *Times* of August 27 contains an interesting letter on this subject from its correspondent in Flushing. He says:

"These Germans are not only sure that they will win. They are convinced also that their cause is a just one, and that the war is not of their making. To Englishmen that must seem an incredible statement; but, from what I have heard them say and from letters that I have seen, I know that it is the plain truth. . . . They are united (he reports a German correspondent as saying) as one man in the resolve to defend their country, and the Social Democrats are heart and soul in favour of the war. . . . It seems to me important that people in England should realise that this is the true state of the case. It is a national attitude that must greatly increase the fighting strength of the armies opposed to us, and any tendency to discredit it, or to assume that the Germans are instinctively conscious that they are in the wrong, would be a fatal mistake. They think nothing of the sort."

The case for Germany is essentially the same as the case for Austria. It was felt that a great conflict of Teuton and Slav was inevitable sooner or later; that if Servian agitation was not stopped, Austria-Hungary would break up, and the Teuton would be weakened before the great conflict had begun. It must not be supposed that this conflict is, on the part of the Teuton, aggressive in substance, whatever it may be in form. In substance it is defensive, the attempt to preserve Central Europe for a type of civilisation indubitably higher and of more value to mankind than that of any Slav State. The existence of the Russian menace on the Eastern border is, quite legitimately, a nightmare to Germany, and a cause of much of the militarist talk by which Germans attempt to conjure away their fears. If we were exposed to the same menace, is it to be supposed that peace propaganda would have much success among us?

The Germans and Austrians accordingly thought the chastisement of Servia essential to their safety and to the preservation of their civilisation—so essential as to make it worth while to *risk* war with Russia on this account. But the White Paper shows conclusively that they did not *expect* war with Russia. "Ministry for Foreign Affairs here (in Vienna) has realised, though somewhat late in the day, that Russia will not remain indifferent in present crisis," Sir M. de Bunsen telegraphs on July 29 (No. 94). "German Ambassador had a second interview with Minister for Foreign Affairs at 2 a.m., when former completely broke down on seeing that war was inevitable," Sir G. Buchanan telegraphs from St. Petersburg on July 30 (No. 97). Sir E. Goschen, on July 31, reporting a conversation with the German Chancellor, telegraphs to Sir E. Grey: ". . . His Excellency was so taken up with the news of the Russian measures along the frontier . . . that he received your communication without comment. He asked me to let him have the message that I had just read to him as a memorandum, as he would like to reflect upon it before giving an answer, and his mind was so full of grave matters that he could not be certain of remembering all its points" (No. 109). None of these extracts suggest the mood of deep plotters whose machinations are being crowned with success; they suggest the despair of those who have played a desperately risky game and lost. The one Power which, on the showing of the White Paper, marched on calmly and imperturbably throughout, was Russia.

The Germans could not stand by passively while Russia destroyed Austria: honour and interest alike made such a course impossible. They were bound by their Alliance, and they felt convinced that if they were passive it would be their turn next to be overrun by the Russian hordes. Thus Germany was drawn in by motives which must appear irresistible to every German, and which have, in fact, convinced even the peace-loving Social Democrats, who, with the encouragement of the authorities, had held anti-war meetings down to the very last moment.

THE WESTERN VIEW

The Western war has not the same ethnic inevitability as the war in the East. It is due, at bottom, to a former crime and a recent folly on the part of Germany, both of which (*mutatis mutandis*) all patriots here are urging us to imitate. The crime was the excessive humiliation of France in 1870; the folly was the building of a powerful Navy while the position on land was far from secure. Fear of a repetition of 1870 compelled the French to ally themselves with Russia—an alliance which, by a singular irony, is now bringing upon France a great part of the evils it was designed to avoid. Fear of the Germany Navy led us to ally ourselves with France and Russia. A wiser policy and a more moderate spirit on the part of Bismarck and his successors might have saved Germany from the enmity of France and England in its life-and-death struggle with Russia. We are being invited to humiliate Germany as completely as France was humiliated in 1870, and to develop by conscription a great military force in spite of the fact that all defensive purposes are served by our Navy. If we follow this advice, we shall prepare for ourselves on some future day a nemesis similar to that which now seems likely to overwhelm the heirs of Bismarck. And so long as many among us tender such advice, we cannot without hypocrisy blame Germany overmuch for having followed it.

In all the nations involved, with the exception of Russia, the one motive that makes the populations acquiesce is Fear. Germany and Austria fear Russia, France and England fear Germany. The fears of Germany, Austria, and France are only too well grounded; those of England are much less so, and have had to be carefully nursed by the naval scare of 1908 and the General Election campaign of January, 1910. (In that election I came upon a voter who firmly believed that, if Liberals won, the Germans would be in the country within a fortnight, and similar beliefs were widely prevalent in the working classes.) These two events, together with a continuous stream of attacks on Germany in newspapers and magazines, have made men feel the Germans capable of any act of sudden brigandage or treacherous attack. Plain men have seen a confirmation of these feelings in the violation of Belgium, though every student of strategy has known for many years past that this must be an inevitable part of the next Franco-German war, and although Sir E. Grey expressly stated that if it did not occur he could still not promise neutrality.

THE FAILURE OF THE POLICY OF ALLIANCES

It is the universal reign of Fear which has caused the system of alliances, believed to be a guarantee of peace, but now proved to be the cause of world-wide disaster. Fear of Russia led to the Anglo-Japanese alliance and to the alliance of Germany and Austria. The need of support in a long tariff war with France led Italy to ally itself with Austria, from fear that otherwise Austria would seize the moment for an attack on Italy. Fear of Germany led France and England into their unnatural alliance with Russia. And this universal fear has at last produced a cataclysm far greater than any of those which it was hoped to avert. Whoever is technically victorious in this war, all the nations concerned, victors and vanquished alike, must lose a large proportion of their manhood, all the economic reserves which make it possible to bring some happiness into the lives of the wage-earning classes, and all the surplus of leisure which produces the arts and the creative thought of peaceful times. None of us, whatever the outcome, can hope to return during our lifetime to the level of happiness, well-being, and civilisation which we enjoyed before the war broke out.

A LEAGUE OF PEACE AS AN ALTERNATIVE

If civilisation is to continue, Europe must find a cure for this universal reign of fear with its consequence of mutual butchery. One way in which it might be cured is that the civilised nations, realising the horror and madness of war, should so organise themselves as to make it practically certain that no advantage can be gained by initiating an attack. For this purpose it would be necessary to avoid exclusive alliances and to form a League of Peace, which should undertake, in the event of a dispute, to offer mediation, and, if one party accepted mediation while the other refused it, to throw the whole of its armed support on the side of the party accepting mediation, while, if both parties refused mediation, the League should throw its weight against whichever party proved to be the aggressor. If a sufficient number of nations entered into such a League, they could make aggressive war obviously doomed to failure, and could thereby secure the cessation of war.

It is in precisely this way that private war has been brought to an end. When two private citizens have a dispute, it is no longer considered derogatory to their honour to submit to the law courts, because the citizens as a whole are prepared to enforce the preservation of peace. Within a single State, a man no longer secures respect by murder, and peerages are not conferred upon the most successful murderers. In barbarous countries the relations of individuals are regulated just as the relations between States are still regulated, and the blood-feud introduces precisely the same tinsel "honour" as a motive to secret assassination as is now urged in favour of wholesale slaughter on the field of battle. In Somaliland, I am told, no native can obtain a wife until he gives clear proof of having committed at least one murder. In the same way, in Europe, no State is respected unless it periodically murders large numbers of citizens belonging to some other State. This condition of things can be ended, and will be ended, as soon as the civilised nations honestly and whole-heartedly desire to end it. All that is necessary is that the nations which desire peace should organise themselves into a police force, and announce and enforce their determination to suppress any disturbance of the peace among the great nations of the world. They have the power to do it; only the will is lacking. If—which I hardly dare to hope—the horror of this war should produce the will for peace, it will not have been fought in vain.

NON-INTERVENTION

But if—as I fear we must expect—the will for peace is not universal after the war, if some powerful nations still direct their policy by considerations of "national honour" and the lust for "glory," English opponents of war will have to be content, at least for a time, with a more humble aim than the creation of a League of Peace. The only policy, in that case, which can secure that England, at any rate, shall not be involved in war, is the policy of strict non-intervention. This involves not only the avoidance of alliances nominally directed to maintaining the Balance of Power, but also abstention from the attractive Palmerstonian attitude of champions of right against oppression. When the Foreign Office desires to enter into a conflict, it can always, by selecting the facts to be revealed, and by inspiring its friends in the Press, make our intervention appear as a defence of the oppressed against oppression or attack. The only security against a war-fever created by such methods is a fixed resolve to hold aloof, as the United States are now holding aloof, from any struggle not involving direct attack upon some portion of our Empire. For this purpose it must be rendered impossible for the Government to incur obligations to other States without the knowledge of the public and the consent of the House of Commons.

DEMOCRATIC CONTROL

Secret diplomacy must cease. Of all the features in our present methods which tend to defeat the will for peace, and which might be altered without waiting for the consent of other nations, the chief is secret diplomacy. Where a settled policy rather than a sudden crisis is in question, no obligation or debt of honour ought to be created without the full previous knowledge of the House of Commons and the country. So long as this principle is not observed, democratic government is a farce and a pretence. No national or human interest is served by secrecy: the only interest served is that of the official clique who are thus enabled to pursue unchecked a policy entailing terrible liabilities, and to keep the support of men who would execrate their policy if they knew what it was. In regard to foreign affairs, the unlimited power of the Cabinet, or rather of a small section of the Cabinet, must be brought to an end, and the same publicity must be introduced into the relations of nations as into the relations of parties within a single State. The democracy, in England, has acquired control of legislation, and, in great part, over the executive as regards internal affairs. Its next battle, when the war is over, must be to acquire control over foreign affairs, and to use that control in the interest of a stable peace, not of a mere armed truce while the world draws breath to prepare for fresh madness hereafter. Great forces on the side of peace were growing up in every civilised country before the war broke out; temporarily silenced, they will leap into tenfold greater strength as soon as exhaustion has brought an end to the conflict. If that moment is to be used to the full, the world must be awake, when it comes, to the possibility of a freer, more harmonious intercourse between States than the world's rulers have hitherto permitted to the millions whom they are hurling into ruin and death.

V. LENIN

English Pacifism and English Dislike of Theory

Political freedom has hitherto been incomparably greater in England than in the other countries of Europe. Here more than elsewhere the bourgeoisie has become accustomed to rule and knows how to rule. The relations between the classes are more developed and in many respects clearer than in other countries. The absence of conscription makes the people more free in their attitude towards the war, in that everybody is free to refuse to join the army. The government (which in England is nothing but a committee to manage the affairs of the bourgeoisie) is therefore compelled to strain every nerve to increase "popular enthusiasm for the war." This would be absolutely impossible to attain without radically altering the law, were not the proletarian mass entirely disorganised and demoralised by the shifting of a minority of the best-situated, skilled, and unionised workers to liberal, *i.e.,* bour-

This article is reprinted from the *Collected Works,* Vol. 18 (New York, 1930) pp. 162–67. It was written in April–May 1915 and first published in *Pravda* No. 169, July 27, 1924.

Lenin's point is to attack the German Socialist Karl Kautsky, but he makes some interesting remarks about Morel and others in the process of using them as stalking horses.

geois politics. The English trade unions already comprise about one-fifth of the wage workers. The leaders of those trade unions are mostly liberals whom Marx long ago called agents of the bourgeoisie.

All these peculiarities of England help us, on the one hand, better to understand the essence of present-day social-chauvinism, for this essence is *identical* in autocratic and democratic countries, in militarist countries and in such as know no military conscription; on the other hand, they help us to comprehend, on the basis of facts, the meaning of that compromise with social-chauvinism which expresses itself in such actions as extolling the peace slogan, etc.

The most perfect expression of opportunism and of liberal labour politics is undoubtedly the Fabian Society. Let the reader take a glance at the correspondence of Marx and Engels with Sorge. The reader will find there are excellent characterisation of that society by Engels, who treats Messrs. Sidney Webb and Co. as a band of bourgeois humbugs whose aim it is to demoralise the workers, to influence them in a counter-revolutionary direction. One may vouch for the fact that none of the more or less outstanding and influential leaders of the Second International ever attempted to refute this characterisation of Engels, or even to doubt its correctness.

Let us now compare the *facts,* leaving theory aside for a moment. We note that the Fabians' conduct during the war (compare, for instance, their weekly paper, the *New Statesman*) and the behaviour of the German Social-Democratic Party, including Kautsky, are *perfectly identical.* We see the same direct and indirect defence of social-chauvinism; the same combination of such a defence with a readiness to utter sugary, humane, and near-Left phrases about peace, disarmament, etc.

The fact stares one in the face; the conclusion inevitably and irrefutably to be drawn from it, no matter how unpleasant it may be for various persons, is that in practice the leaders of the present-day German Social-Democratic Party, including Kautsky, are exactly such agents of the bourgeoisie as Engels called the Fabians a long time ago. The non-recognition of Marxism by the Fabians and its "recognition" by Kautsky and Co. changes nothing in the thing *per se,* in practical politics; it only proves that with certain writers, politicians, etc., Marxism has turned into Struveism. Their hypocrisy *is not* their personal vice; they may be in individual cases the most virtuous heads of families; their hypocrisy is the result of the objective falsity of their social position, namely, of the fact that they are supposed to represent the revolutionary proletariat, whereas in reality they are agents charged with the duty of conveying to the proletariat bourgeois-chauvinist ideas.

The Fabians are more sincere and honest than Kautsky and Co. because they have not promised to stand for a revolution; politically, however, they are the same.

The existence of time-honoured political freedom in England, and the developed state of its political life in general, of its bourgeoisie in particular, made it possible for various *shadings* of bourgeois opinion to find, quickly, easily and freely, new expression in new political organisations of that country. One of such organisations is the Union of Democratic Control. The secretary and treasurer of this organisation is E. D. Morel, who is now a constant contributor to the central organ of the Independent Labour Party, the *New Leader*. This individual has repeatedly been the candidate of the Liberal Party in the Birkenhead district. When, shortly after the outbreak of the war, Morel expressed himself *against* it, he was notified by a committee of the Birkenhead Liberal Association, in a letter dated October 2, 1914, that his candidacy was no longer acceptable to the liberals, *i.e.*, he had been simply expelled from the party. Morel replied, on October 14, in a letter which he subsequently published as a pamphlet entitled *The Outbreak of the War*. In this pamphlet, as well as in a number of other articles, Morel exposes *his* government, proving the falsehood of references to the violation of Belgium's neutrality as the cause of the war, or to the destruction of *Prussian* imperialism as the aim of the war, etc., etc. Morel defends the programme of the Union of Democratic Control which stands for peace, disarmament, the right of every region to decide its own fate by plebiscite, and a democratic control over foreign politics.

All this shows that Morel, as a person, undoubtedly deserves credit for his sincere sympathy with democracy, for turning from chauvinist bourgeoisie to pacifist bourgeoisie. When Morel proves by facts that *his* government duped the people, denying the existence of secret treaties at a time when such treaties existed; that the English bourgeoisie as early as 1887 clearly recognised the unavoidability of violating Belgium's neutrality in case of a Franco-German war, and decidedly rejected the idea of interfering (Germany then was not yet such a dangerous competitor!); that French militarists like Colonel Boucher, in a number of books published before the war, openly admitted the existence of plans for an *aggressive* war of France and Russia against Germany; that the well-known military authority of

England, Colonel Repington, as early as 1911 recognised in the public press that the growth of Russian armaments after 1905 was a menace to Germany;—when Morel proves all this, we cannot fail to admit that we deal here with an exceptionally honest and courageous bourgeois who is not afraid to break with his own party.

Everybody will have to admit, however, that Morel is a bourgeois nevertheless, that his phrases of peace and armament remain empty words, since without revolutionary actions on the part of the proletariat there can be neither a democratic peace nor disarmament. Morel, who parted ways with the liberals on the question of the present war, remains a liberal as far as all the other economic and political questions are concerned. Why then, when the *same* bourgeois phrases about peace and disarmament are being covered up with Marxist gestures by Kautsky, is this not recognised as hypocrisy but as Kautsky's merit? Only the undeveloped political relations and the absence of political freedom in Germany are in the way of forming, as quickly and easily as in England, a bourgeois league for peace and disarmament with Kautsky's programme.

This being the case, let us recognise, that Kautsky occupies the position of a pacifist bourgeois, and not that of a revolutionary Social-Democrat.

The events we are passing through are great enough to warrant telling the truth with sufficient courage without regard to rank.

Being disinclined to abstract theories and taking pride in their own common sense, the English often approach political questions *more directly,* thus helping the Socialists of other countries to find real contents under the cloak of phraseology of every kind (including the "Marxian"). The pamphlet *Socialism and War* published by a chauvinist paper, the *Clarion,* before the war, is in this respect instructive. The pamphlet contains the anti-war "manifesto" of the American Socialist, Upton Sinclair, and a reply to it by Robert Blatchford, a chauvinist who has long been in agreement with Hyndman's imperialist position.

Sinclair is an emotional Socialist without theoretical grounding. He attacks the question "simply"; he is indignant over the approaching war and seeks refuge from it in Socialism.

> We are told [says Sinclair] that the [Socialist] movement is yet too weak, that we must wait for evolution. But evolution is working in the hearts of men; we are its instruments, and if we

do not struggle, there is no evolution. We are told that the movement [against the war] would be crushed out; but I declare my faith that the crushing out of any rebellion which sought, from motive of sublime humanity, to prevent war, would be the greatest victory that Socialism has ever gained—would shake the conscience of civilisation and rouse the workers of the world as nothing in all history has yet done. Let us not be too fearful for our movement, nor put too much stress on numbers and the outward appearances of power. A thousand men aglow with faith and determination are stronger than a million grown cautious and respectable; and there is no danger to the Socialist movement so great as the danger of becoming an established institution.

This, as can be seen, is a naive, theoretically ungrounded, but deeply correct warning against vulgarising Socialism; it is also a call to revolutionary struggle.

What does Blatchford reply to Sinclair?

That war is caused by capitalist and militarist interests is true, he says. I am no less in favour of peace and of Socialism superseding capitalism than any other Socialist, he declares, but Sinclair will not convince me by "rhetorical and beautiful phrases." He will not be able to do away with the facts. Facts, friend Sinclair, are stubborn things, and the German danger is a fact. Neither we nor the German Socialists have power enough to stop the war, he continues. Sinclair exaggerates our powers tremendously. We are not united. We have neither money, nor arms, "nor discipline." What remains for us is to *help* the British government to increase its navy, for we have no other guarantee of peace, and there can be none.

In continental Europe the chauvinists were never so frank, either before or after the beginning of the war. In Germany we have, instead of frankness, Kautsky's hypocrisy and a play with sophisms. The same is true of Plekhanov. This is why it is instructive to cast a glance at the situation in a more advanced country. There nobody will be deceived by sophisms or a travesty of Marxism. There the questions are placed squarely and more truly. Let us learn from the more "advanced" English.

Sinclair is naive in his appeal, although this appeal is deeply true at bottom; he is naive because he ignores the half-century-old development of mass Socialism, the struggle of currents within it; because he does not see that an objectively revolutionary situation as well as a revolutionary organisation are prerequisites for the growth of an active revolutionary movement. This cannot be replaced by "sentiment." The grim and merciless struggle of powerful currents in Socialism, the opportunist and revolutionary one, cannot be evaded by rhetoric.

Blatchford forges ahead; he betrays the deeply hidden argument of the Kautskyists who are afraid to tell the truth. We are still weak, this is all, says Blatchford, but by this directness he at once reveals and denudes his opportunism and chauvinism. It becomes immediately apparent that he serves the bourgeoisie and the opportunists. In recognising the "weakness" of Socialism, he himself *weakens* it by preaching anti-Socialist bourgeois politics.

Like Sinclair, but in a reverse way, like a coward and not like a fighter, like a traitor and not like one "ecstatically brave," he also ignores the prerequisites for creating a revolutionary situation.

As far as his practical conclusions, his politics (rejection of revolutionary activities, of propaganda in their favour, and preparation of them) are concerned, Blatchford, a vulgar chauvinist, is in absolute accord with Plekhanov and Kautsky.

Marxian words have in our days become a cover for absolute renunciation of Marxism; to be a Marxist one must expose the "Marxian" hypocrisy of the leaders of the Second International, one must fearlessly recognise the presence of a struggle of two currents in Socialism, one must follow the problems of this struggle to their logical conclusion. This is the conclusion to be drawn from the state of affairs in England where we see *Marxian* essence *without* Marxian words.

A. J. P. TAYLOR

The Great War
The Triumph of E. D. Morel (I)

Before 1914 everyone expected that a great European war, if it came, would be decided in the first few weeks. And so it was, though in strange ways. Winston Churchill has written of the battle of the Marne: "The War was decided in the first twenty days of fighting, and all that happened afterwards consisted in battles which, however formidable and devastating, were but desperate and vain appeals against the deci-

From *The Trouble Makers Dissent over Foreign Policy 1792–1939* by A. J. P. Taylor, London, Hamish Hamilton, 1958, pp. 132–45. Reprinted by permission of the author and publisher.

sion of Fate." [1] 5 September was the eve of the Marne; the day also of an event unnoticed at the time that was equally decisive. For it determined that the verdict of war would not be permanent. This event was the founding of the Union of Democratic Control. The U.D.C. succeeded where the Foreign Policy Committee and all its other predecessors had failed. Not only did it establish itself. It launched a version of international relations which gradually won general acceptance far beyond the circle of those who knew that they were being influenced by the U.D.C. Mrs. Swanwick, one of its founders, tells how a Trade Union branch in 1915 passed unanimously a resolution on war aims; and then, on someone pointing out that this reflected the policy of the U.D.C., as unanimously rescinded it. Later on, the resolutions were to be passed, and there was no rescinding.

The Union of Democratic Control sprang from the scattered remnant who had opposed Grey's policy on 3 August. By no means all of them. Morley withdrew from public life, replying to every inquiry with Cobden's words during the Crimean war that he would never again open his mouth while a war was on. John Burns was also silent, though he voted with the "peace" minority in 1916 and 1917. Many of the Radical journalists who had criticized Grey now supported the war, at any rate until 1917. C. P. Scott, of the *Manchester Guardian,* always lived in the present, and was more concerned to win the war than to go back over the past. By an agreeable irony, the Union—devoted to the attack on secret diplomacy—itself began with a private appeal to individuals, and was flushed into the open only by an unauthorized publication of this appeal in the pro-war Press. Four members of parliament were in at the foundation of the U.D.C.: two Radicals, Ponsonby and Charles Trevelyan, and two from the I.L.P., Ramsay MacDonald and Fred Jowett of Bradford.[2] But the M.P.s counted for less than the intellectuals: Hobson, Norman Angell, Bertrand Russell; they were soon joined by Lowes Dickinson, Fellow of King's College, Cambridge. More important still, the Union got E. D. Morel as secretary. In the words of Mrs. Swanwick, its historian: "E.D.M. was the U.D.C., and the U.D.C. was E.D.M."

1. Churchill, preface to E. L. Spears, *Liaison, 1914,* p. vii.
2. Keir Hardie, though a Dissenter of the first hour, was too discouraged by the desertion of his former supporters to make a new effort. He died of a broken heart in September 1915. Philip Snowden was in the Antipodes and returned only in November. He then became an active Dissenter in parliament, but was less closely associated with U.D.C., perhaps because MacDonald was prominent in it.

Morel has never had an equal as organizer and leader of a Dissenting movement. He knew exactly where to look for rich sympathizers; and he took money from them without weakening the democratic character of the Union. Millionaires and factory workers alike accepted his leadership. He knew, too, exactly what was wrong in foreign policy and what should be done instead. He was more than a critic; in his own mind, he was from the first the alternative foreign secretary, the foreign secretary of Dissent. He never left his followers at a loss. Morel saw sharply, clearly, dogmatically. Thanks to him, the Dissent of the war years did not wander complainingly in the void; though a minority, it spoke with a resolute voice. Morel's own writings dealt with pre-war diplomacy in detail, and offered an immediate policy in the present; there was no vague talk of waiting for the Socialist revolution or a change of heart. Not that Morel shunned general disquisitions. For these he turned to the outstanding intellectuals among his associates: Hobson, Brailsford, Bertrand Russell, Lowes Dickinson, Dr. G. P. Gooch.

The Union of Democratic Control had a powerful offshoot in Cambridge, which became a home of intellectual Dissent while Oxford specialized in emotional uplift, supporting the war. The group which had one foot in Cambridge and the other in Bloomsbury was solidly determined to remain sane when all the world was mad. Bertrand Russell wrote a pamphlet against *The Foreign Policy of the Entente;* was imprisoned on a charge of interfering with recruiting; and was deprived of his lectureship at Trinity as a result. You must remember that the civilian enthusiasts for the first World war developed a hysteria almost wholly absent in the second. Lowes Dickinson invented two phrases that were to ring round the world: "the League of Nations" and "the international anarchy." Leonard Woolf, who had married Virginia Stephen, devised one of the first schemes for "International Government." Clive Bell wrote early in 1915 a pamphlet, *Peace at Once,* which I have not managed to see.[3] Lytton Strachey, when before a Tribunal, gave the most famous and telling answer ever made to the question: "What would you do if you saw a German attempting to violate your sister?"[4] One of the Bloomsbury set was out of Cambridge. He was a high official at the Treasury, and remained at his desk even when his friends became conscientious objectors. In atonement he

3. [*Peace at Once* was a straightforward pacifist pamphlet, but nevertheless most copies of it were burned by order of the Lord Mayor of London.—Ed.]
4. [Lytton Strachey's reply: "I would endeavor to interpose my own body."—Ed.]

took "a solemn pledge" to himself that he would build a better world —a pledge that he kept with devastating effect in 1919. He was J. M. Keynes.

The most sensational stroke of this group was to take over *The Cambridge Magazine,* which had started in 1912 as a brighter rival of *The Cambridge Review.* Now academical trivialities took second place; and the *Magazine* gave a dazzling display of Dissent at its most aridly intellectual level. Mrs. Dorothy Buxton, member of a famous Cambridge family, contributed a weekly survey of the foreign Press, which was designed to show that there were plenty of sane and moderate men in enemy countries. This survey became so popular that it had to be continued during vacations as an independent supplement. The *Magazine* had other weapons. Adelyne More, that eccentric female, was one of the gayest ironists since Swift. This was not surprising since her name disguised, though it could hardly conceal, C. K. Ogden, the *Magazine's* editor. Rarely has a University periodical achieved national importance of this kind, at any rate since the decline of theological dispute.

The Union of Democratic Control had however another side. It accepted membership from organizations as well as from individuals; and most of these bodies were working-class—trade union branches, co-operative societies, branches of the I.L.P., women's sections of the Labour party. As Mrs. Swanwick puts it: "The appeal was from the first direct to the workers. . . . They believe in a moral basis for public affairs." [5] In October 1915, 48 out of 107 affiliated bodies came from the Labour movement; by 1921 the U.D.C. had 350 affiliated Labour organizations, representing a membership of over a million. These bodies powerfully reinforced the financial support of the few rich backers. But the ideas which they received were more important than the money that they gave. The I.L.P. and other Labour groups were against the war without knowing why. They jumped at the clear answers provided by Morel. Some of his pamphlets came out under the imprint of the I.L.P.; and all its pamphlets on foreign affairs bore the stamp of his inspiration. The Labour party, too, turned to Morel when it began to have doubts about the war. In fact no member of the Labour movement troubled to work out a Socialist foreign policy—if such a thing be possible—so long as Morel was alive. To paraphrase Mrs. Swanwick: Dissent meant the U.D.C.; and the U.D.C. meant E. D. Morel.

5. H. M. Swanwick, *Builders of Peace,* p. 57.

The Union, as its name implied, was directed primarily against "secret diplomacy," or perhaps against any diplomacy at all. It echoed Cobden's "no foreign politics," though with some elaboration. Three out of its four Cardinal Points were negative: no transfer of territory without a plebiscite; no treaty or undertaking without parliamentary sanction; drastic reduction of armaments and nationalization of the arms-traffic. Even the remaining point was mainly negative; a rejection of the Balance of Power. It added, almost as an afterthought: "the establishment of a Concert of the Powers and the setting up of an International Council whose deliberations and decisions shall be public," with treaties of arbitration and Courts "for their interpretation and enforcement." This was a long way from the plans for a League of Nations which others were soon to elaborate; [6] and it reflected the practical cast of Morel's mind. The I.L.P. took over these points virtually unaltered, except that "a federation of the nations" was incongruously dovetailed in along with "an International Council whose decisions shall be public." [7]

The U.D.C. was convinced that, if there had been less foreign policy, there would have been no war. Its practical task was therefore to show that there had been nothing in German policy before the war to excite alarm. Morel did this in a penny pamphlet for the I.L.P., *How the War Began,* which came out before the end of 1914, and more elaborately in *Truth and the War,* which sold twenty thousand copies in 1916. Both developed his private verdict: *"you are all guilty—everyone."* Germany was represented as the aggrieved Power. "In 1898 Germany began to build a fleet to protect her coast and her commerce." The conference of Algeciras "deliberately threw down the gauntlet to Germany." "From 1904 [observe the date, it is that of the Anglo-French entente], European policy hatched war as a hen hatches chickens." Further, "it is a moral, physical and strategic impossibility to bottle up an elemental force such as that which the German people incarnate. It simply cannot be done." The Dissenters did not stop with justifying Germany. They treated Austria-Hungary also as a German national state, and therefore claimed that she was fighting a defensive war. Brailsford wrote in *The Nation:* "Every proposal to take German provinces and dismember Austria is a justification of the German belief that the position of the

6. Even this half-hearted reference to an international organization was missing from the first private letter which was the prelude to the U.D.C.
7. In 1916 the U.D.C. added a fifth Point, also negative: universal Free Trade. This, too, was endorsed by the I.L.P.

German race in Central Europe is made tenable only by its vast armies." [8] Morel said much the same: "Germany and Austria had the deep-rooted conviction that the national existence was, and is, threatened by a coalition of hostile forces. Nor can I conceive that such a conviction would have survived the sufferings of the war if there was not a substance of fact to buttress it." [9]

The Dissenters challenged the immediate, as well as the remoter causes of the war. Belgium was, of course, the trickiest point. A few extreme advocates of even-handed justice held that, since every war had two sides, Belgium must be as much at fault in resisting the Germans as they were in invading her. For instance, Vernon Lee, also an early member of the U.D.C., argued that to insist on the neutrality of Belgium was like "calling for fair play between one man armed with a stick, and threatened by one man (or rather two men!), and a man armed with a long-range rifle." [10] Bernard Shaw also took this line in a pamphlet called *Common Sense and the War*, a title more than usually impertinent. Shaw argued that Belgian neutrality weakened Germany's strategic position, and was therefore an act of aggression against her. In any case, Belgium had nothing to do with the entry of Great Britain into the war. Grey's policy had been a deliberate trap for Germany, "the last spring of the old lion." Having thus destroyed the moral case for the war, Shaw then defended it on strictly practical grounds as a struggle for survival: England must defeat Germany (or Germany defeat England), and, as Shaw lived in England, he proposed to support the English side of the equation. Shaw enjoyed pricking moral pretensions; he also enjoyed teasing his fellow Dissenters. On the other hand he wished to be secure from the attentions of the police and to be received as an honoured guest at G.H.Q. Supporting the war on immoral grounds satisfied his requirements exactly. Many readers did not understand his intentions. Supporters of the war denounced Shaw, the rigorous Bismarckian, as a pacifist; and Dissenters thought that he had given the game of British morality away. Keir Hardie, for instance, wrote to Shaw: "Your article will produce an elevation of tone in the national life which will be felt for generations to come. . . . My heart throbs towards you with almost feelings of devotion." [11]

8. *The Nation*, 29 August 1914.
9. *The Nation*, 28 October 1916.
10. *The Nation*, 22 August 1914. The sense is clearer than the grammar.
11. W. Stewart, *Keir Hardie*, p. 359.

Most Dissenters shrank from a ruthlessness which rebounded on to their own position. The more usual Dissenting position was to treat Belgium as an innocent victim of rival Imperialist Powers. Brailsford, for instance, wrote: "So long as we heap up armaments and form diplomatic combinations, in order to win colonies and spheres of influence for ourselves and our friends, so long will the relationship of nations remain on the precarious basis of force." But he, too, thought that the Belgians had carried things rather far: "We will not discuss whether the Belgians need have resisted the German invasion. Their courage has been superb; but . . . should we say that a single householder was dishonoured if he did not resist a gang of armed burglars?" In any case, this did not acquit the directors of British policy. A declaration of British support to Belgium, if made before the war, "would have forced the German General Staff, on the assumption that it consisted of sane men, to reverse their strategical plans. . . . But *the navy was mortgaged to France*." [12] This last sentence became the Dissenting refrain. Norman Angell said it: "Belgium had to be sacrificed to the maintenance of the Balance of Power"; so did C. P. Scott: "No doubt we were committed to France, Belgium or no Belgium." Bryce, Morley, Loreburn, Courtney of Penwith, all put their finger on No. 123 in the Blue Book, where the German Ambassador was supposed to have offered to trade Belgium in exchange for British neutrality; and they quoted Gladstone's negotiations of 1870 in order to establish—erroneously in my opinion—either that a British guarantee to Belgium did not exist or that there was an obligation on Great Britain to remain neutral if Belgium was left alone.

The position became easier for the Dissenters when deadlock followed the first few weeks of fighting. Instead of arguing why the war had started, they could discuss how it should be ended; they could even show how to end it honourably. The war, in their view, had been caused by the ententes with France and Russia, not by the German invasion of Belgium; therefore the Germans would gladly restore Belgium, the moment that this country repudiated the aggressive designs of its two partners. The Dissenters had some qualms about leaving north-east France in German occupation; they had no qualms at all about abandoning Russia. Indeed even those who supported the war hoped that Germany could be somehow defeated without Russia's winning. Bernard Shaw wrote:

12. H. N. Brailsford, *Belgium and "the Scrap of Paper."*

> A victory unattainable without Russian aid would be a defeat
> for Western European Liberalism. . . . If we cannot without
> Russian help beat Potsdam . . . then we shall simply have to
> "give Germany best" and depend upon an alliance with America
> for our place in the sun.

—not a bad guess of how things turned out thirty years later. It was
soon an article of faith with the Dissenters that Germany was eager for
peace without victory. Pigou, a Fellow of King's College, Cambridge,
asked: why do the allies not state their peace terms? Is it for fear that
the Germans might accept them? [13] Bertrand Russell answered: "Probably, even now, Germany would be willing to evacuate Belgium and
North-East France, and to come to terms with Russia about the
Balkans." [14]

Clearly the Allies must be harbouring some nefarious design, to
refuse such an attractive prospect. And the Dissenters soon discovered
what it was: the Allies were prolonging the war so that Russia should
gain Constantinople. Charles Trevelyan said in the House of Commons:
"Suppose we knew that Germany would retire from Belgium, and give
an indemnity . . . perhaps give back some of Lorraine . . . give
Serbia back its independence? What then? Have we got to continue this
war until Russia is in possession of Constantinople?" [15] Outhwaite, a
Radical from South Africa, almost outdid Urquhart in his obsession
about Russia:

> This War is . . . a fight in the main for Russia to obtain
> possession of Constantinople. If our object is to drive Germany
> out of France and out of Belgium and compel her to indemnify
> their people . . . , all that seems to me an object within the
> capacity of this country which perhaps has been achieved
> already.[16]

Brailsford pushed this argument to its logical conclusion: if we not
merely kept Russia out of Turkey, but gave it to Germany instead, all
our troubles would be solved. "A German Turkey would not be a graver
menace to the peace of the world than a British India. The chief menace
to the world's liberty is to-day an unsatisfied Germany." If Germany
were given political and economic predominance in Turkey, together

13. *The Nation*, 6 February 1915.
14. *The Nation*, 13 February 1915.
15. 11 October 1916. *Hansard*, fifth series, lxxxvi, 147.
16. 12 October 1916. *Hansard*, fifth series, lxxxvi, 332–4.

with control of the Balkan railways, "we may hope for a solution of the Alsatian, Serbian, and Polish (and, of course, Belgian) problems, on lines of nationality." [17]

These ideas reached parliament in November 1915, when Ponsonby and Trevelyan in the Commons, Courtney of Penwith in the Lords, first called for a peace by negotiation—Courtney bravely declaring that he would refuse to *pay* any indemnity to Germany. The call was repeated in 1916—on 23 February, 24 May, 11 October—and on 12 February 1917. On none of these occasions did the Dissenters divide the House —evidence of their isolation. Their arguments were strictly practical: no discussion of the origins of the war, but solely an insistence that, however it began, it should now be ended by negotiation. On 21 December 1916 the House first heard a constructive alternative, the League of Nations. Lees-Smith, back from the trenches and speaking in uniform, said:

> Security can only be obtained by a scheme by which the nations of Europe and outside agree together that all will guarantee each and each will guarantee all. The purposes of the war will be achieved if there is a League of Nations with an absolute and decisive veto upon any mere aggression, and consideration of any legitimate claims which any of the countries engaged in the War may be able to make good. . . . Go back to the old Liberal tradition and trust yourself boldly to those decent, kindly, humane forces to be found in every man and every nation.[18]

Though the phrase was new to the House of Commons, "the League of Nations" had become common currency since Lowes Dickinson coined it in August 1914. The phrase was used, the idea supported, by many people who believed that the defeat of Germany should come first, including Sir Edward Grey. Yet it was used more persistently and emphatically by those who regarded the League as a substitute both for the defeat of Germany and for traditional foreign policy. In 1916 three men published detailed schemes for a League of Nations— Hobson, Brailsford, Leonard Woolf. All three were members of the Union of Democratic Control. All three treated the League as synonymous with "International Government." . . . Yet this did not mean

17. *The Nation*, 1 January 1916. *The Nation* endorsed this solution editorially on 29 July 1916 and 6 January 1917.
18. *Hansard*, fifth series, lxxxviii, 1728–30.

that the League became an essential part of U.D.C. policy. It was rather a fifth wheel, awkwardly tacked on at the end of the argument. Morel himself was significantly absent from every League committee: he had more urgent business. Time and again, the League was spatch-cocked in as an afterthought. For instance, the U.D.C. devised peace terms in July 1917. Out of the thirteen points, the League got one half-sentence. It appeared as "a means of defence which renders old militarism unnecessary"; but obviously the U.D.C. regarded it as of less importance than its old loves—open diplomacy and disarmament. The Labour party provides another instance. In December 1917 it drafted democratic principles of foreign policy (modelled on those of the U.D.C.) for submission to a meeting of Allied Socialists. The draft embraced everything from territorial changes to economic systems. At the last minute a further paragraph was inserted. This begins: "But it demands, in addition, . . . a Supernational Authority, or League of Nations."

Bertrand Russell provides an even more striking example. The final chapter of *The Foreign Policy of the Entente* laid down Radical principles of foreign policy: no annexations; renunciation of the right of capture; universal arbitration; no alliances or understandings; "we shall not engage in war except when we are attacked." Appended to this is a footnote: "Unless a League of Great Powers could be formed to resist aggression everywhere. . . . In that case, we might be willing to participate in a war to enforce its decisions." [19] The contradiction seems startling; but Woodrow Wilson himself did much the same, when he thought to change the character of the treaty of Versailles by tying the Covenant of the League to its coat-tails. Every advocate of the League weighed with two measures. Their books described at length the misdeeds of statesmen all over the world. Then, in a short final chapter, they assumed that the same statesmen would become persistently virtuous once a League of Nations had been set up.

Moreover the League, like other great phrases in history from the Trinity to the Rights of Man, solved every problem for its votaries while remaining incomprehensible to the detached observer. The members of the U.D.C. believed that it made the defeat of Germany unnecessary. Supporters of the war, such as Gilbert Murray or H. G. Wells, expected it to perpetuate the victory of the Allies. The League would guarantee the security of every country, yet carry through treaty-

19. Bertrand Russell, *Foreign Policy of the Entente*, p. 73.

revision. Pacifists could assert that war solved nothing, yet be confident that a League war would solve everything. The League could cover anything from the Concert of Europe to a system of International Government in which national sovereignty ceased to exist. In 1918 Garvin, the Jingo journalist, thought that a crusade against Bolshevism "in the decisive sense . . . would be the best way in which the League of Nations could begin and would do more than anything else to confirm belief in its real efficiency and prospects of successful development." [20] Yet "a league or concert of nations with an international force" was also advocated by the British Socialist party, the most revolutionary and pro-Bolshevik group in England, which became the nucleus of the Communist party of Great Britain.

Morel ignored the agitation for a League. Ramsay MacDonald did more: he dissented from it. The League, in his own favourite word, was "quackery." "To call national armies an International Police Force seems to me nothing but sticking new misleading labels upon them." [21] He said much the same in the House of Commons:

> Those who look to guarantees in arms, and military, and force and all that sort of thing, are only just reading once again, in a somewhat different phraseology, but in substance precisely the same, all the chapters that have been written in the history of the world, every one of which has ended in a war.[22]

MacDonald also repudiated the analogy with a police force that had already become popular in League circles: "My protection really is, not that there is organized force around me, but that there are involuntary social habits around me. . . . It is not so much the policeman that one depends on as public opinion." [23] MacDonald is often regarded as an empty rhetorician, but he seems in retrospect—despite his style of utterance—the only realist among all the Dissenters. "The need, therefore, was for disarmament, the end of the prevailing political system of Europe, open diplomacy, and the genuine internationalism of socialism. . . . Then we shall want no League of Nations to Enforce Peace, with its dangers and surrenders to militarism." [24]

20. J. L. Garvin, *Economic Foundations of Peace,* pp. 400–2.
21. Ramsay MacDonald, *National Defence,* p. 18.
22. *Hansard,* fifth series, 109, 719–22.
23. *Hansard,* fifth series, 109, 719.
24. *Labour Leader,* 19 December 1916. This, and other quotations are from the invaluable book by Van der Slice, *International Labour Diplomacy and Peace 1914–19* (1941).

MacDonald's own enthusiasm was for "open diplomacy," an endless process of talk and discussion; this gave him his hold over the Dissenters. He said of the old diplomacy:

> The whole corrupting system should be swept away. It stands like a dirty old slum area, full of vermin and disease, in the midst of a district cleared and improved. . . . Open diplomacy will not remove the *causes* of war; it will enable these causes to dissipate themselves without an explosion. . . . The people and reasonableness will settle them as they arise.[25]

And here is his description of the new system, a remarkable proof, incidentally, that his style did not grow on him only in later years:

> The days of peace picnics and polite and meaningless speeches are over. They have been empty. Energy that is sleepless and a policy which is pursued from day to day and with complete detail, watching every move in the diplomatic game and with a thoroughly efficient Intelligence Department and Parliamentary policy, are now required if the men who have died for us are not to have died in vain.[26]

It is tempting to go on quoting MacDonald for ever—there is certainly enough material. I cannot resist two further examples. First, his comment on Alsace-Lorraine, a comment which enabled him to avoid any decision between a plebiscite and return to France:

> Two races . . . have been thrown into the middle of Europe in this devilish sort of way as though an imp of another region had simply done it in order to make peace impossible. . . . I hope that it is going to be kept as an open door year.[27]

And his vision of what should happen when the war ended:

> We hope . . . that the moment a truce comes . . . the peoples of Europe will come together, and in their enthusiasm and their sorrow and pain and suffering will there and then on the spot, before the experience has gone out of their minds, create something which will make it impossible for such a state of things ever to take place again.[28]

25. Ramsay MacDonald, *National Defence*, pp. 115–16.
26. Ramsay MacDonald, *National Defence*, p. 120.
27. *Hansard,* fifth series, xcviii, 2034.
28. *Hansard,* fifth series, 107, 588.

MacDonald only said at greater length what every Dissenter believed: that the peoples of the world had no quarrel with each other and that peace would be secured by democratic government, rather than by the League of Nations.

V

THE LABOUR PARTY IN SESSION

G. D. H. COLE

Labour at War

The Labour Party's Annual Conference was due to meet, at the usual
time, in January, 1915. It was postponed, after a postal ballot of the
affiliated Societies had been taken. No Party Conference met till January, 1916, and before then a good deal more had happened. The I.L.P.,
however, held its Annual Conference at Easter, 1915, in spite of war
conditions. The I.L.P. had opposed Labour participation in the recruiting campaign, and had urged that, if the Labour Party did decide to
help recruiting, this ought to be done from its own platforms and not
at meetings organised jointly with the capitalist parties. When a number
of I.L.P. members ignored this view, branches began sending resolutions
of protest to the I.L.P. National Council, which replied that "while
recognising that such matters as enlistment and the urging of recruiting
are matters for the individual conscience," the Council felt it desirable
"to draw attention to our recommendation that no part in the recruiting
campaign should be taken by branches of the Party" (i.e., of the
I.L.P.). On the other hand, the I.L.P. played an active part in the work
of the War Emergency Workers' National Committee and in the organisation of relief work, including work for Belgian refugees. After the
abandonment of the Vienna International Socialist Congress it pressed
strongly for the maintenance of the International during the war,

From *A History of the Labour Party from 1914,* London, Routledge & Kegan
Paul, Ltd., 1948, pp. 21–31. Reprinted by permission of the publisher.

supported the removal of the office of the International Socialist Bureau from Brussels to neutral territory at the Hague, and pressed for a meeting of the Bureau to be attended by delegates from both belligerent and neutral countries. The removal to the Hague was soon effected, Camille Huysmans, the Belgian Secretary, taking up residence there; and in January, 1915, the Socialists of the four northern countries— Sweden, Norway, Denmark and Holland—held a joint Conference and set up, under Hjalmar Branting, the Swedish leader, a Committee of Neutrals to help in holding International Socialism together and to watch for an opportunity of intervention in the interest of peace.

The attempts of the I.L.P. and of the Bureau officials at the Hague to bring about an international meeting did not for the time succeed. They did, however, provoke, in February, 1915, a first Conference of the Socialist and Labour Parties of the Allied Countries only, called largely to consider what attitude to adopt to the efforts of the neutrals. The British Section appears to have been, at one point, not unfavourable to a full international meeting; but the majority of the French Socialist Party refused to be represented at any Conference attended by German delegates as long as any part of France remained under German occupation. The British Section then took the initiative in convening the London Allied Socialist Conference of February, 1915, over which Keir Hardie presided. The resolutions approved by this meeting, while they were unequivocal in their support of the Allied cause, were very different in tone from the British Manifesto of October, 1914. They described the war as "a monstrous product of the antagonisms which tear asunder capitalist society and of the policy of colonial dependencies and aggressive imperialism . . . in which every Government has its share of responsibility." They expressed the intention "to resist any attempt to transform this defensive war into a war of conquest, which would only prepare fresh conflicts, create new grievances, and subject the various peoples more than ever to the double plague of armaments and war." The Allied Socialists asserted that "they are not at war with the peoples of Germany and Austria, but only with the Governments of those countries, by which they are oppressed." Finally, they asserted the need, on the conclusion of the war, to "establish some international authority to settle points of difference among the nations by compulsory conciliation and arbitration, and to compel all nations to maintain peace." In the meantime, however, the war had to be won.

After this Conference, the neutral Executive of the International

Socialist Bureau, as part of its procedure of holding meetings with the Socialists of all the belligerent nations, invited the British Section to meet it at the Hague, and the Section appointed Henderson and Mac-Donald to go, as representing the rival views. In the event, however, the meeting was not held, owing to objections from the more extreme pro-war group; but the British Section kept up its connection with the International Bureau and advanced money to help it in meeting its expenses during the emergency.

By this time it was becoming apparent that the anticipation of the war causing widespread unemployment and distress as long as it lasted had been very much beside the mark. The first great munitions crisis was beginning, as the armed forces ran short of shells and other equipment, and as the enormous expenditure of munitions involved in modern warfare began to be understood. Unemployment and distress there had been, at the very outset, with peace-time industries closing down. But by February, 1915, many of the closed factories had been re-opened, and the cry was going up for more men to work in more and bigger war factories—and for women as well, to supplement the men's labours and to replace those who enlisted—still voluntarily—in the armed forces. Except in the light metal trades in and around Birmingham and in a few heavier trades in the Black Country, women, up to 1914, had been but little employed in metal-working; and there were strong prejudices against their employment, as well as fears of its effects in cutting the men's wages. But now an imperative demand arose for the use of women to make and fill shells and cartridge cases and to undertake other processes simplified by the sub-division of jobs; and the Amalgamated Society of Engineers found itself under the necessity of sanctioning women's employment, first at the Vickers works at Crayford and then, more generally, under the Shells and Fuses Agreement of March 5, 1915. Such sectional concessions were not, however, deemed nearly enough; and on March 17, Lloyd George summoned the Trade Unions to the first Treasury Conference, at which the Government asked for a suspension for the duration of the war of all Trade Union practices and customs that might impede war production, on a promise that no obstacles would be put in the way of the restoration of the suspended practices when the war was over. It required a further Conference, a week later, at which the Government promised a limitation of profits on munitions work, to induce the powerful Amalgamated Society of Engineers to accept the Treasury Agreement; but the other Unions concerned, except the Miners' Federation, accepted at once, and as soon as the A.S.E. had come in the Government set up a National Labour Advisory Committee, under Arthur Henderson's chairmanship, to advise it on labour problems arising under the Agreement. The terms included compulsory arbitration of war-time disputes as well as the suspension of Trade Union practices as a means to what soon came to be known as "dilution" of labour.

Thus, the Industrial Truce, which had been at the outset a unilateral act of the Trade Unions, became embodied in a formal agreement with the Government (but with the Miners standing out). A few months later, in July, 1915, the Treasury Agreement was given statutory force by embodiment in the Munitions of War Act, under which both compulsory arbitration and dilution of labour acquired legal sanctions. The formal co-operation of the Labour movement in the industrial conduct of the war began, however, with the Treasury Agreement and the setting up of the National Labour Advisory Committee under Henderson. Henderson from that point was attempting to double the parts of Leader of the Labour Party in the House of Commons and *de facto* Industrial Adviser to a Government in which Labour was not represented—to say nothing of his further offices as Secretary both of the Labour Party and of the British Section of the International Socialist movement. So difficult and anomalous a situation could not last. It was ended in May, 1915, by the formation of the first war-time Coalition Government. This was in the main a Coalition of Liberals and Conservatives; for the Irish Party did not come in, and the Labour Party was still too small to be offered more than a scanty share. The Prime Minister, Asquith, invited Henderson to accept the office of President of the Board of Education, but to regard it as a war-time sinecure and to devote his main attention, as before, to acting as the Government's Adviser on Labour questions. Henderson was to be the only Labour representative in the Cabinet; but two other Labour M.P.s were given minor office—the South Wales miner, William Brace, as Under Secretary at the Home Office, and the printer, G. H. Roberts, as a Government Whip.

This invitation to enter a Coalition Government dominated by the capitalist parties caused much searching of hearts. The I.L.P. opposed acceptance, and on this occasion J. R. Clynes was in agreement with the I.L.P. colleagues from whom he had broken on the general war issue. Arthur Henderson himself was uncomfortable about it. Besides his unwillingness to become President of the Board of Education—an office for which he did not feel fit and which he objected to regarding as a sinecure—there was the difficult question whether he would not forfeit his hold on the Labour Party by joining a Government which he could have but little power to influence. He realised that, if he took office, the Government would use him to put across the Labour Party and the Trade Union measures which were certain to arouse resentment, and that the effect might be to antagonise Labour from the war effort instead of strengthening its participation. Nevertheless, pressed by Asquith, he did not see how, as a supporter of the war, he could refuse, unless the Labour Party would refuse for him. He at once consulted both the Labour Party Executive and the Labour M.P.s; and, despite considerable opposition, both gave majorities in favour of participation—an attitude which was subsequently endorsed both by the Trades Union Congress in September, 1915, and by the Labour Party Conference in January, 1916.

It was, however, clear that Henderson, as a Cabinet Minister, could continue to act neither as Secretary to the Labour Party nor as its Parliamentary Leader. The decision was that he should substantively retain both posts; but that an Acting Secretary and an Acting Leader should be appointed for as long as he continued in the Government. Consequently, the Assistant Secretary, J. S. Middleton, became Acting Secretary of the party organisation, and John Hodge, of the Steel Smelters, was elected as Acting Leader of the Party in the House of Commons.

Henderson had not long to wait for the expected difficulties. In July, immediately after the enactment of the Munitions Act, came the strike of the South Wales Miners and its "proclamation" by the Government as unlawful under the terms of the Act. But coal—South Wales steam coal above all—was urgently needed; and it would have been useless, even if it had been possible, to clap 200,000 striking miners into gaol. The Government had to give way, and to grant the miners their terms; and though Lloyd George played the main part in the proceedings, Henderson had to take his share, and can hardly have helped feeling it as somewhat ignominious. There was, however, worse to come. Pledges had been given, when the Coalition was formed, that there would be no conscription for the armed forces; but it soon became evident to many people that the vast numbers of men who would be needed if the war went on for long could not easily be got under the voluntary system. National Registration was enforced in August, 1915, under the asseveration that it had nothing to do with the matter. In September the Trades

Union Congress recorded its unqualified opposition to compulsory military service, which was by this time the subject of an intensive newspaper campaign and was finding strong support in the Cabinet. Later in the month, Henderson had to preside over a special conference of Labour organisations, before which Lord Kitchener, the War Secretary, laid a statement of the Government's demand for recruits. The conference, under pressure, agreed, in the hope of saving the voluntary system, to launch a Labour Recruiting Campaign of its own; and in October the Government inaugurated the "Derby Scheme" of attestation, under which all men of military age were called upon to "attest" for service, whether or not they were engaged on essential work, leaving it to the authorities to judge whether they should be called up for military service or not. This scheme involved strong pressure, though not full compulsion; and no sooner had it and the Labour Recruiting Campaign been set on foot than the clamour for conscription was re-doubled. The Prime Minister, in order to induce married men to attest, gave a pledge that single men would be called up first, thus in effect making conscription unavoidable. The Labour organisations protested in vain: the Government, despite its earlier pledges, decided to introduce a Bill for Compulsory Military Service, applicable to single men only, and represented as necessary in order to give effect to the promise made to the married men; for 600,000 single men, it was reported, had failed to attest.

In these circumstances, the Labour organisations, which had been negotiating with Lord Derby and with the Government mainly through Henderson, decided to call a special Congress representing the entire Labour movement in order to decide what to do. At this meeting, on January 6th, 1915, a resolution in favour of accepting conscription of single men was defeated by 2,121,000 votes to 541,000, and a resolution of uncompromising opposition, put forward by the National Union of Railwaymen and the Amalgamated Society of Engineers, was carried by 1,715,000 to 934,000, and then, on a second vote, by 1,998,000 to 783,000. This resolution called on the Parliamentary Labour Party to oppose the Conscription Bill in all its stages.

Upon this, the Labour Party and the Parliamentary Party met and decided to call the Labour Ministers out of the Coalition. This ultimatum was followed by a meeting of both bodies with the Prime Minister, who well understood the difficulty of enforcing conscription in face of organised Labour opposition. Asquith was lavish with his promises—there should be no conscription of married men, the firmest

safeguards should be provided against any form of industrial conscription, the tribunals to adjudicate on calling-up should be civilian, and
not military, the position of conscientious objectors should be amply
secured. Under these inducements, the Labour Party was persuaded to
withdraw the resignations from the Government, and to refer the whole
matter for decision at the impending Party Conference.

The Conference met at Bristol during the last week of January, 1916.
A general resolution expressing hostility to "Conscription in any form"
was carried by an overwhelming majority. Then the Women's Labour
League and the N.U.R. moved and seconded a resolution in the following terms:

> That this Conference declares its opposition to the Military
> Service (No. 2) Bill [the Conscription Bill] and, in the event of
> it becoming law, decides to agitate for its repeal.

These words were carefully chosen. They did not commit Labour to
positive resistance to conscription; but if they had been accepted the
Labour Ministers could hardly have remained in the Government.
What the Conference did, on the motion of Will Thorne, was to delete
the second half, thus limiting the resolution to a recording of opposition, but by implication agreeing to accept the Bill if it became an Act.
The discussion was confused, and many of those who voted against the
second part of the resolution, as the speeches show, did not understand
what the real issue was. The effect, however, was to allow the Labour
Ministers to remain in the Government, and to leave the opponents of
the Military Service Act protesting but powerless: so that when, despite
the pledges that had been given, Parliament went on in May, 1916, to
pass a further Act applying conscription to married men, the Labour
forces had become sharply divided. In April, 1916, Asquith, Kitchener
and Bonar Law again conferred with representatives of the Labour
Party and the Trade Unions; and, after hearing their statements, the
Parliamentary Committee of the Trades Union Congress agreed to
accept the new Bill. At the meeting of the Labour Party Executive—to
quote the reticent language of the Annual Report—"a resolution emphatically protesting against the extension of compulsory military service was not carried." A proposal that a National Conference of the
whole Labour movement should be summoned was put forward, but
"was not pressed."

Thus Labour came, albeit under protest, to accept conscription for
both single and married men. It was in fact a war necessity, on the

assumption of a fight to the finish on which the war was being fought. Labour speakers might argue, with truth, that the voluntary system had not been given a fair trial, and that they had been tricked into accepting, first attestation, then compulsory service for single men only, and then all-round conscription, largely by men who had intended all the time, despite promises in which they tacitly acquiesced, to go the whole way. All this was the case; but it was also the case that the claims of total war had to be met, if victory were the object, and that the devious course actually followed by the Government was probably the only, and certainly the easiest, way of reaching the required end.

While the conscription issue was being thus handled, serious labour troubles were developing on other issues as well. In January, 1916, a special body of Dilution Commissioners had begun work on the Clyde, largely with a view to securing more men for the forces by more extensive substitution of women on war work. Over their activities and over other factors of discontent arose the Parkhead strike of March 17, 1916, and the spreading unrest which the Government attempted to quell by deporting the leaders of the Clyde Workers' Committee, an unofficial, militant movement based on the shop stewards in the munition works and shipyards of Clydeside, and led by Socialists of the Marxist Socialist Labour Party and the British Socialist Party as well as of the I.L.P. Henderson was not consulted about these deportations, and knew nothing about them until they had been made; but as the Labour member of the Cabinet (though not of the inner War Council, on which the Labour Party had no seat) he got a good deal of the odium arising out of the Government's high-handed proceedings. Hard upon the Clyde deportations followed the Easter Rebellion in Ireland, which cost James Connolly, Sheehy Skeffington and other Socialists their lives, and then the Second Conscription Act.

Meanwhile, the I.L.P. and the anti-war opposition as a whole had been passing through difficult times. Keir Hardie's death in September, 1915, had involved a by-election at Merthyr. Under the Electoral Truce this would ordinarily have meant an unopposed return; but when the South Wales Miners, who claimed the seat, put forward one of their own officials, James Winstone, who took the I.L.P. view, his violently pro-war defeated rival, C. B. Stanton, also an official of the Miners' Federation, resigned his Trade Union office in order to fight the seat, and was elected in November, 1915, by 10,286 to 6,080.

Before this, in August, 1915, there had been extensive raids on the I.L.P., B.S.P., and other anti-war bodies by the police, who seized and confiscated pamphlets and other documents putting the anti-war view. The following month a leading Italian Socialist, Odelino Morgari, came to England on behalf of the Italian and Swiss Socialist Parties in order to urge British participation in an international conference of parties or sections of parties favouring a vigorous peace propaganda. The I.L.P. appointed two of its leaders, F. W. Jowett and J. Bruce Glasier, to attend this conference, which was held at Zimmerwald in September, 1915. The Government, however, refused passports both to the I.L.P. delegates and to the delegate chosen by the B.S.P.; and the famous Zimmerwald Conference, at which Lenin took a leading part, passed off without British participation. The Zimmerwald Manifesto, however, with its vigorous denunciation of the Socialist war-supporters in all countries, reached the I.L.P. with a request for its endorsement. The I.L.P., in its reply, declared its support of the aspirations of working-class action for peace, but expressed its disapproval "of those passages condemning other Socialist groups for the action they have taken in connection with the war." Despite this qualification on its approval, it expressed its wish to be represented at the further Conference that was being called, if passports could be obtained. Even at this stage, how-ever, it was clear enough that in Great Britain, as in other countries, there were really two anti-war oppositions, the one, headed internation-ally by Lenin, revolutionary and entirely unconcerned with the merits of the case advanced by any capitalist Government, and the other either out-and-out pacifist or working for peace by negotiation, but opposed to any attempt to invoke revolutionary violence as a means of ending the war by international working-class revolution. The I.L.P., though it had revolutionaries in its ranks, belonged essentially to the second of these groups; the British Socialist Party, having shed its pro-war section, was moving rapidly towards the first. At the I.L.P. Conference of April, 1916, a resolution calling upon the party to "reconsider its affiliation with the Labour Party" on account of the latter's war attitude was heavily defeated, and a resolution urging Socialists of all nations to "refuse support to every war entered into by any Government, what-ever the ostensible object of the war," moved by a leading pacifist, Dr. Alfred Salter, was carried by 235 votes to 3.

In August, 1916, Arthur Henderson was at length allowed to resign his nominal position as President of the Board of Education, in order to become full-time Labour Adviser to the Government in name as well as in fact. The pressure for further enlistments and for further dilution and substitution of labour—no longer only on munitions work—was more severe than ever; and many discontents were accumulating over the conduct of the war on both the military and the economic side. The Asquith Coalition staggered on for a few months more; but behind the scenes Lloyd George was intriguing hard against his political leader, and by the end of November he had won over both the Tories and a section of the Liberal Party. On December 5, Asquith was forced to resign, and Lloyd George was invited to form a new Coalition Government, in which he was the more anxious to secure the support of Labour because of the increasing factory unrest and the need for further unpopular measures if the war was to be fought through to the bitter end.

Henderson remained loyal to Asquith up to the moment of his resignation, and resisted blandishments to join Lloyd George's intrigue. When, however, the Asquith Government had actually fallen, it had to be decided afresh what line the Labour Party should take. Lloyd George was offering attractive terms—a seat for Henderson in the inner War Cabinet, the establishment of a Ministry of Labour under a Labour Minister, state control of mines and shipping, an improved policy of food distribution, and various other things for which, in face of Asquith's strong *laissez-faire* tendency, Labour had hitherto been pressing in vain. Under these inducements the Labour Party agreed without much difficulty to join the new Coalition, with Henderson in the War Cabinet, John Hodge as Minister of Labour, G. N. Barnes of the Engineers as Minister of Pensions, and William Brace, G. H. Roberts, and James Parker in minor posts. J. H. Thomas, of the N.U.R., refused office. J. R. Clynes, who had opposed Labour's entry into the first Coalition, was now in favour. At the Labour Party Conference, held in January, 1917, the Party's entry into the Coalition was approved by a vote of 1,849,000 to 307,000.

MARY AGNES HAMILTON

Arthur Henderson as Leader

Throughout the years of war the British Labour Party remained a single party. In this it was unique. On the Continent, every Socialist Party split: British Labour never split. The value of this, for the movement as a whole, indeed for the country as a whole, can hardly be exagger-

From *Arthur Henderson* by Mary Agnes Hamilton, London, William Heinemann, Ltd., 1938, pp. 98–105, 112–16. Reprinted by permission of the publisher.

ated. The person who deserves credit for it is undoubtedly Henderson, though it was not the kind of credit he ever claimed or wanted to claim. Had he been merely ambitious, 1914 was his opportunity. Quite easily he could have entrenched himself in the leadership; quite easily, in 1915, he could have driven MacDonald out into the wilderness of fractional opposition. He did nothing of the kind. He did the precise opposite. And it took some doing.

He was able to do it because he was the one person strong on the industrial as well as on the political side. He was chairman of the Joint Board, which he had been mainly instrumental in bringing into existence in 1906, to co-ordinate the Trade Union Congress, the Labour Party Executive, and the General Federation of Trade Unions—a body which, at that date, had still got to be considered; and Trade Unionists looked upon him as one of themselves. This was the more important since, in the Trade Union ranks, there was, at this stage, hardly any division, despite the powerful influence over the miners of Robert Smillie; their response to the national call was overwhelmingly clear and positive. All outstanding strikes were at once settled, by agreement. Within three weeks of the Declaration of War, the Trade Union Congress executive had solemnly proclaimed a truce over the entire industrial field. No conditions were laid down. On the workers' side the mood, at the moment, was wholly one of willing sacrifice. Had it been met, on the other side, with anything like the same singleness of aim, the course of events on the "home front" might have been very different; a vast amount of friction and distress could have been prevented. The Joint Board, soon after its first meeting, instructed Henderson to accept, on behalf of Labour, the call to become a joint president, with Asquith and Bonar Law, of the national Recruiting Campaign Committee. Night after night he spent on familiar platforms, in most unfamiliar company, in the appeal to join up. At this stage, the response was eager and enthusiastic; the flame of patriotism burned high and white.

Round this recruiting issue, the earliest conflict within the Party centred. The I.L.P. was against participation. Although MacDonald's line was by no means always entirely clear on this, that of Keir Hardie, Robert Smillie and Philip Snowden was both clear and, to the majority, intensely provocative. The I.L.P. position developed, as time went on, into an "End the War" campaign, which outraged their colleagues. Henderson had no sympathy with this approach. But he threw the entire weight of his influence on the side of maintaining unity, and absolutely refused either to permit his own association with MacDonald to be broken or to have a line taken by the main body of the Party, either politically or industrially, that would make his position impossible. He disagreed with MacDonald, quite passionately; but the very depth of his own patriotic feeling kept him just to one whose love of country took an alien form. He defended him, and insisted on his right to be heard at a time when voices were loud against him, and he risked his own popularity by doing so.

Absorbed in war preoccupations, he did not forget that war was no permanent state. To him, the big thing was the Party. It had a life beyond the war. To permit the old line of division between I.L.P. and Trade Unions to reappear and develop into a schism—against that he was resolved. Thanks to his action, in 1911, in making MacDonald treasurer when he resigned from the secretaryship, a seat was safe for him on the national executive. That seat he retained. Only in one year was his nomination opposed. To have critics inside rather than outside was always part of Henderson's tactics. In this case, however, his determination extended far beyond any temporary tactics. He was not even moved when he was told, often, that MacDonald and Snowden "compromised" the Party.

His technique for continued co-operation was sternly practical. As chairman of the Joint Board he sent out, at a time when hope still lived of preserving peace, a summons, from Head Office, to a National Conference to prepare measures for meeting the emergency. The gathering that assembled at 1 Victoria Street on August 5th had to address itself to war, not peace. In response to his urgent call, leaders came from national bodies as well as from miners, railwaymen, teachers, transport and textile workers, co-operators, organised women, and Socialist societies; it was, as G. D. H. Cole puts it, "in one sense the most representative Labour body there ever has been, inasmuch as no body contained representatives from so many sections of the Labour movement." It elected a committee—the War Emergency Workers' National Committee—of which Henderson was chairman and J. S. Middleton secretary; while the executive included persons as diverse in their standpoints about the war as Robert Smillie and J. A. Seddon, W. C. Anderson and William Brace, J. R. MacDonald and Sidney Webb, Mary Macarthur and H. M. Hyndman. The composition is significant; as is the fact that this all-embracing committee functioned successfully throughout the first two years of war, on an agenda on which members could in the main agree. Here, Henderson found a new and most effective ally in

Sidney Webb. They had met for the first time at the I.L.P. coming-of-
age Conference at Easter, which Henderson had attended as a fraternal
delegate from the Labour Party and Webb from the Fabians. Different
as they were in background and in training, they had, in political
approach, much in common; they agreed, now, about the war; they
also agreed about party unity and in seeing that the way to prevent
splits was to maintain close working association on concrete tasks. The
Emergency Committee was not there to argue about the war, but to
meet its effects on the lives of millions of ordinary citizens.

The first effect was severe unemployment. The Insurance Act of
1911 covered only workers in certain selected groups; for the mass of
men, as of women, there was no legal provision. The Committee at
once set itself to devise means of assistance, work and relief. Later they
concerned themselves, and that most effectively, with allowances, hous-
ing, prices: indeed, all the multifarious social problems arising out of
the war. They did not trench on Trade Union preserves—the chairman
saw to that; but they made proposals on other matters that anticipated
most of the steps taken much later by Government under pressure of
hardship and bitter discontent. The Committee met, twice, and sometimes three times a week; the work was efficient and business-like, and
served, *inter alia,* as a vital reminder to its members of common concern and common responsibility.

Many of these members were soon to be drawn into the vast machinery of war. From mines and railways, factories and fields, skilled men
and unskilled alike rushed to the colours. Successful recruiting brought
fresh problems in its train. The New Armies had not only got to be
created and trained; they had got to be equipped for modern warfare.
Britain, workshop still of the world, was expected to supply not only
herself but her allies with armament of all kinds, as well as with men.
As the curve of recruitment went up, so did that of the demand for
material. Still the cry was for more food for the guns—human food,
and the material food that only human hands could make. Men had
poured into the armies from the engineering trades; somehow, their
vacant places had got to be filled; somehow, workers had got to be
found, not only to fill vacant places but to cope with a vast and continuous expansion of production. Stage by stage, a progressive mecha-
nisation of production was put through. The problem of manning the
new machines remained; it was complicated by the fact that many
employers saw here a chance to cut rates and make enhanced profits.

They put unskilled men on to jobs that had been rated and paid as skilled; above all, they called in women to take the places of men on the machines, at women's rates.

From February 1915, when unemployment ceased to be a problem and "labour supply" took its place, the story of the war at home is a story of the progressive introduction of women into factories and work-shops, as into transport and distributive services, on to the land, and into banks and government offices. Henderson was absorbed in the varying phases of a slow struggle which centred, in the first instances, on the engineering trades. It was a struggle partly to protect the new workers themselves from excessive hours, starvation wages, and shock-ing conditions of work; and, partly, to maintain intact the standard rates which had been won by half a century of Trade Union effort. On the side of the women his great ally was Mary Macarthur, who fought for them like a lion. It was never a fight in which women and women's interests were alone concerned; throughout, she and Henderson and the others who fought with them, were set not only to win decent standards for the women, here and now, but to prevent the entry of "dilutees," whether male or female, into industries in which they were newcomers, from being used to break down the whole fabric of protection for the worker. There was a danger, and a very real one, that established prac-tices and working conditions, on which a tolerable standard of life depended, would be lastingly broken down. For instance, *The Engineer,* in a leading article of October, 1915, put a point of view only too widespread:

> The fact of the matter is, really, not that women are paid too little, but that men are paid too much for work that can be done without previous training. High wages are paid on the false assumption, now almost obscured by Trade Union regulations, that it takes long to learn the craft. Everyone knows now, as all managers knew long ago, that no long period of training is necessary, and the whole argument of high wages based on long training has been carried by the board.

The high wages of which this article speaks varied, for a skilled fitter, from 30s. in Lincoln to 41s.—the top rate—in Belfast. The workers were not prepared to have these rates "carried by the board." They were prepared to make all sorts of sacrifices now; but not to have them carried over into perpetuity, least of all at a time when there was no talk of any limitation of profits, and enormous profits were being made.

From November 1914 on, the Engineering Unions were in conflict with the employers about dilution. Of these Unions, by far the largest was the Amalgamated Society of Engineers (with 174,000 members in 1914); next came the Boilermakers, with 67,000, and Henderson's own Ironfounders, with 25,000. The Unions held repeated conferences with the Employers' Federation, but failed to achieve any satisfactory safeguards; the employers refused to give any binding undertaking, and the engineers refused to consent to dilution without it. Meantime, the recruiting drive went on, and the Press was full of stories of shortage of munitions. In February, 1915, the Government set up a Committee on Production; its report on Shells and Fuses, while recommending a wide extension of female employment, laid stress on "suitable and proper conditions." But how were such conditions going to be enforced? Employers were interested only in output and profit; they saw a chance to tap a vast field of cheap and unorganised labour. At best, they felt that workers ought, in war-time, to be slaves, and glad to be slaves. Public opinion was hardly aware of the issue. Anyone out of uniform was simply a slacker: there was an immense ignorant hostility to Trade Unions.

The women themselves were, for the most part, simply patriotic; they wanted to be on war work; they also wanted the money they could earn. Outside the ranks of Labour, nobody thought much about their point of view, anyhow.

There were protracted negotiations but no result. Then, in March, under the Consolidated Defence of the Realm Act, the Government took power to assume control over factories; this meant that they could, if they chose, enforce proper conditions. On the assumption that they would do so, representatives of the Trade Union Congress, of the General Federation, and of some thirty-three Unions representing engineering and all the other great industries from transport to textiles, met, on the invitation of Mr. Lloyd George, then Chancellor, at the Treasury. Henderson acted as chairman of the workers' side. He was also made chairman of a committee of seven set up to go into the proposals of the Government and their pledges as to safeguards. An agreement was finally signed laying down terms on which Trade Union practices might be waived for the duration; this, the famous Treasury Agreement, was signed by Arthur Henderson and W. Mosses of the Patternmakers, on behalf of the Unions; by Lloyd George and Walter Runciman on behalf of the Government. In return for certain additional guarantees, the Engineers further came into the Agreement, of which the essence was a procedure under which, in cases of proved necessity, there could be abrogation of existing safeguards. It is a landmark in the history of the war on the home front.

The seven members of the drafting sub-committee were constituted a Standing National Labour Advisory Committee, with Henderson as chairman. Had the Committee been able to get the Government to enforce the terms of the Agreement on employers, or even to set up the machinery providing for Trade Union co-operation locally under a decentralised system of control, all might have been well. This course was pressed, repeatedly, by Henderson. But Mr. Lloyd George, at this stage, was convinced that the only remedy for the munitions shortage was to be himself in charge of supply. He suddenly launched a series of most unjust attacks on the workers, accusing them first of bad time-keeping and then of intemperance. "Drink," he declared, "is a more dangerous enemy than Germany." Under this charge Henderson was not going to allow his fellows to lie; the Advisory Committee went carefully into the allegations, and produced a completely smashing reply. By then, however, the Wizard had moved onto something else. About the middle of May 1915, Colonel Repington, at that time *Times* war correspondent, found him talking of resigning, because of the shortage of shells; and notes: "I was astonished at his ignorance of the facts. He had been on the Cabinet Munitions Committee appointed in October 1914, and was on another special committee assembled in April 1915 to deal with war material. Yet he seemed to know nothing of what was happening." He thereupon proceeded to "post" him; and also the Unionist leaders. The immediate result was the reconstruction of the Asquith Cabinet as the first Coalition ministry.

Henderson had, in January 1915, been made a member of the Privy Council. This gave him distinct pleasure; he was later (Edinburgh, 1922) to describe it as "an honour, and may I say I hope it is the only honour that any Labour man will ever accept. In my opinion, it is the only honour that is pure in the whole of the honours given in this country." Now, in May 1915, Mr. Asquith invited him to become a member of his all-party Cabinet, junior posts being at the same time offered to G. H. Roberts and William Brace. Here was a very serious and difficult decision. He at once submitted the question to the National

Executive of the Labour Party, and, at a separate meeting, to the Labour members of Parliament, whose leader he was. To himself, it was clear that, having undertaken to co-operate in a national emergency of an entirely exceptional character, there could be no drawing back, now, from the fuller responsibility which participation in government involved. It was a duty; not a very agreeable duty; but a duty, like another. At the meetings, there were long discussions. Independence of other parties was the very basis of Labour's existence. This point was strongly taken by J. R. Clynes, who further urged that Labour representatives, in a Coalition where they were going to be hopelessly outnumbered, would have responsibility without power. Against this, however, was the argument of the maintenance of national unity. Finally, by majority, it was agreed that the invitation should be accepted. The Trade Union Congress endorsed this decision when it met, for the first time since the outbreak, in September 1915; so did the Labour Party annual Conference in January, 1916. Henderson became a member of the Cabinet, as President of the Board of Education—a post he was, from the start, unwilling to take; William Brace was undersecretary to the Home Office, and G. H. Roberts a junior Lord of the Treasury . . .

December 1916, produced a first-rate political crisis, skilfully engineered by Lloyd George. On the 6th, after a series of manoeuvres to which Henderson was not privy, there took place the famous meeting of party leaders at Buckingham Palace, to which he was called: the others present being Asquith, Lloyd George, Bonar Law and Balfour. According to Lord Crewe's account, he stressed his view that Asquith should stay on; at the meeting of Liberal Ministers on the evening of the same day, he again urged the adhesion of Asquith, even though the head of the Government were Lloyd George or Bonar Law, "in order that a truly national administration might be formed." His admiration of Asquith never failed; he had, indeed, not long before this, described him as "the indispensable man," and therefore was severely criticised, in some quarters, for finally consenting to remain in a Cabinet out of which Lloyd George had jockeyed him. The Party executive, however, fully confirmed his sense that he ought to accept the membership of the small new War Cabinet of five now offered him; J. R. Clynes, who had opposed entry into the first Coalition, was now in favour. The participation now offered was certainly more substantial: Henderson was to be a member, with L.G., Curzon, Milner and Bonar Law, of the inner Cabinet: John Hodge became Minister of Labour and George Barnes, Minister of Pensions, while junior offices were filled by W. Brace, G. H. Roberts and J. Parker. J. H. Thomas was invited to come in, but refused.

At the Party Conference, held in Manchester in January, 1917, Henderson refused to be dragged into any discussion of L.G. and his tactics: "I am not concerned with the methods by which the old government was terminated," he declared roundly. "What I am concerned with, and what I hope delegates are concerned with, whether they belong to the majority or the minority of the Conference, is the most expeditious way we can adopt to bring the war to a final success."

He reminded them that, in France, there was a majority and a minority. He had attended the French Socialist Congress on Christmas Day: one of the issues taken there was the adhesion of Albert Thomas to the recently reconstructed French Ministry. It was hotly discussed, and the decision was that "in a great war of national defence, in a war for what they deem to be just and right, it was essential that M. Thomas should remain a member of the Government."

> I am quite well aware that the minority feels as strongly with regard to their position as the majority does, and I have never asked them at any time to move from their position, but I do ask that, in view of the terrible sacrifices, in view of the magnitude of the danger, you should try to go through the Conference in a spirit of confidence in the majority of the executive and of the Parliamentary Party, more particularly with regard to the effort to carry the war to a successful issue.

On the direct issue of participation in government, Snowden made an exceedingly powerful and notably bitter speech in opposition: he was supported by Fred Bramley, then rising into prominence as a Trade Union leader. The speaking honours were, on the whole, on this side. On the other, the most effective speech was that of Clynes. He stamped on the allegations freely made that the Government was about to introduce coloured labour, and Henderson had not been able to prevent it. The truth about that incident showed how much a man like Henderson could do, and did do. The Government had sought to introduce coloured labour: Henderson intervened, and, on his initiative, there was a conference between Ministers and representatives of building and general Labour Unions, Clynes being among them. They told the Government they would not have it; thereupon, on the assurance that the workmen would be forthcoming, the project was dropped.

> I know there are people who think that men like Mr. Henderson, in comparison with their own greater capabilities, can be shaped and moulded in any way. The same thing is said about a man like Mr. Hodge. Of all the men in our movement, these are two of the most stubborn kind, and, once they take their stand on any question, they are immovable. . . . The men who have been placed in positions are the best the Labour Movement has been able to produce, and the best form of unity is to show full confidence in them.

When it came to the vote, 307,000 voted against entry, 1,849,000 for. But the mood of the Conference was restless, irritable, suspicious and hostile to Henderson: it fully justified what he had written six months earlier to Mr. Asquith. These feelings came to a head in the debate on events on the Clyde. David Kirkwood, in a passionate speech, gave a highly coloured account of the deportation thence of men like himself, against whom no charge had been made and to whom no trial was offered, and, in his accusation of Lloyd George involved Arthur Henderson, "who by joining the Cabinet has lost our confidence."

The baulked feelings of delegates found relief in cheering Kirkwood to the echo. There was small patience for a suggestion that the Shop Stewards' movement was being run in defiance of the Unions, although Kirkwood admittedly, on the occasion of Lloyd George's visit to Glasgow, had repudiated both J. T. Brownlie, the secretary of the Amalgamated Society of Engineers, and Arthur Henderson. Feeling ran so high that the chairman had difficulty in getting a hearing for Henderson when he rose to explain that he had nothing whatever to do with the deportations, and suggested that there should be an enquiry.

> The deportation was an administrative act, for which I had no responsibility and on which I was not consulted. I want to make that perfectly clear. I am no more responsible for some things done by the Government than are some delegates responsible for what other delegates say in this conference. The position is this—if a decision is taken without my being consulted, my responsibility only begins after the decision has been taken, and when it becomes an actual part of Government policy I have the choice of sending in my resignation or remain-

ing in, and doing everything possible to modify the operation of
that policy. Before I can act on the former line, in regard to this
case, I must have a very full investigation, and know exactly not
only the position of the Government, but the position of the
Trade Unions concerned. Ever since the deportation, I have
been in close association with the executive of the A.S.E., and
they have done their level best to modify the policy. It is due to
the influence exerted that some of the men are now back at
work, and in their homes. I think the executive of the A.S.E.
will be prepared to admit that I have left no stone unturned.

He felt the Trade Union point keenly. The Conference, however,
refused for the moment to be interested in it; what they saw was a
harsh and tyrannical attack on civil liberties, which gave them a chance
to go for Lloyd George. Lloyd George was not present: Henderson,
tarred with the L.G. brush, was. He wanted the investigation "because
not only I and other members of the Government are involved, but the
whole of the management of the A.S.E. and the whole of the methods
of the Trade Union movement are involved." Smillie leapt to his feet,
and in violent speech, asked, "What was going to be the use of an
investigation whose results would not be presented for a twelve-
month?" Henderson replied:

> I do not wish to wait for twelve months. If anybody wants to
> condemn me, don't let him wait three months; if there can be
> proper investigation, I would rather have it over, than wait
> another year. I am entitled to a trial. [Cries of 'So was Kirk-
> wood!'] I have told you already in language as plain as possible
> that I was not a party to that until it had taken place. I have
> been asked why I did not resign. I should be resigning every
> day to please some of you. I am not sure that I should not
> resign, if I were to please myself, but I am not here either to
> please myself or you: I am here to see the war through.

It always came back to that. He was angry and hurt. Trade Unionists
were full of suspicion of him, although they seemed quite powerless to
handle the Shop Stewards' movement, and had not even the courage to
face up to what it meant. They voted to keep him in the Cabinet, in
order that he might be there to be shot at. Certainly the Conference
was "not in a frame of mind to do justice to men like himself." He was
hurt: impossible to help being hurt. He had foreseen this unpopularity
and knew it was bound to increase; but it was one thing to foresee and

another to enjoy it; and he did not enjoy it. But he had to stand it: to shrug his heavy shoulders and see their point of view, if they could not see his.

Annual Conference of the Labour Party, January 1916

REPORT OF THE EXECUTIVE COMMITTEE 1914–1915

THE WAR

It was when the attention of the whole Movement had been rivetted on military and industrial affairs in Ireland towards the end of July, 1914, that smoulderings of diplomatic disturbances in Central Europe suddenly threatened to burst into the blaze that has since enveloped the whole continent. By an ironic circumstance arrangements were being completed for the attendance of British delegates at the International Socialist Congress which was to be held in Vienna in the following month. Suddenly the whole aspect of affairs was changed, and the diplomatic and political consequences of Austria's ultimatum to Servia became startlingly apparent to the British people. Realising the baleful effects that were likely to follow, the International Socialist Bureau held a special session in Brussels, when delegates representing all the European countries met and discussed the dangers that were imminent. It was agreed that all sections should use every possible opportunity to preserve peace among the nations, and on July 29th an impressive demonstration took place, in which Jaurès for France, Vandervelde for Belgium, Haase for Germany, Rubanovitch for Russia, Morgari for Italy, and Keir Hardie for this country, united in voicing the desire for peace. Three days later, on Sunday, August 2nd, the British Section of the International followed this lead and held a striking demonstration in Trafalgar Square, when the call for peace was emphasised with the utmost intensity and the demand for British neutrality in the event of a continental outbreak was strongly urged. On that very evening, however, Germany made common cause with Austria and declared war against Russia and France. On the following day, August 3rd, Sir Edward Grey made his historic speech in the House of Commons, and Mr. Ramsay MacDonald spoke on behalf of the Parliamentary Party. Within a few hours Germany had also declared war on Belgium, and

From the *Report of the 15th Annual Conference of the Labour Party, 1916* (London, no date).

on this breach of Belgian neutrality war was declared by the United Kingdom upon Germany on August 4th.

The Executive Committee of the Party met in London on August 5th, considered the whole circumstances of the situation, and passed the following resolutions, which were subsequently endorsed at a joint meeting with the Parliamentary Party:—

> That the conflict between the nations in Europe in which this country is involved is owing to Foreign Ministers pursuing diplomatic politics for the purpose of maintaining a balance of power; that our own national policy of understandings with France and Russia only was bound to increase the power of Russia both in Europe and Asia, and to endanger good relations with Germany.
>
> That Sir Edward Grey, as proved by the facts which he gave to the House of Commons, committed without the knowledge of our people the honour of the country to supporting France in the event of any war in which she was seriously involved, and gave definite assurances of support before the House of Commons had any chance of considering the matter.
>
> That the Labour Movement reiterates the fact that it has opposed the policy which has produced the war, and that its duty now is to secure peace at the earliest possible moment on such conditions as will provide the best opportunities for the re-establishment of amicable feelings between the workers of Europe.

At the instance of the Secretary a Conference, representative of all sections of the Labour and Socialist Movement, was also held in the House of Commons, on August 5th, when the organisation subsequently known as the War Emergency: Workers' National Committee was formed, and a series of recommendations concerning the industrial and social consequences of the war crisis were unanimous adopted. At a further meeting of the Executive Committee, held next day, the following resolution was unanimously adopted:—

> That without in any way receding from the position that the Labour Movement has taken in opposition to our engaging in a European War, the Executive of the Party advises that, whilst watching for the earliest opportunity for taking effective action in the interests of peace and the re-establishment of good feeling between the workers of the European nations, all Labour and Socialist organisations should concentrate their energies mean-

time upon the task of carrying out the resolutions passed at the Conference of Labour organisations held at the House of Commons on August 5th, detailing measures to be taken to mitigate the destitution which will inevitably overtake our working people whilst the state of war lasts.

THE ELECTORAL TRUCE AND THE RECRUITING CAMPAIGN

The Executive Committee did not meet again until August 29th, when it was decided to engage in the electoral truce by which the Liberal, Unionist, and Labour Parties agreed not to contest any vacancies that might arise during the continuance of the war, but that each seat thus fallen vacant should be retained by the Party to which the late Member belonged. The truce has been renewed from time to time.

It was at this meeting that the Party Executive were asked to consider the following letter which had been sent by the Prime Minister to Mr. Arthur Henderson, M.P., who had been appointed Acting Chairman of the Parliamentary Party upon the resignation of Mr. Ramsay MacDonald, M.P.:—

> 10, Downing Street
> Whitehall, S.W.
> August 28th, 1914
>
> Dear Mr. Henderson,
>   I have asked Illingworth to invite Talbot to co-operate with me in using the Party organisations for the purpose of enlisting recruits—which is the urgent necessity of the moment. He has accepted the invitation.
>   I extend the same invitation to yourself. I should be very glad if the Labour Party would join their forces to the other two parties to secure our common purpose. Your help would not only be of the greatest service, but it would also afford a striking object lesson of the solidarity of our people at this moment of trial.
>
> [Signed] H. H. Asquith

It was reported that on the previous day the Parliamentary Party had approved of the Party Whips co-operating in the proposal, and by a majority the Executive Committee endorsed that decision, agreed to place the Head Office organisation at the disposal of the campaign, and recommended local affiliated bodies to render it all possible local support.

The Recruiting Campaign was undertaken by a joint Parliamentary

Committee to which representatives and officials of the various political parties were appointed. Our own Party was represented by Mr. Arthur Henderson, M.P., Mr. F. W. Goldstone, M.P., and Mr. J. Parker, M.P.; and the National Agent, Mr. Arthur Peters, shared with other party organisers the heavy work entailed in the organisation of the recruiting meetings, publicity campaigns, &c., and his report upon the work appears on later pages.

A joint meeting of the Parliamentary Party and the Executive Committee was held on April 26th when the recruiting policy was reviewed, and after prolonged discussion the following resolution was adopted:—

> That this joint meeting of the Parliamentary Labour Party and the Labour Party Executive expresses its appreciation of the manner in which Members have carried out the resolutions adopted in August last and have assisted in recruiting for the fighting forces and various other ways to further the national cause; and that this meeting desires that those endeavours be continued until Great Britain and its Allies have obtained victory and have concluded the terms of an honourable and abiding peace.

. . .

EUROPEAN WAR

When the trouble between Austria and Servia came to a head and it became known that other nations were likely to be involved and that the peace of Europe was hanging in the balance, the Party met on the 30th of July, and after considering the statements that had been made in the House of Commons, it passed the following resolution which was forwarded to the Prime Minister:—

> That the Labour Party is gratified that Sir Edward Grey has taken steps to secure mediation in the dispute between Austria and Servia, and regrets that his proposal has not been accepted by the Powers concerned; it hopes, however, that on no account will this country be dragged into the European conflict in which, as the Prime Minister has stated, we have no direct interest, and the Party calls upon all Labour organisations in the country to watch events vigilantly so as to oppose if need be in the most effective way any action which may involve us in war.

On the 3rd of August Sir Edward Grey made a long statement of the position and the Chairman, Mr. Ramsay MacDonald, acting on the instructions of a Party meeting, spoke and strongly urged that everything should be done to prevent this country being embroiled. Following quickly on this, however, for the reasons stated by the Foreign Minister which are well known, war against Germany was declared, and the opinion of the majority of the Party, after several meetings to consider the situation, crystallised into a conviction that under the circumstances it was impossible for this country to have remained neutral. In a few days the Prime Minister brought forward a Motion for a War Credit of one hundred million pounds. The Party held a special meeting and, after full consideration, it was decided that no statement be made on this Motion, and as a consequence the Chairman felt compelled to resign his office. For the remainder of the Session Mr. Arthur Henderson, the Chief Whip, was requested to look after the work of the Party.

With the progress of hostilities the Government announced the necessity for a considerable addition to the Army forces, and the Prime Minister wrote to the Party asking it to co-operate with the other two parties in promoting a recruiting campaign. The Party, understanding that speakers in the campaign would not necessarily be responsible for any contrary opinions regarding the original causes of the war, or the chain of circumstances which led up to it, but that all that had to be done was to appeal to the young men of the nation to come to the defence of their country, agreed to authorise the Whips to join the Recruiting Committee, and since then various Members have attended non-Party meetings and assisted in appealing for recruits. It only remains to be said that at these recruiting meetings the Members of the Party, without trenching on party politics in any way, took the opportunity to create and strengthen a public opinion in favour of decent and fair treatment being meted out to those who went on active service and to their dependants. It is safe to say that had not Labour Members been in evidence at these meetings this important point would not have been brought so prominently before the public. Before the close of the Session the Prime Minister announced that an increase would be made in the amount of separation allowance. That increase, if not so much as was desired, was at any rate fairly substantial. With regard to pensions for those disabled and for the dependants of those killed, the Party continued to bring pressure to bear on the Government. After the close of the Session, the Government not having made any announcement on this matter, a Memorial, signed by all the Members and emphasising the need for an adequate scale being established, was sent to the Prime Minister.

. . .

PARLIAMENTARY REPORT, 1915

MINISTRY OF MUNITIONS

MUNITIONS OF WAR ACT

During the Session a Ministry of Munitions, with the Rt. Hon. D. Lloyd George as Minister, was set up to organise and accelerate the supply of munitions for our Army. Several National Trade Union Conferences were held with the Minister of Munitions to consider the setting aside of trade union practices calculated to restrict output, and the establishment of methods to organise and increase the output, and ultimately the Munitions of War Bill was introduced and passed. The Bill was of a very drastic character as affecting the rights and liberties of workmen, and it was only the extraordinary conditions in which the country found itself that induced a Conference of representative Trade Unionists affected to agree to the main outline of the Bill and the Party to agree to its passage through the House. Under the Act, on the one hand, the power to strike or lock-out is suspended, and as regards every Controlled Establishment, any rule, practice or custom which tends to restrict production or employment is suspended, and it is an offence for any person to induce or attempt to induce any other person to comply with any such rule, practice or custom.

On the other hand, the Act protects the position of the workman, as follows:—

(1) The statutory suspension of restrictions is required only in Controlled Establishments, that is to say, establishments in which the employer's profits are strictly limited.

(2) The suspension is for the period of the War only, and every change of working conditions made as a result of the suspension of restrictions must be officially recorded.

(3) In any readjustment of staff after the War, priority of employment must be given to workmen in the owner's service at the beginning of the War who have been serving with the Colours or who were in the owner's employment when the establishment became controlled; that is to say, these men must have preference over the semi-skilled and unskilled labour introduced during the War.

(4) Due notice must be given of any proposed change of working conditions following on the suspension of restrictions, and an opportunity of local consultation if desired.

The Act is therefore equally clear on both sides. All restrictions are abolished and at the same time ample safeguards are provided. When the Act came into operation grievances began to arise, principally in connection with the decisions of Munitions Tribunals. During the passage of the Bill the idea of these Tribunals was that they would be of the nature of domestic courts where the merits of a case against a workman or an employer would be tried on its merits apart altogether from legal formula and legal prejudices. Unfortunately in a number of cases the Chairmen of these Tribunals were of the legal profession, very often conflicting decisions were given, and it sometimes happened that the employers' and workmen's assessors were not properly consulted or their opinions taken into consideration before the decision was given. The administration of these Tribunals and other points, such as the discharging of a workman without giving him his leaving certificate, thus preventing him from obtaining other employment, gave rise to a good deal of irritation amongst munition workers, and later on an Amending Bill was introduced. Before it was introduced, however, another National Conference was held to consider in what particulars the Act ought to be amended, and representations were afterwards made to the Minister of Munitions with the result that many suggestions were adopted and put into the Bill. On one or two outstanding points the Party brought forward amendments, such as the abolition of imprisonment, in the House and succeeded in still further improving the Bill which ultimately passed into law.

One thing more may be stated. At no other time in the history of Trade Unionism in this country have the Trade Unions been taken so much into the confidence of the Government and of those responsible for the carrying on of affairs. This is no doubt due to some extent to the extraordinary conditions prevailing, but it is also partly due to the presence of Trade Union representatives in the Government; and while the Unions by the Munitions of War Acts have relinquished for the time being many of the liberties and rights that have taken a generation to build up, on the other hand, they have come forward and occupied a place in the affairs of the country which will do much to consolidate and strengthen them in the future.

. . .

PARLIAMENT AND REGISTRATION BILL

In order to obviate the necessity for a General Election, which according to the Parliament Act would have to have taken place by the end of January, 1916, the Government introduced a Bill extending the life of Parliament for another eight months and providing for the setting up of a special register prior to the dissolution. The Bill also provided that the additional Session should count as a successive Session under the Parliament Act in order to safeguard the position of the Plural Voting Bill which had already passed two successive Sessions during the Parliament. It is understood that the first proposal of the Government was to enact that the time covered by the War should not be considered as part of the normal life of Parliament, and it is to be regretted that this proposal was abandoned because of the opposition of a section of the Conservative Party. As it is, another Bill will be necessary if the War should extend beyond another Session, unless of course a General Election is allowed to take place.

RECRUITING AND THE MILITARY SERVICE BILL

The Members of the Party have continued their activities in connection with the Recruiting Campaign. They made strenuous efforts to assist in keeping inviolate the Voluntary principle, and there is no doubt the success attending the efforts made had considerable effect upon those who desired Compulsory Service merely for the sake of Compulsion. The Lord Derby Campaign was initiated as a supreme effort to secure the number of men deemed to be necessary by the Government and the military authorities. Unfortunately, whether it was necessary or not, the Prime Minister gave a pledge that single men would have to join first, in order to induce married men to attest, and at the close of the Campaign it was estimated that over 600,000 single men had failed to respond. Consequently, in order to redeem the pledge, the Government decided upon introducing the Military Service Bill, the object of which was to compel those single men to attest under the Group System in the same manner as those who voluntarily attested during the Campaign; that is to say, compel them to attest, after which they would be relegated to their respective Groups according to ages, and before being compelled to join would have the right to appeal to a tribunal. A Special National Conference was called to consider the Bill and the decision was come to that the Bill should be opposed, the Party being recommended to take that course. The Party and the National Executive jointly considered the situation and came to the opinion that if the Party was to oppose the Bill it could not maintain its connection with the Coalition Government. The Party's three representatives in the Government therefore tendered their resignations. The Prime Minister, however, acting on behalf of the Cabinet, invited the Party and the Executive to meet him to discuss the situation. The invitation was accepted and at the interview the Prime Minister gave his solemn assurance that the Bill was a military necessity; that there was no intention whatever under the Bill of introducing industrial compulsion in any form; that, if necessary, safeguards would be put in the Bill to prevent this; and that the Bill was not the prelude to any larger scheme of compulsion. These and other points raised at the National Conference were discussed, and the Party and the Executive afterwards met to reconsider the national situation in the light of the Prime Minister's statement. Opinion on the merits of the Bill was strongly divided, and as the National Conference of the Party was to be held in a very short time, it was decided that the matter be remitted for its decision, the resignations of the three representatives being withdrawn in the meantime.

At the time of preparing this Report the Bill was still before the House of Commons and therefore nothing can be said as to its final form, but the Party decided to do its utmost to secure any amendments considered necessary to meet points of objection that had been raised.

DEFENCE OF THE REALM ACTS

In the early stages of the War Defence of the Realm Acts were passed giving the Government wide powers against any acts calculated to endanger the safety of the country. The legislation, being at the time urgent, was passed through the House of Commons with great haste and insufficient consideration. Part of the phraseology was wide and vague. In large measure the Acts were a kind of skeleton, and the real power has been taken under Orders in Council, Regulations, and legal interpretations. Whilst admitting to the full the need for rigid powers being taken to maintain the safety of the Realm in time of war, we think the administration of the Act has gone beyond what was intended by the House of Commons and in some directions has infringed the constitutional rights and liberties of British subjects. We refer more particularly to the denial of open trial even when there was no question of military secrets being involved, to the suppression of newspapers without trial, to arrests without warrant and imprisonment without trial. It will be the duty of the Party to guard against abuses of the wide powers vested in the Executive Government, and to protect the liberties of the subject to the fullest extent consistent with the safety of the State.

GENERAL

The Government having at the beginning of the Session asked for all time to be appropriated to its business, the Party has had no opportunity of introducing any Bills or securing by ballot time for the discussions of any Motions, and therefore it has had very little power of initiative. It has, however, to the best of its ability taken every opportunity that presented itself of raising matters affecting Labour and Labour's interests, moving amendments to Bills, and securing representation on any Committees appointed to enquire into particular subjects. It has, of course, given general support to the Government in the conduct of the War and has voted for all the Votes of Credit, believing that the main object to-day is the prosecution of the War to a speedy and successful conclusion.

> John Hodge, Acting Chairman
> Charles Duncan, Secretary

. . .

REPORT OF THE EXECUTIVE
THE WAR

The Conference then proceeded to consider the Report of the Executive, and on the paragraph headed "The War," in accordance with the recommendation of the Conference Arrangements Committee,

Mr. James Sexton (Dock Labourers) moved the following resolution standing on the Agenda:—

> That this Conference, whilst expressing its opposition (in accordance with previously expressed opinions) to all systems of permanent militarism as a danger to human progress, considers the present action of Great Britain and its Government fully justified in the present war; expresses its horror at the atrocities committed by Germany and her ally by the callous and brutal murder of non-combatants, including women and children, and hereby pledges the Conference to assist the Government as far as possible in the successful prosecution of the War.

He said the delegates would see that the resolution he was moving was practically word for word in substance and in fact the resolution passed by the Trades Union Congress held in September. The time since then was short, but a considerable amount of political water had run under the bridges in the meantime. In September the Congress was confined to Trade Unions, but at this Conference there were present the I.L.P., the local L.R.C.'s, the Trade Councils, and the Women's Labour League. He entirely subscribed to the statement of the Chairman that any permanent system of militarism could not exist alongside true democracy. Some of his best and truest friends socially and politically disagreed with him on the question of Conscription. But he was always a stickler for executive control—they all were in their Trade Unions because they believed in constitutional action, and he was in favour of following the lead of the constituted authority wherever they thought it necessary to go. If there were any present against the War he would like to know how they were and why they were against it. He was for this War and for all the risks associated with it, for the alternative was worse than any risk. He was going to prefer anything to a German victory. If Germany won, nothing else in God's world would matter! That was where he was, and nobody who understood the question would refuse to recognise that the Government had done wonderful service to the Country; they had made blunders perhaps, but did they ever know an executive that didn't? Eighteen months ago we were not in any sense a military nation fitted for a land war, but this Government of ours had equipped and transported three millions of men, with guns, horses, and munitions, to the lines of communication. When all this business was over, we should have something to face. How were we going to face it? When the boys came home again they would have the same old employer to fight as they had to fight before, but after what they had done in defence of the Country their claim would be so irresistible that no one could refuse their fair share in the products of the country.

The Chairman, before calling on a seconder, said he wanted the rule to obtain all through the Conference that everybody, whatever he had to say, and who kept himself within the range of the decencies of fair debate, should have a fair hearing without interruption of any sort. There were many things about the House of Commons he did not like, but one thing he did like, and that was the long tradition which enabled Members to listen with patience to things they were bitterly opposed to.

Mr. George Milligan (Dock Labourers) seconded the resolution.

They would know by the resolution where they stood. Those whom he represented stood for the War, and he was sure that the people of this country as a whole were also for the War. The Union that he belonged to had about 5,000 members fighting in the Services, and he would be sure they were for this War. He could not account for it, but there was evidently a division of opinion in the Conference on this point. Would any Trade Union secretary dare to go back to his men in the mines, in the warehouse, or at the docks, and say he was against the War and had voted against the War? That summed up his case.

Mr. J. Ramsay MacDonald, M.P. (I.L.P.), said he rose to follow in the spirit of his friend Sexton's remarks. He was sorry that the seconder did not understand how anyone could disagree. He confessed straightway that he did understand why people disagreed with the view he himself had taken, and he had risen not for the purpose of raising a question which must be very controversial, but rather to ask the delegates to consider reasonably where they stood, to exercise that amount of toleration which was such a beneficent characteristic of the Chairman's Address, and to endeavour in every way possible to prevent the difficulties they were all faced with becoming reasons for permanent dispute in their midst. His friends of the Independent Labour Party, one of whose delegates he was, had asked him to speak, and he rose with some reluctance. They were in a difficulty in discussing the origins of the War. They were either too late or too soon—as a matter of fact, they were both too late and too soon. They were too late to discuss origins to have any effect upon the War itself; they were too soon to pronounce that final judgment which could only be pronounced after the lapse of a considerable amount of time. Any decision which they registered that day—it did not matter on which side—was bound to be a decision which would be looked back upon in time to come by eyes more critical than theirs, and by men more charged with the facts of the situation than they could be now. Therefore, they should not divide over the question of war origins. They should not divide over another question. Mr. Sexton had said that he did not want the Germans to win. Who did? Was there any man present who was so unutterably unfair as to believe that any of them wanted the Germans to win? Not at all. Take the question of pro-Germans. Were they really pro-Germans? From one point of view they were the most bitterly anti-German of any section of the nation. One of the reasons why they had taken up the attitude they had taken up was that they hated, they detested from the bottom of their hearts, every characteristic of that Prussianism which had been stamping with such a diabolical heel upon the people of Europe during the War, and which had shown in the course of past years that it was prepared for it. That, in his opinion, was not the expression of original sin planted in the breasts of Germans by the Creator, but was the result of a vicious system of thought which did not finish itself in a day but had got in by secret and silent processes during years and years until at last it had poisoned the whole life of the German people; and he wanted to stop the very beginnings of that. He and his friends might be right or they might be wrong. They had passed resolutions expressing the opinion that the war was the result of Foreign Ministers pursuing diplomatic policies for the purpose of maintaining the balance of power, and so on, as they would see by the Report of the Executive Committee. That was their position today. The differences between them were infinitesimal when they came to realities and facts. He thought Mr. Sexton in his enthusiasm to keep his country safe was taking a somewhat narrow view of how he was going to keep his country safe. The problem was not how to save the country. That was common to every man and woman in that hall. The difference between some of them was that under pressure of events and the present crisis some of their views were narrowed a little bit too much. If they could widen their conception of national service and set the military problem as part and parcel of great political problems dealing with Great Britain, the Continent, and the whole international movement of the future, they would see better what the position of his friends and himself was. The Executive had passed resolutions declaring their position, and the Parliamentary Party had done the same. He thought in those early decisions there was a breadth of vision. There was no statement in the resolutions which said they were not going to help the country. It simply said they recognised the problem as a very wide one, and in doing their immediate duty in defending the country, they were also going to keep their eyes on why they had got into the position. Was the resolution now before the Conference a vote of confidence in the Liberal Government of 1914? Did the endorsing of present action include the Compulsory Service Bill and the Dardanelles? If they were going to pass a resolution to go out to the whole world as a declaration of the Labour Party on the War, that resolution should not be drafted in such a way that at no particular point could they place their finger on precisely what it meant, and what it tied them down to. Let the declaration be as emphatic as possible. Was the passing of that resolution worth anything? It was if it meant what Mr. Sexton said it meant.

But it did not. All he had ever wanted them to do was to protect themselves for the future. He hoped they were going to face the whole of
that question as men who had fought side by side in days gone by, men
who had built up a Party so magnificent in its strength that it could
produce a Conference like that—one of the finest he had ever faced.
Oh, how sad it was, how heart-breaking it was, that some of them had
to stand up and face the Conference with pride in their hearts as to
what it was and doubt in their hearts as to what it was to be! In the
name of everything they held sacred, in the name of everything they
had hoped for, let this be a purely passing affair, let this not be one of
those storms that disturb the most friendly of households and the most
permanent of friendships. Let them go out from the Conference with
teeth clenched and head down on their shoulders determined to go
through the dark days, but equally determined that when they were
over back they would come together in the bonds of cooperation to
fight the common enemy as enthusiastically and successfully as they
had fought him before.

The Conference at this point adjourned for lunch and resumed at
two o'clock.

Mr. David Gilmour (Miners) said that at no other Conference had
he had greater pleasure than he had in rising to support the resolution
before the Conference. He was very proud indeed to be able to say that
in doing so he had the concurrence of every delegate representing the
Miners' Federation of Great Britain. He wished to make that position
perfectly clear. While they had their differences inside their ranks, on
this resolution they were absolutely unanimous. He had followed Mr.
MacDonald's speech very closely. In Scotland they had a national dance
where they laid down two swords and danced all round them. Mr. Mac-
Donald had done that to absolute perfection; he had danced round the
point without calling attention to a single word in the resolution. He
was at a loss to know where Mr. MacDonald was. He had been at a
loss to know, from the very beginning of the War, where the I.L.P.
stood. He liked straight, clean fighting, but he did not think the I.L.P.
were fighting clean and straightforwardly. They had been told by
Mr. MacDonald that they were strong against German militarism; but
he (Mr. Gilmour) judged a man by the actions. He thought that had it
rested with the people who had not assisted the Government, and were
not now even raising a little finger to help the country, the Germans
would be here now. The resolution was that the Conference was against
permanent militarism. Was there a single delegate who did not agree

with that? The next line expressed horror at the atrocities committed by Germany. Was there a delegate present who would not express his horror at the atrocities committed by the Germans? Was there any delegate expressing horror at the sinking of the "Lusitania"? The resolution pledged the Conference to assist the Government in winning the War. If any disagreed, let them say so. The Miners' Federation wholeheartedly supported the Government in the prosecution of the War, and they hoped the Conference would unanimously carry the resolution.

Mr. G. J. Wardle, M.P. speaking for the Executive, said for 18 months the question of the war had been dividing the Labour forces in the country and the members of the Executive Committee. It was time, therefore, that a clear, straightforward pronouncement for or against the War was made on behalf of some large representative body to show whether the majority of the Executive and the majority of the Labour Party had behind them the confidence of the people in the War. They had heard the most extraordinary yet most able and conciliatory speech from Mr. MacDonald, but where did it lead them? What was its effect, and how did it help in any shape or form to settle the differences that there were. They held that this resolution, however they might cavil at some of the words, did give a clear, a distinct, and definite lead to that Conference and was a vote of confidence in the Executive for the way in which it had acted during the War. Mr. MacDonald quoted the resolution adopted at an early meeting just after the War commenced, but he did not add that that resolution was a compromise to which the majority agreed, but it was never carried out by the minority. Since then they had travelled a long way, and although they had not rescinded that resolution the effect of the activities of the Party, and the whole weight of the influence of the Parliamentary Party had all been in the direction of standing by this country in this War and prosecuting it to a successful finish. There was no way of meeting force except by force, and he asked them to ask themselves, what would have happened to this country, to Belgium, to France, to democracy, and to liberty if the whole of the great Labour Movement had adopted the same lines as the Independent Labour Party. Let him put another position to them. It was absolutely necessary that the matter should be cleared up. It was all very well for Mr. MacDonald to come there as he had done and make conciliatory speeches, but there were some of them who scarcely had a week of their lives free from attack, from innuendo, and misrepresentation and some of it of the vilest kind, attacking their honour, their principles, their right to speak on behalf of that great Movement; and they were now asking the Conference to say: Who has the right to speak on behalf of the Labour Movement? Was it the small coterie of the Independent Labour Party or the great Trade Unions of the country who, let him remind them, carried the same resolution with but two or three dissentients in that very city four months ago? That was the position, and when they come to face it they were bound to ask the Conference to adopt the resolution which had been proposed. When they were told they had outraged the hopes and traditions of the Labour Movement, and that they had been traitors to it, it was time they had the opportunity to clear the air. Those who wanted toleration should give it and he wanted to put to the Conference the simple proposition that without going into the origins of the War, which was impossible, there was something more than broad and narrow views at stake there. The instinct of their people leaped at once to what was at issue. There was an instinct which was as true as nature itself, that everything for which they lived, that all the issues for which this country stood, that all the issues for which that Movement stood were damned if the Germans succeeded. That being so, they invited the Conference to express in no unmistakable manner that it was behind those of them who had put their all into the war.

Mr. G. H. Stuart Bunning (Postmen's Federation) said that Mr. Wardle had asked that those who asked for toleration should be tolerant. Those who were opposed to this resolution had been accused of being against their country and opposed to the War. That was an unfounded charge. He was not a member of the I.L.P. but he was against the resolution, and he would put his record as a war worker against that of either Mr. Sexton or Mr. Wardle. Some of those opposed to the resolution were as earnest and sincere in their desire and in their patriotism as any of those supporting the resolution. They had been reminded that they should not be led by a little coterie. Over a million of the Labour forces of this country had voted against the Military Service Bill, and was it forgotten, that within a few days of that vote a small coterie in the House of Commons, against the wishes of the Congress, against the mandate of the people who had the right to give instructions, voted for the Bill? Mr. Gilmour had said that the Miners' Federation supported the resolution. Did the Federation realise that in passing the resolution they expressed absolute and explicit approval of the Compulsory Bill? If they did not realise that let him read some words of the resolution: "Opposed to all systems of *permanent* militarism," but why introduce the word at all? If they distinctly said that at the present moment with a temporary Act of Parliament almost on the Statute Book they were only against permanent militarism, were they not approving of temporary militarism? Somebody said, "No!"—then the English language meant nothing. The resolution was by a mere phrase accepting a Bill which most of them were against, and which had been voted against by a huge majority, even including the Miners' Federation. Why did not the Executive put down a straight resolution? The Executive thought it absolutely necessary to have a straight vote but they had not "savvie" enough to put down a resolution themselves. He hoped that on every possible ground, not only on the ground that they were opposed to the Government's Bill, but on the ground that they ought to have a straight vote—which the resolution did not give them—he hoped the Conference would not pass the resolution.

TIME LIMIT FOR SPEECHES

The Chairman said he had not strictly adhered to the time limit, but he thought it now rested with the Conference to decide whether a time limit should now be observed.

It was moved and seconded:

That fifteen minutes be allowed as a maximum for each speaker in this debate.

To this an amendment was moved and seconded:

That five minutes be allowed.

On the amendment being put it was declared carried.

Mr. A. Bellamy (National Union of Railwaymen) said that he felt it was possible for misunderstandings to arise—misunderstandings not created by the Conference but created first by the procedure adopted and second by the drafting of the resolution itself. He wishes it to be very clearly understood that so far as those for whom he had the privilege of speaking were concerned there were many things in the resolution they agreed with. He feared that the net effect of the resolution, if carried, would be that the whole of the business for the next day would be wiped out, as the Conference would have already decided on those matters. He would like to call attention to one sentence in the resolution where it said that the Conference considered the present action of Great Britain and its Government fully justified in the present War. He did not consider that all the actions of the Government were justifiable. A Special Congress by an overwhelming majority did not think so. He wished to ask those who desired a straightforward vote why they had

brought the matter forward in that way. They should not forget that if
they wanted a clear issue they had it in the Executive's Report and he
was prepared to move that that Report be accepted and adopted, but his
friends and he were not prepared to vote for a resolution which had an
ulterior motive behind it. He did not think it was the intention to have
such a motive, but he would appeal to the mover and seconder of the
resolution to withdraw it in the interests of getting a clear-cut issue on
all the matters coming before the Conference. Let them have a clear
issue as to whether they supported the Party's policy on the War; as to
whether they were going to back the leaders in continuing their association with the Coalition Government; and as to whether they were
now going to agree that even a temporary compulsory military measure
would be acceptable to them. As matters were some of them would be
compelled to vote against this resolution while at the same time there
were some things in it they wanted to vote for.

Mr. J. Stokes (London Trades Council) said he wished to associate
himself with the remark of Mr. MacDonald that when the War was
over they would have to fight the same fight and they would all be
comrades again. But he disagreed largely with Mr. MacDonald's speech.
Mr. MacDonald had had the opportunity of his life to give a clear
expression of his opinions and as to which side of the fence he was on,
but he had not done so. He (the speaker) did not agree with everything
the Government had done, but he did agree in prosecuting the War to
a successful conclusion. He thought that if the word "present" (present
action of the Government) was deleted from the resolution there would
not be a single argument left to those who were opposing the resolution.
Unfortunately the word was there; but if, on the other hand, the resolution was turned down what would be the position of the Labour
Movement so far as the great mass of the people were concerned?
What would they say? That the Conference at Bristol had an opportunity to declare where it stood but refused to do so. They would not
go into the finesse and the clever points made by Mr. MacDonald; they
would say that the Conference was against the country. That was a
point the Conference must remember if they desired unity when the
War was over. He hoped the resolution would be carried.

Mr. Alex. Wilkie, M.P. (Shipwrights) said he still respected his
colleague and friend MacDonald, but he could not understand his attitude. Mr. MacDonald had never said how they could have prevented
the War. The War had been created by the ministers and professors, as
well as the military and naval experts of Germany. That was where it

had been done by this country to prevent it. At the beginning of the War a few of the Party had thought that the country was not in danger but the majority did, and everything that had happened since had proved that the majority were right.

Mr. R. C. Wallhead (I.L.P.) said they had heard from the lips of Mr. Wardle that the Executive were in a measure backing this resolution because they desired a straight fight upon the issues raised. The I.L.P. were asked why they opposed the War. They opposed it on the same grounds as stated by the Executive themselves. Did the Executive say that there were any facts brought to their notice, that they could produce any evidence, which upset the resolution they passed at the beginning of the War, which declared that the War was the outcome of a bad foreign diplomacy into which the country had been dragged behind its back by Sir Edward Grey? That was a statement of the Executive. He accepted that statement and said they were in the War because of these facts. Now the I.L.P. were asked to justify something which the Executive admitted themselves sixteen months ago. The I.L.P. were not doing it. Mr. Wardle had told them that he had been attacked by the Independent Labour Party—by "a small coterie." Had the Independent Labour Party never been attacked? At one time there was industrial trouble breaking out in the North of England and it was said in a speech of one of the Labour Members that the hands of the I.L.P. were reeking with the blood of their brothers in the trenches because of the action they took. It was Mr. G. H. Roberts who said so. The whole idea that members of the Executive could protest against the things that were said about them, but no protest could be made about what they had said against the I.L.P. was grotesque, and it seemed to him that members of the Executive rather protested too much.

Mr. G. A. Olley (Electrical Trades Union) said he was opposed to the War and he hoped he would live to see the traitors who had brought it about wrecked in the middle of the Pacific. The War, however, would have to be fought to the bitter end and he was certain it could be won by the voluntary system. He would like to have a vote of all organised trade unionists—women as well—and then they would see where they stood.

Mr. G. H. Roberts, M.P. (Typographical Association) said he was only going to make one observation in reply to the speech of his friend Wallhead. When a charge was made against a delegate the actual quotation should be read and the source from whence it was derived given. He (the speaker) had no knowledge of the statement attributed to him, and until Mr. Wallhead produced evidence he must ask the Conference to waive judgment. The Conference had to make some pronouncement on the War. It was utterly impossible for any representative present to think that he could get into that state of detachment where he could seek to delude the Conference or the country into the belief that it was not necessary for him to declare his attitude on this, the greatest in the whole of the world's history. The delegates should also bear in mind that the men in the House of Commons were even in a different position to the delegates. The members were responsible to their constituents and their constituents demanded to know where they stood in respect of every live issue. He was never going to adopt the ostrich-like attitude. He told men and women what he believed and he was prepared to accept responsibility for his actions in this War. The country, the civilised world, would watch the decision of the Conference on this resolution. It was no time for mere quibbling about a word of which they might disapprove. The broad issue clearly stood out: Were they for or were they against their country in this great War? He had been a member of the Independent Labour Party for 22 years, as far as he knew he was still attached to that body, and he had done his best in its behalf because he had believed in it, but he had a right to say to them: Where do you stand here? No mere fine word-spinning could ever satisfy the people. Mr. MacDonald had said: Who of us want Germany to win? Mr. Wallhead had said: We are opposed to the War. If they were opposed to the War they were not anxious that their country should win. He believed his country would have been dishonoured eternally had it forsaken its friends and shirked the challenge thrown down to it. Once they had accepted war there were no other means but war to attain victory. Those who were not prepared to supply the men and the means of prosecuting the War were not serving his class by betraying their country in the time of its great stress. The Allies were watching the Conference. He had built up an intimate acquaintance in France and he knew that the decision of the Special Congress was misunderstood there. He understood it. He knew the workers of this country were behind this Government, would be behind any Government so long as it carried the War to a successful conclusion. But if the Conference turned down this resolution consternation would appear in France and in all the allied countries. The greatest enemies of human progress —the Central Powers of Europe—would be encouraged by such a vote, and he begged the delegates not to quibble about a word here or there, but to construe the broad issues of it. The underlying principle of the resolution was support of the War. Votes against it, whatever the purpose animating those who cast them, would be misunderstood. A wholehearted support of the resolution would be an encouragement to our boys in the trenches, to those in training, to those in hospital, would be an encouragement to those in alliance with us, and he begged the delegates to think very carefully before one vote was cast against it.

Mr. A. Bellamy rose on a point of order and asked whether, if the Conference decided to approve in accordance with the terms of the resolution the present action of Great Britain, it would be justifiable after that to raise the other questions as separate issues.

The Chairman replied that that was a question as to the actual interpretation and meaning of the resolution—a thing which a Chairman could not possibly give in a satisfactory way to delegates, but his opinion was that the other questions about which Mr. Bellamy and other delegates were anxious to express their views should be brought before the Conference, which would have a right to decide in regard to them.

It was moved, seconded, and carried:

That the question be now put.

The resolution was thereupon put and there voted:—

For	1,502,000
Against	602,000

and it was declared carried.

Annual Conference of the Labour Party, January 1917

REPORT OF THE EXECUTIVE COMMITTEE
THE PARTY, THE WAR, AND THE GOVERNMENT.

Following upon the endorsement of the Executive Committee's action regarding the prosecution of the War and the Party's association with the Coalition Ministry under the premiership of Mr. Asquith, the Executive, like the Parliamentary Party, have continued to pursue this approved policy. So long as the Coalition Government remained in office, the Party, both inside and outside the House of Commons, rendered its official support, and it was not until early in December that there arose any necessity for reconsidering our attitude. The circum-

From the *Report of the 16th Annual Conference of the Labour Party, 1917* (London, no date).

stances under which the Coalition Government was prevailed upon to
relinquish office are notorious, and the Labour Party, from its officials
in Parliament throughout the vast mass of its rank and file membership,
can derive some satisfaction from the knowledge that the methods by
which the Coalition Government was destroyed and its leaders deposed
were not countenanced by any of its sections or representatives.

On December 6th, when the Executive met in London for the
purpose of arranging details connected with the National Conference
on Food Prices, it was reported that a joint meeting with the Parliamentary Party would be held the following morning for the purpose
of considering the Party's attitude to the new Government which Mr.
Lloyd George had then undertaken to form. It was too late at that
moment to express any opinion upon the desirability of the previous
Government remaining in office. The Executive found the new situation had been created, and, in conjunction with their Parliamentary
colleagues, had to decide their official attitude in a crisis for which
they were not in any way responsible.

The joint meeting with the Parliamentary Party was held on the
morning of Thursday, December 7th, when Mr. Henderson reported
upon the state of affairs then existing and outlined certain aspects of
policy upon which the new Prime Minister proposed to develop his
administration, both as regards the prosecution of the War and the
control of home affairs. After a general discussion it was considered
advisable that an interview should be sought with Mr. Lloyd George,
and this took place at the War Office on the same day at noon. There
was a very representative attendance of both the Executive and the
Parliamentary Party. Mr. Lloyd George gave strong expression to his
opinion that every consideration should be subservient to the relentless
prosecution of the War, that the new Government was being instituted
for that purpose, and that he was desirous of securing the co-operation
of the Labour Party in the responsibilities of office. He indicated the
Offices and Departments to which he proposed Labour Members should
be appointed, and announced his intention to institute State control of
Mines and Shipping. He foreshadowed strong action with respect to
Food Distribution, the mobilisation of labour, and important develop-
ments in the production of home supplies. Considerable discussion
followed, Mr. Lloyd George replying to numerous points of policy that
were raised by various Members of the Party and the Executive, who
subsequently withdrew for the purpose of discussing what was probably

the most serious position the Party has had to face in the whole of its existence.

The joint conference of the Executive and the Parliamentary Party was held in the House of Commons later in the day, under the presidency of Mr. George J. Wardle, M.P., the Chairman of both bodies. After a debate which was remarkable for its frank facing of the issues involved and the general straightforward and unimpassioned declarations of a large number of the Members present, it was finally decided by a majority vote that Mr. Lloyd George's invitation should be accepted, and that the Party should associate itself with the new administration. This was accompanied by an expression of opinion that the opportunity should be seized of endeavouring to secure a satisfactory settlement of the Irish Home Rule issue.

In the course of the week it was announced that Mr. Lloyd George had succeeded in forming his administration, and that the Right Hon. Arthur Henderson, M.P., had been appointed a Member of the War Cabinet of five, Mr. John Hodge, M.P., put in charge of the first Ministry of Labour, and the Right Hon. G. N. Barnes, M.P., appointed to the newly-created Pensions Ministry. These appointments were understood to be of Cabinet rank. Later it was announced that Mr. William Brace, M.P., would continue as Under-Secretary for Home Affairs; Mr. G. H. Roberts, M.P., had been appointed Parliamentary Secretary to the Board of Trade; and Mr. James Parker, M.P., would officiate as a Junior Lord of the Treasury.

. . .

REPORT OF THE EXECUTIVE
THE PARTY, THE WAR, AND THE GOVERNMENT.

THE CHAIRMAN said it was proposed to take the paragraphs under this heading first. They contained a summary and statement of facts with regard to the Party joining the Government. In taking a vote on these paragraphs the resolutions on the Agenda dealing with the same subject would automatically be ruled out.

THE RIGHT HON. ARTHUR HENDERSON, M.P., moved:—

That the paragraphs be adopted.

He said the statement by the Executive therein contained should be read in conjunction with a statement on the same subject in the Report of the Parliamentary Party. It would be seen that the paragraphs contained a record of events that had transpired but a few weeks ago and which would still be fresh in all their memories. It was set forth that a crisis was precipitated, and declared that in the causes that led up to that crisis the Labour Party had no part or lot. It was also stated that as the Executive were in London engaged in connection with the Special Conference on Food Prices they were unexpectedly invited to face this new situation. They did so and held a joint meeting with the members of the Parliamentary Party. He had been invited by the Prime Minister to discuss the new situation with him and to convey to the Executive and the Parliamentary Party the suggestions he (the Prime Minister) proposed to make in the hope of securing the co-operation and perhaps the co-partnership of the Movement in the formation of the new Government. He (the speaker) put before his colleagues as fully and completely as he could the message he had been invited to convey. The Prime Minister had also stated that he was prepared if need be to give fuller information, and that if necessary a deputation could wait upon him. There was a feeling—and a right feeling—that the situation was so critical, that it had such an important bearing upon the present and the future of our country, and that it was of such far reaching importance so far as our Allies were concerned, that it was unanimously decided that all the members of the Executive and of the Parliamentary Party should wait upon the Prime Minister and hear at first hand exactly the proposals he desired to submit, the invitation he desired to extend, and the conditions associated with such invitation. What took place was briefly outlined in the Report. He had endeavoured to show his colleagues that he had tried to profit by the experience of the past eighteen months. In May, 1915, the Party were unexpectedly invited by the late Prime Minister to associate with a new Coalition Government. He wished to make it quite clear that not only the suddenness of the invitation at that time, but the seriousness of the step they were invited to take, was such that he was convinced that only a grave national emergency could have influenced them (the majority) ever to have given a moment's favourable consideration to such an invitation. The invitation was accepted, and they had had 18 months' experience. When he was sent for by the present Prime Minister he determined as far as possible, and he with his colleagues when they waited on the Prime Minister at the War Office also determined as far as they could, to profit from the experience of the past eighteen months. They had been told many times in the days before ever there was a war that they had been guilty of selling the Movement without getting anything in return. When the invitation in 1915 was accepted they were told that they had got very little in return. Personally he had never viewed the matter from that standpoint. He thought that in a national crisis like this, if they had to associate with any form of Government, they ought to concern themselves more with what they were going to give than what they were likely to get. But keeping in mind the statements and suggestions that had been made, he determined to ascertain from the Prime Minister as far as possible the most he was prepared to give, not only by way of position in the Government, but what was of infinitely more importance, the most he was prepared to commit himself to with regard to policy, and especially where that policy might affect the social and economic well being of the masses of those whom the Party represented. The Report outlined some of the things the Prime Minister was prepared, as head of the Government, to try to do, how he was prepared to put into operation with regard to great industries like mines and shipping the principle the Party had advocated—the principle of State Control. He thought he could safely say that the majority of those who heard the Prime Minister were favourably impressed with his statement. Questions were also asked with regard to the offices he proposed to place at the disposal of the Party, and here again the majority were very favourably impressed—(Interruption—"What was the majority?"). In a democratic Labour Party majorities were not questioned, they were ruled by them whatever their size. If necessary, the majority could be given. There was nothing to hide. It was a majority, and whether it was small or large the decision was come to in face of great national responsibilities, and he thought they ought to abide by it, at any rate until the Conference either confirmed it, as he hoped it would, or rejected it. On this second question they were also very favourably impressed, and in the last paragraph he was asking the Conference to adopt there were the names of the Members and the offices to which they had been appointed. It seemed to him that if they had to be associated with the Government, if through representatives of the Party they had to occupy administrative positions, it would be very difficult to select more important positions, so far as the workers of the country were concerned, than those to which most of their members had been appointed. With that explanation he would review the position with which they were faced when for the second time they were invited to join the Government. On the first occasion the position was very difficult, very difficult indeed. He had been for many years connected with the Movement, and had been very closely associated with its official life, but he had no hesitation in

saying that he never knew a more difficult decision to take. Most of
them had assisted in building up the Constitution of the Party and that
Constitution was very rigid, but when they were trying their hands at
constitution-building none of them ever contemplated a national crisis
—a crisis not only involving the democracy of our country, but every
free democracy in the world—they never contemplated such a crisis as
that through which they had had to pass since August, 1914. So, keeping that Constitution in mind, they had to consider very carefully, and,
as he had said before, he could imagine no other set of circumstances
that would have induced them to give favourable consideration to the
invitation extended by Mr. Asquith. But when they were invited on the
second occasion he was not sure that the emergency was not greater; at
any rate, they had had eighteen months' more of bitter experience, they
had had eighteen months more of terrible loss and sorrow, and some of
them knew what that sorrow meant. So they had to face the situation
from that standpoint. At the last Conference this very subject was discussed, not on one resolution, but on two. There were vast majorities
on both resolutions, which were discussed from every standpoint,—
discussed from the standpoint of the Constitution and of the future of
the Party, and from the standpoint of the great world crisis—and at the
close of the discussion two important decisions were taken. The first
resolution confirmed the action of the Executive and of the Parliamentary Party in allowing Labour representatives to enter the Coalition
Government. The second resolution declared that, in view of the unprecedented situation which existed, the best interests of the nation
would be served by the Labour representatives remaining in the Coalition Government. When the invitation came from the present Prime
Minister they could not overlook the decisions of the last Conference,
and he would be very much surprised if the decision that was taken at
the joint meeting by a small majority was not confirmed by the Conference by an overwhelming majority, consistent with the decisions of
twelve months ago. It had been put to him in this way: Did they not by
associating with the present Government to some extent endorse the
methods by which the old Coalition had been terminated? That was an
aspect of the case upon which some minds would care to dwell. He was
not concerned with the methods by which the old Government had
been terminated. What he was concerned with, and what he hoped the
delegates were concerned with, whether they belonged to the majority
or the minority of the Conference, was the most expeditious way they
could adopt to bring the War to a final success. Therefore he hoped

that in view of the fact that they had acted in what they thought were the best interests of the country and consistently with the decisions of the last Conference, the delegates were prepared to confirm that action. But there was another and entirely different point of view from which they ought to look on this subject. For two-and-a-half years they had been closely allied in a great cause with some countries that had done great things for the freedom of democracy. They had been linked, he hoped, in an unbreakable friendship with their French Socialist comrades and the French nation. Along with Mr. Roberts, he had attended the French Socialist Congress in Paris on Christmas Day and there they found, as they found here, a majority and a minority. In France, as here, during the past few weeks they had had a reconstitution of the Government, and in the French Socialist Conference, as here, there came up the question as to the action of the Party in allowing M. Albert Thomas to remain in the French Ministry. There was a heated discussion and a division, but in spite of all that had taken place they came to the decision that in the great War of national defence, in the great War for what they deemed to be just and right, it was essential that M. Thomas should remain a member of the French Government. The point he wished to make was this: They had stood shoulder to shoulder with their French comrades for two-and-a-half years. On February 14th, 1915, they were associated with them at the last Socialist Conference that their late respected comrade, Keir Hardie, presided over, where a most emphatic decision was come to in a declaration that a victory for Germany would be the defeat of democracy and freedom. That decision represented not only the majority but also the minority. The minority representatives helped to shape that resolution, and the general feeling was that they had at last found a common policy. If that policy was right then, it was right to-day. It might be asked: but how would that policy be interfered with by rejecting the paragraphs of the Report he was moving? He would tell them. Any message that went from the Conference giving any of the Allied Countries the impression that they were weakening in their determination successfully to prosecute the War would be a message of discouragement to the Allied Cause, and would, in his opinion, be inconsistent with the position unanimously taken up at the meeting in February, 1915. But he was not in the least alarmed that any such decision was going to be reached. He was quite well aware that the minority felt as strongly with regard to their position as the majority did, and he had never asked them at any time to move from their position, but he did ask that in view of the terrible sacrifices, in view of the magnitude of the danger, they should try to go through the Conference with a spirit of confidence in the majority of the Executive and of the Parliamentary Party, more particularly with regard to the effort made to carry the War to a successful issue. He believed that at the conclusion of the debate the message that would go forth would be that they were not weakening in their position, that they were as determined to-day as they were in August, 1914, to carry the War to a successful termination, and that they believed they could best assist in doing that by allowing the Labour Members in the Government to carry on the work they had undertaken.

MR. E. C. FAIRCHILD (British Socialist Party) moved:—

That the paragraphs be referred back.

He said he thought the argument upon which Mr. Henderson had rested his case and which was set out in the first paragraph of the Report was totally insufficient to warrant the Executive and the Parliamentary Party taking the course they had taken. It was perfectly true that the last Conference endorsed the entry of the Labour Members into Mr. Asquith's Government, but he would remind the Conference that the situation in December last was altogether different to that which prevailed when the entry into Mr. Asquith's Government was endorsed. Mr. Henderson declared a few days before the last Government went out that the one workman who was indispensable in this business was Mr. Asquith. Mr. Henderson stated that no Government at this moment of our history could last six weeks unless Mr. Asquith were a member, and in view of Mr. Henderson's statements and the statements appearing in the Report, he would ask how it was possible to reconcile their entry into the present Government. They should not have done so without consulting the rank and file of the Movement. There were at the time a great number of Labour representatives in London, but they were never consulted, and the Movement would be contributing to their own suicide if they passed by that incident without censure. Were the present Government the friends of Labour? Was it likely they would get much from such men as Lord Curzon or Lord Milner? Mr. Henderson, desiring to accomplish the very best, with such men would accomplish nothing. The Report stated they went into the Government because they believed the Government would take strong action "on certain matters in which the Labour and Socialist Movements not only of this country but of all the world are vitally interested." What strong action? Mr. Henderson had not told them. Did it mean legislation like the Munitions of War Acts, or was there going to be a further instalment of conscription of our labour and our bodies? Was there to be more loan-making at 5¼ per cent. Were these the things that were to constitute strong action? He believed the Party had committed a grievous folly. They would not have imperilled the War nor the interests of the working classes by remaining outside the Coalition Government. The Allied Note was purely aggressive in character and would destroy every confidence the neutral nations ever had in the goodwill of this country. The real function of the Labour Movement was to respond to the demand for peace and to throw its weight into the scale. By going into this Government the Party had sacrificed the independence of the Labour Movement, and he hoped the Conference would compel them to return to that independence from which they should never depart either in peace or in war.

Mr. James Sexton (Dockers) said he would like to ask Mr. Fairchild whether he claimed that all the Socialists of this country agreed with him. He protested against Mr. Fairchild or any Socialist Party claiming to be the repository of all the political and human virtues of the Movement. He wished to protest against the impudence of such men coming to the Conference and talking in the way they did.

Mr. F. Bramley (I.L.P.) supported the rejection of the paragraphs. He agreed with Mr. Henderson that the importance of this matter was not so much what happened to bring about the fall of the last Government but what happened to justify the step taken by the representatives of Labour. He noticed that Mr. Lloyd George announced the offices and the departments to which he proposed the Labour Members should be appointed; he announced his intention to institute State Control of mines and shipping, and foreshadowed strong action with respect to food distribution and the mobilisation of labour. He (the speaker) was not prepared to vote for that paragraph in the Report, containing as it did possibilities of danger, without knowing more about what Mr. Lloyd George actually meant and what he actually stated and promised to the Labour representatives. What, for instance, did Mr. Lloyd George mean by the State control of mines and shipping. Did he put before them any definite proposals as to what form that control should take? If so, how was it that that definite statement had not been published in the Report? Did Mr. Lloyd George state that he meant to bring the coal mines under the Munitions of War Act? Did he mean that? Did the Labour representatives agree to that? If he did not mean that, what did he mean? Again they were told that the Prime Minister foreshadowed strong action with respect to food distribution. Did he

state what action he proposed to take on that question? Did he make
any definite proposals? Did he say he was prepared to accept the terms
of the resolution carried a few months before at one of the biggest
Trade Union Conferences ever held in the City of London? Did the
Labour representatives ask him if that mandate received his approval
before accepting his suggestion? Surely that was a commonsense view
to take. A Labour Conference had stated its opinion on the food question, had outlined its policy on the food question. Was Mr. Lloyd
George asked whether he proposed to take any notice of that mandate?
Was he asked for any explanation of what he really did mean? As a
matter of fact there had been a certain kind of strong action taken.
In February, 1915, the agricultural interests informed the Board of
Agriculture that they could not grow wheat in this country below 40s.
per quarter, implying by that statement that they could grow wheat at
40s. per quarter. The Government had taken strong action with respect
to the food question; they had fixed a maximum price of 60s. per
quarter. In other words, the strong action was to give Government
sanction to a price for wheat 20s. per quarter in excess of the price the
farmers admitted they could grow it at a profit. Strong action was also
foreshadowed with respect to the mobilisation of labour. Did Mr. Lloyd
George say what he meant by that? Did he state in definite terms what
steps he proposed to take? Did he make any reference to C 3 men in
agriculture? Did he say that men were to be recruited and drilled and
taken in battalions on to the land? Was he asked whether he proposed
before taking that step to fix a fair rate of wage for the agricultural
labourers of this country? He (the speaker) wanted to know what
actually took place. When Mr. Lloyd George talked about the mobilisation of labour did he say he was prepared to repudiate the offer which
had been made to bring into this country 60,000 black workers from
East Africa? Until the Conference could get definite and clear answers
to these questions they would be—as had happened many times before
during this War—giving a vote of confidence absolutely blindfold on
the issues raised. In normal times they referred to the dignity of Labour,
and here they had from the responsible Executive of the great united
Labour Party a suggestion that the Conference should endorse a policy
of strong action with respect to the mobilisation of labour in wartime
without knowing what it meant, should endorse a policy of strong action
with respect to food supply without knowing what it meant, and should
endorse the State control of coal mines and shipping without knowing
what it meant. The other delegates could use their own judgment on

this matter, but on a bare bald statement of this kind, full of serious dangers, he absolutely refused to vote for any endorsement of the action taken by the Executive.

At this point the Conference adjourned for lunch.

The Conference resumed at 2 o'clock.

Mr. C. G. Ammon (Bermondsey Labour Party) said that in resuming the debate he wished to continue the discussion in favour of rejection of the paragraphs in the Report. He would remind the Conference that last year he had ventured to point out that even if there was a desire to aid the Government in the prosecution of the War, the Labour Party would have been in a very much stronger position had they maintained their independence like the Irish Party, and events that had happened since that date had strengthened him in that conviction. Mr. Henderson had said that the Parliamentary Party had no part or lot in the overthrow of the Coalition Government. He accepted that statement, but if it be so, the only logical position to give emphasis to the condemnation of the political intrigue that resulted in the overthrow of the Asquith Government was to have remained outside of a Government of the character now in power in the country. Above all things they had nothing in common as a Labour Party with the persons who were in power, from Mr. Lloyd George who had degraded public life as no other man ever had, to Lord Curzon and Lord Milner who had never hidden their contempt for the British working people; above all, such friends of Labour as Lord Devonport and Lord Rhondda who were now found hand in glove with the representatives of the Labour Party. It had been said that they ought to be prepared to accept majority rule. He agreed, but this ought to be applied all round, and some had memories long enough to remember that when a mandate was given to the Parliamentary Party they did not accept majority rule but went diametrically opposite to the policy proposed by a Conference in London. He agreed with Mr. Henderson that they should not take their stand on the point as to how much the Party could get in exchange. He would not be prepared to bargain with these people at all. The position of the Party was distinct and independent and they should maintain their independence. What was the position to-day? Mr. Henderson and the others were simply held as hostages for the good behaviour of Labour. The very first public utterance of the members of the present Government as soon as they got into power was to announce the conscription of labour, that labour was to be ordered about the country to carry on industry on the lines that should be ordained by

their masters in present circumstances. When the second Military Service Bill was introduced, Mr. Asquith gave very definite pledges that it
should not be a step towards industrial conscription, but what concerned them more was that Mr. Henderson followed and very definitely
stated that he agreed wholeheartedly with all Mr. Asquith had said. In
the light of that the only fair thing for Mr. Henderson to have done
was to have stood outside and come away from these people. Everything they had fought and striven for in the past was being taken away
from them. They must take the matter in their own hands, dictate their
own terms that they were not going to have some of their men held as
hostages for their good behaviour. The Labour representatives must
come right out. They had been told that the thing they had to stand for
was the freedom of Belgium and Serbia, but the latest utterances of the
Government had made the freedom of Belgium and Serbia conditional
upon Constantinople going to Russia and concessions on the Adriatic
to Italy. Now the fighting was being prolonged for a nation that had
done everything it possibly could to condemn every movement for
democracy, which, even while the War was going on, had banished and
punished and murdered those who dared to stand for democracy.
Giving the Labour representatives credit for having acted in the very
best interests, having regard to present conditions, he must point out
that the position was such that they would find all their liberties gone,
and with the best will in the world, when the time of Peace came, they
would find they had established a position that meant the enslavement
of the whole people, with no liberties left, and what was more, the
desire for moral power and liberty would also have left the people. The
cry of liberty raises no echo in their hearts, and the love of freedom
was being banished even while they were giving lip service to freedom
on the Continent of Europe.

MR. J. H. THOMAS, M.P. (Railwaymen) said that at the Bristol
Conference he urged that the Labour Party would be stronger outside
than inside the Government. That was immediately following the invitation of the late Government that Labour should join the Coalition.
But by an overwhelming vote the views he then expressed were rejected
by the Conference, and as a democrat he had to accept that verdict.
He did not think they were justified in mixing the issue as it had already
been mixed. He would still join with Mr. Ammon in doing all he could
to fight industrial conscription, he would still join with Mr. Bramley in
doing all he could to deal with mines and shipping, but that was not the
question they were debating. If Mr. Bramley's speech meant anything

at all it meant he was not opposed to Labour being in the Coalition but he was opposed to the terms on which Labour joined. All these questions were raised in a definite form at another part of the Agenda and they would be able to express their opinions on those issues. The mover of the rejection after denouncing Labour for joining the Coalition went on to declare that Labour should express its opinion on Peace terms. He (Mr. Thomas) wanted to know whether this vote was going to be taken on issues of that kind. He submitted that all those side issues were foreign to the real question: Was Labour to retain its position in the Coalition Government? He denounced in Parliament and out of Parliament the circumstances responsible for the fall of the late Government. He had never hesitated to say that he looked upon the Press Dictatorship in this country as one of the most dangerous weapons Labour would ever have to encounter. The moral was that when Labour had its own paper, at a time when it would have been more useful than ever, Labour refused to support it. They could not blind themselves to the fact that if Labour had refused to join the Government it would have been interpreted both by our Allies and by the enemy that Labour was prepared to give up the sacrifices already made. It would have been a grave responsibility upon the Labour Movement for practically saying that all the sacrifices of our young manhood had been sacrifices made in vain. Nothing was more unworthy than the kind of taunt that their men were mere hostages to the Government. He was prepared to say that the posts they now occupied were the posts that were vital to the future of the Labour Movement. They had such an opportunity of serving Labour as no other Labour leader in the past had ever had. If they failed they would fail because the Movement had failed to give them the support they deserved. Let the Conference in no unmistakable manner express its clear and definite views on the issues it would have to deal with, but do not let it sidetrack the real question facing it at that moment. He thought it would be fatal to the best interests of the Movement to reject the Report. That would mean that their men must come out of the Government. There would be no alternative then but a General Election. He was not afraid of an election, but he was afraid of anything that was going to weaken the country, that was going to dishearten those who had already sacrificed so much. They had got to keep that in mind and realise that the spirit of the young men who volunteered in 1914 was the spirit that would save any Movement. The enthusiasm and patriotism those lads displayed, the feelings that prompted them to risk their own lives, was something that was invaluable to our Movement. It was because he believed it would be disastrous to them, because he believed it would have a weakening effect upon the War, and give encouragement to the enemy, that he hoped the Conference would reject the amendment and unanimously endorse the Report.

MR. PHILIP SNOWDEN, M.P.* (I.L.P.) said that those of them who during the last eighteen months had been actively associated with Mr. Thomas in opposing the legislation of the Coalition Government had heard with regret the speech he had just delivered. It seemed that the experience of the Coalition Government had not taught Mr. Thomas the obvious lesson. He thought Mr. Thomas must be included amongst those to whom the Chairman referred in his Address who were "unable to see the obvious things." There were two tests which he thought he might apply to enable them to come to a conclusion as to what their future attitude should be. Mr. Henderson had said that he regarded the question from the point of view not of what Labour might get by join-ing the Government but rather by what Labour might be able to give. The whole policy during the past eighteen months appeared to have been dictated by a desire not to gain but to give, and as the outcome of this they had had under the Coalition Government legislation inim-ical to Trade Union, Labour, and social interests, without a parallel in the legislative history of this country. It had been one long record of sacrifices of all those liberties for which Trade Unionists in the past had fought and suffered. He asked the delegates calmly and dispassionately to consider the record of legislation during that time, and to compare it with the record of legislation anterior to Labour accepting responsi-bility in the Government. What was the position of Labour to-day? The Coalition Government had been justified on the ground that Labour inside would be able to conserve the interests of Labour and of the Nation more powerfully than if they were in an independent position outside. Let them test that by facts. There were a number of questions in which—apart from the vital question of the War, but matters arising out of the War—they were all united, such as, for instance, the question of the cost of living. Before the formation of the Coalition Government, Labour repeatedly expressed opinions and made demands. Surely if Labour was able to exercise more influence inside the Government than outside, one would have expected that their influence inside the Gov-ernment would have had some beneficial effect in regard to this most

[* Philip Snowden became Chancellor of the Exchequer in Ramsay MacDonald's governments of 1924 and 1929. Ed.]

important question. In the first nine or ten months of the War when Labour was exercising an independent influence outside the cost of living rose, but during the eighteen months that Labour had been inside the Government the cost had risen at a far greater rate, and to-day the cost of living was nearly 50 per cent. higher than it was before Labour entered the Government. They had had a crop of legislation as a result of the Coalition unparalleled in the history of the country. What was the first thing that was done in the way of legislation when Labour became responsible for legislation? It was the introduction of a Munitions Bill which was defended from the Treasury Bench by Labour Members of the Government. Then there followed the National Registration Bill which again was supported by Labour Ministers whose speeches as well as the speeches of other Labour supporters of the Coalition Government, had always been received with rapturous adulation by such well known friends of Trade Unionism as Sir Frederick Banbury and Sir Edward Carson. Mr. Henderson gave an assurance upon that occasion that this measure had nothing whatever to do with military conscription, but a few months later the Military Service Act was passed. Mr. Henderson spoke about the right of majorities to rule. He also believed in the right of majorities to rule, but Mr. Henderson had not always carried that admirable precept into practice. Mr. Thomas has said that if the Conference should decide to support the rejection of the paragraphs it would mean that the Labour Ministers would have to withdraw from this Northcliffe * Government. It meant no such thing. They could depend upon it that whatever decision the Conference came to, Labour would still remain in office. In London twelve months ago a conference was held to discuss the Military Service Bill then before the House of Commons. By a huge majority vote it decided to oppose that measure. They were told then, as Mr. Thomas had told them just now, that if the Conference refused to support the measure it would involve the resignation of the Government and of the Labour Ministers. But it did not. They still remained in the Ministry; they still voted for the measure which had been condemned so emphatically by the vote of organised Labour. They were specially put forward by the Government to oppose those Labour Members who were carrying out the verdict of the majority of the Movement in regard to this particular measure. The vote which would shortly be taken would show a large

[* Lord Northcliffe owned *The Times* and *The Daily Mail* and was regarded by some as the power behind the replacement of Asquith by Lloyd George as Prime Minister in December 1916. Ed.]

majority in support of the action the small minority then took, but nobody knew better than Mr. Henderson that the Conference vote would
not indicate the proportion of opinion in the rank and file of the Party.
The Conference was already packed with huge block votes, the disposal
of which had been decided upon before ever a single word had been
said in the debate, and they were going to have a unanimous vote of
one Union who in their own delegation had carried it only by a majority
of one. That would show the value of the majority which the supporters
of the Northcliffe and Lloyd George Government would be able to
secure. Mr. Henderson had advanced as a reason why the action taken
should be supported, that if Labour decided against association with the
Coalition it would have a disastrous effect in the countries of our Allies.
He was afraid that that was placing the influence of the Labour Members of the Government upon far too high a level. In Russia, our
glorious ally—Russia, who through all the ages had been the champion
of small nations and of civil liberty, Russia, which changes its government at every full moon—it was putting the influence of the Labour
Members of the Government too high to assume that it would influence
Russia in the slightest degree as to whether Labour was or was not in
association with Lord Northcliffe. But did it never occur to Mr. Thomas
and Mr. Henderson that if the withdrawal of the Labour Party from
the Coalition would have a disastrous effect upon the Allied countries,
the withdrawal of Mr. Asquith, Lord Grey, the men who had conducted
the War during two and a half years of its most critical time would
probably have had some effect upon opinion in the Allied countries?
The self-importance of some people was of colossal dimensions! He
was not by any means finished in his recital of the benefits derived from
the Coalition Government. He had left his previous statement at the
introduction of the Military Service Act, and was pointing out that notwithstanding majority rule, notwithstanding Mr. Henderson's democratic views and democratic sympathies, in spite of the overwhelming
vote of the Conference, Mr. Henderson and his friends remained in the
Government and continued to oppose the very policy formulated by
that highly representative Conference. He himself was present at that
Conference and he knew there was considerable hesitation on the part
of many Trade Unionists to support that Bill owing to the fear that it
might ultimately involve industrial conscription. Might he point out
that it was not the Labour Members of the Government who first
pointed out the danger of that development? It was that small, despised,
negligible, Independent Labour section of the Labour Party. Mr. Hen-

derson, speaking in the House of Commons on the first Military Service Bill, tried to assuage the fears of those who thought there might be found in it the germs of industrial conscription and said their fears and doubts were wholly without foundation. They were assured that the Military Service Bill was not the prelude to an extension of military conscription, but a few months later, with the support of the Labour Members of the Government it was extended to married men. Again assurances were given that there was no danger of industrial conscription. But the "Rake's Progress" still continued. On a certain Friday evening Mr. Henderson declared that Mr. Asquith was absolutely indispensable—a phrase with which many had been very familiar during the last twelve months in the administration of the Military Service Act —he understood by the way that many of those Trade Union leaders who so heartily supported the conscription of other men were subsequently very actively engaged in saying that they themselves were absolutely indispensable—on a certain Friday evening Mr. Henderson announced to the world that Mr. Asquith was the one indispensable man to govern the country, and within a week Mr. Henderson was a member of the Northcliffe-Lloyd George Government. He understood that Mr. Henderson still regarded Mr. Asquith as indispensable—in opposition. Believing that the Labour Members were indispensable he (Mr. Snowden) thought they would be much more useful, much more influential, much more indispensable in opposition than in office. He wished to submit that this record would not have been compiled if Labour had been outside the Government. They appeared to have forgotten everything they had been saying to the working classes during the last sixteen years. There was not a single man present in the Conference who had been associated with the Party during those years who had not over and over again justified the existence of an independent Labour Party on the ground that it was far more influential outside the Government than inside. Let him point out what might have been done. Mr. Thomas in his concluding sentence said he believed that in the Offices to which Labour Members had been appointed they would be able to render great service to the nation and to the interests the Party was anxious to promote. Well, why had they not done it during the last eighteen months? Was Conscription one of the great causes Labour wanted to promote? Was industrial slavery under the Munitions Acts one of the great causes Labour wished to promote? Was the suppression of civil liberty and the right of public meeting a cause in which they were interested? The fact of the matter was that the freedom of action of the

Labour Members in the Government had been shackled during those eighteen months, and the action of the Party had been hindered and hampered. They were called disloyal when they criticised or opposed legislation introduced by the Government and for which the Labour Ministers were responsible. It had been said that it was a great thing for Labour that Mr. Barnes should be Minister of Pensions. Mr. Barnes knew quite well that there was no other man in the Labour Movement for whom he (Mr. Snowden) entertained a higher regard, and he believed that in a Labour Government the appointment of Mr. Barnes to a position would have been admirable. He knew Mr. Barnes would bring to the consideration of his duties a wide knowledge and sympathy with the conditions of those concerned, but he denied altogether that Mr. Barnes would be able to render greater service to those people as Pensions Minister than in an independent position, and he would prove it to the Conference. A few weeks ago Mr. Henderson was the Pensions Minister. Mr. Henderson, who was a man of wonderful energy and remarkable versatility, occupied for some time the Office of Labour Adviser on such questions as the importation of coloured labour, but in his capacity of Pensions Minister he introduced a Bill into the House of Commons, and that Bill was so riddled by the criticism of independent Members of the House of Commons that it had practically to be withdrawn and re-cast, the demands made by those who were free to criticise the Government having to be conceded. That was something won by independent action, and had those Members not been independent Mr. Barnes would not have been Minister of Pensions to-day with the power he possesses. Take the case of the Irish Party. He wondered what Russia and Serbia would think of the refusal of the Irish Party to join the Coalition Government. Surely they would regard that as a lamentable instance of the lack of national unity. The Chairman in his Address had said that the Labour Party lacked the political experience of older political parties. That at least was one part of his Address with which he (Mr. Snowden) agreed, and the reason why it lacked that experience was because of its incapacity to see the things which were obvious. The Irish Party were a more experienced Party than the Labour Party. They knew of the dangers of coalition and they refused to join the Coalition eighteen months ago. They would not even consider it two months ago. The Irish Party knew that an independent party outside in time of peace and in time of war were able to serve the interests of their own people far better than if bound to the feet and legs of men who were strong enough to drag them in the opposite direction to that which they wished to go. What had the Irish Party got? During the last eighteen months there had been prosecutions in this country under the Defence of the Realm Act against expression of opinions mild in the utmost degree compared with the opinions constantly being expressed in organs of the Government like the *Daily Mail.* What protest had the conscriptionist Labour Members made in the House of Commons against this? They had been dumb dogs. During recent months representatives of the Irish people had been imprisoned without trial. The Irish Party did not join the Northcliffe Government, they exercised their independent power in the House of Commons, with the result that the Government had been compelled to concede everything they wanted. Mr. Thomas said that the Offices to which our Members had been appointed were those in which they would be able to render great service to the causes the Party had at heart. One of the Labour Members had been appointed to the Board of Trade, and already they had an instance of the great benefits the general public were going to derive from his administration of that important office. The first thing announced in the House of Commons was that under the Lloyd George scheme of public control of the railways the travelling public were to have an impost of 50 per cent. on the rates. He was looking forward with interest to seeing the same beneficial control extended to mines and shipping, and he expected they would have announcements by the respective Ministers that the present shipping rates were to be increased by another 50 per cent., and that the price of coal for the benefit of Lord Rhondda—another democratic member of this Northcliffe Government—another great friend of Labour—was to be increased another 50 per cent. He certainly ought not to forget that they had at last a Labour Ministry, and there was an announcement of the policy of this Labour Minister in two remarkable speeches two days ago. Well, he supposed it was never too late to mend, it was never too late to become wise, and he certainly had a great admiration for a man who discovered—to use the eloquent language of the Minister of Labour, language so befitting the dignity of a Minister of State—that when a man realised what a big fool he had been he had the courage to announce the fact to an admiring and sympathetic public. What was the new policy of the Minister of Labour? It was a combination of the employers and the workmen in the steel trade to establish protection for that industry and use their protective powers to exploit and rob the country. Mr. Thomas thought that the alternative to the endorsement of this policy was a General Election? Mr. Thomas said he had no fear of a General Election, but it was not those who had opposed this War, it was not those who had opposed military conscription and the taking away of the industrial and social rights of the people, who feared a General Election. If a General Election was the alternative to Labour continuing in a Government like this, then by all means let them have a General Election. Mr. Thomas knew quite well there was not a shadow of substance in a statement like that. If a change in Government involved a General Election, why was there not a General Election two months ago when the Government was weakened by the withdrawal of every responsible Liberal Minister? Was the withdrawal of the Labour Members going to be regarded as a matter of great national importance? He had spoken about the colossal self-conceit of certain of those who were dependent on Labour Party support of the Government. He could admire the colossal conceit of any man who said that the withdrawal of the Labour Members of the Government would be regarded as a far greater national calamity than the withdrawal of Mr. Asquith and every other influential member of the Liberal Party. He could admire that colossal conceit, but he could never hope in the highest flights of his imagination to be able to emulate it. They need not fear to support the rejection of this part of the Report. There would not be a General Election. He had not got to the end yet of the "Rake's Progress" which he had been describing. Did they think that the ambition of Lord Northcliffe was now satisfied? In one of his organs already there was announced the successor Lord Northcliffe intended to appoint to the present Dictator at no distant date. It stated that Lord Derby had now followed Mr. Lloyd George as Secretary of State for War, and in the natural course of things he must follow Mr. Lloyd George in the position of Dictator-in-Chief. What were they going to do then? They were going to support him and probably the price of their support would be raised. They might get another Member in the Cabinet—the Cabinet which had ceased to exist. Possibly they might get a Secretaryship of State, but they would get a stronger dose of industrial servitude than they had yet had. Mr. Bramley had made certain definite statements as to the promises given by Mr. Lloyd George. Those promises were never necessary. He would be betraying no secrets when he said that Mr. Lloyd George gave only one definite and unequivocal pledge, and that was his determination to introduce industrial conscription. He believed Mr. Henderson had said that the majority of the Labour Members came away from that interview satisfied. Many of the delegates had had experience of interviews with Mr. Lloyd George. Did they ever know a deputation which was not perfectly satisfied when they left Mr. Lloyd George? They were all satisfied in haste and left to repent at leisure! It was true that Mr. Lloyd George foreshadowed some State control of certain industries and Mr. Lloyd George had already redeemed that pledge. He promised there should be some control of shipping and he at once appointed one of the largest shipowners in the country to control that industry. He promised some measure of Land Reform—he immediately set to work to redeem that pledge and appointed for the carrying out of his Land Reform programme the Agent of the Duke of Bedford who made such complimentary references to Mr. Lloyd George three years ago. This was the way the pledge was being redeemed. He was not making this speech under the mistaken idea that he was going to influence many votes, and he was quite indifferent what the vote of the Conference would be upon the question. He was prepared to bide his time, and when this War was over and they could look at these things through an atmosphere unclouded by the smoke of battle and uninfluenced by the fitful passions of the moment, he had no doubt as to what the verdict of his own fellow countrymen would be on the attitude taken up. (Interruption: "What are you doing?") What was he doing? He was defending those sane principles he had advocated on public platforms for the last twenty years. He was supporting principles which if they were right for times of peace were right for times of war. He was not there in obedience to a popular passion. He was not there to have his policy dictated by newspapers owned and controlled by men of no political principle but of insatiable ambition, men who would not enter the Government because they preferred to make and unmake Governments from Carmelite Street. He knew his views would be beaten in the vote, but he and his friends would not be dismayed by that. They would go on carrying out the policy they had carried out during the last few years, confident that by and bye the principles they had decided to sustain would be carried to a crowning triumph.

Mr. J. R. CLYNES, M.P. (National Union of General Workers) said that the speech to which they had just listened had convinced him at least of one thing, and that was that anything he could say would not make any difference in the vote to be given from that particular quarter of the hall. It was a speech which showed that where they were they are. It was a speech uttered as though there were no war. Events may change and circumstances of great moment alter, but that section was immovable. A speech like that just delivered by Mr. Snowden made

him certain that Mr. Snowden was conscious of knowing how high was
the intellectual altitude from which he had spoken as compared with
the lower level of the standpoint of others. But even so accomplished a
master of gibes and sneers as Mr. Snowden would not expect anyone
who followed him in the debate to deal seriously with most of the
trivial points of sarcasm made by him. Mr. Snowden was in the happy
position of not considering that there was any work to do while this
War was on. The Party took the stand of this being the moment in our
nation's history in which action was the supreme necessity. Criticism
could wait for a later day, deeds were required now, and they could not
stand aside from national activities and see the world and the War roll
on and then come in and claim that they above all others had the right
to say what the terms of peace should be. If they were to take part they
must take part now. He was one of those who eighteen months ago
could not see his way on the facts and merits of the case as he could
then understand them to approve the entry of the Party into the Coalition Government. Events since then had had some impression upon his
mind. He could not afford to settle these things upon a rough and ready
plan of first principles: events did have an effect upon his mind. He
could recall the recorded doctrine of the Independent Labour Party
that it was the duty of Members of the House of Commons to settle
questions on the merits as they arose, and he had tried to settle his
attitude on the merits. The offer to Labour eighteen months ago did
not appear to him to be worth the great responsibility, but the political
and military situation had changed vastly in this period, and after the
interview with Mr. Lloyd George he came away undecided. Many of
the points used on I.L.P. platforms since that time could have been
used by Mr. Snowden when he was face to face with Mr. Lloyd
George. They came away from the interview and jointly with the Executive had to decide their policy. Even in the Party Room Mr. Snowden
and most of his colleagues sat silent. The others did not have the
benefit of their views. As they could not extract from Mr. Snowden
even in the Party Room any exchange of views, he felt justified in
making as impersonal a reference as possible to another matter. A few
days after they had decided their course of action Mr. Snowden, in an
article in the *Labour Leader,* wrote as follows:—

It was the offer of offices; neither the call of patriotism nor
the programme of the new Government had decided the matter.
When the Coalition Government was destroyed by as vile a

conspiracy as ever disgraced English political life, the Liberals officially withdrew from association with the authors of the plot. Labour had no sense of honour or decency which compelled it to stand apart from the men who had brought about this result. With the instinct of the Vicar of Bray these Labour Members were determined to have the offices no matter who was Prime Minister.

After that appeared, Mr. Thorne, a member of the Party, brought the matter forward at a Party meeting, quoting the passage just read. Mr. Snowden was there and said not a word. He appealed to Mr. Snowden but there was no response, and Mr. Thorne, stung no doubt by the taunts thrown at colleagues, turned and said in effect that Mr. Snowden had had as many plums from the Liberal Party and the Liberal Government as any man. He took that to refer to expenses which Mr. Snowden had received for various public work he had done. When Mr. Thorne made that charge what happened? Mr. Snowden wrote the following letter to Mr. Thorne, whose honesty would stand the test of any man:—

> Dear Thorne,
>   At the Party meeting last Wednesday you raised the matter of certain remarks of mine in the *Labour Leader* about the action of the Labour Party in joining the new Government. I declined to be drawn into any controversy on this matter, as I deny the right of either yourself or the Labour Party to interfere with my freedom to say what I like and where I like.
>   But there was one observation you made to which I must direct your attention. You said:
>   "Friend Snowden had had as many plums from the Liberal Party and the Liberal Government as any man."
>   I must ask you seriously to make this statement in public where it can be reported, and then I will at once give you an opportunity of proving it in a Court of Law.
>   Believe me, yours sincerely,
>   (*Signed*) Philip Snowden

They had been told that they were moved by motives of personal gain and that the bribe of office was the thing which governed their acts, and then when Mr. Thorne turned and threw back a sneer Mr. Snowden yelled out for the policeman and told Mr. Thorne he would have the law of him—the law was to be invoked in order that the integrity and honesty of Mr. Snowden should be proved. A good deal had been said about the way the downfall of the Coalition Government had been finally accomplished and Mr. Snowden properly sympathised with Mr. Asquith. Mr. Asquith will no doubt be happy to know that he is reconciled to his old enemies of the I.L.P., who not so long ago referred to him as "Featherstone Asquith." The Party was not under any obligation to Mr. Asquith so great as to stand aside from its duty, and while they joined with others in condemning the movement which was largely the cause of the break up of the Government, their business was to consider the attitude of Labour towards the Government that must again be set up. He sympathised freely with the men who had accepted office in Labour's name. He looked forward twenty or more years ago to the period when the great Labour Movement could put these men in high offices of State. Time had brought that earlier than they thought. But if he had to choose between asking the workers to wait for power until they had got all the power, until they could get a Labour Government, and asking the workers to state their attitude in war time as to taking part in the Government, he could not make so great a draw upon the patience and honesty of the workers as to ask them to wait. There had been times when they had been taunted with giving the Movement away and told they should never give support unless they got something in exchange. When in exchange for that support they received positions of power and authority the jeer was that they had taken those posts because of private gain and because of the quality of the bribe. Mr. Bramley made one or two points in his speech that he would like to refer to, especially the one about black labour. Mr. Bramley did not make it clear as to whether he and his colleagues would, if they were completely satisfied on details, change their minds at all upon the main issue. Mr. Bramley wanted to know whether they had asked for this, that or the other. He might just as well turn to Mr. Jowett and Mr. Snowden and Mr. Anderson and others and ask them why they did not ask.

MR. F. W. JOWETT, M.P., interrupting, said they put more questions than the other sections of the Party and they could not get a clear reply to any, except the one with respect to labour mobilisation.

MR. CLYNES, resuming, said there was on record a full account of what took place at the interview, and if Mr. Jowett liked to raise the issue and question his statement at the Party meeting he should be glad to meet him. But he did not quite understand whether, if the terms were ample and sufficient the attitude of the I.L.P. delegates would be changed.

MR. R. C. WALLHEAD (I.L.P.), interrupting, said his attitude would not be changed.

MR. CLYNES said that was just the position. What then became of all their arguments? For instance, on the question of wheat at 40s. per quarter, could Mr. Anderson, in view of his recent experiences on the Food Prices Committee, say that any such price as things are was not totally out of the question? With regard to black labour he had better briefly state the facts. Labour was consulted because it was a matter concerning Labour. Ministers of State with Mr. Henderson took the first step by inviting a conference drawn from the building trades of the country. As representing a section of the building trades he was there. The question was put seriously as to the urgent necessity of a great increase in the volume of labour and the introduction of coloured labour for certain work in certain districts. They told the Government they would not have it. It was not put to them as something other than an alternative. The Government stated they must have this labour from abroad or at home. If it could be found at home they would take it, and the conference undertook to see that the necessary supply of labour should be forthcoming. That was a brief statement of the facts. Finally, he believed that in entering the Government Labour men had done the right thing as a matter of prosecuting the War to a successful issue, and especially had done a just thing for the immediate claims of organised labour. By what arguments were they to conclude that Labour could do as well dispossessed of power as it could with the power it had assumed? There was the question of the end of the War and the terms of settlement. Was it of no value to Labour to have a man of great Trade Union experience like Mr. Henderson having a voice and taking part in the terms of settlement as he had in the general prosecution of the War? He knew there were people who thought that men like Mr. Henderson, in comparison with their greater capabilities, could be shaped and moulded in any way. The same thing was said about a man like Mr. Hodge. Of all the men in the Labour Movement those were two of the most stubborn kind, and once they took their stand on any question they were immovable. He asked that Labour should be given an opportunity to prove its capacity to serve. Of all the times through which the Movement had passed, this was the time above all others when Labour could not afford to stand aside from the rest of the national activities. On the many important questions affecting Labour they would be more certain of Labour being served than if Labour merely stood always in the position of being able to criticise, never particularly caring what the result would be. The men who had been placed in position were the best the Movement had been able to produce, and the best form of unity was to show full confidence in them.

MR. E. BEVIN * (Dock, Wharf, Riverside and General Workers' Union) said he wished to emphasise some of the fears with regard to Labour joining the Government. He was not concerned with the dialectics of a clever man like Mr. Snowden who could use terms about the "drink-sodden democracy" and say the workmen were wrong when they went on strike. The cheap gibe, which usually came from the blackleg in the industrial field, that they were in the Movement for what they could get out of it, was a gibe which ought never to be used. He was apprehensive as to the attitude of the Party towards those with whom they were associated. If Mr. Snowden was opposed to dictatorship why was he a member of the Liquor Control Board, which was not responsible to Parliament and wielded the most degraded form of government ever introduced into this country? It had been stated that the Party had joined the Government purely on the ground of the national crisis. If the crisis was so urgent and the difficulties so great, surely they ought to have considered the character of the people who were going to deal with such problems. They ought to have remembered that the man who was forming the Government had lied to Labour at the Bristol Trades Union Congress. Of all the men in politics, that man did not represent the sane portion of the citizens of this country. Then there was Lord Rhondda. Supposing the crisis had been a crisis in the Labour Movement and the representatives had asked Lord Rhondda to help in solving their problems, suspicion would have been aroused in the minds of the rank and file. Then there was Lord Devonport whose treatment of the kiddies in the East London strike was as bad as anything Von Bissing had done in Belgium—a man who refused arbitration to the employees of the Port of London Authority, and who, just before the creation of the new Government, stated in the House of Lords that the country could save millions of money by cutting down the allowances of the wives of the men who had gone to shed their blood. These were not the kind of men Henderson should associate with. If a crisis had to be faced, let them face it with men whose character and citizenship they could respect even if opposed on certain points in politics. Then there were Lord Derby, who called the

[* Ernest Bevin became a great trade union leader, and Foreign Secretary in the 1945 Labour Government. Ed.]

postmen "blood-suckers" when he was Postmaster-General and Lord Milner, the "damn-the-consequences" man. He could not understand why, when Labour decided to join the Government, it did not receive assurances as to whom they were expected to associate with.

It was moved and seconded:

That the question be now put.

On this motion being put it was declared lost.

MR. D. GILMOUR (Miners' Federation) said this was the one country in the world where they could have had such a free debate. The Labour Party since its inception had been expected to carry out the lesson he had learned as an individual trade unionist on the very first day—to endeavour to carry out the decision of the majority. They could discuss inside their own circle the rights and wrongs of a question, but when the vote was taken the individual members of the Party ought to accept the decision of the majority. What was Mr. Snowden doing? He had gone on his own just as his Party, the I.L.P., had done on other questions decided by the Conference. The last Conference decided not to agitate for the repeal of the Military Service Act, but from that time till now the I.L.P. had not observed that decision. They had not yet learned as a body to sink their own opinions and bow to the majority. The delegates of the Miners' Federation had met and discussed the Agenda of the Conference, and now they were subjected to the taunts and sneers of Mr. Snowden because they were there to carry out the decision of their own conference. This was not a packed Conference. Mr. Snowden had gone out of his way to write articles in the capitalist press when trade unionists were fighting a life and death struggle. It was left for Mr. Snowden to use the capitalist press to endeavour to beat them. There was no loyalty in that. If there was to be loyalty from the Trade Unions there would have to be loyalty from everybody. The Miners' Federation believed that the action of the Party was best in the interests of Labour. They had got now in addition a Minister of Labour, Mr. John Hodge, about whose position in the Trade Union Movement no man could say a wrong word, as well as Mr. Barnes as Pensions Minister. Personally, he agreed with what the Party had done, and he strongly objected to the criticisms of Mr. Snowden and other irresponsible men.

MR. T. SHAW (Textile Workers) said he was not concerned as to whether Mr. Henderson was a kind of semi-idiot without brains, without will, and without initiative, or as to whether Mr. Snowden was a God-gifted intellectual who could perceive in the first moment everything that was best for the Movement, but he was concerned about the principles he imbibed twenty years ago and the results of which he wished to see. In all their discussions at Conference there had been a remarkable type of individual in evidence, an individual with only one lobe to his brain and only one eye capable of seeing every fault of the Allies and absolutely blind to the faults of the other side. In the International Movement the two resolutions which were always passed with acclamation were in favour of reduction of armaments and international arbitration. When this struggle came along what was the position of affairs? It was Germany, the greatest opponent of any attempt to reduce armaments, the opponent of international arbitration, that brought about the War, and where were Mr. Snowden and the others when these things ought to have been pointed out? They were silent. They had done everything to hinder an advance of the principles they all held dear. The answer as to what the Labour Movement wanted at the beginning of the War was given by the workers when they voluntarily enlisted to fight for a cause they thought was the cause of freedom. Labour was not Mr. Snowden, nor Mr. Henderson, nor Mr. Gilmour, nor himself, it was the men who paid the piper all the time. The Labour Party was composed of the men and women in the mines and the workshops. Those people had decided, and approved that decision, that they believed the War to be a just war. The question he asked himself was: Was it a good thing for Labour men to go into the Cabinet or was it not? What were other nations doing? In Germany universal military and industrial conscription had been introduced with the consent of the Socialist Party. Only 19 votes were cast against it, and the Socialist Party was the largest individual party in the State. There was a people united to fight. To fight what? To fight the lads who had gone from this and other countries and were fighting in the defence of the principles that Socialist Congresses, National and International, had laid down for the last quarter of a century. He was not a Jingo. He detested the man who said his country ought to be defended right or wrong. The only thing that was worth defending was the right. He detested the man who believed in his country right or wrong, but the miserable person who believed that his country was always wrong and tried to make it always wrong was the object of his special detestation. He did not know how they were going to get a better state of things for the lads who had gone to fight and for those whom they ought to consider first and foremost than by a concentrated effort on the part of every party. Did anyone doubt that the withdrawal of the Party would have a bad effect? Did anyone doubt the fact that their withdrawal would stop peace from coming as soon as it might? There were faults in this Government as in every other. Had they a Government of Snowdens, or Jowetts, or Andersons, or MacDonalds, there would still be just a tiny fault here and there. But because a fault was found, to want to spoil the efforts of the country was a wrong thing to do. He heartily supported the acceptance of the Report.

It was moved, seconded, and carried:

That the question be now put.

It was then put:

That the five paragraphs be referred back.

There voted:

For   307,000
Against   1,849,000

and the Chairman declared that the paragraphs were accepted.

VI

STOCKHOLM

Minutes of the War Cabinet, July–August 1917 (excerpts)

JULY 26, 1917

. . .

16. With reference to a Foreign Office telegram from Mr. G. M. Young, through Lord Bertie, and a telegram from Mr. Arthur Henderson, Lord Robert Cecil raised the question of issuing passports to the Right Hon. Arthur Henderson, M.P., Mr. Wardle, M.P., and Mr. Ramsay Macdonald, M.P., to enable them to proceed to Paris on 27th July accompanied by four Russian Sovyet delegates, in order to confer with the French Socialists regarding—

(*a.*) The proposed Allied Socialist Conference in London on 8th and 9th August;

(*b.*) An International Socialist Conference at Stockholm early in September.

He pointed out that the Italian Government had reaffirmed their objection to allowing representatives to attend the latter, and it was decided that—

Mr. Henderson should be asked to confer with his colleagues in the War Cabinet at 7·30 P.M. that evening, with a view to their ascertaining from him how far the proposed action

(1.) Committed His Majesty's Government to assent to British

Socialist representatives meeting enemy Socialist representatives at Stockholm;

(2.) Whether the inclusion of Mr. Ramsay Macdonald, M.P., among those to be allowed to proceed to Paris implied official recognition by the British Government of Mr. Ramsay Macdonald's status as a representative of British Socialists.

WAR CABINET, AUGUST 1, 1917

Prior to Mr. Henderson's arrival, the other members of the War Cabinet discussed the question among themselves . . . Mr. Henderson demurred to this procedure, as he was invited to attend at 4·30 and had waited one hour, and even then was not invited into the Cabinet, but it was explained that it had been adopted with special regard to Mr. Henderson's interest and feelings, and that no slight had been intended . . .

Mr. Henderson reminded the War Cabinet that the question of the Stockholm Conference had never been discussed by those who were specially entitled to a view in the matter, namely, the Allied Socialist Parties. The proposal had originally been made by the Russian Soldiers' and Workmen's Committee without conference with their Allies. The policy of the British Labour Party towards it had been to postpone it as long as possible; in fact, they had adopted precisely the same attitude towards it as that of the Government towards the Russian Government's proposals for a Government Conference on War Aims.

Mr. Henderson recalled that, before he had left England, the War Cabinet themselves had agreed that if a Conference at Stockholm was held at all it would be advisable that British representatives should be present . . . Circumstances had, he admitted, changed considerably since then, but until he met his colleagues he had no information that their attitude on the subject had changed.

He himself had returned from Petrograd somewhat under the influence of the daily discussions he had had with the Russian Foreign Secretary, who had insisted very strongly, and almost up to the moment of his departure, on the great importance that the Russian Government attached to the holding of the Stockholm Conference as a means of clearing away the suspicions that existed in Russia of British Imperialistic designs. The Russian Government had wished the Stockholm Conference to precede the Government Conference on War Aims, their reason being that an Allied Socialist Conference, as proposed by the British Labour Party, would not exercise any influence on the

Governments concerned, whereas they considered that the Stockholm Conference would.

Owing to the inability of the British Government to send a warship to bring him back from Norway, Mr. Henderson said that he had been delayed three or four days on his journey, with the result that the Prime Minister had left for Paris before he reached London. On his arrival he had found himself confronted with an invitation from the French Socialists to the Russian Socialists and the British Labour Party to proceed at once to Paris to discuss the Allied Socialist Conference and the Stockholm Conference. Before he had met his colleagues in the War Cabinet, he had had to attend a meeting of the British Labour Party's Executive, and at this meeting it had been decided to accept the invitation of the French Socialists and to proceed to Paris, and Mr. Henderson himself, as Secretary of the British Labour Party's Executive, together with Mr. Ramsay Macdonald, the Treasurer, and Mr. Wardle had been selected as representatives. Immediately this decision was reached, he had telegraphed it direct to the Prime Minister at Paris, and on the afternoon of the following day he had met his colleagues and frankly discussed the whole question with them at the War Cabinet.

Mr. Henderson justified his acceptance of a nomination to go to Paris by pointing out that, as the Russian Socialists had accepted, it was eminently desirable that British representatives should also attend. Further, as Mr. Ramsay Macdonald, as Treasurer of the British Labour Party's Executive, was selected, it was desirable that those who held different views from him should be represented.

At Paris the Stockholm Conference had been discussed as a matter that was already settled in principle, and Mr. Henderson himself had taken the line which he had decided on his return from Russia to be best calculated to promote the national interests, that is to say—

1. To postpone the Stockholm Conference as long as possible.

2. To do his utmost to ensure that it should not be a Conference to take decisions, but merely a consultation at which the British and French delegates could expound the British and French case.

At Paris he had stood out against the Russian and French Socialists for this point of view. The French had wished the Socialist parties of the various nations to be bound by the decisions of the Conference, because they had thought that by these means they could secure French aims in regard to Alsace and Lorraine. He himself, however, had explained that Great Britain was confronted with special difficulties in the matter of war aims, and that the British Labour Party could not permit themselves to be bound by the decisions of the Conference. He had stated that he would have to reconsider his position in regard to the Conference if he found the resolutions were to be binding, and eventually he had succeeded in securing the adoption of his point of view. He had also succeeded in obtaining the postponement of the Conference from the 15th August to the 10th September in order to give time for the representatives of the United States Labour Party to attend the Allied Conference that was to precede the Stockholm Conference.

On the question as to whether he himself, if selected by the British Labour Party to attend the Stockholm Conference, could accept nomination, Mr. Henderson urged that he could not give an immediate answer. He had always realised that it would be very difficult for him to proceed to Stockholm as a Member of the British War Cabinet. Consequently, if he should receive a nomination for the Conference, he would have to reconsider the whole position according to circumstances. By that time, he pointed out, the situation might have entirely changed, as, indeed, it had already changed since the War Cabinet itself was inclined to favour British representation if a Conference should be held at Stockholm.

The War Cabinet then discussed with Mr. Henderson the immediate Parliamentary situation. It was generally agreed that the House of Commons was less concerned in the Stockholm Conference than in the fact that Mr. Henderson, a Member of the War Cabinet, had proceeded to Paris in company with Mr. Ramsay Macdonald, who only a day or two before had made himself conspicuous as the leader of the pacifist group in the debate on war aims.

It was generally agreed that Mr. Henderson could dispose of criticism in the House of Commons by pointing out that the difficulty had arisen from the fact that he held a dual position as a Member of the War Cabinet and as Secretary of the Executive Committee of the British Labour Party. It might be frankly admitted that, on the present occasion, this had entailed some misunderstanding, but it must be borne in mind that it also possessed great advantages. It had enabled Mr. Henderson in the past to keep in the closest possible touch with the views of the Labour Party, and so, by first-hand information, to assist the Government in preparing its war measures on lines which would be acceptable to labour. Moreover, it had enabled Mr. Henderson to attend the previous Conferences of Allied Socialists with good results. For example, only last Christmas he had attended a Socialist Conference in Paris, where he had met with considerable opposition, but had eventually induced the Conference to take the view which he shared with the British Government in regard to the prosecution of the war. Further, he could point out that members of the French and other Allied Governments occupied a position similar to his own. On balance, therefore, the dual nature of his position had been an advantage. Mr. Henderson could also remind Parliament that this was not the first Conference which he had attended in company with Mr. Ramsay Macdonald. It was true he had not been with him to Paris before, but he had travelled with him to Manchester. In fact, as Secretary of the Executive Committee of the British Labour Party, he could not refuse to take part in official missions in company with its treasurer. This was an inevitable part of his dual position already referred to. Moreover, neither he nor Mr. Ramsay Macdonald had any illusions as to the views which each held with regard to the war.

By taking some such line as this, and by combining it with a strong war speech, on the lines of the speech he had made to the Comité Parlementaire d'Action à l'Étranger in Paris, it was felt that Mr. Henderson should succeed in satisfying the House of Commons.

AUGUST 8, 1917

The War Cabinet discussed two points:—

(a.) Whether the Government should allow British delegates to proceed to Stockholm.

(b.) Whether there should be an announcement in Parliament of the Government's decision.

On the first question the War Cabinet were agreed that, since May . . . when our main object was to sustain the Russian Government, decisive changes had taken place. It was now clear that the influence of the Soviet in Russia was steadily declining, and that the attendance of the British delegates in Stockholm was less important than formerly. It was felt, however, that it would be much more convenient to the Russian Government, and more conducive to the maintenance of good relations between the British Government and the Labour Party, that the working men themselves should refuse to attend rather than that the Government should announce their decision and thereby appear to dictate to the Labour Party. This course, it had been ascertained by personal enquiry, was also acceptable to the French Government. From this point of view the best course appeared to be to leave the final decision until after the meeting of the Labour Party on Friday the 10th August. As an objection to this course, however, it was pointed out that there was at present no certainty that the Labour Party might not cast a vote in favour of attendance at the Stockholm Conference, and that, in this case, the Government would be placed in a difficult position. The fact that the Trades Union Congress, to be held on the 3rd September, might oppose representation at Stockholm, was felt to be too uncertain a factor to rely upon, since the Government would be bound to announce their decision long before that date.

During the discussion the War Cabinet received a communication to the effect that the United States Government had refused to grant a passport to Mr. Morris Hillquist to proceed to Stockholm, which indicated that they were opposed to participation. They were also informed that, whatever the decision of the other Allies, the Italian Government had no intention of allowing representatives of that country to attend.

The War Cabinet decided that, in replies to questions in the House of Commons, Mr. Bonar Law should state that—

(*a*.) The attendance of British delegates at the Conference would be illegal;

(*b*.) Such a Conference could not be attended by British delegates without the permission of the Government;

(*c*.) The whole question was being examined by the Government;

(*d*.) It was obviously one which concerned not this Government alone; and

(*e*.) A full statement would be made on Monday the 13th August.

AUGUST 10, 1917, AT 11:30 A.M.

. . .

12. With reference to War Cabinet 207, Minute 5 [August 8, 1917], the Secretary of State for Foreign Affairs reported the receipt of a communication from M. Nabokoff, of the Russian Embassy, dated the 8th August, conveying a message from the Russian Foreign Minister to the effect that, although the Russian Government do not deem it possible to prevent Russian delegates from taking part in the Stockholm Conference, they regard this Conference as a party concern and its decisions in no wise binding upon the liberty of action of the Government.

A copy of this message has been sent to Mr. Henderson before the meeting of the Labour Conference to-day.

AUGUST 10, 1917, AT 6:15 P.M.

1. With reference to War Cabinet 207, Minute 5, of the 8th August, 1917, the War Cabinet discussed the situation created by the resolution of the Labour Party's Conference giving 1,846,000 votes against 550,000 votes in favour of representation at the Stockholm Conference.

The War Cabinet decided—

Not to permit British representation at the Conference.

2. The War Cabinet further decided that—

The Secretary of State for Foreign Affairs should send an urgent telegram to the British Ambassadors in Paris, Rome, and Washington instructing them to inform the Governments to which they were accredited that on Monday the British Government would announce that no British representative would be permitted to attend the Stockholm Conference, and that it would greatly assist them if they could announce at the same time that the French, Italian, and United States Governments respectively intended to adopt the same attitude.

3. The discussion centred mainly on Mr. Arthur Henderson's speech at the Labour Party's Conference, shorthand notes of which were available. It was pointed out that this speech had been misleading, particularly in regard to two omissions:—

(1.) That no mention had been made of the fact that Mr. Henderson's colleagues in the War Cabinet were strongly opposed to British representation at Stockholm, which had been made perfectly clear at the meeting held on the 8th August.

(2.) That Mr. Henderson had not communicated to the Conference the gist of M. Nabokoff's communication in regard to the altered attitude of the Russian Government towards the Stockholm Conference (War Cabinet 210, Minute 12), although, by the Prime Minister's instructions, Mr. Sutherland had drawn his attention to the important bearing of this communication on the Labour Party's discussions.

The general lines of the discussion are indicated in the letter from the Prime Minister to Mr. Henderson, the terms of which were agreed to by the War Cabinet.

It was decided, however, to postpone the despatch of this letter until it had been ascertained from M. Nabokoff whether the substance of his urgent and strictly confidential communication No. 1328, dated the 8th August, setting forth the present attitude of the Russian Government towards the Stockholm Conference could be included in a published letter.

4. In the course of the discussion a communication was read from M. Albert Thomas, the French Minister of Munitions, stating that a telegram had been received from Petrograd to the effect that the Provisional Government had disinterested itself in the Stockholm Conference, and that M. Kerensky desired that it should not meet.

5. The Secretary was instructed not to summon Mr. Henderson to future meetings of the War Cabinet, nor to circulate War Cabinet documents to him.

AUGUST 11, 1917

1. With reference to War Cabinet 211, the War Cabinet continued their discussion on the situation created by the Labour Party's vote in favour of representation at the Stockholm Conference.

Two new factors had arisen since the previous evening: (1) Mr. Henderson had tendered his resignation, and at the same time had informed the Prime Minister that he continued to share his desire that the War should be carried to a successful conclusion, and trusted that in a non-Government capacity he might be able to render some little assistance to this end. [During the meeting, the Prime Minister received information that His Majesty the King had given his permission for the acceptance of Mr. Henderson's resignation.] (2) M. Nabokoff, the Russian Chargé d'Affaires, had given the Prime Minister full authority to include in a published letter the Russian Government's communication in regard to the Stockholm Conference (War Cabinet 210, Minute 12), as well as anything mentioned in his letter of the 8th August (No. 1328), so long as his name was not mentioned.

There was some discussion as to whether, after Mr. Henderson's resignation, it would be advisable for the Prime Minister to send the proposed letter to Mr. Henderson, as decided the previous day (War Cabinet 211, Minute 3). It was suggested that there was no precedent for such action; that it was important, particularly in view of Mr. Henderson's offer of continued assistance, not to make a wider breach with him than could be avoided; and that it might be better to confine action to a statement in the House of Commons. Against this it was urged that no time ought to be lost in making public in some form, the two points mentioned in War Cabinet 211, Minute 3. During the discussion on this point, information was received that Mr. Henderson, in view of the suggestions of bad faith on his part which had been made in the morning papers, was himself preparing a statement for publication, and that he proposed to make use of certain official telegrams.

The War Cabinet took note, however, the consent of His Majesty the King, obtained through a Secretary of State, would be necessary before Mr. Henderson could make public official documents, and decided that—

The situation would best be met by re-drafting the proposed letter from the Prime Minister to Mr. Henderson, and that it should be somewhat modified in tone. Apart from changes in form, the main alteration in substance in the original draft was the inclusion of an acknowledgment of Mr. Henderson's offer of assistance. The letter, as finally approved by the War Cabinet, is printed in the Appendix.

2. In regard to publication, the War Cabinet agreed that—
The correspondence should be published in Sunday's newspapers (Sunday, 14th August), Mr. Henderson being informed of this. The Prime Minister's Private Secretary to take the necessary action.

3. It was generally agreed that the action of the Labour Party was likely to damage this country in the eyes of foreign Powers, who would say that British democracy had by its vote shown itself tired of the war, and that it would also be a serious blow to the Government. The view was expressed, however, that the situation might very likely be retrieved at the Trades Union Congress to be held on the 3rd September, by which time the facts given in the Prime Minister's letter would have become generally known. It was also pointed out that the effect of an important success by our arms in Flanders during the current offensive would have a most beneficial effect on democratic opinion.

In this connection it was suggested that one way of meeting the situation might be that the Labour representatives in the Government should go to their constituencies, which action would be tantamount to a miniature General Election, asking for a vote of confidence in the Government. The objections to this course appeared to be that it would be looked upon as a farce, as merely an effort of the Government to obtain a majority, and as being a partial appeal to the Labour Party and not to the country at large.

To meet the latter objection it was suggested that a General Election should be held immediately, without waiting for the new Register, in order that the direct authority of the whole country might be behind the Government in their future conduct of the war. But it was urged against this course that women would be discontented if they had no vote, and would regard themselves as being betrayed by the Government, and that the consequence of an election at the present moment might, in two years' time, be a reaction in the other direction.

It was also brought to the notice of the War Cabinet that the present moment, which was one of really critical importance, when proposals for peace had actually been made by the Pope, and other proposals of a plausible nature but tending towards an unsatisfactory peace were in the air, was most inopportune for a General Election, and that it would cause difficulties with our Allies.

After consideration of these points it was decided that—
The question of having a General or partial Election should be further considered at a convenient moment, after time had been allowed for the opinion of the country to be fully educated, as to the real situation in regard to the Stockholm Conference, by the information made public in the Prime Minister's letter to Mr. Henderson.

AUGUST 13, 1917

. . .

17. It was suggested that the important point on which the Government must be prepared with their reply to Mr. Henderson was the answer to the question of what new factors had arisen to make the Government change the attitude taken by them on the 21st May, 1917, when, with the agreement of the War Cabinet, telegram No. 1027, dated the 21st May, 1917, had been sent by the Prime Minister to M. Thomas, rather favouring the representation of the Western Allies at Stockholm (see also War Cabinet 141, Minute 15, of the 21st May, 1917).

The reason for this change of attitude were, that in May the Russian Government was in the hands of the Workmen's and Soldiers' Committee, and, under its influence, were then inclined strongly in favour of the Stockholm Conference, and that the British Government were in this matter, to a great extent, influenced by their desire to support the authority of a newly formed body which had not yet firmly established itself. The consequence of the influence exerted by the Soviet, however, had been to shatter the discipline of the Russian army and the organisation of the nation, and the Russian Government was at the moment taking measures to re-establish discipline in their forces by means which were absolutely contrary to the principles of the Soviet, and showed that the policy of the extreme revolutionaries had been discredited.

To permit the attendance of British representatives at the Stockholm Conference, which was tantamount to countenancing fraternisation between one section of the Allied British public and one section of the enemy public, would be very prejudicial to the policy which the Russian Government was engaged on and was pressing forward, the very first item of which was the prohibition of fraternisation between Russian troops and those of the enemy.

It was recognised that no difficulty would be found in proving, on the above lines, that the conditions had completely changed since May 1917, but that there would be considerable difficulty in doing so without embarrassing M. Kerensky.

The War Cabinet felt that the Prime Minister would himself have to use the greatest discretion in dealing with this matter in Parliament, that he should intimate to the House the difficulty in which the Government were placed, and should bring out clearly the great disservice which Mr. Henderson had done, both to M. Kerensky and the Russian Government, in raising this question at this precise moment.

18. The point was raised as to what answer should be given in the House if Mr. Henderson asked what difference there was between the attitude of the Russian Government, as evinced in telegram No. 1180 of the 2nd August, and as described in M. Nabokoff's message. It was pointed out that, while the former was merely an expression of Sir George Buchanan's personal belief as to the opinions of particular elements in the Russian Ministry, the latter was a formal and official statement of the considered views of the Russian Government as a whole.

APPENDIX I

MR. Henderson submitted his resignation to the Prime Minister at 10·45 on Saturday, the 11th August. At the same time he instructed me to make enquiries from the private secretary of a Minister recently resigned in order to ascertain what papers he might take away with him and what papers should be left for his successor. I pointed out to Mr. Henderson that there was no precedent which covered his position, because he was the first member of the War Cabinet, being Minister without portfolio, to resign, and the usual distinction made between papers sent to the Minister as Head of a Department and as a member of the Cabinet could not be made in his case. Mr. Henderson cited the case of Mr. Asquith, and suggested that if he took with him all the papers of the War Committee that would form a satisfactory precedent. It seemed to me that the two cases were not analogous.

After long consideration Mr. Henderson decided that his proper course would be to take with him all papers which had been issued to him whilst he was a member of the War Cabinet and present in this country. At the same time, he is quite prepared to return any papers if the War Cabinet consider that he should do so. I attach a list of the papers which I despatched on Saturday afternoon by motor-car to his private house.

G. M. Hodgson.

August 13, 1917

APPENDIX II
M. Nabokoff to Mr. Balfour
(No. 1328. Urgent and Strictly Confidential.)

Russian Embassy, London,
August 8, 1917

Your Excellency,

In a telegram I sent to the Russian Foreign Minister three or four days ago I gave him an account of the statements made in the House of Commons by the Prime Minister and Mr. Henderson concerning the latter's visit to Paris, as well as of Mr. Bonar Law's statements regarding the Stockholm Conference and of the discussions which were taking place in the different labour organisations of Great Britain as to the desirability of sending delegates to Stockholm. I also drew the Russian Foreign Minister's attention to the reply given by the American Federation of Labour to the French Confédération générale du Travail. In conclusion I said the following: "I consider it absolutely necessary, with a view to safeguarding the stability and closeness of our union with Great Britain, where the majority of public opinion is adverse to the Conference, that I should be in a position to declare most emphatically to Mr. Balfour that the Russian Government, as well as His Majesty's Government, regard this matter as a party concern and not a matter of State, and that the decisions of the Conference, should it be convened, would in no way be binding on the future course of Russian policy and of Russia's relations with her Allies."

In reply to this message I have just received the following telegram: "I entirely approve of the declaration to be made to His Majesty's Government in the sense suggested by you, and you are hereby authorised to inform the Secretary of State for Foreign Affairs that, although the Russian Government do not deem it possible to prevent Russian delegates from taking part in the Stockholm Conference, they regard this Conference as a party concern and its decisions in no wise binding upon the liberty of action of the Government."

I hasten to lay before you the above information, as I fear that the impression has hitherto prevailed that, in the words of one of the London newspapers, "Russia ardently desired the Stockholm Conference," and this argument has been put forward in order to influence British public opinion in favour of the Labour and Socialist Parties of Great Britain participating in the Conference.

I have, &c.
(Signed) C. Nabokoff

AUGUST 17, 1917

. . .

16. The attention of the War Cabinet was drawn to telegram No. 1258, dated the 15th August, 1917, from Sir George Buchanan, with reference to complications which have arisen in Petrograd as a result of the correspondence between the Prime Minister and Mr. Arthur Henderson on the subject of the Stockholm Conference, and of the action taken by the Russian Minister in London.

It was pointed out that neither in the correspondence with Mr. Henderson nor in his statement in the House of Commons had the Prime Minister stated that M. Kerensky was opposed to the holding of the Conference.

With reference to a suggestion put to Sir George Buchanan by some journalists that the Russian Government should request His Majesty's Government to allow British Socialists to attend the Stockholm Conference, it was urged that it was most undesirable that any such request should be made. His Majesty's Government and the Allied Governments of France, Italy and the United States, had to consider public opinion in their respective countries, just as the Russian Government had to consider public opinion in Russia.

The action of M. Nabokoff had been fully considered by the War Cabinet on the 13th August, and it was important to adhere to the undertaking then given (War Cabinet 213, Minute 14).

Mr. Philip Kerr was requested to draft a telegram on the above lines to Sir George Buchanan, for submission to the Secretary of State for Foreign Affairs.

Annual Conference of the Labour Party, January 1918

REPORT OF THE EXECUTIVE COMMITTEE

INTERNATIONAL

During the past twelve months the work of the Executive Committee has been dominated very largely by its interests in democratic diplomacy, and serious and strenuous attempts have been made to secure common agreement upon war aims among the Socialist Parties of the Allied Nations with a view to the ultimate presentation of a unified peace policy to an International Conference. Differences in our own Movement at home, paralleled by similar dissensions in the ranks of our Socialist colleagues in the Allied Nations, together with the tremendous change occasioned in the whole International outlook by the success of the Russian Revolution in March, have rendered the task of the Executive difficult in the extreme.

Almost immediately after our Party Conference at Manchester the French Socialist Party endeavoured to secure a Conference of Allied Socialists in Paris on March 13th. The Executive, in the first instance, agreed to appoint ten delegates, but subsequently the situation was reviewed and the decision rescinded by a small majority, with the result that the Conference was postponed.

In the meantime, the Headquarters of the International Socialist Bureau had been removed to Stockholm where the Dutch members, with Camille Huysmans, the secretary, in response to an invitation from the Swedish and Danish Socialist Parties, agreed to co-operate in the forming of a Dutch-Scandinavian Committee presided over by Hjalmar Branting, the leader of the Swedish Party, and one of the most prominent supporters of the Allied Nations' policy in the neutral nations. This Committee sought to arrange consultations at Stockholm with delegates of the various nationalities engaged in the War. An invitation was received by the various affiliated sections in this country in May, and was very carefully considered by the Party Executive in the light of the resolutions and discussions on the "International" at the Manchester Conference of the Party in January, 1917. It was ultimately decided that the invitation should not be accepted, but that an attempt should be made to convene a meeting of the Labour and Socialist Parties of the Allied Nations in London, preferably at the end of June, [it] being understood that the American Federation of Labour

From the *Report of the 17th Annual Conference of the Labour Party, 1918* (London, no date).

should be invited to participate. It was also agreed that all majority
and minority sections of the Allied Parties should be invited, and that
no resolutions of a binding character should be carried, but that
differing policies should be discussed and placed on record.

Within two or three days of this decision an announcement appeared that the Russian Council of Workmen's and Soldiers' Deputies
—the organisation representing the forces responsible for the Russian
Revolution—had decided to issue invitations to the Socialist and Labour Parties of all nations to a Conference with a view to securing the
adoption of a general Working-Class Peace Policy. The Executive
were unanimously of opinion, when this invitation was reported, that
arrangements for the proposed Inter-Allied Conference should be
suspended until further information regarding the Russian proposal
was forthcoming. A deputation was appointed to proceed to Petrograd for this purpose, and, if desirable, with permission to consult
with Branting and his colleagues at Stockholm. Owing to reasons with
which delegates will be familiar, the official deputation (Messrs. G. H.
Roberts, M.P., and W. Carter) did not leave for Petrograd. The Executive Committee thereupon agreed, before deciding on any further
action, to await the return of Mr. Henderson, who had proceeded to
Petrograd at an earlier date on a Government mission. Mr. Henderson
returned to London and arrived at the same time as four representatives of the Russian Council of Workmen's and Soldiers' Deputies
(Messrs. Roussanoff, Erlich, Smirnoff, and Goldenberg). Consultations with the Party Executive were immediately arranged, . . . and
it was proposed to hold the International Conference at Stockholm
whether the British Party decided to be represented or not, and that
there were important reasons for it being convened without delay.

The Party Executive also agreed that the Inter-Allied Conference
should be proceeded with, recommended that it should be summoned
by the British Section of the I.S.B. for August 8th and 9th, and that a
Special Party Conference should be called for the purpose of receiving
a report of the Inter-Allied Conference and to decide whether the
Party should be represented at the International Conference at Stockholm. The Executive agreed, by 5 votes to 2, to recommend to the
Special Conference that the invitation should be accepted condition-
ally upon the gathering being of the nature of a consultation and that
no binding resolutions should be adopted.

The conditions governing the International Conference were as unsatisfactory to the French Socialist Party as to the Party Executive,

and when the Executive met on July 25th an invitation was reported from the French Socialist Party for a deputation from the Executive to accompany the Russian delegates to Paris to examine the new invitation. Messrs. Henderson, Wardle, and MacDonald were appointed for this purpose, and, in company with the Russian delegates, proceeded to Paris on July 27th. Consultations there took place upon the Russian invitation, with the result that a series of resolutions regarding the procedure of the Conference was decided upon and a recommendation made that it should be postponed until September 9th. It was also decided that the Inter-Allied Conference, which the British Section of the I.S.B. had already summoned, should be postponed until August 28th and 29th. These changes were endorsed by the British Section and the Party Executive and the postponement of the International Conference was accepted by the Organising Bureau of the Conference.

Under all these circumstances the Executive decided that a Special Party Conference should be held as originally proposed, and this took place at the Central Hall, Westminster, on Friday, August 10th, 1917. Mr. W. F. Purdy presided, and Mr. Henderson made a lengthy statement on the whole position of affairs.

In accordance with its majority decision the Executive recommended

> That the invitation to the International Conference at Stockholm be accepted on condition that the Conference be consultative and not mandatory.

To this the following amendment was moved:—

> That this Conference, having heard the statement of the Right Hon. Arthur Henderson, while agreeing that he was actuated by a sincere desire to serve the best interests of the British democracy, is of the opinion that no case has been made out for the appointment of delegates to the Stockholm or any other Conference which would include delegates from enemy countries, and that this Conference do now adjourn *sine die*.

After discussion the amendment was defeated by 1,651,000 to 391,000, and upon the Executive's resolution being put as a substantive motion, it was adopted by the overwhelming vote of 1,846,000 to 550,000.

The Executive then recommended

> That the Party delegation consist of 24 representatives, the Executive to appoint eight, the Parliamentary Committee of the Trades Union Congress to be invited to appoint eight, and the present Special Conference to appoint eight; this sectional representation to be equally reduced should circumstances necessitate.

To this, on the initiative of the Miners' Federation of Great Britain, the Conference, by 1,813,000 to 432,000, decided to add

> but no further additions thereto shall be permitted from any affiliated or unaffiliated body in this country.

As this latter condition infringed the terms of the invitation to the Stockholm Conference, in so far as it restricted the representation of Minority Parties, after some discussion the Conference was adjourned until August 21st.

The Executive also submitted to the Special Party Conference a Draft Memorandum on War Issues which it proposed should be submitted, after agreement, to the Inter-Allied and Internationalist Social Conferences as representative of the general view of the British Movement respecting the Peace settlement. This document was circulated to the delegates, to the Press, and to affiliated societies with a request for amendments with a view to a detailed discussion taking place at the adjourned Conference.

The decisive vote of this Special Conference to accept the invitation to the Stockholm Conference came as a great surprise to the Government, as well as to large sections of the Press and public. Mr. Henderson was widely attacked as being guilty of withholding information from the Conference respecting the alleged change of view on the Stockholm proposal held by the Russian Revolutionary Government, and also by the Prime Minister (Mr. Lloyd George) with a breach of faith as a member of the War Cabinet. He therefore resigned office as a member of the Government on August 11th in the following terms:—

> Offices of the War Cabinet
> 2, Whitehall Gardens
> August 11th, 1917

Dear Prime Minister,

At our interview last night I gathered you had reached the conclusion that my retention of the post of Secretary to the

Labour Party was no longer compatible with my membership of the War Cabinet. Recent experiences have impressed me with the embarrassing complications arising from this duality of office. In these circumstances, therefore, I deem it advisable to ask you to release me from further membership of your Government.

I continue to share your desire that the war should be carried to a successful conclusion, and trust that in a non-Government capacity I may be able to render some little assistance to this end.

I remain,

Yours sincerely,
Arthur Henderson

The adjourned Conference met in London on August 21st, when it was reported that the Dutch-Scandinavian Committee had accepted the conditions governing the Stockholm Conference as laid down by the Paris Delegation.

It should also be put on record that after the Conference on August 10th the Government announced that no passports would be issued to British delegates desiring to attend the Stockholm Conference, and it was made apparent that this decision had been come to by the Government prior to the holding of the Conference on August 10th, but the announcement had been withheld in order not to prejudice the decisions of the Conference. . . .

INVITATION TO THE INTERNATIONAL SOCIALIST CONFERENCE
AT STOCKHOLM ON THE 15TH AUGUST AND FOLLOWING DAYS
WORKERS OF ALL COUNTRIES! UNITE!

The War has been going on now for three years and we do not yet see the end of the conflict.

It is the need to pave the way for this which has led the Council of Workmen's and Soldiers' Delegates to summon, under the flag of the Russian Revolution, an International Conference of the Socialist World.

This proposal, which had been preceded by similar suggestions from many Socialist Parties, has been sanctioned by the All-Russia Congress of the Councils of Deputies. Its aims is to unite all the forces of the international proletariat in order to obtain a peace without annexations or contributions, and based on the right of peoples freely to dispose of themselves.

To enable it to succeed in its work the delegation of the Russian Councils has been assured of the effective collaboration of the Dutch-Scandinavian Committee, which has merged its plans in the Russian initiative, and which had already elucidated numerous questions by separate conferences with most of the Socialist Parties in order to prepare for the General Conference. It has created an Organising Bureau composed of delegates of the Russian and Dutch-Scandinavian Committees. This Bureau has decided, in order to avoid disputes, to respect as strictly as possible the procedure followed at the ordinary Congresses of the International as regards both admissions and the allocation of votes.

The Delegation of the All-Russia Congress of Workmen's Deputies and the Dutch-Scandinavian Committee therefore invite to the General Conference all the parties affiliated to the International Socialist Bureau; also those who, during the War, have been connected with the Berne Commission—majorities and minorities, as well as the oppositions which, in the course of recent events, have formed themselves into distinct Parties. They also invite the occupational organisations affiliated to the Trades Union International. The Congress will be held at Stockholm on August 15th and following days.

The provisional programme of the Conference has been drawn up as follows:—

1. The World War and the International.

2. The Peace Programme and the International.

3. The ways and means of realising this Programme and bringing the War rapidly to an end.

The organisers of the General Conference are deeply convinced that in order to bring about the end of the World War the International ought to induce all the Socialist Parties and all the Trade Union organisations to abandon any co-operation with Governments which refuse to indicate their War aims, or which have adopted Imperialist aims in an open or disguised manner and refused to renounce them.

Convinced that your organisation also approves of these views, and that it is ready to undertake to put into practice without hesitation or deviation the resolutions of the General Conference conforming to these principles, the Delegation of the Russian Council and the Dutch-Scandinavian Committee beg you to take an active part in the International Socialist Conference and to send representatives.

In the event of your organisation desiring to have placed on the

Agenda any question which does not appear in the Programme of the Conference, a communication containing the proposal, accompanied by a report, ought to be addressed to the Organising Bureau of the International Conference, Uplands-gatan, 14, Stockholm, and be in the hands of the Secretary before August 5th.

Socialist and fraternal greetings.

For the Delegation of the Russian Congress of Deputies of Soldiers and Workmen:—

H. Erlich.	N. Roussannoff.
J. Goldenburg.	A. Smirnoff.
W. Rosanoff.	

For the Secretariat:—

Camille Huysmans.
Arthur Engberg.

For the Dutch-Scandinavian Committee:—

P. J. Troelstra.	H. J. Branting.
H. H. Van Kol.	E. Soderberg.
J. W. Albarda.	G. Moller.
(Substitutes:	F. I. Borgbjerg.
W. H. Vliegen,	(Substitute:
F. M. Wibaut.)	Nina Bang.)
	J. Vidnes.

Stockholm, July 11, 1917.

Supplementary Declaration of the Russian Delegation:—

The Delegation of the All-Russian Congress of the Councils of Workmen's and Soldiers' Deputies notes with regret that it has been unable to obtain the collaboration of the International Socialist Commission at Berne in the preliminary work of the General Conference.

The Delegation believed that it was its duty to make sure of the assistance of the Commission, not only because it had strict instructions to do so, but also because all the active Socialist Parties in Russia are affiliated to the Zimmerwald Union.

The participation of the Berne Commission in the preliminary work of the Conference appeared to the delegates especially necessary for another reason, that a considerable number of large Parties in Russia and abroad, affiliated to the Berne Commission had already expressed a desire to take part in the Conference proposed by the Council of Workmen and Soldiers.

Be that as it may, the International Socialist Commission, composed for the moment of four members who are at Stockholm, has refused to take part in the preliminary work, without, however, refusing to give the Delegation technical assistance.

The Zimmerwald Conference, where the question of participation at the General Conference will be considered, will be held five days before the meeting of the latter.

REPORT OF MEETINGS OF REPRESENTATIVES OF THE BRITISH LABOUR PARTY, THE EXECUTIVE COMMITTEE OF THE FRENCH SOCIALIST PARTY, AND DELEGATES OF THE RUSSIAN COUNCIL OF WORKMEN'S AND SOLDIERS' DEPUTIES

A meeting of the representatives of the British Labour Party (Messrs. Henderson, Macdonald, and Wardle), the Delegates of the Russian Council of Workmen's and Soldiers' Deputies and the Executive Committee (the "C.A.P.") of the French Socialist Party, was held on Sunday, July 29th, 1917, at the offices of the latter (37, Rue Sainte-Croix-de-la-Bretonnerie, Paris) to consider the conditions on which the British and French Socialist and Labour Movements would be prepared to attend the International Socialist Conference convened jointly by the Dutch-Scandinavian Committee and the Council of Workmen's and Soldiers' Deputies.

M. Dubreuihl, the Secretary of the French Socialist Party, outlined the steps that had been taken since the question of holding a Conference had been raised by the Russians at the end of May, 1917. A prolonged discussion then took place on the constitution of such a Conference, especially on the point whether it was to be held strictly on the lines of the International Conferences formerly convened by the International Socialist Bureau, or whether it was to be an *ad hoc* meeting under its own rules.

Mr. Wardle moved that a small sub-committee should be appointed to decide the basis of representation at the Stockholm Conference, its date, and place. This was carried, and a sub-committee was formed accordingly consisting of Mr. Henderson and Mr. Macdonald; M. Longuet and M. Renaudel; M. Elrich and M. Goldenberg.

The sub-committee met on Monday, July 30th, and decided to recommend to the full Conference the eight following resolutions:—

(1)

The meeting expresses its cordial approval of the initiative taken by the Soviet and supported by the Dutch-Scandinavian Committee, the result of which is the joint invitation of the two organisations to the working class of all nations to meet at an International Socialist and Labour Conference.

(2)

The organising bureau, consisting of the Russian delegation and the Dutch-Scandinavian Committee, with the technical assistance of the Secretariat of the International Socialist Bureau, is to have sole charge of all communications with the national sections for the purpose of the Conference.

(3)

All bodies affiliated to the International shall be invited to take part in the Conference.

(4)

Where, since the War, these bodies have been divided, the minorities as well as the majorities shall be invited in those cases where the minorities have formed themselves into separate Parties.

(5)

Trade Union organisations not affiliated to the I.S.B., but affiliated to the International Trade Union Bureau, shall be invited, provided that they are not already represented through organisations affiliated to the I.S.B.

(6)

The invitations to each fraction of each national section shall be issued by the Organising Bureau, through the national sections of the International, and any appeal from the decisions of these sections shall be made to a Bureau to be elected, two representatives from each nation present, representing majority and minority, at the International Conference.

(7)

The future and action of the International being dependent on the loyalty with which the resolutions passed by the Conference will be adhered to, the national sections who will take part in the Conference hereby undertake, after the general decisions have been taken, to declare definitely at the meeting of the International what effect they intend to give to such decisions.

(8)

The sub-committee recommends that this meeting suggests to the organisers of the Conference that it should be held in Stockholm from September 9th to 16th. If there is any practical difficulty preventing this, the organisers should be requested to hold it in Christiania or elsewhere on the dates named.

These resolutions were afterwards placed before a meeting of the British and Russian delegates and the Committee of the French Party, and were carried.

Discussion also took place on the agenda of the International Socialist Conference, with special reference to the statement contained in the official invitation, that the provisional programme was to consist of:—

1. The World War and the International.

2. The Peace Programme and the International.   •

3. The ways and means of realising this Programme and bringing the War rapidly to an end.

ADDRESS BY THE RIGHT HON. ARTHUR HENDERSON, M.P., AT THE SPECIAL PARTY CONFERENCE ON AUGUST 10TH, 1917

In rising to address this Special Conference on so momentous an occasion, I do so with a deep sense of my own personal responsibility. I desire to make what I hope will be a fair yet a frank statement of the position. It appears to me the more necessary to do so, partly because your Executive were undoubtedly influenced by information I supplied in making the recommendation before the Conference, and partly because of the grave doubts which have been cast upon my own attitude in the matter. In order to make clear my position I must appeal to the delegates to bear in mind the fact that the political situation in Russia is, and has been, constantly changing. Unless that is borne in mind justice cannot be done either to the merits of the case as a whole or to my own personal actions. I want to say quite freely that before I went to Russia some ten or twelve weeks ago I was opposed to the holding of an ordinary International Conference. On my arrival in Petrograd I met the Executive of the Workmen's and Soldiers' Council. I met them on invitation, and though in Russia, as I distinctly told them, on a Government mission, I said I was going to speak to them as the Secretary of the Labour Movement. I put before them what I conceived to be the attitude of organised Labour to the War. I gave them the decision of the Manchester Conference against holding an international Conference in the form then declared. The question of their proposed Conference for which invitations had already been issued was discussed. I pointed out to them how impossible it would be for British Labour to accept an invitation under the conditions laid down or under any conditions until the Manchester decision had been reversed.

When I was presented with the statement of the Executive of the Workmen's and Soldiers' Council and the invitation they had already issued, it appeared to me that there were three courses open. One was definitely to decide on the rejection of the whole matter. I have no hesitation in saying that, having regard to the condition of public opinion in Russia at that moment, that would have been about the most fatal position that I could have taken up, either in a Government capacity or as the representative of the great British Labour Movement. The second course open was to have informed them that I would come at the earliest possible opportunity and advise the Labour Party to reverse its decision, and accept the proposal for a Conference on their conditions. I made it unmistakably plain that I could do no such thing, and I hope before I sit down to give you the reasons why. The third course open to me was to intimate to them that if they were prepared to change completely the conditions of their Conference, turning it from an obligatory Conference to a consultation for the purpose of exchanging views, I would come and recommend the great Labour Movement so far to reverse its decision as to make such a consultation possible. As everybody knows, except those who have been misled by the garbled statements in the Press, that was the position I took up, and that was the position which I shall show presently I maintain. Let me emphasise the fact that the Russians clearly had it in their mind that they wanted a binding Conference for the purpose of discussing actual terms of peace. British Labour, I stated, could only attend the Conference where their representatives would make a full and frank statement as to why they had supported the War, and as to what were the aims and objects in the hope of achieving which they still continued to support the War. I made it as plain as I was capable of doing that if a Conference was held in which we participated there could be no question of negotiating peace terms. I pointed out that the Socialists and Labour Parties in this and other countries were not yet the nation, and that the only people who were responsible for negotiating actual peace terms were the Governments of the respective countries, for upon them rested on behalf of the people the entire responsibility. I pointed out that there could be no binding decision of any kind, that it was absolutely impossible for us to contemplate entering the Conference where the decisions should be made mandatory and binding. I said that the Conference could be no more than an opportunity for an exchange of views. I went further. I said that in order that this might be effectively carried out it was absolutely necessary that representatives of all the Allied Countries should be present, including the United States of America.

I may be asked why I did not immediately reject all idea of British representatives attending such a Conference. The reason is simple. In my opinion, our case has never been properly stated and is certainly not properly understood to this day in Russia, and to have point blank refused to consider the question would have done incalculable harm.

As I have been opposed to an International Conference I would like to state why it was that I was influenced to take up the position that I have already indicated. One of the reasons was that I found the most confused ideas were current in Russia as to the aims for which our country continues the struggle. I even found not only confused but prejudiced ideas against the great Labour Movement, because of the mistaken notion of our attitude in supporting the War. Our objects have been perverted, and these perversions I found were being utilised to the full by enemy agents. It seemed to me that the proposed Conference under the conditions that I laid down, once they had been approved by you, would form a useful opportunity for a frank statement of our case, always provided—and I emphasise the reservation —that satisfactory conditions could be laid down for the attendance of our best representatives. I must ask the delegates, whatever be their views, to remember the condition of affairs in Russia at the moment of which I am speaking. It is no exaggeration to say they were positively appalling, and it is difficult to say whether they have improved at the moment. But we must have regard to the fact that Russia was an Ally, and had been an Ally for three years, and I for one am not going to judge Russia by the unfortunate failure of the present instead of by the bravery of her troops in the past. I had to keep in my mind that British Labour—I do not say it disrespectfully—had manifested a desire to assist Russia by almost every section competing one with the other to send delegations to that country. It will be said that they were anxious to try to consolidate the fruits of the Revolution. So was I. It may be said we were anxious to go and assist them to organise their forces against the onslaught of a cunning and ruthless enemy. So was I. Further, you must remember that the Provisional Government at that time was in favour of a Conference, and several of its members pressed me more than once to use all the influence I had with British Labour to secure their attendance at the Conference.

Believing, as I did, that a Conference had become inevitable, owing to the determination of the Russians, I concluded, after great thought, that it would be highly inadvisable and perhaps dangerous for the Russian representatives to meet representatives from enemy and neutral countries alone. Unless, therefore, I was prepared to shut my eyes to the facts of the situation, I had no alternative but to lay before the Executive and—on my suggestion—before you the information I had gained, and to recommend that British representatives should attend the Conference provided satisfactory conditions were first laid down and accepted by the promoters of the Conference.

So much for the position as it was when I was in Russia. I desire now to examine the position in order to see how far it remains the same or how far it has been modified. It would be a great mistake, I think, for any of us to try to persuade ourselves that there has been no change in Russia since the time of which I have just spoken. We are bound to recognise that there has been a tremendous change. The Provisional Government then in power is no longer in office. It has been replaced by an almost entirely new Coalition under the leadership of that brave soul Kerensky. I admit that such evidence as I have, though it is very slight, suggests that there has been some modification of the position of the new Government as compared with the old on the question of the proposed Conference. For instance, M. Terestchenko, the Foreign Minister, has stated that at the present moment it is impossible to talk of peace. Tseretelli, with whom I was repeatedly in conversation, and who is one of the most influential members of the Socialist Movement, and who has not joined the new Government, preferring for, I believe, very satisfactory reasons, to remain at the head of his own Party, has now declared, with regard to the foreign policy of their country, that there is only one course, and that is, a continuation of the War until the Russian people have thrown off the shame lying on them and the freedom gained by the Revolution has been duly secured.

Now, from the purely British point of view there are some points which ought not to go unnoticed: An important factor that we Britishers cannot possibly ignore is the decision of the American Federation of Labour and of the Belgian Socialists not to take part in the Conference. I do not know the reasons why the American Federation of Labour has decided in this way, but I do know that the Belgian Socialists were prepared to take part in a Conference provided satisfactory conditions could be laid down. I think I am not going too far when I say that the French Socialists were prepared to take part in a Conference provided satisfactory conditions were laid down. But I ought to be perfectly frank, and to say that both these Parties took up a position entirely opposite to my own. They wanted not conditions of freedom, but conditions absolutely binding, and when in Petrograd I discussed it with my colleagues who were there, M. Thomas and M. Vandervelde. I laid it down that I was totally opposed to anything in the nature of a binding Conference, no matter what the conditions were. Now the absence of these colleagues and representatives of these Parties must influence our point of view, however disappointing it may be to many of the delegates. Nor can we overlook the fact that 40 Socialist representatives in the French Parliament have recently made a protest against participation in the Conference on the conditions laid down. Another very important point is that the form of the Conference, or consultation, as I prefer to call it, at which we—I mean your Executive and myself—have been aiming, does not now appear possible, owing to the attitude of the Russian Socialists. They still demand a binding Conference. We continue opposed to a binding Conference. In this connection, may I submit to the delegates what M. Rosanoff, who represents the Workmen's and Soldiers' Council on the committee that is now making arrangements for the Conference in Stockholm, says in giving his report to the Workmen's and Soldiers' Council, as recently as last Saturday. He says: "The Dutch-Scandinavian Committee, which at first wished that the resolutions of the Conference should not be obligatory, on the point of view of their being put into practice, finally renounced this wish, and also adopted the Russian programme." When you get time to peruse the documents that have been circulated this morning, you will find that Appendix 1. consists of the Russian programme. Let us see exactly what that programme is, with all its binding character, because it has been accepted up till now, and we have not been able to get any change—it has to be accepted now without hesitation or equivocation. It would mean that the Stockholm Conference would have to be held under conditions that are far from being in accord with the views of your Executive and myself when we determined to make the recommendation. If you will examine the first resolution to be moved to-day you will see that it makes an indispensable condition that any Conference that we attend, or that any representatives of the British Movement attend, must be consultative and not mandatory. We had always hoped to be able to secure a drastic change in the conditions of the Conference. We had hoped that we would be able so to alter them as to bring them into harmony with the actualities of the International situation. If we were to fail in obtaining such drastic alterations, let me show the delegates briefly what it would mean. It would mean the acceptance of the Russian programme, and that, in my judgement, would place British Labour in a most dangerous position—a position which, as I have shown, we have done everything to avoid. It would mean that, whatever resolutions were carried at the Conference, they would be binding on all of us who might be represented. What is more, I believe that any attempt to do that at a first Conference would destroy the effectiveness of the Conference, lead to angry recriminations, and make the Socialist and Labour Parties the laughing-stock of the world. Let me again repeat that, when in Petrograd, on every occasion, and when in Paris, about which you have heard so much, I strongly opposed the ideas of the Russian programme. I strongly insisted on no departure from our conditions, and I gave both the Russian Socialists and the French Socialists to understand that, so far as I, at any rate, was concerned—and I believe I was speaking for the whole Executive—it was a fundamental condition that the Conference should be a free exchange of opinions and not in any sense obligatory.

Notwithstanding all the opposition to the idea of a Conference, I am convinced that under proper safeguards a consultation such as I had in mind would have been productive of much good. Our case, as far as I know, has never been properly stated either to the German Socialists or to those of the Neutral Countries. In Russia, as I have already said, there is the most confused idea regarding the aims for which we, as a country, are continuing the struggle. If I am correct in my estimate of the position, surely a frank statement of our case presented by working-class representatives would have assisted in dispelling the mist from the minds of the Socialists in Russia and in Neutral Countries, and would probably have provided the German Minority Socialists with important new facts which have been purposely withheld from the German people. It was for these reasons, and these reasons only, that I advised your Executive to take the positions set out in the first resolution to be submitted to the Conference. I hope the delegates will dismiss from their minds the suggestion that any of us—and I put in the plea for myself—have been in any way influenced by either unworthy or unpatriotic motives. Convinced as I was that the Conference was inevitable, it was surely not unpatriotic for one who had supported the War as I had done—not so unpatriotic as some people and some Press representatives appear to imagine—to try to prevent a bad impression being continued or a worse impression being formed on the minds of the Socialists of one of our own Allies. In my opinion, at any rate, our case is so strong—in fact, the case of the whole of the Allies is so strong—that if it were presented by responsible working-class representatives it would materially assist in convincing the German people that it was the crime of their rulers that caused the War, and it is the crime of their rulers that now prevents its just settlement. It appeared to me that to adopt such a course as I have indicated could not be other than valuable, provided it did not involve—and I attached the greatest importance to this qualification—any interference with military effort or sacrifice of any of the fundamental aims for which the Western democracies are fighting. I do not think I am going too far when I say it has been very frequently stated of late that it would be much easier for this country and the Allies to negotiate a peace settlement if a real democratic Government were installed in Germany and Austria. We have become familiar with the statement. Surely then it could not be other than advantageous to the Allied cause for responsible leaders of Democracy, organised Labour, and Socialism from the Allied countries to press home this declaration on the minds of the German people, and especially the German Socialists. I have not wavered in the slightest degree in my attitude to this War, nor have I changed my mind as to the need of a final and complete settlement, but I want to say that in a War in which losses of such terrible magnitude are being imposed on all the Nations it appears to me not only wise but imperative that every country should use its political weapon to supplement all its military organisation, if by so doing it can defeat the enemy. That is why I continue in favour of a consultative Conference with proper safeguards and conditions. May I make another present to some of my opponents? I fully realise that the course I have taken the responsibility for advising is not entirely free from difficulty, and I with others can suspect a certain amount of danger in it. This is bound to be the case where so many different countries are allied together. In this connection we do not fail to appreciate the great need there is for the Socialist and Labour Parties of all the allied Countries to continue, if it be at all possible, to support a common War policy. But, however desirable such a position may be, I want to say this, that the absence of complete agreement should not prove an impediment to sound propaganda through a consultative Conference.

I have now stated my case, and I freely and frankly leave the decision to this great Conference. There is no disguising the fact that it is one of the most momentous decisions you have ever had to take, and I join with the Chairman in appealing to you to settle it, not merely from Party considerations, but from the standpoint of national interests. Let us try to take our decisions without being influenced in the slightest degree by what I cannot characterise in any other way than as the unscrupulous agitation that has been carried on outside. Let us be influenced by the interests of the nation of which we form a part and for which the workers have done so much during this War. Let us remember poor struggling Russia, whose great miracle we all welcomed with such delight a few weeks ago, and of whom it was universally admitted that it had done the finest thing that had ever been done during the whole War. Let us remember poor Russia, and if we cannot give the newest Democracy, the infant of Democracies, all she asks, I beseech you not to give her an entire point blank refusal. Of this I am convinced, and I want to say this with all the seriousness and deliberation of which I am capable, that if we to-day, representing as we do the great British Labour and Socialist Movement, determine for the whole period of the War, not to use the political weapon to supplement our military activities, not only shall I regret it, but I will venture to predict that you as a Movement will regret it hereafter. My final word to the Conference is: Let us by all means at our disposal, whether they be military or whether they be political, strive to secure such a victory as will ensure for the world a lasting, honourable, and democratic peace.

In the House of Commons, August 13, 1917, Arthur Henderson and Lloyd George

MR. ARTHUR HENDERSON: In rising to make a personal statement, I must ask the indulgence of the House for an opportunity to speak at much greater length than, I think, is usual under such circumstances. This is due to the fact that my relations with the War Cabinet and my actions at the Labour Party Conference on Friday have been made the subject of what I can only describe as an unprecedented and dangerous Press campaign. I venture to say it would be difficult, if not almost impossible, to find a precedent in all the Ministerial resignations for the conduct pursued by the present Prime Minister and his

Hansard, Fifth Series, Vol. 97, Cols. 909–32.

colleagues in regard to my case during the present week-end. May I
say in passing that the Press campaign to which I call attention was
organised with such perfection that the first intimation I received that
my resignation had been accepted came not from the Prime Minister,
but from the columns of the "Pall Mall Gazette"; and I should emphasise the fact that never during the whole of the time since I sent
my resignation to the Prime Minister had I left the office of the War
Cabinet. Having made that preliminary statement, may I say a word
or two in regard to the actual resignation? After the decision of the
Labour Conference on Friday I had an interview with the Prime
Minister. I am not going to explain, or go into detail with regard to
that interview, except to say this: that the Prime Minister made it
clear that my retention of the position of Secretary of the Labour
party was no longer compatible with my remaining a member of the
War Cabinet. . . . May I now deal with the circumstances of the
resignation? As everybody knows, it has arisen out of the question of
the Stockholm Conference. If the complete story of Stockholm is to
be told I am doubtful—and I want the House to appreciate the point
—if the telling of that complete story would at this moment assist the
national interests. I shall, therefore, be content to join the interesting
list of ex-Ministers who are awaiting an opportunity to state the full
facts of their case when they can do so without prejudice to the interests of the nation. But the attacks in the Press—and they have been
plentiful—the suggestions of bad faith, or—shall I say—of conduct
much more reprehensible, compel me to deal with certain recent
events, whatever be the consequences. It appears to me that it would
be to the advantage of the House and all concerned if I made a plain,
unvarnished statement to the House and kept it as far as possible in
chronological order. On July 24th I reached London, having completed the mission on which I had been sent on behalf of the Government. On 25th July a meeting of the Labour Party Executive was held,
at which I was present in my capacity as secretary. The question of
the proposed Stockholm Conference came up for consideration, and,
as the result of my experiences in Russia, I felt compelled to give
advice to the Executive. I advised them first of all to put the whole
question before a special National Labour Conference. I went further.
I recommended that the invitation to Stockholm be accepted under
conditions that I had previously laid down. It was also decided at that
meeting that the invitation of the French Socialists that a delegation
should be sent to Paris should be accepted . . .

On my return from Russia, the question of the Stockholm Conference and of my proposed visit to France—I hope the House will take notice of the point—were the subject of consideration at a special meeting of the War Cabinet twenty-four hours before I left for Paris. The Prime Minister was unavoidably absent, being then in Paris. Immediately the decision of the Labour Party Executive was taken I wired to the Prime Minister informing him of the position, and yet I am compelled to make this comment, that the Prime Minister and colleagues who have issued the document to the Press that is now known to the world, charging me with withholding information from the Conference, stand convicted before this House in having intimated to it that the whole of the arrangements for my going to Paris were done without their knowledge.

The PRIME MINISTER (Mr. Lloyd George) rose——

MR. SNOWDEN: Sit down!

The PRIME MINISTER: I should like to ask my right hon. Friend what he means by saying he sent a wire to me to Paris stating what the position was? He does not mean to suggest he wired to me to Paris to tell me what decision was taken by the Labour party? The only wire I had was a telegram stating he was going to Paris with four Russian delegates, Wardle and Macdonald. I received that, I think, on Thursday. Nothing about business—not a word.

MR. HENDERSON: The statement that I made is in strict harmony with the position. I intimated to the House that, after the decision had been taken in regard to the visit to Paris, I intimated that to the Prime Minister, and that it was the subject of a special meeting of the Cabinet. No one can challenge either of those statements.

The CHANCELLOR of the EXCHEQUER (Mr. Bonar Law): I really think I must put the facts before the House. My right hon. Friend the Prime Minister was absent. His colleagues here had no knowledge whatever from my right hon. Friend of his intention to go to Paris with the Members mentioned. We discovered it first in this telegram which was circulated to us. On receiving it, in the absence of the Prime Minister, I summoned the Cabinet to deal with it. We clearly expressed to our right hon. Friend our disapproval of the course he had intimated to us it had been decided upon and he must go. In these circumstances, as I said to the House at the time, I was not able to interfere further than that.

MR. HENDERSON: I have not a word to say with regard to the explanation given by the leader of the House. I accept every word of

it. That does not clear him. It does not clear the Cabinet from the—
I am not going to say guilt; I am not going to make such a charge
—from the fact that they intimated to this House, in reply to a question, that all the arrangements were made without the knowledge of
the Cabinet.

MR. BONAR LAW: I am sure the House will understand. I am very
sorry to interfere with the speech of my right hon. Friend, but, on the
contrary, in one of the supplementary questions put to me it was said,
Did the right hon. Gentleman conceal from us he was going? I at once
replied that we did know he was going, but we only knew it after all
the arrangements had been made.

MR. HENDERSON: I leave this matter with the House. The one point
that cannot be challenged is this: This House did not know, notwithstanding all the questions that have been submitted, that there ever
was a special meeting of the War Cabinet between the Labour party
coming to this decision and my leaving for Paris. I want to refer to
this special meeting a little further. I must refer to it because it was
the first opportunity I had of stating the decision of the executive of
the Labour party the previous day. It was the first opportunity since
my return from Russia to put my own position with regard to the
Stockholm Conference. I also went the length of intimating that it was
upon my responsibility—upon my advice—that the executive had
taken its decision to make a recommendation to the Conference that
the invitation to go to Stockholm should be accepted. I think I ought
to say that there was a very sharp division of opinion. I know that I
am treading on delicate ground, but, in view of the fact that the
Leader of the House has intimated what took place at that particular
Cabinet, I cannot see that I can do other than follow him. [An HON.
MEMBER: "Out with it!"] There was a very sharp division of opinion,
I admit, and, as the result of that sharp division, having given advice
to my executive, although the whole of my colleagues present were
against me, I offered to end the difficulty by expressing my willingness
at once to tender my resignation. I think the Leader of the House will
agree with me.

MR. BONAR LAW: Quite.

MR. HENDERSON: I had to bring that point out because it has something to do with the question raised, to which I shall have to refer
later, in the Prime Minister's letter. On my return from Paris on 1st
August, I immediately saw the Prime Minister. I gave him a very full
and, I hope, very faithful statement as to my own personal position.

I gave him the reasons why I had reached the conclusions that it was
in the interest of the Allied cause and of our own country, so far as
our relationships with Russia were concerned, that we should be
represented at the Stockholm Conference, if we could make it of a
consultative and not of a mandatory character. At the close of our
conversation—and that was the day upon which the Debate on the
Paris visit took place—the Prime Minister invited me to attend a
special Cabinet at four o'clock. I complied with his request, but, to
my surprise, when I turned up at the Cabinet, I was informed by
the Secretary of the Prime Minister that he wanted me to wait in the
Secretary's room for some time. I waited for a full hour, and, at the
end of the hour—I leave the House to form its conclusion of the
treatment—the Minister of Pensions was sent out to make a statement
to me. I intimated to my right hon. Friend the Minister of Pensions
that I did not do business in that way. I put what I thought was a very
pertinent point: "I am either a member of the Cabinet or I am not.
If I am a member of the Cabinet, and I have anything to say to my
colleagues, I will say it to them when they are all present." He returned and told my colleagues what I had said, and I was at once
invited in, the Prime Minister making the statement—I will be perfectly fair and frank—that I had been kept waiting out of regard for
my personal feelings. I put in my protest, as I thought I was perfectly
entitled to do, for I will venture to say it will be difficult to find another precedent, so long as a Cabinet Minister has not tendered his
resignation to the Prime Minister, that when that Cabinet Minister's
conduct was being investigated he should be kept in another room.
[An HON. MEMBER: "We are getting on!"] Having made my protest,
we discussed the question of my visit to Paris, having regard to the
Debate that was going to follow the same evening. After the Debate—
and this is a very important point because Stockholm did loom very
large in that Debate—there were some very strong opinions expressed,
especially on the opposite side of the House, against the whole business of Stockholm, and I very naturally expected, having regard to
the Debate, that a very early opportunity would have been presented
for going into the merits or demerits of the whole question of the
proposed Stockholm Conference in the Cabinet. But to my surprise
the week ended and the subject was not raised. On the following Tuesday, the Tuesday of last week preceding the Labour conference, I
asked the Prime Minister when we were going to consider the question
of the Stockholm Conference, and he replied that he hoped at the next

Cabinet, but I had better see him first. So that on Tuesday, the 7th of August, I did see the Prime Minister by himself by appointment at Downing Street, and we talked over matters at some length. I ventured to make two suggestions at that interview. On that day the Attorney-General's legal opinion with regard to the Conference had been circulated to Members of the Cabinet, and I said to the Prime Minister, if the Government is going to act upon this legal opinion, I would suggest that an immediate announcement of that fact be made to-morrow. I attached very great importance to it because, if I had to remain a member of the Government, if there was going to be a legal side of the case, if it became the policy of the Government publicly announced through this House, I would have had to have gone to my labour committee and my conference and pointed out to them, as I undoubtedly would have done, that this legal position would compel me to consider my personal position, and choose between either giving up the secretaryship of the Labour party or giving up my membership of the War Cabinet.

I made a second suggestion. I suggested that the Cabinet ought to allow the Labour party conference to decide, and apart altogether from the legal aspect of the case, if they decided in favour of sending a delegate to Stockholm, we should consent to their going; but in order that the Government might officially dissociate itself from the conference, I suggested that no member of the Government should form part of the delegation, even including myself. The suggestion with regard to the announcement of the legal aspect of the case was the subject of discussion between my labour colleagues in the Government the same evening. I found for one reason or another they were unanimously opposed to any statement with regard to the legal aspect of the case being made before the Conference. I want to say quite frankly that as they were unanimous I at once weighed the position that I had taken up earlier in the evening with the Prime Minister on that aspect of the case, and I telephoned immediately after they had intimated their unanimous decision intimating to him that on the legal aspect of the case we were unanimous that no announcement should be made before the conference, but that the conference should be left absolutely free from Government influence to come to a decision. This aspect of the case came before the Cabinet the following morning. I again put in the decision that I had reported to the Prime Minister over the telephone the evening before. The legal aspect was again discussed, and notwithstanding the intimation that I had made on behalf of my labour colleagues, a decision was taken that an announcement would be made on the question that was then on the Order Paper in the name of the hon. Baronet who represents Blackburn (Sir H. Norman) that in reply to that question then on the Order Paper the Government should state the legal aspect of the case, with a further intimation that the matter did not alone concern the British Government, and that a full statement would be made to the House to-day.

That was the last Cabinet decision on this question that I know anything about, because I think I am right in saying I have not attended a Cabinet since. I believe I am right in saying that, although owing to pressure of work, I have not been able to follow the answers to questions, I believe I am right in saying that that decision, as come to that morning, was not reported to the House, and unless it has been reported to the House to-day, a decision that was reached that day whilst I was there that it should be announced, that decision was not carried out. The reason why it was not carried out has never in any syllable been reported to me by the Prime Minister or any of his colleagues. I have done my best, Mr. Speaker, to deal with this aspect of the case in chronological order, and I want to make one very emphatic statement. I want to say that during the whole of the time I have referred to in my speech I never hinted to any of my colleagues, either collectively or individually, that I was going to do otherwise than continue the course to which I had committed myself, as I stated in this House on 1st August. Moreover, during the whole of this time no request was made that I should state the position for the Government at the Labour party conference, and what is more, having regard to all that had gone on, having regard to the advice that I myself had given, having regard to the fact that that advice had been placed on the agenda paper of the Conference that had been sent out when the invitations were published, if such a request had been made definitely, as I think it ought to have been very definitely and very clearly, then there would have been no alternative for me but to have definitely tendered the Government my resignation.

This brings me to the very strange proceeding on the part of the Prime Minister of issuing to the Press a letter that appeared in the late editions of Saturday night, certainly the Press of yesterday and to-day. In that letter the question is very definitely put why it was, knowing as I did the views of my colleagues, I did not resign. I want to face that issue and that challenge, and deal with it as faithfully as it is at all possible. My first reply to the challenge is, I did not do so having regard to the fact that at the special meeting of the Cabinet before going to France, as the Leader of the House has just admitted, I recognised the differences between us, and offered to tender my resignation. Moreover, owing to the unsatisfactory answers that were being given, and had been given ever since I went to Paris with regard to that visit—answers, let me say, that placed me in a false position, because it was being gossiped in the Lobby that Henderson sneaked away to Paris without his colleagues being made aware of the fact that he was going—having regard to these answers, I said to my colleagues in the most emphatic language, "If on this question you want my resignation, you will have to ask for it." It would have been a very fine thing for these questions to have been asked in the early days and answered in the way they were answered.

As the business of that Cabinet has been referred to, I want to say not only was my visit to Paris mentioned, but I want to go further. The fact that the four Russian delegates were going was mentioned, and I ventured to say to my colleagues—and, mark you, I would not have given the history of this Cabinet, I would have mentioned the fact that it was held and nothing more if the Leader of the House had not risen and made the statement he did—that the Russian delegates were going, and I said they were the guests of the Labour party, and it appeared to me that the Government might do well in looking after them to the extent of seeing that they had facilities to get to Boulogne. I was authorised to make the arrangements. I made the arrangements, but, unfortunately, a question was asked about the expenses to Russia, and, in order to make the answers fit, I was invited, through the instrumentality of the Minister of Pensions, conveying a message from the Chancellor of the Exchequer—and these are the people that talk about loyalty to colleagues—that I might see to it that the whole of the money that had been expended should be returned, and the money was returned, and, though I was authorised to look after the Russian delegates, and did look after them up to this moment, their expenses have come out of my own pocket.

I want to go further. I want to deal with this question of resignation. The letter of the Prime Minister would suggest to the public that they did not know that I had ever committed myself on this question of a Stockholm Conference, and that I ought to have resigned. Let us see what would have been the effect of my resigning upon the great Labour Conference that had to be held two or three days afterwards.

It would have shown that there were strong differences, or, in other words, that the Cabinet were opposed to the business. Does not the Prime Minister, of all men, realise that for me to have gone to the Conference as a resigned Minister on the question of Stockholm would only have had one effect? I think my Labour colleagues who are in the Government, and who were so anxious that the Conference should not in any way be influenced by the action of the Government, would be the first to admit that, large as the vote was, it would have been larger if they had felt that I had had to resign. I know what would have been said then. It would not have been admitted that it was a vote on the merits of the question. Oh, no! It would have been said that it was a vote on Henderson's resignation. I will leave the House to judge, having regard to all that I have said, of the course that I have adopted, having once offered my resignation, having told the Government that if they wanted it on Stockholm they would have to ask for it, having made that position unmistakably clear, and having told them that I had advised the executive. I leave the House and the public to judge whether there was anything in the nature of the conduct attributed to me in the letter sent, I think, with undue haste and with a lack of consideration, as it was on Saturday morning.

With regard to the fact that I spoke at the conference as I did. This is a very important question, and the Prime Minister makes the most of it in his letter. He rather gives the impression that I undertook to speak as a member of the Government. I venture to say, if Members will keep in mind the history that I have tried to recite, they will see that it was impossible for me to have done so. If I had done so, I should have had to resign the secretaryship. There is not a shadow of doubt about that. . . . I prepared my case finally on Thursday night and on Friday morning, and I want to claim before this House that I made an honest attempt—and I hope that I shall be able to show that I did so—to put before the conference an accurate summary of the position, even as it affected the Russian Government. May I trouble the House by quoting from the notes that I practically read, because I was so anxious to present the case with all accuracy to the delegates attending the conference:

> So much then for the position as it was when I was in Russia. I desire now to examine the position in order to ascertain how far it remains the same or how far it has been modified.

And this is what I said to the delegates:

> It would be a mistake for us to try to persuade ourselves
> that there has been no change. We are bound to recognise that
> there has been a tremendous change in the position so far as
> Russia is concerned. The Provisional Government which was
> then in office during my stay has been replaced by a new
> Government under the leadership of Kerensky. Such evidence
> as we have, though it is slight, suggests that there has been a
> modification in the Government's attitude towards the Con-
> ference.

I could not quote any Government telegrams. I was speaking as the
secretary of the Labour party. I have been twice reminded since my
resignation that I had no right to quote telegrams without the consent
of His Majesty through a Secretary of State. Therefore, I did not say
anything that I was quoting Government telegrams, but I did say this,
and I honestly think that I lifted the strongest thing from the telegrams:

> The Minister for Foreign Affairs——

I was referring to M. Terestchenko—

> has stated that at the present moment it is impossible to talk of
> peace.

I quoted that on behalf of the Russian Government. Could I have
quoted a stronger statement, mark you, against the case that I was
advising? I was advising the conference to talk of peace, and to talk
of the position, and here was a quotation that this was no time to talk
of peace. In order to put this case frankly and fully I went further,
and quoted the opinion of M. Tseretelli, who was, at the time that I
was in Russia, one of the leading members of the Government, and
who has now returned to the leadership, I think, of the Socialist party.
What did he say? He now declared, with regard to the foreign policy
of their country, that there was no other course save a continuation of
the War till the Russian people had thrown off the shame lying upon
them, and the freedom gained by the Revolution had been duly
secured. Then I am charged with withholding the crucial facts as
affecting the Russian Government. If hon. Members will keep in mind
this very definite statement of the Russian Foreign Minister that at
the present moment it was impossible to talk of peace, and if they will
compare that with the telegram that I was supposed to be withholding,

they will be able to satisfy themselves as to which statement was most material from the standpoint of the Government of Russia. Let me remind the House of the statement I am charged with withholding. Listen to it:

> Although the Russian Government do not deem it impossible [sic] to prevent Russian delegates from taking part in the Stockholm Conference, they regard this Conference as a party concern, and its decisions in no way binding on the liberty of action of the Government.

Now to me the most important part of that statement is that "the decisions will be in no way binding upon the Government." What did I say in trying to put the Russian position, and the position of our own Government if you will, before the conference? On this point I told the conference that there could be no question of negotiating peace terms as the responsibility for this rested solely on the countries engaged in the War. If I had quoted the telegram which I am charged with withholding, how could I have escaped from quoting other telegrams? I could not have quoted the telegram without getting the consent of His Majesty through a Secretary of State. I should have had to invite permission to quote another telegram. I was going to quote that telegram to-day, but, very properly I think, I was informed by the Secretary of State that I could not do so, and I was given a formula which I have accepted. I am not complaining. I am going to read the formula.

The PRIME MINISTER: Hear, hear!
MR. HENDERSON: Just let me read.
        The Russian Government of that date——
That is 2nd August——

> were certainly of opinion that if the Conference was held, Russian Socialists must be allowed to attend, and that if Russian Socialists attended it they would like the Socialists of Allied countries to attend it also, so that the Russian Socialists should not be isolated and the field thus left clear for the Germans.

I said all that in my speech.

> Good observers earnestly hoped that British Socialists would attend the Conference, as they were of opinion that the refusal

to allow British Socialists to attend would expose us to attack and misconception in Russian Socialist circles.

MR. SNOWDEN: Is that the telegram from Russia?

MR. HENDERSON: No, I am going to keep loyal with the permission that I was given. If the hon. Member or any other Member desires to point out any further information, it must come from the Government, and not from myself. Having dealt with this question, it brings me to what I cannot otherwise describe than the most unfortunate position arising out of the Prime Minister's communication to me on Friday. The Press, as is usual on these occasions, have been all—not all, but nearly all—largely on one side. There is no better Press Bureau in this country than the one controlled by the Prime Minister.

MR. PRINGLE: He runs the Press, if he does not run the War.

MR. HENDERSON: Before I resigned I had an overdose; since I have resigned I have had a super-dose; and though I have appealed, as I was bound to do, to the Press and to the public to suspend judgment until I had had an opportunity of stating my case in the only place where such cases ought to be stated—and that is in this House—I have been a subject of a shameful attack, and I say when you take up your newspaper and read at the headlines of charges of breaches of faith, of withholding crucial facts and the comments that have been made upon these things in these articles, I say I have strong ground for complaint. I think that this House ought to have been the judge and the jury, and if the House says that these statements were true after they have been properly made and properly examined and properly replied to, I would have been quite prepared to accept the verdict of the House. Now, it is difficult as you read the papers, to follow exactly what took place. The suggestion has been thrown out that I received a telegram on Friday, the day of the conference, from Kerensky. I want to make it clear exactly what did take place. I understand that a telegram from Kerensky did come. I never received it; I was told at seven o'clock on Friday night, while I was waiting in the Secretary's room at No. 10, Downing Street, that a telegram had been received since the conference closed, through the French Embassy, saying that Kerensky dissociated himself from the conference. I did not receive that telegram. I have not received that telegram yet, and the only knowledge I have of that telegram is the statement made by Professor Mantoux whilst I was waiting in the Secretary's room. He is on the staff of the French Embassy and acts as interpreter. Now, what actually took place regarding the communication from the Prime Minister was this. I am sorry with regard to the misunderstanding arising out of that communication. What took place was this: On Friday, just as the Conference was adjourning at midday—adjourning, dispersing, going away, going where they liked in order to discuss what had taken place in the morning in their separate sections—just as I was leaving the platform an envelope was handed to me which I saw at once was from the Secretary of the Prime Minister. I opened it and I found the telegram, the exact copy of which I had had before me, and to which I have already referred, when I was preparing my speech on the Thursday night and on the Friday morning. I had a little time during the adjournment. We adjourned, I think, at twelve, and had to reassemble at two. I had my lunch to get and one or two things to attend to, but I did try to write to the Prime Minister and return him his document, and in my hurry—I am quite prepared to admit that in my hurry I did perhaps not fully explain the position. But I did say that I had informed the conference that there had been a modification in the position taken up by the new Government as compared with the old Russian Government. I am not going to take that matter further. Whatever be the verdict of the House upon this statement, I am prepared to claim, and claim most emphatically— claim now and claim at any time hereafter—that the last intention I had—and I hope that hon. Members in all parts of the House will accept it—that the last intention I had was the intention of withholding any information that I was legally entitled to use from the conference. I ought, in fairness to myself, to say that some of the delegates claimed that after I had concluded my speech they could not but think that, whilst I had advised in one direction, my speech was an overwhelming case against going to Stockholm. So it is very difficult to understand why, if I made such a speech, that those who heard it thought the speech was against the conclusion I myself said I had reached, and it is somewhat surprising that the charge should have been preferred that I had withheld information against the interests of the Russian Government. I have trespassed at considerable length upon the patience of the House, and I said at the beginning of my speech, as I said in my statement which I issued to the public on Saturday, that in anything I had to say at this juncture I would have to have regard to the national interest. I have tried faithfully to deal only with any question that might affect the national interest, because of the serious aspersions made upon my own honour in the Press and in the letter sent to the Press by the Prime Minister. I understand now that as the Government have moved the Adjournment of the House the whole question may be fully considered. I wish with all my heart that such a Debate could have been impossible. I have not told the full story of this Stockholm business. I do not intend to tell the full story of this Stockholm business.

MR. HOGGE: Why not?

MR. HENDERSON: Because I believe honestly, in the interests of the nation in this great crisis, it is highly inadvisable that that story should be told at this moment. To adopt any other course, to follow the course of a general Debate at this moment, I want to warn the House, means opening up questions regarding this Stockholm Conference that have been hanging over for several months, and in view of the evidence of unrest in the country, in view of the difficulty that I believe the Government will have to face before this Stockholm Conference question is finally disposed of—

MR. SNOWDEN: Hear, hear!

MR. HENDERSON: I think it is highly inadvisable, in the public interest, that this question should be opened up any more than is necessary for those who have been forced to clear themselves of the charges made. My last word is as I have said in the letter to the Prime Minister. The House knows my desire to see this War carried to a successful conclusion. I have endeavoured—though I claim it for myself—I have endeavoured ever since the War began, at great risk occasionally, at great risk in the ranks of my own movement, to do only that which I thought would lead to victory for the Allied cause and for a lasting and honourable, and, I hope, a people's peace. It is because of that that I deeply deplore the necessity for saying some of the things I have been compelled to say to-day, and I wish to repeat that the moderate position I have taken up in the brief letter I sent to the Prime Minister could have been reciprocated, for that course, in my judgment, would have been in the best interests of the nation, and I have been compelled to make this statement in self-defence against gratuitous attacks upon my honour. I am now content to leave the matter with the House and the public.

The PRIME MINISTER: Whatever anyone in the House may think about the major part of my right hon. Friend's speech I am sure they will respond to the last appeal he made for unity in the securing of victory for this country, but with regard to about three-fourths of his speech I think I should consult the interests and the wishes of the

House by not making any comments upon them because they are not in the least relevant to the great issues that have arisen. I do not wish to use the word "triviality," but they are not issues which are large enough to merit the attention of the House—for instance, as to whether my right hon. Friend had been kept waiting for an hour. I can assure him that we were anxious to treat him with every possible courtesy. After hearing my right hon. Friend's speech I am not sure it is necessary for me to say anything more than repeat the statements which have already been made in the public Press.

They have been challenged categorically by him in respect to one matter. My right hon. Friend says that he never gave any indication to any of his colleagues of any change in his mind, or opinion, or intentions with regard to Stockholm. All I can say upon that is that I have seen every member of the Cabinet who was present on the day of that discussion. I have asked each of them what impression was left on his mind, and the impression of each is identical with that left on my mind. It was that my right hon. Friend had made up his mind, for reasons which were indicated to us, that he would use the whole of his influence to turn down the Stockholm Conference at the Friday meeting. There is not a member whom I have consulted—and there are two or three of them present here to-day—whose memory is not identical with my own. My right hon. Friend had about an hour's conversation with me on Tuesday, and that is the impression he left on my mind. The two reasons which induced him to change his mind were, first of all, the opinion of the Attorney-General that it would be illegal for British subjects during war-time to meet the enemy, and the second was the change that had taken place in Russia itself, which had influenced not merely his own mind, but the minds of some of the French delegates with whom he as well as myself came into contact during their visit here. That was the impression left on the mind of every member of the Cabinet who heard what my right hon. Friend said on Tuesday.

Mr. HENDERSON: Will the right hon. Gentleman quote the Cabinet minute on the subject?

The PRIME MINISTER: I have not got the Cabinet minute here, but I could quote some of the words my right hon. Friend used, and which were recorded. I have refreshed my memory by referring to the actual discussion that took place in the Cabinet, and no man reading that discussion could come to any other conclusion than the conclusion to which we all individually and collectively came—that my right hon. Friend had made up his mind on Friday to turn down the Stockholm Conference.

MR. HENDERSON: Did I say so? Is there a record in the Cabinet minutes?

MR. PRINGLE: Did he say so?

The PRIME MINISTER: Certainly.

MR. HENDERSON: I want to ask the right hon. Gentleman if I made the statement that I was going to do other on Friday than what I had done at the executive, and if there is a record of that statement in the Cabinet minute?

The PRIME MINISTER: We have got a record of the Cabinet minute. A discussion took place, and undoubtedly that was the effect of the words used by my right hon. Friend on Tuesday, and on Wednesday morning, and of the words which he used to me on Tuesday. May I just point this out to my right hon. Friend? What is the meaning of his letter——

MR. HENDERSON: May I ask the right hon. Gentleman a question? I have referred to the conversation on Tuesday. May I ask the right hon. Gentleman, in view of what he is now stating, whether I did make to him the suggestion that it would be best, if the Labour Conference decided to go to Stockholm, that we should allow the delegates to go, but that no member of the Government should be included in the delegation?

The PRIME MINISTER: I have no recollection of that. I know my right hon. Friend suggested in the course of various discussions I had with him that he should not go, but that delegates should go. I said that so far as I was concerned I should not assent either to his going or to any delegate going representing the people of this country.

MR. HENDERSON: I have admitted in my speech that was the position of the Government, but I want to ask the Prime Minister when the conversation took place that he referred to, because he tells the public we had several. I say we had one, the one he is now referring to, and he says I had mentioned these words to him more than once. Will he tell the House when we had the other conversations?

The PRIME MINISTER: I cannot now, but I can tell my right hon. Friend that the most important conversation was the one we had on Tuesday. What I want to put to the House——

MR. HENDERSON: But will the right hon. Gentleman——

MR. SPEAKER: The Prime Minister is in possession of the House.

The PRIME MINISTER: It is not a very pleasant matter to have differences of opinion of this kind with colleagues. All I can say is this —and I want the House and the country to realise it—that the impression left on the minds of eight persons, some of them members of the Cabinet, and some who are not members of the Cabinet but who were present, who have each of them been seen individually by me —the impression left on their minds no doubt that the statement of my right hon. Friend was that on Friday he meant to turn down the Stockholm Conference. After all, eight men would not have had that impression unless there was justification for their coming to that conclusion. The same impression was left on the minds of the right hon. Gentleman's Labour colleagues in the Ministry, who had seen him separately. May I call my right hon. Friend's attention to the actual terms of his letter—the letter he wrote to me after he had made this speech.

> I think I ought to inform you that after the most careful consideration I came to the conclusion that I could take no other course than to stand by the advice I had given the day after my return from Russia.

If we were all under the impression that he had always been of that mind, that that was the course he intended to take right through, what was the point of his writing that to me? As a matter of fact, my right hon. Friend refers to the Press. There were statements in two newspapers on Friday morning that my right hon. Friend intended taking this course, the course which he did take.

Mr. HENDERSON: On a point of Order, may I say that this statement had to be made to the Press because of a statement that went round the previous day's issues of the Press that I had changed my mind.

The PRIME MINISTER: Here are statements that appear in the Press. My right hon. Friend says he thought it was necessary to communicate to the Press, in order to correct a false impression. It was with surprise that I read them. I did not believe them, neither did my colleagues believe them, because we had been given the other impression. What I want to know is this. Here were statements given on Thursday to the Press. [An HON. MEMBER: "Who gave them?"] My right hon. Friend says he thought it necessary to do so in his own defence. Why were they not given to the Cabinet? Why was not I told? Why were not my colleagues told? It would have made a very considerable difference. What difference would it have made? It would have made this difference: That, in the first place, my right hon. Friend could not have gone to that conference to declare, not only as Secretary to the Labour party, but as a member of the body responsible for the direction of the War, his opinion that we ought in the interests of Russia to send delegates to Stockholm. My right hon. Friend says that, if the Labour conference on Friday had known that the War Cabinet took a different view, the vote would have been overwhelming. What does that mean? Is it really conceivable—I do not believe it—that the responsible Labour leaders of the kingdom, knowing that those who are responsible for the conduct of the War thought it was a dangerous expedient under present conditions in Russia to send delegates to Stockholm, knowing that those who are responsible for the direction of the War in France, in Italy, and in the United States took that opinion—is it conceivable that, having heard that, they would flout it by a bigger majority? I say it is really an insult to intelligent people to ask them to believe that. . . . Without quoting any secret information, it is obvious to everyone who reads the newspapers about what is taking place in Russia that there has been a most drastic change in the whole policy of the Government in Russia. There has been an end put to the fraternisation which has destroyed the morale of the Russian Army. There have been most drastic changes, introduced with a view to restoring the fighting efficiency of the Army, to make it a better fighting machine, and to restore discipline. Naturally, under these conditions there would be a different feeling with regard to holding a fraternising Conference with the enemy. What was the meaning of that telegram which came on Thursday? No one can read the telegram without seeing the change that had taken place. Under the old conditions the Russian Government was supposed to be not merely in favour of the Conference, but to be promoting it. What did this telegram mean? It meant that as far as they were concerned they as a Government had nothing whatever to do with the Conference, but they felt that they could not possibly prevent delegates from attending it. Let anyone read that telegram and see what a difference there is between the attitude of the Russian Government as to Stockholm——

MR. HOGGE: From whom is the telegram?

The PRIME MINISTER: From the Russian Government. Then there are the concluding words of the covering letter.

MR. SNOWDEN: Who wrote that?

The PRIME MINISTER: I am not going to say. It is enough to say that it came from the Russian Embassy. Let the House remember what the words were which I quoted in my letter—that he hastened to send this to the Government, because there was an attempt being made to create the impression in this country that the Russian Government was anxious to get this Conference. Does anybody imagine that if that document had been read to the conference on Friday it would not have made a great difference? Let the House remember what was said on Friday. The hon. Member for Leicester (Mr. Ramsay MacDonald),

> after welcoming Mr. Henderson into another fellowship, said my hon. Friend the member for South-West Ham asked: Did Kerensky invite the Powers?
>
> Mr. MacDonald: Yes, he did. Mr. Kerensky's view is that the Conference at Stockholm is absolutely necessary if his hands are to be strengthened.
>
> Mr. Will Thorne: I wish Kerensky were here to repudiate that.
>
> Mr. MacDonald: Nothing would have delighted me more than to have him here alongside me.

Those are the statements that influenced the conference on Friday —the belief not that the Russian Government found it impossible to prevent delegates going there, but the belief that the great leader of the Russian democracy was anxious that there should be a conference in order to strengthen his hands. Could anyone have believed that after reading that telegram? That is the point of the telegram. My right hon. Friend says he did not get it in time. All I can say is that it was sent in time, and if it did not reach his hands before he was due to leave the platform I do not know how to explain it. But that is not enough. My right hon. Friend had this telegram himself on Thursday night. He, in his letter to me, said he had already read it.

MR. HENDERSON: I told the House so.

The PRIME MINISTER: So it was not necessary that he should have had it from me. Besides, he read my communication before the vote was taken. I think it would have been right to the delegates, who were coming to a very important decision on the representation that the Russian Government were anxious to have this conference, for him to get up and say, "A communication was received last night from the Russian Government to say that it was a party concern, and they would have nothing to do with it." Why was not that done? I think I have dealt with the two facts which I put in my letter. The first is

that my right hon. Friend had given us the impression that he was
going to take a different line on Friday. That is the impression of the
eight men who were present at the Cabinet discussion. It is the impression of his Labour colleagues, and it is borne out by that statement in his letter, written after he delivered his speech. I come to the
second point, that my right hon. Friend had my communication from
the Russian Government which made it clear that, at any rate, they
were not promoting the conference and that the only view they took
was that if there were a conference they could not prevent delegates
from going there. Although my right hon. Friend had it in his possession on Thursday, he never gave that impression to the conference.
He did not read it, although he had a personal request from me to do
so, and he had my personal request in his possession before the vote
was taken. That was a telegram which would have made a substantial
difference in the views of, I say, the vast majority of those who were
present at that meeting.

MR. SNOWDEN: Take another vote, and see!

The PRIME MINISTER: With regard to the general position, I have
only one thing to say. Whatever may have been my right hon. Friend's
views about the conference when those who were promoting it were
practically in complete command, he himself admitted that there was
a change within the last few days when efforts were being made to
restore the discipline of the Army. Nothing could be more fatal to
those conditions than to hold conferences with the enemy at the very
moment when the first step in the restoration of discipline is to prevent fraternisation with the enemy on the Russian front. That is the
conclusion to which four Allied Governments have come. I had rather
not say anything for the moment about the opinion of the Russian
Government itself; it has got its difficulties. The United States of
America have decided that they cannot allow delegates to go there.
That is a great democracy, a great Republic. The French Republic,
they have come to the same conclusion. Italy has come to the same
conclusion. The British Government have come to the same conclusion. The four Allied countries have come definitely to the conclusion
that if peace terms are to be discussed, they must be discussed by the
representatives of a whole nation and not merely a section. I am the
last man to disparage the power of Labour. I am the last man to say
anything derogatory to their influence and to their weight and their
power in the community, but they are not the whole community.
When peace comes to be made, it must be made by the nation as a

whole. In Russia there is a Socialist Government; at any rate, it is a Government the majority of whose members are Socialists. It is a Socialist Government that has got the whole of the facts, and when you come to get peace terms to discuss you must not merely have the authority of representatives of the nation, but you must have those representatives in full possession of all the fatcs which enable you to come to a decision upon the subject. To have a sectional discussion of peace, whatever may be said about that being necessary in order to preserve unity with Russia, when it becomes clear that the Russian Government have no responsibility for the Stockholm Conference, I say we should not be doing our duty to the Alliance, but we should be doing our duty least of all to Russia in her difficulties if we were to countenance such a project.

The Russian Government's Attitude

(Henderson, back in England, went before the Labour Party Conference on August 10 (N.S.) to recommend it accept the Stockholm invitation, which it did by an overwhelming majority. In the meantime, Nabokov had received, at his request, a telegraphed statement from Tereshchenko that "although the Russian Government does not deem it possible to prevent Russian delegates from taking part in the Stockholm Conference, they regard this Conference as a party concern and its decisions in no wise binding upon the liberty of action of the Government." With Tereshchenko's authorization, the text of this note was communicated to Arthur Balfour, who laid it before the Cabinet, including Henderson. When Henderson made no reference to it in his speech before the Conference, Lloyd George, who had asked that he do so, requested and received Henderson's resignation from the War Cabinet, publishing the correspondence between them in the press. In his letter accepting the resignation, Lloyd George quoted the above excerpt from Tereshchenko's telegram, having received permission to do so from Nabokov on Nabokov's own initiative. Lloyd George had also received a telegram from Thomas in Paris that "Kerensky ne veut

An excerpt from *Daily Review of the Foreign Press* (Moscow), Ser. 4, No. 14, August 17, 1917, reprinted from *The Russian Provisional Government 1917*, Vol. II, pp. 1183–5, documents selected and edited by Robert Paul Browder and Alexander F. Kerensky, with the permission of the publishers, Stanford University Press. © 1961 by the Board of Trustees of the Leland Stanford Junior University.

pas de Conférence." The source of Thomas' information is not clear.

These revelations, plus the decision of the British Government, announced on August 13 (N.S.), that it would not issue passports to the Stockholm delegates, caused considerable excitement in Russia and embarrassment to the Provisional Government, as the following documents indicate. [R.P.B. & A.F.K.])

With regard to the statements which have appeared in the foreign newspapers on the subject of the Provisional Government's attitude towards the Stockholm Conference, the following statement is made (Aug. 15) from an authoritative source:—

"The Provisional Government considers that the solution of questions affecting war and peace appertains exclusively to it, in union with the Governments of the Allied countries, supported by the Allied democracies.

"The Socialist conference at Stockholm, as the Russian Government has pointed out on various occasions, is a conference of particular political parties, and, as such, can lay no claim to formulate decisions which could in any way bind the Government.

"The Government has always been far from intending to refuse Russian Socialists passports for Stockholm, its view being that it is useful that questions concerning war and peace should be submitted for discussion to the Socialist Internationale, and in the person of the Prime Minister as well as of the Minister for Foreign Affairs, has similarly informed the Allied Governments that it considers it undesirable to raise any obstacles whatever to the participation of Socialist organisations in the Conference.

"Nevertheless, while not denying the political bearing of the Socialist Conference with a view to the clearing up of the fundamental questions which have been raised by the war, the Provisional Government cannot admit that the decisions formulated by the conference can have a character which must exclusively and solely beyond [sic] to the decisions of the Allied Governments."

In this connection it may be noted that Kerensky stated, in the course of an interview with a British journalist, when asked if it were true that he was opposed to the Stockholm Conference:—

"There has been serious misunderstanding. They are drawing a wrong deduction from our Note. We meant simply to state our position. We are a Coalition Government and, therefore, since the Conference is a party matter, we cannot, as a Coalition, be bound by its decisions. Our Conference, the Conference of Governments, is the London Conference. [The Inter-Allied Conference, scheduled for the fall, was later shifted to Paris.] The Swedish Conference is a conference of Labour Parties. That is all we wished to say. That does not mean we are opposed to it. It is not our business to be opposed to it or in favour of it."

I said: "But it has been said that M. Albert Thomas declared you said that you personally are opposed to the Stockholm Conference."

"Nothing of the sort. I think it of great importance, although personally I think it would have been of greater importance if it had taken place while we were advancing instead of it in the present conditions. But I am not opposed to it. No. I have insisted again and again that any opposition offered to it by the Allied Governments, any difficulties put in the way of the delegates, is simply playing into the Germans' hands." . . .

"Say this. Say that the Russian Government regards the Swedish Conference exactly as you regard it—that is as a Conference not of Governments but of parties. As a Coalition Government we can be neither for nor against the Conference called by one of the parties which are in coalition. For that reason, personally as President of the Coalition, I have made no speeches about it. But we consider that no obstacles should be put in the way of it, and we shall regard the Conference itself as an extremely important and significant expression of public opinion. It is an entirely wrong deduction to say that we are opposed to the Conference."

G. D. H. COLE

The Labour Party During Stockholm

A new phase of the first World War began in December, 1916, with the formation of the Lloyd George Coalition. On November 19, President Wilson had addressed a Peace Note to the warring Powers; and on December 18, soon after the change of Government in Great Britain, German Peace Proposals were received from the American Ambassador in London. Two days later, an Amercan Note to the

From G. D. H. Cole, *A History of the Labour Party from 1914,* London, Routledge & Kegan Paul, Ltd., 1948, pp. 31–44. Reprinted by permission of the publisher.

British Government suggested that it should formulate its war aims with a view to a negotiated peace. The Allied answer was sent on 30th December, banging the door; but in effect the decision had been made, as far as Great Britain was concerned, when Lloyd George overthrew the Asquith Coalition. The very basis of the new Government's policy was that the war should be fought out to the bitter end, even if some of those who supported Labour's entry into the new Coalition were far from realising the truth. Little more than three months after the sending of the Allied answer, the pursuance of the campaign of "unrestricted" submarine warfare by Germany brought the United States into the war.

In the meantime, while peace talk, however unreal, was in the air, the Labour movement had begun thinking seriously about post-war problems. On March 6, 1917, a Labour Party deputation visited Lloyd George to present to him the resolutions on domestic reconstruction passed by the Party Conference in January. These resolutions, drafted by Sidney Webb, were largely based on a series of reports prepared during 1916 by the War Emergency Workers' National Committee. It was in reply to these resolutions, which dealt with the post-war use of war factories, the prevention of unemployment, the nationalisation of mines and railways, the assurance of a living wage, and a number of other economic questions, that Lloyd George uttered his characteristic, but hollow, incitement to the Labour deputation to be "audacious." "I am not afraid," he said, "of the audacity of these proposals. I believe the settlement after the war will succeed in proportion to its audacity. . . . If I could have presumed to be the adviser of the working classes . . . I should say to them, Audacity is the thing for you."

That, of course, was said before the Revolution in Russia; and Lloyd George was careful to give no specific approval to the Labour deputation's individual proposals. There was nothing that he could be held to afterwards, when the issues actually arose. He was simply bidding for Labour support for the measures which he regarded as necessary for military victory, in the knowledge that there would be no victory if the Labour front were to crack.

Within a month or two further combing out of the war factories for the armed forces and the extension of dilution, coupled with grievances especially among skilled workers who, tied to their skilled jobs, saw unskilled "dilutees" earning higher wages than they were allowed to receive, led to a sequence of strikes, culminating in the widespread "May Strikes" under the leadership of the now nation-wide Shop Stewards' Movement. This agitation was at an early stage when, on March 12, 1917, the first Russian Revolution broke out, leading to the enforced abdication of the Czar and to the attempt to carry on with a moderate Liberal Government under the leadership of Prince Lvov. This Revolution had an immense effect on Labour opinion. Most Labour men had been uneasy at the war alliance with the re-actionary Czarist Government; and the Revolution was hailed as a grand liberation for the consciences of Allied Socialists as well as for the Russian peoples. Moreover, the Russian workers, feeling for the most part no sort of obligation to carry on the Czarist war policy and aware besides that the whole country was on the verge of military as well as of economic collapse, at once began to demand a negotiated peace, and to urge the Socialists of the belligerent countries to force a peace policy upon their several Governments. These sentiments added to the enthusiasm of the elements in the British Labour movement that were hostile to Lloyd George's war policy; and there went up from the Labour left wing a demand that the British workers should form Workers' and Soldiers' Councils on the Russian model and should take the task of making peace and re-making Great Britain into their own hands. At the unofficial Leeds Conference of June 3, 1917, organised by George Lansbury's *Herald* followers in conjunc-tion with nearly all the left-wing groups, delegates saw the incon-gruous spectacle of Ramsay MacDonald, Snowden, and other I.L.P. leaders making flamboyant speeches to the cheers of revolutionary shop stewards and other left-wing Socialists of whose behaviour they at bottom thoroughly disapproved. The Conference decided in favour of the formation of local Workers' and Soldiers' Councils throughout the country, with purposes that were but vaguely defined. But when the shouting was over, nothing much happened. Neither the Labour Party nor the Trades Union Congress would have anything to say to the doings at Leeds. The Labour Party kept its place in the Coalition Government; and when the Government had appointed, in June, a number of Commissions on Industrial Unrest, to report upon the causes of the May strikes and the troubled state of the country, there was a pause, during which the Whitley Committee issued its first Report on the Relations between Employers and Employed, recom-mending the establishment of Joint Industrial Councils, and the Government announced the setting up of a Ministry of Reconstruction to prepare the way for the post-war settlement of home affairs.

The pause was short. Early in 1917 the Scandinavian-Dutch Committee of neutral Socialists under Branting's chairmanship had begun to make tentative preparations for the calling at Stockholm of an International Socialist Conference, to include the Socialists of the belligerent countries, with the object of laying down peace terms which the workers' organisations would then proceed to force upon their respective Governments. After the first Russian Revolution, the Russian Workers' and Soldiers' Councils took up the cry, and demanded a Conference at Stockholm to reach decisions which should become binding upon all the Socialist and Labour Parties throughout the world. In May the Labour Party, sharply divided on the Stockholm issue, decided to send a delegation—G. H. Roberts, William Carter of the Miners' Federation, and Ramsay MacDonald—to Russia to explore the situation with the Russian Socialists and to report back on the line which the Party should take. At this point the Russian Government fell, and was replaced by a semi-Socialist Government under Kerensky's leadership, which proceeded to ask for an Allied Conference for the discussion of war aims, while maintaining an ambiguous attitude to the proposal of the Workers' and Soldiers' Councils for an all-in Socialist Conference. The British Government thereupon decided to send Arthur Henderson on a special mission to Russia, to report on the situation and to suggest the steps necessary to keep the Russians from making a separate peace. Henderson, from Petrograd, cabled advising that MacDonald should be allowed to go to Russia; and the Government at length issued passports to the Labour delegation—which was, however stopped at Aberdeen by the refusal of Havelock Wilson's Sailors' and Firemen's Union to allow MacDonald to proceed.

In June, while Henderson was in Russia, the Kerensky Government, under strong pressure from London and Paris, launched its ill-fated offensive against the Germans, only to be faced almost at once with the collapse of its forces owing to lack of transport, munitions, and other supplies—to say nothing of the sheer war-weariness of most of the Russian soldiers. The collapse came while Henderson was on his way home, fully convinced that the Russians were in no mood or condition to follow Lloyd George's "fight-to-a-finish" exhortations, and that, in order to prevent a separate peace, it was essential for the

Allied Governments to allow the Stockholm Conference to be held, and to use it as a means of fostering the peace movement inside Germany and of bringing pressure from within upon the German Government.

An extraordinary series of confusions, cross-purposes, and mutual recriminations followed Arthur Henderson's return from Russia. In his absence, the leaders of the Labour Party had been debating the Stockholm invitation without reaching any decision, but with a tendency for those who supported war to the bitter end to be hostile. Henderson, on his way back, had met a group of Russian delegates who were on their way to England; and these delegates now joined their voices to his in pressing that the invitation should be accepted. Indeed, they wanted the Stockholm Conference, in accordance with the terms of the original invitation, to be authorised to arrive at binding decisions, whereas Henderson (and Albert Thomas in France) favoured only a consultative conference. Henderson, even with this reinforcement, found difficulty with his own Executive; and it was decided that he, MacDonald and G. J. Wardle, the Acting Chairman of the Parliamentary Party, should go to Paris to talk matters over with the French Socialists before any decision was taken, and that the question of going or not going to Stockholm should be decided by a specially summoned Labour Conference in the light of the results of this visit.

Henderson, however, had to reckon not only with the Labour Party and the Trade Unions, but also with his colleagues in the War Cabinet. When he got back from Russia, Lloyd George was absent in France; and when he reported to the other members that he proposed to support the Stockholm project he found them solidly hostile—so much so that he proffered his resignation, which, with Lloyd George away, they were not in a position to accept. Lloyd George, who had at an earlier point been converted to the Stockholm proposal, had now changed his mind and, on his return, had high words with Henderson. This was partly because Henderson's visit to Paris in company with MacDonald had been widely denounced in the press as a pacifist manoeuvre; but it was even more because Lloyd George had come back from his consultations with the French in a new mood, and was dallying with the idea of allowing Germany to do what it pleased with Russia, provided that the other Allies got all they wanted. The last thing the Prime Minister desired just then was to be faced with a set of War Aims accepted by the Russian, French and British Socialists—and perhaps by the German Socialists as well—and to be forced to define the Government's attitude to these aims.

Henderson, however, had fully made up his mind. At Paris, he had secured, with a good deal of difficulty, agreement that the Stockholm Conference should be regarded only as consultative, and not as mandatory; and on these terms he was determined to proceed, whether the War Cabinet approved or disapproved, if only he could get his own party to agree. When the emergency Labour Conference met, on August 10, 1917, to decide the issue, Henderson argued strongly for Stockholm, and was able to secure a large majority vote in its favour —1,846,000 to 550,000—which means that most of the big Trade Unions voted on his side. There was, however, an important and even destructive rider; for the Labour Conference also voted, on the motion of the Miners' Federation, that the British delegation to Stockholm should consist entirely of nominees of the Labour Party and the Trades Union Congress, and that the other bodies affiliated to the International Socialist Bureau—the I.L.P., B.S.P. and Fabian Society —should not be allowed to send independent delegates, though it was of course open to the Labour Party to include some of their members among its own delegation. This resolution ran directly counter to the terms of the Stockholm invitation, which had insisted on the representation of minority as well as majority groups from each country invited; and it drew emphatic protests both from the I.L.P. and from the Russian delegates in England.

For the moment, however, this awkward problem was pushed into the background by the news that Henderson had resigned—or rather had been forced to resign—from the War Cabinet. This was a sequel to the celebrated "doormat" incident of August 1, 1917, when Henderson, on his return from Paris, was kept waiting outside the Cabinet room while that body, with G. N. Barnes taking his place (as he had done during Henderson's Russian visit) discussed his iniquity in persisting with the Stockholm project and in going to Paris to discuss it with the French Socialists in MacDonald's company. The public—and even Henderson's Labour colleagues—knew nothing of this incident at the time; nor did they know that during the ten days between the incident and the Labour Conference there had been pressure on Henderson from more than one quarter, or that the Government had at least half made up its mind to refuse passports to any British delegates who might be sent to Stockholm by the Labour Conference. All this came out only later: the delegates who voted for Stockholm on August 10 had no idea that their representatives would be refused permission to go or that Henderson's position in the Cabinet was at stake. And it appears that, up to the very last moment, Lloyd George himself had hoped, or even expected, both that Henderson would withdraw his proposal and that, if he did not, the Labour Conference would turn it down.

The Labour Conference's decision, procured largely by Henderson's advocacy, made his position in the Cabinet untenable; and he resigned in justifiable anger at his colleagues' treatment of him, and particularly at Lloyd George's tergiversations. This, however, did not mean that the Labour Party came out of the Coalition, or that Henderson tried to bring it out. On the contrary, G. N. Barnes was allowed to take his place in the War Cabinet without protest, and outwardly Labour's place in the Coalition remained unaffected by the withdrawal of its leader, who automatically resumed his position both as Secretary to the Party and as Leader in the House of Commons. He soon, however, asked for release from the parliamentary leadership, on the plea that he wanted to devote all his energies to reorganising the party machine with a view to the post-war struggle, but also because, in his new position as leader of an anti-government group working for the resumption of international Socialist relations, he found the position of parliamentary leader difficult and hampering. Wardle, the previous Acting Leader, had joined the Government on Henderson's resignation, and the Parliamentary Party chose the innocuous William Adamson, of the Scottish Miners, as Chairman and Leader in Henderson's place.

The decisions of August 11 had not in fact settled the Stockholm issue. The Miners' resolution concerning the choice of delegates had led to an impasse, as the Conference had no power to exclude the Socialist Societies from appointing delegates to Stockholm if they wished. The Conference had therefore decided to adjourn until August 21, in order to give time for the Executive to deal with the situation, and to meet again on that date for the purpose of choosing its delegates. The Russians and the Branting Committee in Stockholm were strongly opposed to the exclusion of minority representation; whereas a strong Trade Union group in Great Britain was determined to wreck the Conference rather than allow the I.L.P. and the B.S.P. to be represented at it. Between August 10 and August 21 a furious controversy raged both in the Labour movement and in the Press over the whole

Stockholm issue; and it became plain that when the Conference reassembled the basic decision to send delegates would be again challenged.

It was challenged, to such effect that the resumed Conference, while agreeing to protest against the Government's decision to refuse passports, carried the proposal to send delegates only by the tiny margin of 1,234,000 votes to 1,231,000, and, in spite of the Executive's pleadings, reaffirmed by a large majority its ban on delegates attending on behalf of the Socialist bodies. This was carried by 2,124,000 against a mere 175,000.

These votes were in effect the end of Stockholm—for they had their parallel in France. The Inter-Allied Socialist Conference which met in London on August 28, and had been intended to carry an agreed policy for presentation at Stockholm, in effect broke down in face of keen disagreements. A majority there insisted on minority representation as *sine qua non;* and there was a babel of voices for and against every possible attitude. The British delegation had prepared a statement of Allied War Aims, which had been approved by the Conference of August 11; but even this failed to secure endorsement, though it was agreed by a narrow majority to set up an Inter-Allied Committee to draft an amended statement for presentation to a further Allied Conference. Thus, what came out of it all was not a Socialist Conference, to be attended by neutrals and by belligerents on both sides, but only a prospect of a further Allied Socialist Conference, at a date still to be settled, at which Allied Socialist differences would be further debated and, if possible, reconciled. The Stockholm proposal was dead, though it still stood as formally approved, some months before the Bolshevik Revolution altered the entire face of International Socialist relations.

It is easy enough to see now that there was never much, real chance of success for the Stockholm project. The Trades Union Congress in September, 1917, wrote its epitaph by declaring that the Conference, however desirable, "at the present moment could not be successful." The T.U.C.'s Parliamentary Committee expressed the view that "general agreement of aim amongst the working classes of the Allied Nations" was "a fundamental condition of a successful International Congress"—and such agreement clearly did not exist. At the same time the Trades Union Congress declared emphatically in favour of an International Congress as "a necessary preliminary to the conclu-

sion of a lasting and democratic peace," and instructed its Committee
to work with this object in view. But it also re-affirmed that "the
voting shall be by nationalities, sectional bodies within nationalities
to be governed by the majority of the nationality," or that, if minority
delegations were allowed, "each section should be given voting power
according to the number of persons actually represented"—i.e., that
the I.L.P. and B.S.P. should have only their 40,000 or so votes as
against the millions of the Labour Party and the T.U.C.

For a month or two after the burial of the Stockholm project the
main centre of interest shifted back to home affairs, which had been
temporarily overshadowed. Unrest was still widespread among the
munition workers; and in September the local Shop Stewards' Committees came definitely together into a Shop Stewards' National
Committee. The Reports of the Commissions on Labour Unrest were
followed, in October, by the abolition of the Leaving Certificates
which had been so acute a source of grievance, and by the concession
of a wage bonus of 12½ per cent to skilled time-workers in the munitions industries, in order to bring their earnings up to a better relative
level. Unfortunately for the success of this concession, the problem of
defining a "skilled worker" gave rise to so much difficulty that presently the bonus had to be granted to unskilled men as well, where they
were on time-work; and this in turn upset the piece-workers, who had
to be given 7½ per cent to keep them quiet. The entire purpose of
the original grant was thus defeated; but for a little while the hubbub
over the bonus took the attention of the shop stewards—the most
militant section of the Trade Unions—off political issues.

Their attention was sharply recalled in November—by the Bolshevik
Revolution, which was speedily followed by the announcement that
peace negotiations were to be opened between Russia and Germany.
On the heels of this announcement came Lord Lansdowne's letter,
proposing a negotiated peace, and the publication by the Bolsheviks
(and the republication in the *Manchester Guardian* in December) of
the hitherto unknown, though not unsuspected, secret treaties made
among the Allies in 1915. Before this, early in December, President
Wilson had addressed to the United States Congress the first of his
famous Messages on War Aims. Despite the failure of the Stockholm
project, peace talk was in the air. The German Reichstag had passed
its peace resolution in July, and though the new German Government
under Michaelis was in effect controlled by the High Command and

not by the Reichstag, it began to seem possible that the advocates of a fight to the finish on both sides might be overborne. Then, in the middle of December, came the news that the negotiations between the Germans and the Russians at Brest-Litovsk had broken down. On January 2, 1918, the new Russian Government made proposals to the Allies for a general peace: on January 8, President Wilson produced his famous Fourteen Points as a basis for a peace without annexations or indemnities.

Just before, on December 28, 1917, a further Labour Conference in London had approved a revised Statement of War Aims for presentation to an Allied Labour and Socialist Conference which was to meet in February, 1918. Henderson, baulked of Stockholm, was endeavouring to weld together the Socialists of the Allied countries in a demand for a reasonable peace, and was now acting as closely as he dared with MacDonald and the I.L.P. group against the extreme anti-German section of his own party. He was also pressing ahead with his promised plans for the reconstruction of the party with a view to the coming political struggle. At the Annual Labour Party Conference held at Nottingham in January, 1918, a comprehensive new statement of policy, *Labour and the New Social Order,* was presented and a new Party Constitution was put forward, designed to transform the Party into a nation-wide organisation capable of offering a real challenge to the Tories and Liberals at the next General Election. This new Constitution . . . represented the real break with the Lloyd George Coalition, even though the Labour Ministers retained their seats in the Government right up to the conclusion of the war. The enactment of the Representation of the People Act, enfranchising practically all men and many women, on February 6, 1918, defined the greatly enlarged electorate to which the new Labour Party would be able to appeal.

Meanwhile, in Russia, the Bolsheviks had convened the Constituent Assembly for which they had been calling before the Second Revolution, only to dissolve it at once, and to replace it on January 27, 1918, by a Congress of Soviets which declared itself the supreme governing authority of the new State. The Soviet system had begun, and the Soviet leaders, realising the impracticability of either resisting the Germans or securing a general peace, were making the best of a bad bargain at the resumed negotiations at Brest-Litovsk. The Brest-Litovsk Treaty, which took Russia definitely out of the war, was signed on March 3, 1918, and ratified twelve days later. In Germany, the wide-spread strikes which had broken out at the end of January had been repressed. At the beginning of March, the great new German offensive in the West was launched.

Even before this, in January, the man-power position in Great Britain had become acute, and an extensive new comb-out had begun. This accentuated the unrest, especially among the munition workers, and helped to give the Shop Stewards' Movement a more definitely political twist. This movement, concerned at first primarily with industrial grievances, grew more and more political as the emphasis shifted from dilution designed to increase output to the combing-out of more reluctant workers for military service; and the Second Russian Revolution gave the more left-wing leaders a more coherent revolutionary purpose than the first Revolution had imparted. There was as yet no Communist Party in Great Britain and no Communist International to proclaim a policy of World Revolution. But Bolshevik Russia was already becoming a focus of loyalty for the extreme left in all countries—and at the same time, of course, a focus of opposition for the right, whose friends among the Russian Socialists had been driven from power and in many cases were fleeing into exile and uttering fierce denunciations of Lenin and his associates as betrayers of democracy, both in Russia and in world affairs.

In Great Britain, whatever the shop stewards might feel, the leaders of the Trade Unions, of the Labour Party, and of the I.L.P. were at one in their dislike of the Bolsheviks. MacDonald and Snowden loved Lenin and Trotsky no better than did Henderson or Sidney Webb —the two chief architects of the new Labour Party. The Russian Revolution was still acclaimed; but the phrase meant one Revolution to the established leaders, and another to the left wing. The British Socialist Party, having already shed its old Social Democratic leaders, was ready to acclaim the Bolshevik Revolution, though not, as appeared later, to accept without an internal struggle the Bolshevik doctrine of "democratic centralism." The I.L.P. was sharply divided, its best-known leaders more and more anti-Bolshevik as the character of the second Revolution became more plain, its rank and file somewhat bewildered and for the most part wishful to go leftwards without ceasing to be a parliamentary party working within the Labour Party on constitutional lines. Even the small, militant Socialist Labour Party was divided, between an "old guard" which was not prepared to let anything—even World Revolution—impair the purity of its cherished doctrine, and a shop steward group which eagerly embraced the new Leninist gospel.

In March and,April, in face of the German offensive, the manpower crisis became more acute than ever. The Government forced through an Act raising the age of military service to fifty and even attempted to impose conscription on the Irish people. This measure undoubtedly did much to increase the strength of anti-war feeling. The Labour Party's further Conference, held in June, 1918, voted by 1,704,000 against 951,000 in favour of putting a formal end to the Electoral Truce and resuming its freedom to fight by-elections against Government candidates of the other parties. This Conference also passed a series of resolutions covering the main ground of home reconstruction policy, as the complement to the declaration of international policy already embodied in its Memorandum of War Aims. Individual Trade Unions were also by this time formulating their post-war demands. The National Union of Railwaymen had done this as early as November, 1917, when it put forward a plan for the nationalisation of the railways, with workers' representation on the public boards to which control was to be entrusted on behalf of the people. Now, in July, 1918, the Miners' Federation, at its Southport Conference, scrapped its older nationalisation plan, in which it had proposed a simple taking over of the mines by the State, and put forward instead a complete plan of public ownership combined with workers' control. Guild Socialism was rapidly gaining adherents in the Trade Unions: workers' control was being demanded by more and more Trade Unionists—though those who made the demand meant different things by it, as was to appear presently when British Communism emerged as an organised movement.

Early in August, 1918, a delegation from the Trades Union Congress and the Labour Party, headed by Arthur Henderson and C. W. Bowerman, proposed to attend a meeting in Switzerland, convened by the International Socialist Bureau, for the purpose of hearing and considering the replies of the Socialists of the enemy countries to the Allied Labour Memorandum on War Aims, which had been transmitted to them through the Bureau. The Government, however, refused passports, and the delegates were unable to go. Strong protests were made at the Jubilee Trades Union Congress, held early in September, and at a further Allied Labour and Socialist Conference, which met in London on September 17. This meeting, from which the

Socialist Societies were again excluded, was notable for the attendance of a delegation from the American Federation of Labor, including Samuel Gompers. The Americans put forward their alternative draft of War Aims, based mainly on President Wilson's Fourteen Points; and they abstained from voting on the composite Statement which was finally adopted by the Conference. They agreed, however, that an International Labour Conference, representing all nations, ought to meet simultaneously with the Peace Conference when the war was over. In the meantime, they put forward a resolution, which was heavily defeated, "urging that we [i.e., the Allied Labour movements] will meet in Conference only those of the Central Powers who are in open revolt against their autocratic governors." The Americans agreed, however, to appoint a representative [Gompers] to serve on a Joint International Committee which was to approach the various Allied Governments in order to ensure that Labour representatives should be included in the official delegations attending the Peace Conference, and was also to organise the World Labour Conference that was to meet at the same time.

This September Conference met the day after the reception of the Peace Note from Austria-Hungary, which heralded the collapse of the Central Powers. Little more than a fortnight later, Prince Max of Baden became German Chancellor, and it became plain that the end was near. In mid-October the German Government announced its preparedness to accept President Wilson's terms. Peace was evidently imminent when Henderson, in company with Camille Huysmans, the Secretary of the International Socialist Bureau, left London to attend a meeting of the Joint International Committee, which had been called to meet in Paris on October 26. They were stopped at Folkestone under orders from the National Sailors' and Firemen's Union, which refused to let its members sail with them on board. This, as we have seen, was not the first occasion on which such action had been taken. Havelock Wilson, the Sailors' leader, summoned before the Congress Parliamentary Committee, said that his objection was to Huysmans, who had been meeting the German Socialists, and not to Henderson; but he refused to give any pledge against a repetition of the incident. It was in fact repeated, against Huysmans, later in the year; but no further interference was attempted with the movements of British Labour delegates.

On November 1 came the Austrian Revolution, and on November 6 the German naval revolt at Kiel. A Republic was proclaimed in

Bavaria on November 7, and two days later the Kaiser abdicated, and the majority Socialist, Ebert, became the first Chancellor of the German Republic, which was formally proclaimed on November 11, the day that the Armistice was signed. On November 14 a specially summoned Labour Party Conference in London, at which Bernard Shaw made a memorable speech, decided by a vote of 2,117,000 against 810,000 to leave the Coalition at once and to resume complete independence as a party.

The majority in favour of this decision was large; but the minority was considerable. The latter had, moreover, the support of the Parliamentary Labour Party; and it was on that body's behalf that Clynes moved an amendment to the Party Executive's resolution in favour of resuming independence. Clynes and those who supported him— including James Sexton, Tom Shaw, and Will Thorne—argued that Labour should remain in the Coalition Government in order to have a share in making the peace. The Coalition, they said, was popular; and Labour, in leaving it, would be inviting disaster at the polls. Hardly anyone doubted that Lloyd George would rush on an election and do his best to fight it on the prestige of victory; and probably few Labour men expected that, under such circumstances, the Labour Party could poll well. Nevertheless, though a few of the big Trade Unions were on Clynes's side, there was no doubt about the views of the great majority of the delegates. Shaw twitted Clynes with coming empty-handed to ask Labour to surrender its freedom. Lloyd George, he said, had made large concessions to the Tories, but was offering Labour nothing except a promise to "consider" its claims. "Sympathetic consideration" was what the governing classes always offered the workers. "Mr. Clynes has come from Mr. Lloyd George and done the best he can. I ask you to send Mr. Clynes back to him with the message 'Nothing doing!' "

The Conference, having made its main decision, proceeded, on MacDonald's motion, to demand Labour representation at the Peace Conference and to vote for a World Labour Conference to meet at the same time and place. Robert Smillie seconded. The leaders who had been in eclipse were already stepping back into their places. But the next hurdle before them was the General Election.

The Labour Ministers did not all obey the Conference's orders. Clynes loyally resigned at once from his office as Food Controller, which he was loath to leave. Four, however, fought the General Election as Coalition Labour candidates, and stayed on to be gradually

discarded. These were G. N. Barnes, who attended the Paris Peace
Conference as the Government's Labour nominee; G. H. Roberts, who
succeeded Clynes as Food Controller; James Parker; and G. J. Wardle.
The rest, including John Hodge, rejoined their Labour colleagues in
opposition.

MARY AGNES HAMILTON

Henderson's Position

The position of one who was at once secretary to the Labour Party
and member of the War Cabinet was always difficult. It had, by now,
become almost impossible. The workers distrusted Lloyd George more
and more: anyone associated with him was to them suspect. They
knew, and Henderson too knew, that he was no match for L.G. L.G.
had all the gifts he had not. He could never best him. As he put it
later, "L.G. was the War Cabinet, and no one else really counted. He
threatened to resign, like a spoilt child, whenever he was opposed, and
as his resignation would have brought the whole thing down, the rest
always gave way." Little as he trusted him, he believed that L.G.'s
resignation "would have brought the whole thing down": that he was
the only man who could win the war. For him, nothing mattered, in
comparison with that; because of that, he had got to stand by him,
whatever it cost. Yet he was unhappy about it, very unhappy. The
fact that the war, despite L.G.'s brilliant improvisations, was, in 1917,
going worse than ever, with no gleam of hope of ending, only fortified
his hard decision. He had to stick to his post, uncomfortable as he
was, and doubtful of his personal effectiveness.

Issues, of course, arose from time to time, on which he came down
with effect, but they were not, as a rule, directly connected with the
conduct of war: he never fell into the folly of amateur strategy. Such
an issue came up in connection with the new Representation of the
People Bill. Curzon was against any extension of the franchise; above
all, he was against any admission of females. On this, Henderson
thumped the table: Did he want the workers to get their rights by
compromise, or by revolution? As for the women, it would be an
abominable breach of faith if they were not brought in, and he, for
one, would not stand for it. But for him and Cecil, who backed him

From *Arthur Henderson* by Mary Agnes Hamilton, London, William Heinemann,
Ltd., 1938, pp. 117–25, 134–48, 152–62. Reprinted by permission of the publisher.

stoutly, the women would almost certainly have been left out. On such a point he could be and was his natural dominant self. Even here, however, he had to be acutely aware of the gulf separating him from his associates.

His position, as well as his natural outlook, was, of course, profoundly different from that of the other members of the Cabinet. He was in constant contact with the ordinary people, the workers and the soldiers whom Lloyd George and Curzon, Bonar Law and Milner, talked of as "man-power." He knew their sufferings and their grievances. He had, constantly, to meet MacDonald and Snowden, Anderson and Smillie in personal talk, at executive meetings, on the floor of conference; he had to see the case, as they saw it, even if he did not agree; he knew how sincere their views and how strong their hold was on the rank and file, and how silly it was to dismiss them as "traitors," as his Cabinet colleagues, and the Press, liked to do. He knew how they were being helped by the discontent bred of the harsh working of Conscription and the Munitions Acts, and the sense that the war was going on for ever. Now and then, he tried to make the Cabinet realise how much this last factor counted in "unrest." Our war aims were good and generous; why not state them? They stared at him: was Henderson becoming tainted with pacifism? When, on January 22nd, 1917, President Wilson made his famous "Peace without Victory" speech, declaring that the aim was, or should be, a peace of reconciliation and democracy, something not imposed by victors on vanquished, his words sent a thrill of sudden hope through the hearts of the slaves of the war machine. The official British view, however, was that he had dropped a terrible brick, and the less said about it the better. Here, again, Henderson felt an "outsider" in the Cabinet.

No one can, to-day, read the Memoirs and Diaries of governing statesmen in the various countries at war without a sense that their minds became numbed by the very vastness of the machines of which they were in charge, as by the constant pressure upon them of external events. Inevitably, almost, purpose disappeared, in their mechanistic absorption. By 1917, anyhow, war had become an institution: part, as Colonel Repington naïvely observed (August 1917), "of the natural law of our being"; for questions as to what it was for or how and when it was to be ended, its directors, literally, had no time to think. Anyone who did dare to raise them was disloyal, unpatriotic, defeatist. "Not to think" summed up practical duty; the mark of the odious pacifist was precisely this—that he went on using his head. Henderson certainly would, at this stage, have been insulted and very angry, if anyone had called him a pacifist; but he could not stop using his head. If, to those who encountered him, early in 1917, he seemed rather aloof, and more than a little self-important, they missed him and did not get much below the surface. His son's death was a pain that went on. It did not lessen the pain to have to realise it as common. On the contrary, it was terrifying to know that pain like this was part of the texture of life, now, for millions, and that every day that passed added to its dreadful weight. This was what war meant. The thought turned in him, like a knife. He could not, did not, talk of it, but it went on and on. Yet he could not see what to do about it.

. . .

In Henderson's career, his visit to Russia in the summer of 1917 marks a definite turning-point. It altered no settled conviction, disturbed no deep-seated idea. But it did change the proportion of his outlook, and affect, and that in far-reaching fashion, his judgment as to necessary action. It did this wholly within the framework of his determination that the war had got to be won. That never varied. Only there were released, from below the dense overlay of war emotion, elements in his normal thinking and feeling till then resolutely kept under: elements, above all, in his thinking about peace and its terms.

The Revolution of March 1917 in Russia suddenly broke across Western absorptions and lit up the murky sky of endless war like a fiery meteor. Always mysterious to Britishers, Russia had not become less so during two years of war. The collapse of the front, the shortage of munitions, the appalling hardships endured by Russian soldiers— these things were in the newspapers: but about the home front, no one knew much. The Ambassador in London, Count Benckendorff, was but vaguely aware of what was going on: the Russian Foreign Office "never took the trouble to keep the Russian representatives abroad informed. We learnt the news of happenings in Petrograd from casual visitors"—such is the account of M. Nabokoff, chargé d'affaires in London, who carried on after Benckendorff's death in January 1917, expecting the new chief who never arrived. The British Government could have known a good deal had it been willing to heed the voices of those able and ready to report the truth, among them that of the British Ambassador, Sir George Buchanan; but it does not appear that it heeded either Buchanan or Samuel Hoare. The latter, in December 1916, in his capacity of intelligence officer, sent a despatch in which he uttered warning of a political drift "from bad to worse"; in other words, "a very great majority of the civilian population of Russia is in favour of peace." Sir Samuel Hoare was still in Russia when there arrived the Inter-Allied Mission of which Mr. Bruce Lockhart says, tartly: "Rarely in the history of a great war can so many important ministers and generals have left their country on so useless an errand." For the British, there was Lord Milner, accompanied by Lord Revel-stoke, Sir Henry Wilson and other eminent persons. Lord Milner had a conversation with Prince Lvov, who told him that, unless the Tsar changed his attitude, revolution was inevitable. He also saw Peter Struve, who handed him a most grave memorandum, in the same sense. Lord Milner listened, but, although he regarded the situation as hopeless, from a military point of view, he did not believe in revolution, and told the War Cabinet so on his return.

The events of March, culminating in the abdication on March 15th of the Tsar and the establishment of a Provisional Government, including several Socialist ministers, came therefore with a shock of surprise to the British Government. To most of its members it was a painful shock. To Henderson, however, the event wore a very different face. He could not, of course, foresee all that this tremendous change was going to mean, but he did hail with enthusiasm the advent of democracy and the fall of Tsardom in Russia. Alliance with the old, autocratic Russia had been a bitter pill to swallow, in 1914. How talk convincingly of crusades against military despotism and for free government, in that companionship? Now, freedom in Russia rejuvenated and recharged every ideal purpose in the great struggle. The news of the bloodless March days gave to his burdened spirits a much-needed lift. At last, some good had come out of the horror. At last, it was possible to feel that free peoples were indeed fighting side by side against a common foe. The establishment in Russia of a largely Socialist and wholly democratic Government, and the statement by that Government, of war aims that were neither Imperialist nor annexationist; this he welcomed, with a full heart. On this, he felt as did every member of the Labour Party, from extreme Left to extreme Right; in enthusiasm for this, they were completely at one. Russia free, in mid March; the United States entering the war, on the first day of April—the uniform blackness of the sky knew vivid streaks of hopeful light, at last.

Early in April, the British Ambassador reported that the Russian Press was beginning to accuse the Allies of waging a Capitalist war;

could "English Labour leaders be induced to send a telegram to the leaders of the Duma, urging Russia to go on with the war?" To this appeal, Henderson at once responded. "Organised labour in Great Britain," he wired, "is watching with the keenest sympathy the efforts of the Russian people to deliver themselves from the power of reactionary elements which are impeding their advance to victory." In this message, he correctly reflected the feelings of the majority of Labour, which welcomed the revolution, first on its own account, as ending an abominable tyranny; and, secondly, as giving new force to Russian cooperation in a war of liberation. In this outlook he represented the great central body of opinion, on whose either side were very different and very violent views. To the Right were those who agreed with the British Press in denouncing Kerensky's abolition of capital punishment in the army, and viewed Russian events solely in their bearing on the military position; to the Left, those who rejoiced when they knew that the slogan that had brought the crowd out into the streets of Petrograd and called the soldiers to fraternise with it, had been, not victory, but "Peace and Bread!" What they hoped was that Russia might now help to bring the war to an end. While Henderson was wholeheartedly in sympathy with Kerensky's passionate effort to recharge weary and weaponless soldiers with fresh fighting spirit by giving them a worthwhile objective, MacDonald and the I.L.P. were all for the Soviets with their cries: "No annexations or indemnities! Peace Now!"

On May 10th came the news that the Council of Workers and Soldiers' Deputies in Petrograd (the Petrograd Soviet) was about to issue invitations to a world-wide International Socialist Conference to be held in Stockholm, for the definition of war aims.

Stockholm was, now, the headquarters of the International; for a Conference there, invitations had already been sent out over the names of Mr. Branting, the great Swedish leader, Mynheer Troelstra of Holland, and Camille Huysmans, the brilliant secretary of the International Bureau. This proposal the Russian Government now took up; and the mighty change in their country gave it a wholly new complexion.

Miliukov, Cadet Foreign Minister in the Provisional Government, telegraphed officially to ask that facilities should be granted to enable British delegates to attend. When the executive of the British Labour Party received this intelligence, there was a long and most animated discussion. The I.L.P. had put forward more than once—and no later than January 1917—the summoning of a meeting of the International;

but the Manchester Conference had then firmly refused. Now, while MacDonald was all for accepting the Stockholm invitation, and G. H. Roberts was equally strong for blank refusal, the majority of the executive took the cautious view that it would be well to know rather more than anyone did at present both about actual conditions in Russia—was it a Socialist revolution or no?—and about the conditions and basis of the Conference, as to which the terms of the Russian message were anything but clear, before they committed themselves to sending a delegation. It was true that Will Thorne, James O'Grady and W. S. Sanders were already on their way to or in Russia, but they had been sent at the suggestion of the War Cabinet, on the news that a French Labour delegation was *en route*. Finally, the executive decided to send three of its own members: G. H. Roberts, representing the Right wing, W. Carter of the Miners, representing the centre, and J. Ramsay MacDonald, representing the left. They were to go to Petrograd and to Moscow to establish friendly contact with the new Government, and to report.

This on May 20th. Next day Henderson reported this decision to the Cabinet. On that day, they also had before them the news that Miliukov had fallen, and the Russian Government was reconstructed under Kerensky. Sir George Buchanan shortly after conveyed the news that the new Foreign Minister—Tereschenko—a young and very able Socialist—was asking for an Allied Conference to define war aims, and also requesting facilities for a visit to Russia from Ramsay MacDonald. Sir George explained that he had talked with Emile Vandervelde and James O'Grady while in Russia, and after hearing from them what MacDonald's views actually were, supported this request on the part of M. Tereschenko.

Here was difficult and indigestible matter for the War Cabinet. Although it is impossible to gain any clear picture of their standpoint from Mr. Lloyd George's account—written very much *ex post facto,* and omitting more than it includes—it does appear that they were thoroughly annoyed and distinctly hot and bothered. It was inconsiderate of the Russians to have had a revolution at this juncture. These suggestions of conferences and statements of war aims were exceedingly ill-timed. The whole affair was probably more interesting to Mr. Lloyd George than to others. He was a Liberal: he felt a theoretic [sic] with revolution in Russia and could not yet be sure that there was not going to be something in it—if one only knew what! The French were sending Albert Thomas: the British ought to do at least as well. Henderson had been getting a bit prickly; why not send him? Why not even send him there for good? We had an ambassador; but "he was an object of suspicion and mistrust to the new administration which has been set up under Kerensky with the support of the Soviet."

This was not the case; but the statement is there to give an excuse for the decision to send Henderson to replace Buchanan, which is implied, though not stated. As a reflection either of a completely muddled approach at the time, or a determination, after it, to conceal what really happened, the following two sentences could hardly be bettered. The first runs:

> In view of the prospect of German Socialists going to Stockholm and fraternising there with the Russians, it was suggested that there might be an advantage in sending a strong delegation, even one headed by Henderson.

This "suggestion" can only have come from the Premier. To his colleagues, the very thought of Stockholm, of an International Conference of Socialists in a neutral country, was abominable, and there is no indication that any of them ever held any other view about it. The significance of this sentence—which, of course, becomes quite clear when the telegram is read which, on May 22nd, the P.M. sent to M. Thomas, and only then—is masked by that which follows:

> Alternatively, it might be worth while to send Mr. Henderson to Petrograd on a special mission, similar to that being carried out for the French by M. Albert Thomas.

This was, of course, not an alternative; the only point in common with the two suggestions is that both of them removed Mr. Henderson. If there were anything important going on in Russia, it could prove a shrewd and sympathetic-seeming stroke to send him thither. Moreover, he might get on with these odd revolutionaries. And, if not . . .

On the 29th, therefore, Henderson, who had not been present at the meeting at which the "suggestions" were thrown out, was told that the Cabinet wished him to go on a special Mission to Petrograd and to start to-morrow. And, if he thought fit, he could stay there as British Envoy.

"What about Buchanan?" asked Henderson, with his inconvenient habit of going straight to the point. "If I am to replace him, he must be so informed." The Foreign Secretary, Mr. Balfour, had a right to attend Cabinet meetings; this was an F.O. matter. Under the impression that a F.O. message to Sir George Buchanan would precede him, Henderson departed. The message actually sent, however, merely suggested to Buchanan that he might care for a short period of leave, and added: "There is no question of your being recalled."

. . .

Events of which he knew nothing were moving against him. Just before he left Petrograd, a new offensive had been launched under the transitory influence of Kerensky's fiery eloquence. As he had stated in his report to the Cabinet, written while he was still in Russia, the prevailing opinion in Petrograd, in June, was that "an offensive would be attempted, but that it would be rendered abortive by the failure of transport and industry behind the front." While he was on sea, this forecast proved correct; the Brusiloff offensive, after a dashing start on June 29th, collapsed in failure.

In London, meantime, air raids intensified, and the effect on nerves was not good. There had been one of the recurrent reconstructions of the Ministry, with a good deal of moving; General Smuts had been added to the War Cabinet, and Clynes had come in as deputy food controller. Towards the end of July, an imposing but ineffective Inter-Allied Conference was held in London. There were high military and political chiefs from France and Italy and practically the entire British Cabinet present; for Russian representation no provision had been made. This was the more remarkable that the first item on the agenda was a proposal from the British P.M. that "A stern protest be despatched to the Russian Government against the continuation in Russia of disruption and anarchy"—a message more likely to be helpful to Lenin than to Kerensky, to whom it was transmitted in official but entirely intelligible terms. Had Henderson known of this, he would have realised how far the volatile mind of the Prime Minister had moved from the enthusiasm which, only two months earlier, had made him eager for Stockholm. Yet every argument good in May was stronger now—unless he was light-mindedly preparing to write Russia off, on the strength of the Brusiloff failure.

Late on the evening of July 23rd, landing in Aberdeen to board a train for London, he found that he had, as fellow-passengers, four Russians. Messrs. Rousanoff, Erlich, Smirnoff and Goldenberg had been sent by the Council of Workers and Soldiers' Deputies—the Central Soviet—to make arrangements for Stockholm and, to that end, were going to Paris. After some talk, Henderson persuaded them that they should meet the British Labour Party before proceeding on their journey, and then cross to Paris with him, as he was going thither for an Inter-Allied Socialist meeting. He did not want the Russian delegates "nobbled" by the Left, or a wrong complexion would be given to the affair from the start. When at King's Cross he saw MacDonald on the platform, he was glad he had taken this precaution.

He made straight for No. 1 Victoria Street, where the headquarter offices of the Labour Party were then housed. There, he talked frankly and fully with his colleagues, making no secret of the profound impression that what he had seen and learnt in Russia had made upon his mind. Next day, Wednesday 25th, there was a meeting of the executive. He recalled that, at the Manchester Conference, he had opposed the MacDonald-Snowden proposal for summoning the International; to an ordinary meeting, he remained opposed. But he did now think that British Labour ought to be represented at the Conference being organised by Branting, Troelstra, Huysmans and the Russians to meet at Stockholm to discuss war aims, if they could get it made a consultative Conference. The Russians were determined: the Conference was going to take place. Whether or no he thought or they thought that it was a good thing or a bad thing was now irrelevant. With them or without them it was going to take place. The only question was: Should they be there? He thought, Yes, they should be there; it was, in his view, a duty. If not, they were abandoning Russia to the Bolsheviks at home and to the Germans abroad. He urged that a special Conference of the Party should at once be summoned, to discuss the single specific issue of participation in Stockholm, as a consultative conference. He wanted the executive, further, to put before that Conference a definite recommendation. To that, he would be ready to speak.

There was an animated discussion. There was opposition: the opposers, of course, twitted him with having crossed into the camp of the Left, whose support was more ardent than helpful. "Are we ashamed of stating our war aims?" he asked the patriots: "I am not." Finally, by a majority, it was agreed that the special Conference should be called for August 10th, in London. The Russian delegates were then brought in, and it was arranged that Henderson, as secretary, MacDonald, as treasurer, and G. H. Wardle, then acting-chairman of the Parliamentary Party and a leading spokesman of the Right, should go with them to Paris. The meeting there had been called by the French United Socialists, the majority section of the

Socialist Party in France, of which Albert Thomas was a leading member: its original purpose had been to lay plans for an Inter-Allied Socialist Conference, which had, indeed, been under discussion ever since May, before his departure for Russia, and had hung fire in his absence. Now, the threads could be picked up and tied; out of the Paris meeting he hoped to get a common Anglo-French front for Stockholm, and a majority front. To get that, he must obviously go himself. Since MacDonald was going, minority views would have a brilliant spokesman; but a minority Stockholm would be no good.

Having discovered that the Prime Minister was in Paris, he wired to him on this same 25th, informing him of his action and proposed course. On the 26th he attended a War Cabinet meeting, and explained his plans. Cold and pronounced disapproval met him there. This, from Bonar Law, Milner and Curzon, did not surprise him; none of them brought any imaginative understanding to the Russian situation; the very word Stockholm frightened them. If they could, they would have stopped his going even to Paris. But they were in a by no means unusual dilemma. They did not know which way their eminent leader, the Goat (to use Sir H. Wilson's name for him), was going to jump. Not so long ago he had been all for Stockholm; he might, for all they knew, be so again. Or he might not; there was no knowing. His account of the meeting is:

> The members of the War Cabinet told him how thoroughly they disapproved of the course which he proposed to take. Mr. Henderson was in an aggressive mood, and informed them that it was on his initiative that the Executive of the Labour Party had now decided in favour of sending delegates to Stockholm. This met with unanimous disapproval from the Cabinet, and Mr. Henderson told them that if they insisted he was willing to tender his resignation from the Cabinet. Naturally, they could not press him to do this, for they knew that I valued his membership.

The Cabinet therefore sulked. Henderson's position, on the other hand, was entirely clear. He told his colleagues frankly what he proposed. He explained the unexceptionable purpose of the Paris meeting —a consultative meeting of the Allied Socialists, called at the instance of the French. He put the Stockholm position before them, and stressed the importance of getting agreement in Paris as to the consultative character of that Conference. He reminded them that Russia was still an ally. He reminded them also that he was going to Paris, not as a member of the War Cabinet, but as secretary of the Labour Party.

On the 27th, he, MacDonald and Wardle went to Paris. The meeting was useful, both in that it permitted a valuable exchange of ideas between the British and the French, and as clearing the ground for Stockholm. Hitherto, efforts to bring about an inter-allied meeting had failed, on some point of mutual misunderstanding; now, those points were cleared; a common front was secured; a date was fixed for a formal and general meeting. This was very important, both in the present and for the future. Moreover, agreement was finally secured on the point which Henderson regarded as vital, about Stockholm itself. The Russians were insisting that resolutions passed at that Conference should be binding; the French were inclined to take the same view, because they wanted a resolution about Alsace-Lorraine. He persuaded both to modify their stand on this; he got a compromise and a resolution generally accepted such as he could, with a perfectly good conscience, recommend British Labour to accept. He also got the date of opening shifted from August 15th to September 10th, in order to give the British movement time to come to calm decisions, and to enable the American Federation of Labour to attend, if attend it would. It was not likely. The A.F. of L. was violent in its militarism and definitely anti-Socialist.

These were valuable results. He returned to London, after a strenuous week-end, well satisfied.

Wednesday, August 1st, the day of his return to London, was to be a hectic day—first of a fortnight of hectic days. He at once saw the Prime Minister, himself not long back from Paris. The latter was in one of his recurring phases of reconstructing the entire strategy of the war. He was full of hatred of Haig and Robertson; angry that the first-fruits of his premiership appeared to be a costly stalemate in the West, and especially angry with the Russians. They had let him down. Having told the Imperial War Cabinet in March (by way of defiance of Wilson's impertinent Peace without Victory speech) that punishment and restitution were the aims of the war, he was, now, toying with the notion of saving the West by allowing Germany to compensate herself in the East at the expense, of course, of Russia. His domination by this idea—shared with Milner—was at this stage causing real distress to Liberal friends like C. P. Scott. This being so,

Henderson, full of the idea of saving Russia as ally and democracy, was pursuing a peculiarly inappropriate line: one none the more acceptable that it had, only two months earlier, been his own. Quite intolerable to have him pointing out that to refuse to go to Stockholm was to play nobody's game save Lenin's, and would certainly be used to suggest that Lenin was right about British war aims, and that they were such that we dare not send responsible delegates to state them openly—which was absurd. Nothing but irritation in hearing him repeat the argument of his own May telegram, and reminding him that the Russian Government wanted, even needed, the Conference, and well-informed and cautious Ambassadors of the stamp of George Buchanan and Esmé Howard strongly endorsed its appeal.

What account of his own present view the Premier gave Henderson on this occasion is not on record. In his *Memoirs* he says that he took him to task: "I could not disguise the unpleasant nature of the situation he had created by his action." The members of the Cabinet whom Henderson had defied at the special meeting held on the 26th before going to Paris were certainly in a quandary: but Mr. Lloyd George gives no hint of his own view of Stockholm or of his rejoinder to the "very full and, I hope, very faithful statement as to my own personal position," which Henderson (Hansard, August 13, col. 915) gave him: or to "the reasons why I had reached the conclusion that it was in the interest of the allied cause and of our own country, so far as our relationship with Russia was concerned, that we should be represented at the Stockholm Conference, if we could make it of a consultative and not of a mandatory character." At the close of the conversation the Prime Minister invited him to attend a special meeting of the Cabinet at 4 o'clock; a debate on the Paris visit—as to which rumours of the most extraordinary character had been flying about—was to take place in the House that evening.

At 4 o'clock he accordingly presented himself, only to be asked, to his amazement, to wait. He was kept waiting for an hour. Then G. N. Barnes (who had taken his place in the Cabinet, while he was in Russia) came out, to convey a statement to him. . . .

This was, of course, the famous "door-mat" incident, of which the public heard a fortnight later. He was, not unnaturally, very angry; and in anger formidable. Mr. Lloyd George describes him as "in a highly resentful frame of mind." He had told the Cabinet on the 26th, when they had tried to put obstacles in the way of his going to Paris, that he was ready to resign; now, "there was no longer any question of his offering to resign. On the contrary, he challenged us to demand his resignation—which, as I have said, was the last thing that I wished to do." Before it came to that, there were preparations to be made, a scene to be set; without that, Henderson could be dangerous— dangerous, above all, because, in his action, he was animated by a strong and settled conviction of public duty. "He stressed the value of the agreement reached in Paris on making Stockholm a consultative conference": he "declined to say whether he would himself propose to go to Stockholm, if invited by the British Labour Party. . . . He would have to consider the whole position according to the circumstances." This the Cabinet had to take. Nothing ambiguous, either in general or in detail, about his position; no possible dubiety as to where he stood, or what he was going to do. He was going ahead. In the House, the debate had already started; the temperature was reported to be rising; it was agreed that the Prime Minister should pour as much oil as possible on the troubled waters, and confine himself, in the main, to indicating the difficulties and advantages of the combination in one person of the offices of member of the Cabinet and secretary of a political party.

In the House, excited and amazingly ill-informed speeches were being made, in an atmosphere made tense and suspicious by Mr. Bonar Law's efforts, in reply to the earlier fusillade of questions, to refrain from giving any information about anything. In the minds of excited M.P.s and journalists, the very word International was, at this date, sheer treachery; conversations between Socialists, even Allied Socialists—there were no others, of course, in Paris—at once translated themselves, in their febrile imaginations, into "hob-nobbing with the enemy." The home-keeping fire-eaters were in a frenzy; they smelt fire and brimstone. They hated Russia: had rejoiced, openly, when Havelock Wilson's men stopped MacDonald and Roberts at the port; regarded the members of the I.L.P. as pro-Germans, anyway, and persons who ought to have been interned *en bloc:* they were not, at bottom, much happier about the Labour Party, cat's-paw of Trade Unionists who refused to make munitions while their wives strutted about in fur coats. Viscount Duncannon, who moved the adjournment, insisted that his intention was not to attack Henderson personally, but the Government "which allowed the Rt. Hon. Member to take a prominent pacifist member of this House to Paris. . . . We are entitled to demand explicit statements from the Government, here and now, that they will not allow any Englishmen to go and meet

Germans at Stockholm during this war, and that, if the Rt. Hon. gentleman, the Member for Barnard Castle, has committed himself to a conference at which Germans are to be present he will either retract that, or the Government will ask him to resign his office."

Henderson's own speech was plain and simple. He pointed out that any difficulty that might arise out of the fact that he functioned in a dual capacity was shared by his eminent colleague, Albert Thomas. He further strove to give to the House a picture of what had been done in Paris that should carry understanding to their minds; and attempted to clear from those minds some of their misapprehensions about Stockholm. The Conference there was going to take place. The Russians were set on it, so were the neutrals. For the Russians it was of life-and-death importance. It was going to take place: the question was: Was it to be a Conference at which the Russians were to meet neutral and enemy Socialists only, or Allied Socialists, who could convince them that Allied war aims were worthy and so induce them to continue fighting? In his view, there would be grave disadvantage to the Allied cause if it were not represented at Stockholm by men who believed in it. Let them, anyhow, clear from their minds any notion that actual terms of peace were to be settled. There was no question of that.

> But I do say this—when this war is settled, it will be settled
> on lines which meet with the approval of the common people
> of each of the countries. [An Hon. Member: "Representing a
> majority, not a minority."] In view of the fact that the news-
> papers have given a good deal of space, and a good deal of
> attention to myself, of which I am not worthy, I think hon.
> members might give me an opportunity of stating my case.
> It is quite true we may be a minority. We have our point of
> view. We have our ideals. We are an organised movement.
> I do not mind saying that I have always felt that if you have
> a certain amount of organised propaganda work going on, and
> provided—I always make that a condition—that it in no way
> interferes with your military effort, then I think it is well to
> have running on parallel lines your military effort and your
> political propaganda. I think, as the circumstances of the war
> change, the more you can educate the people to the new posi-
> tion the better. I think there has been too little of it. I think
> that British interests have suffered because, since recruiting was
> no longer necessary, propaganda has almost come to a stand-
> still.

Until he went to Russia, he had thought that British war aims were understood by everybody: now, he knew that they were quite misunderstood in Russia, and he suspected quite unknown to the Social Democrats of Germany. Since he believed in them, he wanted them to be known. Here, and throughout, he had done what he felt to be his duty, "not in the interests of a party, but in the interests of the country —the only interests that have moved me since the commencement of the war."

Mr. Lloyd George, later on, made a very clever speech, in which he said nothing. A contribution of serious note came, however, from J. H. Thomas. Making it quite plain that he was not a pacifist, he also made it plain that Labour was not going to tolerate "The view that we, giving our sons by the thousand and the million, are not going to be allowed to discuss what may lead to peace. . . . Labour, rightly or wrongly—in my opinion, rightly—is determined that the part it is playing in waging this war demands that in the settlement of the terms of peace it shall be consulted." About Stockholm, Labour had not yet decided; but, in his view, they would decide for it, and they would be right.

Of this statement, the Cabinet would have done well to take heed. They knew, of course, that the special Conference to decide was set for the 10th; they knew Henderson's view, and his authority over the Party. But their mood would seem to have been that a tiresome fence had been surmounted, and that was that. There were plenty of other troubles to worry about. Most of them regarded the whole business as secondary, anyhow. However this may be, the week passed: the matter was not raised again in Cabinet. . . .

It seems more than doubtful whether the straight issue of Stockholm, merits or demerits, was discussed then, or at any Cabinet save that of August 26th. On this, it is, of course, not possible to speak with precision: Cabinet minutes are confidential. Henderson loyally handed back all his papers. Moreover, his sense of collective responsibility, always keen, was sharpened, not blunted, by war. There was a major obligation, here, which he never forgot: not even in private conversation. By him, nothing was said to anyone, so long as the war was on. The provocation was extreme, when attacks developed based on a partial use of material which he felt himself precluded in honour from quoting in full; but he resisted it, without flinching. When the war was over his mind had moved on to issues to him more important than any personal question: what was past was

over and done with, for him. Therefore, except for what he felt free
to say in the House—which was not much—and what Mr. Lloyd
George says in the chapter devoted to Stockholm in the fourth volume
of his *Memoirs*—which is a good deal, but most carefully arranged
and selected—there is a paucity of direct evidence on the transactions
of the next few days, crucial as they are.

Mr. Lloyd George is an artist, building up a picture. He does not
record what was said in the long talk of the 7th; instead he draws an
extremely effective, if tendencious, portrait of his interlocutor:

> Fresh from the glow of that atmosphere of emotionalism
> and exaltation which great revolutions excite, Mr. Henderson
> was out of tune with the stern but frigid sense of responsibility
> and self-control which was dominant here. When he came back
> from Russia, the fine steel of his character was magnetised by
> his experiences. He was in an abnormal state of mind. He had
> more than a touch of revolutionary malaria. His temperature
> was high, and his mood refractory.

This portrait is inserted where it is inserted in order to convey an
impression. It records its author's swift response, in May 1917, to the
vision of revolution rather than anything that happened to Henderson
in Russia. He did not like revolution. It would, no doubt, have exalted
Lloyd George to be there; in Henderson, it increased the "stern but
frigid sense of responsibility and self-control" of which there was far
more in him than in his eminent chief. His sense of responsibility to
democracy in Russia—struggling for its life, and in imminent danger
—and for the war, liable to be gravely prejudiced if Russia went out—
compelled him to a slow but firm conviction about Stockholm, wholly
unlike the vivid enthusiasm that had lit the Prime Minister, with
spark-like fervency, and then died down, leaving no trace, hardly even
a memory. What Mr. Lloyd George met in him, now, was not any
excitement, but that quality which his friend and colleague, J. R.
Clynes, had seized on, when he had said of him and of John Hodge:
"of all the men in our movement, these are two of the most stubborn
kind, and when they take their stand on any question, they are immovable." On Stockholm, he had taken his stubborn stand; he was
immovable.

That being so, it seems likely that the straight issue of Stockholm
was not discussed, either at this interview, or at the Cabinet meeting
of the next day, the 8th. It did not need to be. Henderson's attitude

was known; by now even familiar. Nobody wanted to go hurling himself on that rock a second time. What was discussed, on both occasions, was the issue of passports: and the passport problem arose, directly, out of the assumption that, at the Labour Conference on the 10th, Henderson's known view was going to prevail. It generally did prevail; that was why he was in the Cabinet. Before the 7th, the question about passports—should they be granted to British delegates for Stockholm?—had been submitted to the Law Officers: on the 7th the Attorney General's legal opinion against their issue had been circulated to members of the Cabinet. Henderson, first, urged most earnestly that the Cabinet should not make any such decision; he pleaded with the Prime Minister to grant passports to delegates, if the Labour Party Conference decided to send them. He himself, as a member of the Government, should not, of course, form part of the delegation; but the arguments for sending a delegation were of a political urgency of the highest kind, and the Cabinet ought not to allow the matter to be settled on a purely legal basis. Getting nowhere on this line, he then took the ground that if the Cabinet, as a Cabinet, were going to act upon the Attorney's opinion, the decision should be announced before the Conference of the 10th, since such a decision would "compel me to choose between giving up the secretaryship of the Labour Party or giving up my membership of the War Cabinet."

Later in the same day—the 7th—he had a consultation with his Labour colleagues in the Government: in first line, with Barnes, Hodge and Roberts. He found that they all took the view that, if the Conference of the 10th was to come to a responsible decision, the fact that passports might be refused ought not, previously, to be announced, since that must materially prejudice debate. This was a genuine point, which came all the more strongly from men who were against Stockholm, as were these three. He saw its force and accepted it, although that was going to put him, personally, in a dilemma; he at once telephoned to the Prime Minister to inform him that the Labour Ministers' view was that, even if passports were to be withheld, the fact should not be given out till after the Friday.

That the passports situation was discussed at the Cabinet meeting on the 8th, Wednesday—the last he attended—is matter of common knowledge. Despite his report as to the unanimous views of his Labour colleagues, which he loyally supported, it was decided to make the announcement at once. For some reason—one more among the minor

mysteries of these tense days—it was, in fact, not made till the 11th
—the day after the Conference.

On the evening of August 9th, while he was preparing his speech
for the morrow's Conference, Henderson received a message from the
Russian Embassy.

At this point, a curious and rather pathetic figure enters the story,
M. Constantin Nabokoff, the Russian chargé d'affaires, who, since
Benckendorff's death early in 1917, had been acting as Ambassador,
although there was the minimum of contact between him and Petrograd. As he records in his memoirs, *The Ordeal of a Diplomat,* the
Embassy learnt the news of the Revolution "from casual visitors";
Miliukov did not send him a single letter; such telegrams as he did
later get from Tereschenko were "invariably late, and always over-
optimistic." "After a time, I ceased to read these telegrams. Reports
from the Petrograd correspondents of the leading journals were more
truthful and more up to date." Well-bred and personally attractive, he
was a popular figure in London society; his views were those of his
English friends. At the end of July he became seriously afraid that
sympathy in British Government circles was going to be finally alien-
ated from Russia by the belief that the Russian Government was
pressing for Stockholm.

"So, bearing these considerations in mind, and in view of the fact
that a Labour Conference was due in London on August 10th, I sent
the following telegram to M. Tereschenko on August 3rd:

> The question of the participation of representatives of the
> British Labour Party in the Stockholm Conference will be
> decided next Friday. There is a strong agitation within the
> Party against participation, and the opposition to British par-
> ticipation will undoubtedly be strengthened by the reply of the
> American Federation of Labour to the French Federation. It is
> stated categorically in this reply that the Conference cannot,
> at the present moment, have useful results, and that the Ameri-
> can Federation do not intend to send delegates to Stockholm.
> Mr. Bonar Law stated yesterday in the House of Commons
> that the Government would not send delegates, that the ap-
> proval of the Conference depends not only on the Government
> but on the Labour Party, expressed the hope that this approval
> would not be given, and pointed out that the Government had
> not decided whether anybody would be allowed to take part in
> the Conference. The Leader of the House added that "This
> permission will not be given without serious consideration and

will probably be refused." I consider it absolutely necessary, with a view to safeguarding the stability and closeness of our union with Great Britain, where the majority of public opinion is adverse to the Conference, that I should be in a position to declare most emphatically to Mr. Balfour that the Russian Government as well as H.M. Government regard this matter as a party concern and not as a matter of State, and that the decisions of the Conference, should it be convened, would in no way be binding on the future course of Russian policy and of Russia's relations with her Allies. I shall be questioned by Mr. Balfour on this subject and therefore expect you to give me definite instructions.

The wording of this telegram is important, in interpreting the reply. That reply, which arrived on August 9th, takes up the two points stressed by Nabokoff: first, the distinction being drawn in Britain—so M. Nabokoff tells the Russian Foreign Minister, who was, of course, entirely dependent on him for information on such a point—between a "party concern" and a "matter of State"; and, secondly, the non-binding character of the Stockholm Conference itself. Accordingly, what M. Tereschenko wired was:

> I entirely approve of the declaration to be made to H.M. Government in the sense suggested by you, and you are hereby authorised to inform the Secretary of State for Foreign Affairs that although the Russian Government does not deem it possible to prevent Russian delegates from taking part in the Stockholm Conference, they regard this Conference as a party concern, and in no way binding upon the liberty of action of the Government.

To those who knew conditions at both ends, as Henderson did, the meaning of this carefully worded document was plain. As to the non-binding character of the Conference, he had always been for that; he had never had any idea of its decisions being binding on Governments. He quite understood, further, that any Russian Government—and, above all, a coalition, such as was at the moment in the saddle—had got to keep itself right with the British Government. If that British Government was against the Conference, the obvious way out, for the Russian, was to agree to the view suggested for it by Nabokoff, that the Conference was a party concern, and stop there. It is noteworthy that Tereschenko does stop there. He says: "The Government regard this Conference as a party concern." He does not go on to take up the other half of Nabokoff's antithesis, and say that it is "not a matter of State." He could not do so, since, in Russia, the handy distinction between "party concern" and "matter of State" had, as no one knew better than M. Tereschenko, no validity. What the Soviet wanted, the Government had got to take—although they need not say so. Henderson knew this; he knew that, in Petrograd, a party concern was a matter of State, and realised that Tereschenko was too honest to imply that it was not.

This message therefore told him nothing new. Nor did he attach any importance to Nabokoff's personal addendum to his letter to the British P.M. "I hasten to lay before you the above information, as I fear the impression has hitherto prevailed that, in the words of one of the London newspapers, 'Russia ardently desires the Stockholm Conference,' and this argument has been put forward in order to influence British public opinion in favour of the Labour and Socialist parties of Great Britain participating in the Stockholm Conference." Henderson knew that, were a Russian Government to come out against Stockholm, that Government would fall. When he had interpolated into the statement he was preparing the sentence—"I admit that such evidence as I have, though it is very slight, suggests that there has been some modification of the position of the new Government as compared with the old, on the question of the proposed Conference"—he felt he had dealt quite fairly with M. Nabokoff.

· · ·

> Offices of the War Cabinet
> 2, Whitehall Gardens
> London, S.W. 1
> August 10th, 1917

My dear Prime Minister—

Mr. Sutherland forwarded me the telegram signed by Nabokoff on your instructions. I had already seen it, and in the course of my speech I took the opportunity of intimating that there had been a modification in the attitude of the new Government as compared with the old to the proposed Conference.

The Conference has adjourned till two o'clock with no debate, in order that the different sections can take counsel as to the course they propose to support when we resume this afternoon.

I think I ought to inform you that, after the most careful consideration, I came to the conclusion that I could take no other course than to stand by the advice I had given the day after my return from Russia. I endeavoured to make a statement of the position as I found it in Russia and since my return, both pro and con. It is absolutely impossible to estimate what decision the Conference will reach. If you would like to see me at its conclusion, I shall leave myself at your disposal for an appointment.

Yours sincerely,

ARTHUR HENDERSON

After the lunch interval, the Conference resumed and an animated debate, on a high level of realism and seriousness, took place. The executive's resolution in favour of participation in a consultative conference was moved by W. C. Robinson, of the Textile Workers, and seconded by W. Carter, of the Miners. The rejection was moved by James Sexton, who said that to go to Stockholm was to go to meet men who had not repudiated masters whose hands were red with the blood of Nurse Cavell, Captain Fryatt, and the crew of the *Belgian Prince*. It was seconded, in a very able speech, by G. N. Barnes, Minister of Pensions. He ridiculed the distinction between a consultative and a mandatory conference, and said: "The main fact is that, if you go there, you will be going to discuss terms of peace." The rest, he said, was all phrase-mongering. "I believe that the only way of ending this war is the way in which our brave boys at the front are trying to end it." G. H. Roberts, supporting the rejection, said that Stockholm would only be an embarrassment to Kerensky. Referring to MacDonald's speech, a little earlier, he ironically congratulated Henderson on his welcome into the "new majority." MacDonald roused the opposition to great anger by following up his statement that Russia needed their help to consolidate its democracy by suggesting that the democracies of Europe should now make a clear statement as to where they stood on peace terms, and: "Then," he cried, amid cheers and protests, "we can ask our German friends how far they agree and far they disagree." A powerful and effective speech came from J. H. Thomas. "I hope," he said, "that we shall not hear any more about the enemies of our country and the friends of our country. I am not afraid of meeting Germans. I am as true a patriot as anybody, and I am satisfied that no German will browbeat me or compel me to do anything contrary to the best interests of my country."

When the vote was taken, there were 1,846,000 votes for Stockholm, to 550,000 against—a more than three-to-one majority.

By the Press the result was received with something like stupefaction. Fed from the Downing Street bureau with stories that Henderson was going to oppose, convinced that, whether or no, Stockholm was going to be beaten, they had, on the morning, gone all out against him. The afternoon editions travestied his speech; notably, there appeared what may in origin have been a mistake of hearing, but was persisted in and used with suspicious insistence. He had said that they should *supplement* military by political effort; "supplement," however, was printed as *supplant*. This went on being used against him, for months, nay years. Stockholm itself was, of course, described—as the Prime Minister was himself to describe it in the House next Monday—as "a fraternising Conference with the enemy." A tornado of accusations of bad faith, treachery, betrayal of his country, defeatism and dishonour whirled round Henderson's head, in the evening papers. On the Saturday morning, these charges were repeated and supported with a wealth of curious detail. In particular, it was stated, categorically, that the Russian Government was now against the Conference, and that Henderson knew it. Thus *The Times* solemnly declared: "We have every reason to believe that the Russian Government have now dissociated themselves from the whole project, and that Mr. Henderson was aware of the fact when he made his speech." The *Daily Express* was even more specific. They were "able to state, on the best authority, that M. Kerensky and his colleagues are entirely indifferent to the Conference." The indifference of Saturday had, by Sunday, become definite hostility: Kerensky is against the Conference—that was the refrain in pretty nearly every paper.

Interest in Kerensky and Russia, however, was pale and remote, compared with that created by the news flashed all over the country, and indeed the world, on the Saturday evening—Henderson's resignation. On the Friday evening, after the Conference, he had an interview with the Prime Minister, of which there is no record. As a result, he wrote, early on the Saturday morning, and sent round by hand, the following letter:

> Offices of the War Cabinet
> 2, Whitehall Gardens
> August 11th, 1917

Dear Prime Minister—
  At our interview last night I gather you had reached the conclusion that my retention of the post of Secretary to the Labour Party was no longer compatible with my membership

of the War Cabinet. Recent experiences have impressed me
with the embarrassing complications arising from this duality
of office. In the circumstances, therefore, I deem it advisable
to ask you to release me from further membership of your
Government.

I continue to share your desire that the war should be carried
to a successful conclusion, and trust that in a non-Government
capacity I may be able to render some little assistance to this
end.

I remain,
Yours sincerely,
ARTHUR HENDERSON

Mr. Lloyd George at once sent this to the Press, with a much
longer covering letter of his own, in which he repeated and amplified
the newspaper charges of deceiving the Labour Conference, and added
to them the equally grave charge of having misled colleagues in the
Cabinet.

This was jam for the evening and Sunday papers. They went all out
against Henderson, who was denounced in quite unmeasured terms as
a traitor, a liar, and a pacifist—worst term of abuse then current.
During the week-end the charges reverberated, accumulating momen-
tum by their noise. . . . On July 26th, Henderson was ready to resign
on the Stockholm issue. On August 1st, he dared the War Cabinet to
demand his resignation, again on this issue. On August 7th, when he
told Mr. Lloyd George that a refusal of passports for Stockholm
would compel him to choose between his membership of the Cabinet
and his secretaryship of the Party, there was no doubt in his mind, and
can have been none in the Prime Minister's, which he would sacrifice.
It may have occurred to the latter's nimble intelligence that he could
be made to lose both, but he knew that he would not give up his
Labour association; that was unthinkable. At the Cabinet of the 8th
the issue discussed was passports. From this fact, the natural infer-
ence to be drawn is that Henderson's view on Stockholm, or the
Cabinet's view, was not discussed, for the simple reason that both
were by then entirely familiar. That passports were discussed further
suggests that it was also accepted that Henderson was going to advise
the Conference to go to Stockholm; only in such case would the
demand for passports arise. If he advised the Conference against
Stockholm, there could be little doubt in the mind of any member of
the Cabinet that the Conference would reject it; only on the assump-

tion that he was going to advise for it did a decision in its favour, and therefore the issue or non-issue of passports for delegates to go, come into the picture.

Nor does Mr. Lloyd George, in charging Henderson with a sudden change of front on the 8th, suggest any arguments that could have motived it. The reader of the *War Memoirs,* although the atmosphere has been subtly prepared for him by the picture of a magnetised and malaria-stricken man, already quoted, meets the reported change with surprise; looks back to see whether he has not missed or overlooked something, and fails to find it. There is, of course, no refuting an account of Cabinet transactions. Henderson tried to defend himself on this, in the House; he jumped up, more than once, calling for minutes, but Mr. Lloyd George swept on. Inviolability of discussion and loyal observance of collective responsibility are vital to democratic government; no one took this view more strongly than Henderson; at no stage did he reveal what passed at Cabinets, not even in the interest of his own defence. The one issue known to have been raised on the 8th is that of passports. True a sentence in the letter he wrote from the Conference was used by Lloyd George to imply that he had changed; but that sentence can at most be read to mean that the writer, on reflection, felt a doubt as to whether he had, in face of massed opinion against him, permitted his colleagues to gather, by default, an impression that he agreed with them. He was not, in committee, at this period, quick in the uptake; he may, by silence, have allowed an impression to arise. More cannot be read into the letter. To read even that, or anything like it, always seemed to him ridiculous. A last-minute shift of ground on his part is, anyhow, a psychological improbability; the fact that Mr. Lloyd George, in charging him with it, found it necessary to buttress his theory up by going on to suggest that he misled his Labour colleagues also, is significant.

For this second charge was a piece of manufacture—most ingenious manufacture, since, while little was directly stated, everything was most cleverly implied, and truth and untruth so inextricably wound together that detachment is not easy, even now. According to Lloyd George—in the House of Commons in 1917, and in his book twenty years later—Henderson was informed by him, on the morning of August 10th, that the Russian Government had changed its position. In the House of Commons, although not in his book, he caused members to believe, as he had caused readers of the newspapers during the week-end to believe, that the form of this intimation was a telegram to the effect that Kerensky—key figure in the whole picture, since he was almost the only Russian minister whose personality England had grasped—was, now, against Stockholm. He had sent Henderson a message, on the morning of the 10th; but it was not from, nor about, Kerensky: his name was not mentioned in it. He spoke after Henderson, and refused to permit himself to be interrupted, when the latter endeavoured to get him to admit that he had seen no message from Kerensky. What Henderson said was:

> Now, it is difficult, if you read the papers, to follow exactly what did take place. The suggestion is thrown out that I received a telegram on Friday, the day of the Conference, from Kerensky. I understand that a telegram from Kerensky did come. I never received it. I was told at seven o'clock on the Friday night, while I was waiting in the Secretary's room at No. 10, Downing Street, that a telegram had been received, since the Conference closed, through the French Embassy, saying that Kerensky dissociated himself from the Conference. I did not receive that telegram. I have not received that telegram yet. The only knowledge I have of the telegram is the statement made to me by Professor Mantoux while I was waiting in the Secretary's room.

On this, he could only set his word against Lloyd George's. The verdict of the House of Commons majority—which regarded the very idea of Stockholm with horror—was that L.G. made mincemeat of him. Certainly that was the intention. Master in a kind of tactics in which Henderson was no match for him, Lloyd George conveyed the impression that, if Henderson liked to lie about the Kerensky message, he was, as likely as not, lying also about what happened in the Cabinet. There were, in fact, *two* Russian messages, one which Henderson had seen and the other which he had not. Moreover, the one which he had not seen was bogus.

On this second message, light is thrown by M. Nabokoff, author of the first. In his interesting, if pathetic, *Ordeal of a Diplomat,* he says:

> On the next morning (August 10th), I was invited to Downing Street. I found the Prime Minister in a very angry mood. He showed me a telegram from Albert Thomas—"Kerensky ne veut pas de conférence." A copy of my note to Mr. Balfour was in the hands of the Prime Minister, who said to me, "This note is a document of the highest importance."

Nabokoff goes on to say that, to him, the origin of this Albert Thomas telegram was "mysterious." He did not for a moment treat it as authentic. He knew that, whatever Kerensky might privately think, he dare not, and could not, say in Russia that he regarded Stockholm as a nuisance. To him, it would be a disaster to have such a telegram published, whether forgery or no. Mr. Lloyd George must have known this, too; yet the words "Kerensky ne veut pas de conférence" that evening (10th) went the round of the newspaper offices—sent out, from Downing Street, after it was known that the Labour Conference was voting for Stockholm. So soon as he saw it, Kerensky denied its authenticity. He had not sent it or said what it reported him to say; he was not against Stockholm. The first message from him, repudiating it, came while the debate was going on in the House of Commons. Who in fact sent the telegram has not been disclosed: but Kerensky had nothing to do with it.

Henderson, anyhow, knew nothing of it, until he read the vaguely veiled accounts of its purport in the Press, on the 11th. Though sent out from Downing Street on the evening of the 10th, it was not shown to him by the Prime Minister when he visited him there that night. On the morning of the 10th, the Prime Minister had sent him a quite different message: Nabokoff's note. He used the confusion between the two to destroy Henderson. Not till the end of the week did denials from Kerensky and the Russian Government, specific and definite as they were, suggest to a few analytically disposed minds the explanation of the puzzle presented by the apparent dishonesty of an honest man. There were two messages; the Prime Minister had deceived the public and the House into believing there was only one.

He was as well aware as was Henderson, or Nabokoff, that it would be highly detrimental, and even dangerous, to Kerensky to publish anything which suggested that he was against Stockholm. To involve him in this risk, on the basis of an anonymous message, which the only Russian who saw it dismissed, at once, as fraudulent, was, literally, to stab him in the back. But on the 10th, as Nabokoff naïvely records, "The Prime Minister was very angry"—with Henderson. He saw what a weapon against him was in his hands, and that was all he cared to see at the moment. Nabokoff had his consolations. On August 13th (day of the debate) he had his second interview with the P.M.

He appeared to be fully aware of the fact that the declaration of the Russian government in regard to the Stockholm

Conference, which had enabled him to take the action he considered as being in the best interests of the Allied cause, was
due to my initiative. He also realised that I had taken this step
in face of the bitter opposition of the Soviet. Mr. Lloyd George
therefore expressed his appreciation of the service I had rendered in very warm and complimentary terms. This was the
last occasion on which I had the honour of meeting the P.M.

He had served his purpose.

On the 13th appeared Kerensky's denials; on the 15th Tereschenko
wired to Nabokoff that "It is desirable that you should confine yourself to transmitting to the Government to which you are accredited the
exact text of our declarations on matters of principle." Nabokoff's
reply that he "thought it necessary to give whatever assistance I could
to the British Government" crossed telegrams from Tereschenko in
which he stated that "No declarations against the Stockholm Conference could be made by M. Kerensky." These protests were immediate;
but they were vain; as vain as the enthusiastic congratulations transmitted to Arthur Henderson by Tseretelli on his own behalf and on
that of the Soviet. Stockholm was killed.

It was too late; a great opportunity had been blindly destroyed.
Had the Conference taken place, with good will, in the autumn of
1917, the war might have been shortened, and the peace might have
been worthy of its countless sacrifices. As it was, the dangers Henderson had foreseen—that Russia would go Bolshevik, and that, to the
advantage of Germany, it would go out of the war—were realised
before the year was out. The Stockholm Conference never took place.
Instead, the Second Revolution took Russia out of the war and lost it
for democracy. He would gladly have paid more than his position in
the Cabinet could he have averted this. The Stockholm issue had
stirred him, profoundly. For a time, he was torn by a sharp conflict
of loyalties. But from the hour in which he reached the conclusion
that, since Stockholm was going to take place, British Labour ought
to be there, he did not waver in a decision whose possible price he
foresaw.

Where, in these transactions, he did fail was, not in the integrity of
his own attitude, but in his rooted inclination to attribute a similar
integrity to others. He was too simple to fight Lloyd George. Out of
the entire nexus of incidents, what remained to hurt him was the
revelation of trickery and duplicity where he had believed in loyalty
and good faith. In the early autumn of that year, the Order of Com-

panions of Honour was created by the King. The following letter says all that need be said:

> Dear Prime Minister—
> I have to acknowledge receipt of your undated note intimating that His Majesty has been graciously pleased to approve that I should receive the honour of Companion of Honour.
> Under other circumstances, it would have been my pleasure to accept His Majesty's gracious pleasure, but in view of the charges you have thought fit publicly to make against me, I must ask you to ask His Majesty to excuse my non-acceptance of His Majesty's gracious offer.
>
> I remain,
Yours sincerely,
ARTHUR HENDERSON

Lloyd George's Position

Fresh from the glow of that atmosphere of emotionalism and exaltation which great revolutions excite, Mr. Henderson was out of tune with the stern but rigid sense of responsibility and self-control which was dominant here. When he came back from Russia the fine steel of his character was magnetised by his experiences. He was in an abnormal frame of mind. He had more than a touch of the revolutionary malaria. His temperature was high and his mood refractory. The Executive of the British Labour Party offered to nominate him, as its Secretary, to go along with its chairman, Mr. Wardle, and its Treasurer, Mr. Ramsay MacDonald, as their delegates to Paris with the Russian Soviet emissaries. He accepted the nomination. It was a profound blunder. As a Member of the British War Cabinet, he had no right to go off to Paris without even consulting his colleagues in the Cabinet, arm in arm with Ramsay MacDonald, who was openly opposed to the War and to all measures for its effective prosecution, and had been organising pacifist propaganda, to talk over with French Socialists the arrangements for an International Conference of which his own Government did not approve, and to which our Allies, the French, the Italians and the Americans, were strongly opposed.

From "Stockholm and Mr. Arthur Henderson" in *War Memoirs of David Lloyd George*, Vol. IV, Boston, 1934, pp. 148–67. Reprinted by permission of the Beaverbrook Trust.

Mr. Henderson failed to put in an appearance at the meetings of the War Cabinet on the 25th and 26th of July. At the latter meeting, the question was raised of his proposed visit to Paris, which had come to the knowledge of the Foreign Office through the application of the Labour Party delegates for passports. Mr. Henderson had not notified the War Cabinet of his intentions, though he cabled me in Paris where I was at the time, stating that he was coming to Paris with four Russian delegates and Messrs. Wardle and MacDonald—not, however, stating their business.

The War Cabinet was naturally a good deal perturbed at the news of Mr. Henderson's intended trip and decided that Mr. Henderson should be asked to confer with his colleagues in the War Cabinet at 7.30 P.M. that evening, with a view to their ascertaining from him how far the proposed action committed His Majesty's Government to the meeting of British Socialist representatives with enemy Socialist representatives at Stockholm; and whether the inclusion of Mr. Ramsay MacDonald among those chosen to proceed to Paris implied official recogntion by the British Government of Mr. Ramsay MacDonald's status as a representative of British Socialists.

This conference with Mr. Henderson was duly held, and the Members of the War Cabinet told him clearly how thoroughly they disapproved of the course he had decided to take. He intimated to them that he had made up his mind and his arrangements for the visit, and could not and would not draw back. Mr. Bonar Law and his Cabinet colleagues were in a difficult position, for they could hardly prohibit Mr. Henderson from going, nor yet demand his resignation from the War Cabinet as a condition of his action; and yet it was clear that they would be blamed by Parliament and the country for allowing the Cabinet to be mixed up, through one of its members, in a discussion between Mr. Ramsay MacDonald and French and Russian Socialists, about arrangements for a World Socialist Conference where Germans would discuss with British pacifists how to end the War and on what terms to arrange peace. Mr. Henderson was in an aggressive mood and informed them that it was on his advice that the Executive of the Labour Party had now decided in favour of sending delegates to Stockholm. This met with unanimous disapproval from the Cabinet, and Mr. Henderson told them that if they insisted he was willing to tender his resignation from the War Cabinet. Naturally they could not press him to do this, for they knew that I greatly valued his membership and appreciated the help he had rendered the Government in our relations with Labour. So amid this atmosphere of disapproval he went off to Paris.

His behaviour at Paris was hardly of a nature to reassure public opinion here. Along with Mr. Ramsay MacDonald, he became a member of a small sub-committee to examine and revise the proposed arrangements for the Stockholm Conference. The other members were a left-wing and a right-wing French Socialist, and two of the delegates from the Russian Soviet—Messrs. Ehrlich and Goldenberg, from the right and left wing respectively of Russian Socialism. On this committee Mr. Henderson tried hard to secure agreement that the Stockholm Conference should not go further than mutual consultation as to the war aims of the respective belligerent countries, and the lines on which they might be willing to make peace, and that it should not proceed further to pass binding resolutions on these matters, where neutrals and the enemy might outvote British Socialists upon issues vital for this country. He had some success in this effort, but the fact that then and subsequently this question seems to have been unresolved, and that there was a strong wish on the part of a number of the national Socialist groups proposing to attend Stockholm to make it the occasion for authoritative pronouncements, shows how recklessly Mr. Henderson was plunging in supporting the scheme.

He returned to England on August 1st, and had an interview with me at which he recounted his proceedings. I could not disguise the unpleasant character of the situation which he had created by his action. At the same time I was extremely unwilling to lose him from the Government. He had been a loyal and courageous colleague. He had done some very fine work for the country as a member of my own Cabinet and of the preceding one, in helping us to keep in touch with Labour and in getting the Trade Unions to coöperate with us in necessary war measures. I also had a warm personal esteem for him. So I decided to talk the whole thing over with the rest of the War Cabinet and seek their agreement with the course of retaining him with us, if at all practicable. I asked him to come round to the Cabinet that afternoon at half-past four, to discuss matters with us.

It was of course inevitable that the other members of the War Cabinet would wish to express their views in this discussion with considerable frankness, and we decided to get this part over before asking Mr. Henderson to join us. As a result, he was asked on his arrival to wait a while in my Secretary's rooms. This was the famous "doormat" incident. Unfortunately the delay, which was designed solely to spare him personal unpleasantness, lasted about an hour, and when at the end of that time Mr. Barnes went out to speak to him about what had been taking place, he found Mr. Henderson in a highly resentful frame of mind. There was no longer any question of his offering to resign, as he had done at the Cabinet meeting before he left for Paris. On the contrary, he challenged us to demand his resignation—which, as I have said, was the last thing I wished to do. He recounted the circumstances of his decision to visit Paris, and urged that his course there had been on wise lines, particularly in regard to making the Stockholm Conference a consultation and not an assembly at which binding decisions should be taken. As to whether he himself would propose to go to Stockholm if invited by the British Labour Party, he declined to give a definite answer. "He had always realised that it would be very difficult for him to proceed to Stockholm as a Member of the British War Cabinet. Consequently, if he should receive a nomination for the Conference, he would have to reconsider the whole position according to circumstances."

We made it clear to him that we wanted to retain him in the Cabinet, and examined with him how the case could best be stated in Parliament, which wished to discuss the matter that evening on the adjournment. It was generally agreed that Mr. Henderson could dispose of criticism in the House of Commons by pointing out that the difficulty had arisen from the fact that he held a dual position as a Member of the War Cabinet and as Secretary of the Executive Committee of the British Labour Party. It might frankly be admitted that, on the present occasion, this had entailed some misunderstanding, but it must be borne in mind that it also possessed great advantages. It had enabled Mr. Henderson in the past to keep in the closest possible touch with the views of the Labour Party, and so, by first-hand information, to assist the Government in preparing its war measures on lines which would be acceptable to Labour. Moreover, it had enabled Mr. Henderson to attend the previous Conferences of Allied Socialists with good results. For example, only last Christmas he had attended a Socialist Conference at Paris, where he had met with considerable opposition, but had eventually induced the Conference to take the view which he shared with the British Government in regard to the prosecution of the War. Further, he could point out that members of the French and other Allied Governments occupied a position similar to his own. On balance, therefore, the dual nature of his position had been an advantage.

We recognised that the House of Commons was less concerned at the moment about Stockholm than with the fact that Mr. Henderson, a Member of the War Cabinet, had gone off to this Paris meeting in company with Mr. Ramsay MacDonald, who only a day or two earlier had been making himself conspicuous as the leader of the pacifists in a debate on war aims in the House of Commons and who, in the Manifesto of Aims of the Leeds Conference, which he had a leading part in summoning, had declared that its purpose was to make this country like Russia. But we suggested that Mr. Henderson could remind Parliament that this was not the first conference to which he had gone in MacDonald's company. Their association on such occasions was inevitable, since one was Secretary and the other Treasurer of the British Labour Party. If he also reaffirmed his war attitude on the lines of some of his recent speeches, he should satisfy the House.

Mr. Henderson had to face a rather unfriendly Chamber that evening, when on the motion for the adjournment he was called to give an account of his conduct to the House of Commons. In his defence he urged that one important part of his Paris visit had been to make arrangements for an Inter-Allied Socialist Conference; that, as to the Stockholm proposal, he had found, when in Russia, that the Russians were strongly in favour of it, so he had willingly accepted the invitation of the Labour Party to be a member of the Delegation to Paris to make arrangements for it; that the anomaly of his doing so while a member of the War Cabinet was inherent in his dual position. He had accompanied Mr. Ramsay MacDonald to Paris and on to the sub-committee there, because he wanted to keep him in order. "I deemed it of the highest importance that I should go on the sub-committee to assist in keeping my Hon. Friend the Member for Leicester right. . . . If there had to be a representative of the Minority, and if that representative was elected by the Executive of the Party, then I was not going to demur. I was going to accept the position, and do what I could, if I found him going astray. . . ." And apart from his duty of chaperoning Mr. MacDonald and keeping him out of mischief, Mr. Henderson urged that if there was going to be a Stockholm Conference, it was his duty to see that it was held at a date when the Americans could be present if they wished, and that it was a consultative, not a binding assembly. He suggested that there might be considerable advantages in the holding of such a conference, but at the same time made it clear that his own views on our war aims and the need of fighting till we could win them were unaltered.

A little later in the debate I myself spoke warmly in Henderson's defence. I paid a tribute to his war services to the Government and justified the anomaly of his dual status as Member of the War Cabinet and Secretary of the Labour Party on the ground of its proved practical utility. In France, M. Albert Thomas occupied an analogous position. I promised that the Government would give this problem its careful consideration and would consult about it with France. The Government was not committed to Stockholm. The Inter-Allied Conference in London was a different matter, and we thought this very desirable. In conclusion, I begged the House not to take a line which might increase the troubles of the Russian Government, which was just then facing extraordinary difficulties.

My speech had the desired effect of moderating the temper of the House. The motion for adjournment was talked out and the difficult corner safely rounded. But the affair left Mr. Henderson in a stubborn and defiant temper which was before long to cause further trouble. A combination of pugnacity and sensitiveness is not easily appeased.

At this time the situation in Russia was causing us grave anxiety. For a good while past, its government had borne a most indefinite and unreliable character. While the official Executive was preaching a continuance of the War, it was allowing the utmost civil and military disorder. Bolshevist Commissars, representing the left wing of the Soviet, incited the troops to abandon the War and shoot their officers. They persuaded workmen to leave their tasks in munition factories. There was no certainty who was really governing Russia. At the beginning of August, the whole government fell into chaos, and on August 4th, Sir George Buchanan told us in a cable "We are at present without a Government, so that there is no one to whom I can speak." A telegram of the same date from the Military Attaché at Petrograd informed us:

> As things stand at present, this country is travelling straight to ruin. No real measures have been taken during the last fortnight to reëstablish among the troops in the rear, either the authority of the officers or discipline among the ranks. Until discipline in the rear has been established and the troops are made to fight, there is not the slightest hope of an improvement in the conduct of the Army at the front. And while there is no discipline in the Army, the men in the railway repair shops and in the mines cannot be made to work.

If things are allowed to go on as at present, there will be a

general breakdown of railway transport in the winter, and that
will result in a famine in Petrograd and in the Army. The only
man at present with any magnetic influence among the Ministers is Kerensky, and he does not yet understand the necessity
of discipline. Among his immediate military advisers, none are
men of character. The Socialists would prefer to run a class
war rather than the national war, and to the mass of the
soldiers this appeals as being not so dangerous. . . .

A few days later, Kerensky formed a coalition government in
which the Soviet was only one of the groups represented. Its influence
was to some extent overpowered and held in check by the other
groups.

At the meeting of the War Cabinet on August 8th we discussed
once again the question of the Stockholm Conference. We had learnt
both from the United States and the Italian Government that they
were not going to allow representatives from their countries to go to
Stockholm. We were also opposed to the Conference, as was France.
The Attorney-General had circulated to the Cabinet on the previous
day the information that it would be illegal for any British subject to
engage in conference with enemy subjects except with the authority of
the Crown. Mr. Henderson was at first inclined to urge that this
decision should be forthwith published, but after consulting with his
Labour colleagues, he found that they were unanimously opposed to
this being done before the Labour Party conference, which was to take
place on August 10th, and he informed me that he agreed with this
decision. He suggested, however, that instead of the Government
announcing its opposition to the Stockholm Conference, we should
wait until after the Labour Party meeting, for if this turned down the
proposal, nothing further would be necessary. This idea was discussed
with him at our Cabinet meeting on the 8th, and it was felt that it
would be much more convenient to the Russian Government, and
more conducive to the maintenance of good relations between the
British Government and the Labour Party, that the working men
themselves should refuse to attend rather than that the Government
should announce their decision and thereby appear to dictate to the
Labour Party. This course, it had been ascertained by personal
enquiry, was also acceptable to the French Government. From this
point of view the best course appeared to be to leave the final decision
until after the meeting of the Labour Party on Friday, August 10th.
We decided that in replying to any questions on the matter in the

House of Commons, Mr. Bonar Law should confine himself to stating that:

(*a*) The attendance of British delegates at the Conference would be illegal.

(*b*) Such a Conference could not be attended by British delegates without the permission of the Government.

(*c*) The whole question was being examined by Government.

(*d*) It was obviously one which concerned not this Government alone, and

(*e*) A full statement would be made on Monday, the 13th August.

Mr. Henderson was present at this Cabinet meeting, and took part in the discussion which ended in the decisions which I have here set out. Apart from him and myself, there were also present the other members of the War Cabinet—Lord Curzon, Lord Milner, Mr. Bonar Law and General Smuts—and in addition, Mr. Balfour, Lord Robert Cecil, Lord Derby and Sir William Robertson. I am not speaking alone from my own recollection, but from that of all these eight responsible statesmen, when I say that the impression we all had was that Mr. Henderson at this discussion recognised the impossibility of pressing the Stockholm Conference and agreed with us that it must be abandoned. Indeed, he assured us that he expected the Labour Conference would turn it down "by a fair majority."

Our surprise therefore may be judged when in the Press on Friday morning there appeared the statement that Mr. Henderson was still in favour of sending British delegates to Stockholm, and would urge that view in the Labour Conference to be held that day. We were of course aware that Mr. Henderson held to the idea that Stockholm was greatly desired by the Russians, particularly by Kerensky. But it so happened that the last few days had seen a considerable change in the Russian situation. The power of the Soviet for the time being had been greatly reduced, and Kerensky's need to conciliate it by supporting its desire for the Stockholm Conference was now far less urgent. This fact, and the circumstance that the Russian Government was no longer concerned about the holding of the Conference, were communicated in a letter from the Russian Embassy which we received on Thursday morning, and which was promptly circulated to members of the Cabinet. It was in Mr. Henderson's possession on Thursday evening, by his own subsequent admission, when he was preparing his speech for the Friday meeting of the Labour Party. . . . The Russian Government was now no longer under the heel of the extreme Socialists of the Soviet, by whom the renewed move for a Stockholm Conference had been fathered, and was striving to shake free from their domination still more. The holding of the Stockholm Conference at their instigation would not strengthen Kerensky's hands in his struggle with them.

Knowing this; knowing too, that the War Cabinet of which he was a member was definitely opposed to the Stockholm Conference, and that it would be illegal for British subjects to attend it, Mr. Henderson went to the Labour Conference on Friday morning and delivered a passionate oration in favour of British Socialists sending representatives there. News of this was brought to me, and I promptly sent him round a further copy of M. Nabokoff's letter with a request that he would communicate it to the Conference. He did not do so, holding apparently that he had sufficiently covered the ground in his speech when he stated that there had been a tremendous change in the position in Russia since he was there, and that "Such evidence as we have, though it is slight, suggests that there has been a modification in the Government's attitude towards the Conference." . . .

In the voting at the afternoon session the effect of Mr. Henderson's plea was to persuade the British Labour Party to reverse its previous decision and resolve by more than three to one in favour of being represented at Stockholm.

The War Cabinet considered this situation the same evening. Mr. Henderson was not present. He had avoided the meetings of the Cabinet since the one on Wednesday, August 8th, to which I have referred, when he had learned that no delegates could legally go to Stockholm, and that the Cabinet was opposed to British representation there. In face of the report of the Labour Conference vote, the Cabinet renewed their determination not to allow British representation at Stockholm, and decided to approach the French, Italian and United States Governments informing them of our decision.

At this meeting a communication was read from M. Albert Thomas, stating that a telegram had been received from Petrograd to the effect that the Provisional Government had disinterested itself in the Stockholm Conference, and that M. Kerensky desired that it should not meet.

There remained to be considered the position of Mr. Henderson. Feeling in the War Cabinet was very strong as to his action in thus publicly urging upon British Labour the adoption of a course to which we were definitely opposed, and one which we considered, in common with our Allies, to be detrimental to our position and war interests. Although I was profoundly unwilling to ask for his resignation, it seemed in the circumstances impossible to avoid taking firm action. We decided that I should send him a letter of remonstrance, the terms of which were agreed by the War Cabinet, and that for the time he should not be summoned to Cabinet meetings nor have Cabinet documents circulated to him. Before actually dispatching the letter, however, we agreed to make further enquiry from the Russian Embassy about the use which could be made of M. Nabokoff's communication of August 8th.

When we met again on Saturday morning, August 11th, there were two new factors in the situation. Mr. Henderson had tendered his resignation, at the same time informing me that he continued to share my desire that the War should be carried to a successful conclusion, and that he trusted to be able to still assist us to this end in a non-governmental capacity. And M. Nabokoff had given us full permission to publish the communication from the Russian Government, so long as his name was not mentioned.

I replied to Mr. Henderson's letter of resignation as follows:

11th August, 1917

My dear Henderson,

I am in receipt of your letter of this morning, tendering your resignation of your position as a member of the War Cabinet, and have received the permission of His Majesty, to whom I submitted your resignation, to accept it. My colleagues and I have received with satisfaction the assurance of your unabated desire to assist in the prosecution of the War to a successful conclusion, and they greatly regret that you can no longer be directly and officially associated with them in that enterprise. There are, however, certain facts with which it is essential that the public should be acquainted in order that they may form a correct appreciation of the events that have led to this regrettable conclusion.

The first is that your colleagues were taken completely by surprise by the attitude which you adopted at the Labour Conference yesterday afternoon. You knew that they were, in the present circumstances, unanimously opposed to the Stockholm Conference, and you had yourself been prepared to agree to an announcement to that effect some days ago. At your suggestion however, and that of your Labour colleagues, it was decided to defer any such announcement until after the meeting yesterday.

I was under the impression, after several talks with you, that you meant to use your influence against meeting enemy representatives at Stockholm. What has happened in Russia during the last few weeks has materially affected the position in reference to that Conference. You admitted to me that the situation had completely changed even within the last fortnight, and that whatever ground you might have thought there was for delegates from Allied countries attending such a Conference a fortnight ago, the events of the last few days had shown you the unwisdom of such a course. That was clearly what you led me to believe; it was also the impression left on the minds of your colleagues in the Cabinet and of your Labour colleagues in the Ministry. It was therefore with no small surprise that I received a letter from you yesterday afternoon stating that you "ought to inform me that after the most careful consideration you had come to the conclusion that you could take no other course than to stand by the advice you had given the day after your return from Russia," and that your colleagues subsequently read the speech which you had delivered.

Surely this was a conclusion of which you ought to have informed the Cabinet before you entered the Conference. When you spoke at that Conference you were not merely a member of the Labour Party, but a member of the Cabinet, responsible for the conduct of the War. Nevertheless, you did not deem it necessary to inform the Conference of the views of your colleagues, and the delegates were accordingly justified in assuming that the advice you gave was not inconsistent with their opinions.

The second point is this. Yesterday morning we received a most important communication from the Russian Government, in which we were informed that "although the Russian Government did not deem it possible to prevent Russian delegates from taking part in the Stockholm Conference, they regarded it as a Party concern and its decisions as in no wise binding on the liberty of action of the Government." And further the covering letter which accompanied this communication contained these words: "I hasten to lay before you the above information, as I fear that the impression has hitherto prevailed that, in the words of one of the London newspapers, 'Russia ardently desired the Stockholm Conference,' and this argument has been put forward in order to influence British public opinion in favour of the Labour and Socialist Parties of Great Britain participating in the Conference."

Immediately on receipt of this intimation, I sent it over to you with a request that you should communicate it to the Conference. You omitted to do so. It is true that in the course of your speech you made a very casual reference to "some modification" in the attitude of the Russian Government; but there is a manifest difference between the effect which would necessarily be produced upon any audience by an indifferent summary of that description and the communication to them of official information showing that the attitude of the Russian Government towards the Stockholm Conference was very different from what had been supposed.

In these circumstances, your action does not appear to have been fair either to the Government or to the delegates whom you were addressing. They were left in ignorance of a vital fact which must necessarily have affected their judgment.

I am sending a copy of this correspondence to the Press.

Yours sincerely,

D. LLOYD GEORGE

It was of course inevitable that the Parliament should discuss the situation which had arisen, and a debate upon Mr. Henderson's resignation took place as soon as the House of Commons began its Orders of the Day on Monday, August 13th. In preparation for this debate the Cabinet reviewed the situation that morning, and decided that Mr. Balfour should have a personal interview with Mr. Henderson before he made his statement, to arrange with him how far he could make public use of the private official information concerning the issue. We felt that Mr. Henderson, being on his defence, should be given all facilities for utilising as much of the information as was necessary to his case and compatible with the public interest.

In the course of our Cabinet discussion, we reviewed the circumstances which had brought it about that while in May we were prepared to consider allowing delegates to go to Stockholm, in July we were definitely opposed to the Conference. We noted that the reason for this change of attitude was that in May the Russian Government were in the hands of the Workmen's and Soldiers' Committee, and, under its influence, were then inclined strongly in favour of the Stockholm Conference, and that the British Government were, in this matter, to a great extent influenced by their desire to support the authority of a newly formed body which had not yet firmly established itself. The consequence of the influence exerted by the Soviet, however, had been to shatter the discipline of the Russian Army and the organisation of the nation, and the Russian Government were at the moment taking measures to reëstablish discipline in their forces by means which were absolutely contrary to the principles of the Soviet, and showed that the policy of the extreme revolutionaries had been discredited.

To permit the attendance of British representatives at the Stockholm Conference, which was tantamount to countenancing fraternisation between one section of the Allied British public and one section of the enemy public, would be very prejudicial to the policy which the Russian Government were engaged on and were pressing forward, the very first item of which was the prohibition of fraternisation between Russian troops and those of the enemy.

It was recognised that no difficulty would be found in proving, on the above lines, that the conditions had completely changed since May, 1917, but that there would be considerable difficulty in doing so without embarrassing M. Kerensky.

This last point was the really difficult aspect of the problem. M. Kerensky was still struggling with the power of the Soviet, and to some extent dependent on its good will. He dare not announce his open opposition to it without putting himself in the gravest peril from a body which was always rousing the mob with the cry of a danger of counterrevolution, and used bomb and revolver freely to dispose of opponents. Indeed, he found it necessary to declare an interview published a few days later by the *Daily News* that he was not opposed to the Stockholm Conference, and in fact that he thought it of great importance. Any other statement would probably have shortened his life.

The debate in the House on the Monday afternoon added little fresh to the story. The chief fact that emerged from Mr. Henderson's statement was that evidently he had stubbornly made up his mind to press through the decision in favour of the Stockholm Conference, and that the various contretemps, such as the friction with his Cabinet colleagues before he went to Paris, and his detention on the doormat of the Cabinet room after his return thence, had only stiffened his determination. He failed to make it clear why he had lain low and said nothing of this resolve at the Cabinet meeting, where it had been clearly settled that delegates would not be allowed to go to Stockholm. He suggested that if we had forced him to resign on the issue of Stockholm before the Labour Conference on Friday, it would have made the vote in favour of Stockholm only more emphatic.

My own speech was carefully restrained, for I did not want to add any avoidable bitterness to the situation. I expressed regret that Mr. Henderson had left his colleagues in ignorance of his real attitude on the issue. I regretted that he had seen fit to slur over the important communication from Russia, despite my request to him to communicate it to the Conference, and I hinted the strong reasons, based on the Russian situation and the attitude of our other Allies, for abandoning the Stockholm proposal.

VII

THE LABOUR PARTY IN 1918

A. J. P. TAYLOR

The Great War—
The Triumph of E. D. Morel (II)

1917 was in every country the great year of discussion for a negotiated peace; it was also the year which saw the dawn of the New World—in more senses than one. The earthly home of this Utopia still stands, as derelict as an abandoned Sandemanian chapel. When next in Soho, push your way through the parked cars and the equally stationary, though more aged, whores; brave the mixed smell of Continental cooking and exotic barber shops; and stand reverently before No. 5 Gerrard Street. There above a bakery was the 1917 Club, home of idealist enthusiasm: founded to commemorate the great year of liberty, and perishing appropriately in 1931, when J. A. Hobson, withdrawing in protest against the confusion of the accounts, fell heavily downstairs.

Two great events caused this Dawn. One was the entry of the United States into the war; the other was the Russian Revolution. Together they determined the shape of the world in which we still live. Both marked the triumph of idealism. The war to make the world safe for democracy eclipsed the conflict of rival Imperialisms. At the beginning the Russian Revolution counted for more with the Dissenters.

From *The Trouble Makers Dissent over Foreign Policy 1792–1939* by A. J. P. Taylor, London, Hamish Hamilton, 1958, pp. 145–56. Reprinted by permission of author and publisher.

A democratic Russia was "the virtual solution of the problem of the war" [1]—the problem, that is how Germany could be defeated without Russia's winning. Snowden said: "It has given us a new hope in democracy and revived our faith in Internationalism." [2] Not that it converted the Dissenters to support of the war. On the contrary it made them more convinced than ever that the war was unnecessary. They had long regarded old Russia's claim to Constantinople as the one obstacle to peace. New Russia had dropped this claim. The Radicals still believed that Germany was prepared to withdraw from Belgium and north eastern France. Soon they heard rumors of the Austrian peace offer, supposedly made in April 1917. Russia, Germany, Austria-Hungary all wanted peace. Yet it was not made. Why? The fault could only lie with the governments of England and France. France received most of the blame now that tsarist Russia was out of the way. The suspicions of Agadir were revived; and France appeared as an Imperialist Power, fighting for the left bank of the Rhine, with which Alsace-Lorraine was easily confused. But the British government did not escape condemnation. *The Nation* regarded the British demands for Mesopotamia and the German colonies as the principal obstacle to peace.[3] Ponsonby told the House of Commons that the British government had "prostituted the original disinterested motives with which you entered the war and . . . substituted a mean craving for gain and an arrogant demand for Imperial aggrandisement and domination, without the consent of the people, and behind the backs of the people." [4] . . .

Opposition to the war recovered its moral force. Before 1917 the Dissenters, pure pacifists apart, had been sane and rational, but they had been battling against the moral current. The Russian revolution, the Austrian peace offer, and finally the publication by the Bolsheviks of the so-called secret treaties, branded the supporters of the war as cynical and imperialist. Even Wilson's Fourteen Points did not restore the moral superiority of the war-makers; for the British and still more the French government were accused of planning to evade them—an accusation which swelled during the actual peace-making later. During 1917 the Dissenters repeatedly divided the House—a striking sign that they had recovered confidence. Thirty-two voted in favour of the

1. *The Nation*, 24 March 1917.
2. *Hansard*, fifth series, xciii, 1625.
3. *The Nation*, 30 June 1917.
4. 19 December 1917. *Hansard*, fifth series, xciii, 1999.

Russian peace terms on 16 May; 19 in favour of the Reichstag peace resolution on 26 July; 18 in favour of the Stockholm conference on 16 August; and 28 for a declaration of war aims on 13 February 1918. The figures are not impressive—always less than the support which Fox and Charles Grey received during the war against revolutionary France. But they were an immense improvement on the four or six who had raised their voices in the first two years. All the same, the Dissenters were embarked on a strange course. These votes were cast in support of what Noel Buxton called "an anti-annexationist and restoration settlement," [5] in other words a return to the *status quo* of 1914. Radicals of an earlier age would have been amazed to see their twentieth-century descendants marching under the banner of the Restoration and insisting that in international affairs, as in everything else, the best thing was to stand still, or rather to go back. The Radical Utopia now lay in the past, not in the future.

The movement for a peace of restoration reached its climax with the appeal for peace made in November 1917 by Lord Lansdowne —grandson of the Lord Henry Petty who had won Fox's admiration by demanding the liberation of Europe in 1806. Lansdowne was an extreme Conservative. To his bewilderment he was taken up by the Radicals. He found himself in the company of Noel Buxton, F. W. Hirst, Massingham of *The Nation,* and the business men from Liverpool who had once backed E. D. Morel's campaign over the Congo. These men formed the Lansdowne Committee for a peace by negotiation; their agitation flourished until the decisive victory of the Allies in the late summer of 1918. It was a strange end for the middle-class Radicals that they should rally under the leadership of a man who had broken with Gladstone over the Irish Land Act of 1881, had forced the crisis over the House of Lords by his uncompromising opposition to Liberal legislation, and now came hotfoot from wrecking the last chance of settling the Irish question by consent. The "weird combination" [6] went further. Lord Milner, sometimes called the second figure in the War Cabinet, also favoured "a peace of adjustment," and approached the Webbs through Haldane, in hope of securing the support of the Labour party. Milner's "adjustment" was that Germany should be allowed a free hand in Eastern Europe, on condition she surrendered her conquests in the West; the treaty of Brest-Litovsk was to be

5. 19 December 1917. *Hansard,* fifth series, c, 2040.
6. Wedgwood, 16 May 1918. *Hansard,* fifth series, 106, 610.

the foundation for a partnership to protect Western civilization against Bolshevism.

Once upon a time the Labour party would have been delighted to co-operate with Germany against Russia. With the fall of tsardom that time had passed. Milner's overture met with no response. Moreover it had come too late. The Labour party was at last beginning to devise its own foreign policy for "the democracy"; it no longer needed guidance from Lord Milner or anybody else. The process had taken a long time. In 1914 the Labour party supported the war almost unanimously. The Dissenters of the I.L.P. were forced into alliance with the few remaining Radicals, and away from the trade union leaders. When Allied Socialists met in February 1915, the Labour party agreed without discussion that, while capitalism caused wars, this particular war had been caused by the German invasion of Belgium and France. There was another striking breach with the pre-war Dissenting outlook on Keir Hardie's death in September 1915. The electoral truce was broken at Merthyr, his constituency; and a bellicose follower of Hyndman defeated the official Labour candidate, who had been nominated by the I.L.P. Most Labour leaders welcomed this ostensible defeat for their own party. In 1916 the party conference, the first since the outbreak of war, supported the war without a division. MacDonald, explaining that he was an opponent of secret diplomacy, not a friend of Germany, lamented: "Oh how sad it was, how heart-breaking it was, that some of them had to stand up and face the Conference with pride in their hearts as to what it was and doubt in their hearts as to what it would be!"

The Labour party was pushed into independence, willy-nilly, by the changed political circumstances which followed Lloyd George's seizure of power at the end of 1916. Asquith's government had been parliamentary even when it became a coalition; and since there were few Labour M.P.s, the party had little influence on policy. Lloyd George's government was made outside parliament, or even against it; for Asquith still commanded a powerful majority at the moment of his fall. Lloyd George owed his position to "public opinion," which in this case meant newspaper proprietors from Riddell and Northcliffe to C. P. Scott. He was more popular in the country than in parliament, which he rarely attended; and he defined his policy in public speeches, not in the House of Commons. He dealt directly with the great "interests," not with parliamentary votes; and the greatest of

these interests was "Labour." Henderson secured a seat in the War
Cabinet as the voice of this interest, not as leader of the few Labour
M.P.s. Moreover Lloyd George endorsed the view that Labour spoke
for "the people" and that they, as the old Radicals held, were peculiarly pacific and enlightened. He told the Labour party executive: "It
seemed inconceivable that any Minister should make terms of Peace
without consulting representatives of Labour"; and he hoped for, or
perhaps promised, Labour representation at the peace conference:
"I think nothing could conduce more to getting a satisfactory peace
. . . because you want above everything else to ensure that there will
be no more wars in the future." Here was a clear invitation to the
Labour party to formulate its own foreign policy.

A second, and more powerful, impulse came with the first Russian
revolution. Democratic Russia denounced the secret treaties and called
for a peace with "no annexations and no indemnities." This was a challenge to Socialist parties in other Allied countries. It seemed at first as
though the only response would come from the extreme Left. In June
1917 the I.L.P. and the B.S.P. set up the United Socialist Council—
the first appearance of the Popular Front, though by no means the
last; and this body summoned a Convention at Leeds, the name re-
calling the Chartist Convention of 1839 or even the Convention of the
great French Revolution. The Leeds Convention was intended to in-
augurate the British revolution. Its chief resolution, supported by
MacDonald and Snowden among others, called for the setting up of
Workers' and Soldiers' Councils—Soviets in fact. The Convention also
endorsed the Russian peace programme and instructed the British government to do the same. A historic moment. Previously British Radicals
had railed against alliance with Russia. Henceforth advanced Dissenters defined their foreign policy as endorsement of whatever Russia
happened to be doing at the moment. This was the only achievement at
Leeds. The eleven hundred delegates dispersed. The Convention vanished into limbo, taking the United Socialist Council along with it.

Nevertheless Henderson did not ignore the warning that Labour feeling was moving towards independence. He moved with it. The occasion
for his break to freedom was the proposed Socialist conference at
Stockholm, where Allied representatives would meet Germans for the
first time since the outbreak of war. Henderson at first opposed the
conference, then swung round in order to strengthen the flagging bellig-
erence of the Russian people; or, as he put it, "using the political

weapon to supplement our military activities." He was in an odd position—at once a member of the War Cabinet and leader of the most important Labour movement on the Allied side. He found no conflict in this. He could be the Rt. Hon. Arthur Henderson one day, and close associate the next of such trade union leaders as Robert Williams, who told a party conference: "I say, praise God when there will be a notice 'to let' outside Buckingham Palace!" Henderson was happiest in double harness. We always think of him as one of a pair. Webb and Henderson devised the constitution for the Labour party in 1918; MacDonald and Henderson were denounced by Lenin as the two Socialist lackeys of Imperialism; J. H. Thomas replied "Me or 'Enderson" when asked who would be the first Labour Prime Minister; Lansbury and Henderson saved the soul of the Labour party in 1931. So now, in 1917, Henderson thought that he could work with Lloyd George to win the war, and with the Dissenters to win the peace.

The War Cabinet did not stomach this arrangement. When Henderson went over to support of the Stockholm conference, he found himself "on the mat" and was forced to resign. "I refused to do what I never will do, namely, desert the people who sent me into the government." He did not go into opposition. Though he resolved never again to join a government where Labour was not in a majority, he successfully resisted a proposal that the remaining Labour ministers should withdraw, on the ground that it would embarrass the government in its prosecution of the war. But his own path was fixed: though not in opposition, he was independent and intended to remain so. The Labour delegates were prevented from going to Stockholm; nevertheless the Labour movement, under Henderson's guidance, set out to create its own foreign policy. Thus resolved, where could it turn for ideas? Only to the U.D.C. The Union had staked its claim to provide an alternative foreign policy. Now it struck gold.

MacDonald was the most important link. His influence obviously increased when the Labour party drifted towards independence. His hand can be seen in the phrase in the party programme against "the old entanglements and mystifications of Secret Diplomacy and the formation of Leagues against Leagues." But all the intellectuals of the U.D.C. streamed into the Labour party, packing its Advisory Committee on International Questions—a sort of rival foreign office. Only Morel himself was absent. He was too independent to work under the guidance of others; and in any case was out of the way at this moment, sent to prison on the most forced charge ever trumped up against a critic even by the British government.[7] Not that the Labour party limited itself to the U.D.C. The Advisory Committee also contained members who supported the war—Toynbee, Hammond, J. L. Stocks, on one occasion a memorandum from Namier; and future Communists—Palme Dutt and Saklatvala. But the U.D.C. set the tone for them all.

The outcome was a statement of war aims, issued by the Labour party and the T.U.C. on 28 December 1917. Apart from a few changes of phrase, it was indistinguishable from proposals which the U.D.C. had made in July. There was the same repudiation of the old diplomacy, the same refusal to discriminate between enemies and allies, the same emphasis on reconciliation with Germany. But soon the Labour movement ran into a characteristic tangle. Henderson still wanted international action despite the failure of Stockholm. In February 1918 the T.U.C. and the Labour party organized an Inter-Allied Labour and Socialist conference—thus excluding the I.L.P. and the B.S.P. who would have had to be invited if the meeting had been called by the International Socialist Bureau. The conference turned the December statement upside down, largely under French prompting. The League of Nations was placed at the beginning, instead of appearing as a grudging addition, and military sanctions were added to it; Poland received special and mandatory recognition "with free access to the sea"; and a clause was put in, recognizing "the claims to independence made by the Czecho-Slovaks and the Yugo-Slavs." All this was in flagrant contradiction with the policy of the U.D.C. It caused endless confusion that the Labour party, true to Henderson's spirit, never decided between the two outlooks. It pursued both at once: approving the national claims to independence and sympathizing with the German grievances which these claims caused; demanding Poland's access to the sea and denouncing "the Corridor"; preaching pacifism and sanctions, disarmament and security. This is tiresome for those who want men and events to fall into a simple pattern, but this is how it was. If the Labour men were full of contradictions, so were their Radical predecessors; and so, for that matter, is everyone else.

Few noticed the contradiction at the time. The Labour party had

7. Morel sent a copy of *Truth and the War* to Romain Rolland who, he thought, was in France, but was actually in Switzerland. It was an offence to send printed matter to a neutral, though not to an allied, country; and on this thin charge Morel was sentenced to six months' hard labour. It is a wonder that the government did not manufacture evidence against his sexual morality.

spoken on foreign policy with one voice abroad and another at home even in Keir Hardie's days; and the habit was never lost. Now the declaration of Allied Socialists was clearly marked For Export; Labour policy continued to be found in the statement of December 1917 so far as the British public was concerned. This statement was to achieve a remarkable success. The government had hitherto evaded all demands for a definition of British war aims; and no doubt Lloyd George would have held out longer if parliament alone had been concerned. But he was anxious to keep the Labour movement in a good temper. On 5 January 1918 he called a meeting of trade union leaders and informed them that the government's policy was identical with that of the Labour statement, if in slightly different words.

MARY AGNES HAMILTON

Arthur Henderson Out of Office

Resignation was an order of release—moral release. He was busier than ever; the amount of constructive work put through in the six months after leaving the Government is astounding. But he was busy, now, in an atmosphere quite different from that in which he had been stifling during the previous months: a cleaner atmosphere. From the hothouse of Whitehall, where war had become an institution—as Colonel Repington puts it, "part of the natural law of our being"—he came back into bracing contact with the cold and grim reality of war as experienced by workers and soldiers. His natural idealism was charged with a new sense of purpose. Sacrifice must not be wasted; it must not be allowed to go on for ever, because nobody had the intellectual vitality and the common courage to reduce to terms what it was for: what victory meant.

When, in his letter of resignation, he said that he hoped still to be of service in the prosecution of the war, he meant it; but he was not prepared to accept war as "the natural law of our being," to be pursued for its own sake: to let the infernal machine run on till it ran down. He wanted victory expressed in selfless and democratic terms, and believed both that such expression would keep allies fighting and call forth a response from elements on the enemy side. This is the real issue

From *Arthur Henderson* by Mary Agnes Hamilton, London, William Heinemann Ltd., 1938, pp. 163–72. Reprinted by permission of the publisher.

behind his resignation. On this issue, Labour, under his renewed leadership, was largely converted in 1917 and 1918.

From August 1917, on, down to the end of the war and beyond that,
he was, for the Press, and even for sections of the ignorant public, the
villain of the piece. He was, of course, accused of crookedness; but
the real sting was not in this accusation, in which no one who ever
encountered him could believe. His crime was "defeatism." For *The
Times* and its satellites, the mark of defeatism was a demand for a
statement of war aims.

There were plenty of persons who took the view, quite simply and
sincerely, that to make any such demand was to play the enemy's
game. Up to August 1917, this was the view of a majority, both in the
Labour Party and among Trade Unionists; after August 1917, a large
minority went on in this view. . . . For Henderson, however, the issue
remained one of right, and never became one of indomitability. The
thing was a horror: a horror only justifiable in so far as, and for so
long as, it had a purpose, and a noble purpose. The institutional view
of war was, to him, hideous, even blasphemous. War was an abomination, even while he saw it as a necessary abomination, compelled by
human wickedness. He had, at no time, any kind of enjoyment in it. . . .

The effort to mobilise a diplomacy of democracy was his object now;
it was to go on being his object, to the day of his death. By far the
most important long-range result of his Russian experience is here. The
ideas he had learned to apply in industrial negotiation and conciliation,
he now began, slowly and steadily, to apply to the larger field of international relations. His international outlook, before dim and rather
conventional, now gradually became vivid and personal, and never
again left him. Stage by stage, too, the ideas he reached, and the
processes by which he reached them, were shared. He put them with
complete candour and a total freedom from any desire to "shine" by
difference, into the common pool. What he learned, that he communicated; as he learned, he also taught. He was always a little, but not too
far, ahead; he never got out of step with comrades whom he trusted
and in whose collective judgment he sincerely believed.

In September, the Trade Union Congress met at Blackpool. He went
as fraternal delegate from the Labour Party, and, so the official record
states, "was welcomed with a warmth of demonstration without precedent in the history of these gatherings." There was great applause when
he got up: an ovation positively tumultuous when he sat down. He
defended Stockholm. Stockholm might be dead; the idea of an Inter-

national Conference of workers was not dead. It "could be the finest expresssion of a League of Nations because it would be a League of the Common Peoples throughout the civilised world." He stated bluntly—some people, he knew, and said, would not like it—that, in his view, absolute government had got, first, to be replaced by free democracy:

> Is it too much to say that this great world conflict, which has entailed such tremendous sacrifices in blood, treasure and effort, can only be finally successful—and I emphasise that word finally, for I am afraid that some people mistake military victory for the final and complete success—can only be finally successful when autocratic government has been completely and for ever destroyed?

But—and here again he recognised that some would disagree—this was why—

> I would rather consult with the German minority before peace than I would with the representatives of a discredited government when a military victory has been secured. . . .

Smillie, like Hardie, MacDonald, Snowden, Anderson, had been critical of the war from the start; but Thomas and Clynes, Tom Shaw and John Hill had not. On war responsibility, division still yawned wide between the I.L.P. and the Trade Unions, and Henderson, on this, thought as the Trade Unions did. But, on the finding of "less humanly costly way" of achieving a good ending, the two sides were beginning to draw together. Henderson's resignation consolidated and accelerated a shift that had already begun; his weight behind the centre strengthened its pull; gave it a majority that steadily grew. So, the solid Trade Unionists at Blackpool hailed him, enthusiastically, when he took up the Stockholm challenge:

> The promoters of the Stockholm Conference in Great Britain were prepared to leave the settlement of the peace conditions to the Governments, who alone are responsible to the entire nation. But we of all classes have suffered so much—and which among us at these tables have not got lying beneath the sod a son or someone else who was near and dear to us?—we belong to the class which has given most and suffered most, and we shall not allow this matter to rest in the hands of diplomatists, secret plenipotentiaries, or politicians of the official stamp, unless they are prepared to have some regard for the opinion

of the common people. . . . The common people, the democracy, did nothing to create the conditions out of which the war
came; but the common people have done everything to realise
the ideals for which we entered the war.

I do not withdraw one word of what I have said. I stand by
my position. I am not here as an unofficial member of the House
of Commons merely because I supported the Stockholm Conference. I am here—as Gosling said—in "a position of greater
freedom and less responsibility" because I refused to do what
I never will do, namely, desert the people who sent me into the
Government.

The people who sent him into the Government in 1915 and again in
1916 were determined, now, that the objects of the war, as they had
believed in them, should be restated. They were beginning to feel real
doubts as to whether they had not been betrayed. Faced by any challenge they could see as a challenge of danger, they were there, staunch
and self-sacrificing as ever. There was no failure of nerve when the
"backs-to-the-wall" message came from Haig in the spring of 1918. But
refusal to state war aims was beginning to seem to them suspicious.

From the time of the Blackpool meeting, Henderson had the majority
of rank-and-file Unionists with him. His stand on Stockholm, and the
unjust abuse meted out to him, roused a passion of loyalty; the warmth
of welcome given him showed that, and also their gladness that he
was among them, not as a stuffy Cabinet minister, but as one of themselves. It earned the whole Party, and especially the Trade Union side,
plenty of abuse from the Press. But they were used to that.

At Blackpool, he brought the political and industrial wings, which
had been getting seriously out of touch with one another, into contact;
and, from this time on, he was at pains to keep that contact. Here,
Thomas, Clynes and Smillie were entirely at one with him. At a
meeting between the execuitves of the Party and the T.U.C., it was
agreed that the Labour movement should hammer out a statement of
its own on war aims, and then endeavour to secure Allied Socialist
agreement. From such Allied agreement, if it could be secured, they
would move on to the effort to bring about a full international Socialist
meeting—a Stockholm of their own, in fact. Henderson believed that
the working men of Germany and Austria would be shaken, if they
found that their comrades were intent on liberating, and not on en-
slaving, them. A sub-committee of the two executives was therefore

appointed to formulate a statement to be put before a special Labour Conference, if possible before the end of 1917.

This decision in itself represented a big forward move. Before the December Conference met, two events occurred which potently assisted the process of conversion to democratic diplomacy. On November 7th, the second Revolution in Russia took place. Lenin at once asked the Germans for an armistice; on the 24th, he issued an appeal to the world for a general truce. On November 29th, the *Daily Telegraph* published in its columns the famous Lansdowne letter: a temperate and far-seeing plea for a restatement and revision of war aims by the Allies. Lord Lansdowne showed great courage. He was, of course, denounced, as Henderson was denounced, as a defeatist and a traitor. But, although his plea met with little but abuse in England, it produced its effect; and the *Manchester Guardian* noted a fact not elsewhere revealed—the *Temps* and the other French journals welcomed it. M. Briand, indeed, told Colonel House, in Paris at the time for one of the recurring Inter-Allied meetings, that the Allies were now using force without brains, and the war would end sooner if the world were now plainly told on what terms Germany could have peace. "What is still lacking," Colonel House wrote to President Wilson, "and what this Conference has not brought about, is intelligent diplomatic direction." He agreed with Briand in wanting a "broad declaration of war aims that would . . . knit together the most unselfish opinions of the world."

At such a statement Henderson and his colleagues were at work. But how little the "most unselfish opinions of the world" were reflected in Cabinets, and why these Cabinets were unwilling to state their aims, and denounced anyone who asked to know them, was made plain when, on December 13th, 1917, the *Manchester Guardian* published the texts of a series of Secret Treaties between the Allies, mostly concluded in 1915. These the Bolshevik Government had released from the archives of the Russian Foreign Office. Here, nakedly revealed, were the "Imperialistic designs" that were attributed to Germany. The publication helped to set the stage for the special Labour Conference that met just after Christmas, 1917.

To the delegates, representing some three and a half million workers, a letter was read from the Premier, solemnly warning them off the grass. "A statement with regard to the war aims of the Allies can, of course, only be made in agreement with the other nations who are fighting together in the "war." Since an Inter-Allied Conference had just met and agreed on nothing, this *non-possumus* attitude was neither very helpful nor very sincere. Anyhow, within ten days, Mr. Lloyd George was to make the statement, which he, on December 28th, solemnly declared neither could nor should be made. The delegates listened to his letter, and then passed on to the business of the day— the full and very clear statement of war aims prepared by the joint committee. This was moved by Henderson. The document itself is a notable one. While frank and definite on the outline of a just territorial settlement, clear about Belgium and Alsace-Lorraine, and un-ambiguous about self-determination, it goes much beyond that, to lay down the framework of lasting peace. . . .

In the debate that followed, there were, of course, dissentient voices, loudly raised. A powerful section held to the view that any formulation of aims was a weakening in the face of the enemy. But the new co-operation of MacDonald and Henderson, Smillie and Thomas was telling; the Statement of Aims was accepted by 2,132,000 votes to 1,164,000.

Statement of War Aims of the Labour Party

As adopted at a joint conference of the societies affiliated with the British Trades Union Congress and the British Labour Party at Central Hall, Westminster, on December 28, 1917

1. THE WAR

The British Labour movement sees no reason to depart from the declaration unanimously agreed to at the Conference of the Socialist and Labour Parties of the Allied Nations on February 14, 1915, and it reaffirms that declaration. Whatever may have been the causes of the outbreak of war, it is clear that the peoples of Europe, who are necessarily the chief sufferers from its horrors, had themselves no hand in it. Their common interest is now so to conduct the terrible struggle in which they find themselves engaged as to bring it, as soon as may be possible, to an issue in a secure and lasting peace for the world.

2. MAKING THE WORLD SAFE FOR DEMOCRACY

Whatever may have been the causes for which the war was begun,

the fundamental purpose of the British Labour movement in supporting the continuance of the struggle is that the world may henceforth
be made safe for democracy.

Of all the war aims, none is so important to the peoples of the
world as that there shall be henceforth on earth no more war. Whoever triumphs, the people will have lost unless some effective method
of preventing war can be found.

As means to this end, the British Labour movement relies very
largely upon the complete democratisation of all countries; on the
frank abandonment of every form of Imperialism; on the suppression
of secret diplomacy, and on the placing of foreign policy, just as much
as home policy, under the control of popularly elected Legislatures; on
the absolute responsibility of the Foreign Minister of each country to
its Legislature; on such concerted action as may be possible for the
universal abolition of compulsory military service in all countries, the
common limitation of the costly armaments by which all peoples are
burdened, and the entire abolition of profit-making armament firms,
whose pecuniary interest lies always in war scares and rivalry in preparation for war.

But it demands, in addition, that it should be an essential part of
the treaty of peace itself that there should be forthwith established a
Supernational Authority, or League of Nations, which should not
only be adhered to by all the present belligerents, but which every
other independent sovereign state in the world should be pressed to
join; the immediate establishment of such League of Nations not only
of an International High Court for the settlement of all disputes
between states that are of justiciable nature, but also of appropriate
machinery for prompt and effective mediation between states at issue
that are not justiciable; the formation of an International Legislature,
in which the representatives of every civilised state would have their
allotted share; the gradual development, as far as may prove to be possible, of international legislation agreed to by and definitely binding
upon the several states, and for a solemn agreement and pledge by all
states that every issue between any two or more of them shall be submitted for settlement as aforesaid, and that they will all make common
cause against any state which fails to adhere to this agreement.

3. TERRITORIAL ADJUSTMENTS

The British Labour movement has no sympathy with the attempts
made, now in this quarter and now in that, to convert this war into

a war of conquest, whether what is sought to be acquired by force is territory or wealth, nor should the struggle be prolonged for a single day, once the conditions of a permanent peace can be secured, merely for the sake of extending the boundaries of any state.

But it is impossible to ignore the fact that, not only restitution and reparation, but also certain territorial readjustments are required if a renewal of armaments and war is to be avoided. These readjustments must be such as can be arrived at by common agreement on the general principle of allowing all people to settle their own destinies, and for the purpose of removing any obvious cause of future international conflict.

(A) BELGIUM

The British Labour movement emphatically insists that a foremost condition of peace must be the reparation by the German Government, under the direction of an International Commission, of the wrong admittedly done to Belgium; payment by that Government for all the damage that has resulted from this wrong, and the restoration of Belgium to complete and untrammelled independent sovereignty, leaving to the decision of the Belgian people the determination of their own future policy in all respects.

(B) ALSACE AND LORRAINE

The British Labour movement reaffirms its reprobation of the crime against the peace of the world by which Alsace and Lorraine were forcibly torn from France in 1871, a political blunder the effects of which have contributed in no small degree to the continuance of unrest and the growth of militarism in Europe; and, profoundly sympathising with the unfortunate inhabitants of Alsace and Lorraine, who have been subjected to so much repression, asks in accordance with the declarations of the French Socialists that they shall be allowed under the protection of the Supernational Authority, or League of Nations, freely to decide what shall be their future political position.

(C) THE BALKANS

The British Labour movement suggests that the whole problem of the reorganisation of the administration of the peoples of the Balkan Peninsula might be dealt with by a Special Conference of their representatives, or by an authoritative International Commission, on the basis of (a) the complete freedom of these people to settle their own

destinies, irrespective of Austrian, Turkish, or other foreign dominion;
(b) the independent sovereignties of the several nationalities in those
districts in which these are largely predominant; (c) the universal
adoption of religious tolerance, the equal citizenship of all races, and
local autonomy; (d) a Customs Union embracing the whole of the
Balkan States; and (e) the entry of all the Balkan National States into
a Federation for the concerted arrangement by mutual agreement
among themselves of all matters of common concern.

(D) ITALY

The British Labour movement declares its warmest sympathy with
the people of Italian blood and speech who have been left outside the
inconvenient and indefensible boundaries that have as a result of the
diplomatic agreements of the past been assigned to the kingdom of
Italy, and supports their claim to be united with those of their own race
and tongue. It realises that arrangements may be necessary for securing the legitimate interests of the people of Italy in the adjacent seas,
but it has no sympathy with the far-reaching aims of conquest of
Italian imperialism, and believes that all legitimate needs can be safe-
guarded without precluding a like recognition of the needs of others or
an annexation of other peoples' territories.

(E) POLAND, ETC.

With regard to the other cases in dispute, from Luxembourg on the
one hand, of which the independence has been temporarily destroyed,
to the lands now under foreign domination inhabited by other races—
the outstanding example being that of the Poles—the British Labour
movement relies, as the only way of achieving a lasting settlement, on
the application of the principle of allowing each people to settle its
own destiny.

(F) THE JEWS AND PALESTINE

The British Labour movement demands for the Jews of all countries
the same elementary rights of tolerance, freedom of residence and
trade, and equal citizenship that ought to be extended to all the inhabitants of every nation. But it further expresses the hope that it
may be practicable by agreement among all the nations to set free
Palestine from the harsh and oppressive government of the Turk, in
order that the country may form a free state, under international guarantee, to which such of the Jewish people as desire to do so may

return and may work out their own salvation, free from interference by those of alien race or religion.

(G) THE PROBLEM OF THE TURKISH EMPIRE

The whole civilised world condemns the handing back to the universally execrated rule of the Turkish Government any subject people which has once been freed from it. Thus, whatever may be proposed with regard to Armenia, Mesopotamia, and Arabia, they cannot be restored to the tyranny of the Sultan and his pashas.

The British Labour movement disclaims all sympathy with the imperialist aims of governments and capitalists who would make of these and other territories now dominated by the Turkish hordes merely instruments either of exploitation or militarism. If in these territories it is impracticable to leave it to the peoples to settle their own destinies, the British Labour movement insists that, conformably with the policy of "no annexations," they should be placed for administration in the hands of a commission acting under the Supernational Authority or League of Nations. It is further suggested that the peace of the world requires that Constantinople should be made a free port, permanently neutralised, and placed (together with both shores of the Dardanelles and possibly some or all of Asia Minor) under the same impartial administration.

(H) THE COLONIES OF TROPICAL AFRICA

With regard to the colonies of the several belligerents in tropical Africa from sea to sea—whether including all north of the Zambesi River and south of the Sahara Desert, or only those lying between 15 degrees north and 15 degrees south latitude, which are already the subject of international control—the British Labour movement disclaims all sympathy with the imperialist idea that these should form the booty of any nation, should be exploited for the profit of the capitalist, or should be used for the promotion of the militarist aims of governments. In view of the fact that it is impracticable here to leave the various peoples concerned to settle their own destinies, it is suggested that the interests of humanity would be best served by the full and frank abandonment by all the belligerents of any dreams of an African empire; the transfer of the present colonies of the European Powers in tropical Africa, however the limits of this area may be defined, to the proposed Supernational Authority or League of Nations herein suggested, and their administration under the legislative council of that authority as a single, independent African state, with its own trained staff, on the principles of (1) taking account in each locality of the wishes of the people when these can be ascertained; (2) protection of the natives against exploitation and oppression and the preservation of their tribal interests; (3) all revenues raised to be expended for the welfare and development of the African state itself, and (4) the permanent neutralisation of this African state and its abstention from participation in international rivalries or any future wars.

(I) OTHER CASES

The British Labour movement suggests that any other territories in which it is proposed that the future safeguarding of pacific relations makes necessary a transfer of sovereignty should be made the subject of amicable bargaining, with an equivalent exchange, in money or otherwise.

4. ECONOMIC RELATIONS

The British Labour movement declares against all the projects now being prepared by Imperialists and capitalists, not in any one country only, but in most countries, for an economic war after peace has been secured, either against one or other foreign nation, or against all foreign nations, as such an economic war, if begun by any country, would inevitably lead to reprisals, to which each nation in turn might in self-defence be driven.

It realises that all such attempts at economic aggression, whether by protective tariffs or capitalist trusts or monopolies, inevitably result in the spoliation of the working classes of the several countries for the profit of the capitalists; and the British workmen see in the alliance between the military Imperialists and the fiscal Protectionists in any country whatsoever, not only a serious danger to the prosperity of the masses of the people, but also a grave menace to peace.

On the other hand, if unfortunately a genuine peace cannot be secured, the right of each nation to the defence of its own economic interests, and, in face of the world shortage hereinafter mentioned, to the conservation for its own people of a sufficiency of its own supplies of foodstuffs and raw material cannot be denied.

The British Labour movement accordingly urges upon the Labour parties of all countries the importance of insisting, in the attitude of the Government towards commercial enterprises, along with the neces-

sary control of supplies for its own people, on the principle of the
open door, on customs duties being limited strictly to revenue purposes, and on there being no harsh discrimination against foreign
countries. But it urges equally the importance, not merely of conservation, but also of the utmost possible development by appropriate Government action of the resources of every country for the benefit not
only of its own people, but also of the world, and the need for an
international agreement for the enforcement in all countries of the
legislation on factory conditions, hours of labour, and the prevention
of sweating and unhealthy trades necessary to protect the workers
against exploitation and oppression.

5. THE PROBLEMS OF PEACE

To make the world safe for democracy involves much more than
the prevention of war, either military or economic. It will be a device
of the capitalist interests to pretend that the treaty of peace need
concern itself only with the cessation of the struggle of the armed
forces and with any necessary territorial readjustments. The British
Labour movement insists that in view of the probable world-wide
shortage after the war of exportable foodstuffs and raw materials, and
of merchant shipping, it is imperative, in order to prevent the most
serious hardships and even possible famine, in one country or another,
that systematic arrangements should be made on an international basis
for the allocation and conveyance of the available exportable surpluses
of these commodities to the different countries in proportion not to
their purchasing powers, but to their several pressing needs, and that
within each country the Government must for some time maintain its
control of the most indispensable commodities in order to secure their
appropriation, not in a competitive market mainly to the richer classes
in proportion to their means, but systematically to meet the most
urgent needs of the whole community on the principle of "No cake
for any one until all have bread."

Moreover, it cannot but be anticipated that in all countries the dislocation of industry attendant on peace, the instant discharge of millions of munition workers and workers in war trades, and the de-
mobilisation of soldiers—in face of the scarcity of industrial capital,
the shortage of raw materials, and the insecurity of commercial enterprise—will, unless prompt and energetic action be taken by the several
Governments, plunge a large part of the wage-earning population into
all the miseries of unemployment more or less prolonged. In view of

the fact that widespread unemployment in any country, like a famine, is an injury not to that country alone, but impoverishes also the rest of the world, the British Labour movement holds that it is the duty of every government to take immediate action, not merely to relieve the unemployment when unemployment has set in, but actually, so far as may be practicable to prevent the occurrence of unemployment.

It therefore urges upon the Labour Parties of every country the necessity of their pressing upon their governments the preparation of plans for the execution of all the innumerable public works (such as the making and repairing of roads and railways, the erection of schools and public buildings, the provision of working class dwellings, and the reclamation and afforestation of land) that will be required in the near future, not for the sake of finding measures of relief for the unemployed, but with a view to these works being undertaken at such a rate in each locality as will suffice, together with the various capitalist enterprises that may be in progress, to maintain at a fairly uniform level year by year, and throughout each year, the aggregate demand for labour, and thus prevent there being any unemployed. It is now known that in this way it is quite possible for any government to prevent, if it chooses, the very occurrences of any widespread or prolonged involuntary unemployment, which, if it is now in any country allowed to occur, is as much the result of government neglect as is any epidemic disease.

6. RESTORATION AND REPARATION

The British Labour movement holds that one of the most imperative duties of all governments immediately peace is declared will be the restoration, so far as may be possible, of the homes, farms, factories, public buildings, and means of communication in France, Belgium, Tyrol and North Italy, East Prussia, Poland, Galicia, Russia, Rumania, the Balkans, Greece, Armenia, Asia Minor, and Central Africa, that the restoration should not be limited to compensation for public buildings, capitalist undertakings, and material property proved to be destroyed or damaged, but should be extended to setting up wage earners and peasants themselves in homes and employments, and that to insure the full and impartial application of these principles the assessment and distribution of the compensation so far as the cost is contributed by any international fund should be made under the direction of an international commission.

But the British Labour movement will not be satisfied unless there

is a full and free judicial investigation into the accusations so freely
made on all sides that particular governments have ordered, and particular officers have exercised, acts of cruelty, oppression, violence and
theft against individual victims for which no justification can be found
in the ordinary usages of war. It draws attention in particular to the
loss of life and property of merchant seamen and other non-com-
batants (including women and children) resulting from this inhuman
and ruthless conduct.

It should be part of the conditions of peace that there should be
forthwith set up a court of claims and accusations, which should investigate all such allegations as may be brought before it, summon the
accused person or government to answer the complaint, to pronounce
judgment and award compensation or damages, payable by the individual or government condemned, to the persons who had suffered
wrong, or to their dependents. The several governments must be
responsible, financially and otherwise, for the presentation of the cases
of their respective nationals to such a court of claims and accusations.

Labour Party Constitution of 1918

1.—NAME.

The Labour Party.

2.—MEMBERSHIP.

The Labour Party shall consist of all its affiliated organisations,*
together with those men and women who are individual members of a
Local Labour Party and who subscribe to the Constitution and Programme of the Party.

3.—PARTY OBJECTS.

NATIONAL

(a) To organise and maintain in Parliament and in the country a
Political Labour Party, and to ensure the establishment of a Local
Labour Party in every County Constituency and every Parliamentary

* Trade Unions, Socialist Societies, Co-operative Societies, Trades Councils, and
Local Labour Parties.

Borough, with suitable divisional organisation in the separate constituencies of Divided Boroughs;

(*b*) To co-operate with the Parliamentary Committee of the Trades Union Congress, or other Kindred Organisations, in joint political or other action in harmony with the Party Constitution and Standing Orders;

(*c*) To give effect as far as may be practicable to the principles from time to time approved by the Party Conference;

(*d*) To secure for the producers by hand or by brain the full fruits of their industry, and the most equitable distribution thereof that may be possible, upon the basis of the common ownership of the means of production and the best obtainable system of popular administration and control of each industry or service;

(*e*) Generally to promote the Political, Social, and Economic Emancipation of the People, and more particularly of those who depend directly upon their own exertions by hand or by brain for the means of life.

INTER-DOMINION.

(*f*) To co-operate with the Labour and Socialist organisations in the Dominions and Dependencies with a view to promoting the purposes of the Party and to take common action for the promotion of a higher standard of social and economic life for the working population of the respective countries.

INTERNATIONAL.

(*g*) To co-operate with the Labour and Socialist organisations in other countries, and to assist in organising a Federation of Nations for the maintenance of Freedom and Peace, for the establishment of suitable machinery for the adjustment and settlement of International Disputes by Conciliation or Judicial Arbitration, and for such International Legislation as may be practicable.

4.—PARTY PROGRAMME.

(*a*) It shall be the duty of the Party Conference to decide, from time to time, what specific proposals of legislative, financial, or administrative reform shall receive the general support of the Party, and be promoted, as occasion may present itself, by the National Executive and the Parliamentary Labour Party: provided that no such proposal shall be made definitely part of the General Programme of the Party unless it has been adopted by the Conference by a majority of not less than two-thirds of the votes recorded on a card vote.

(*b*) It shall be the duty of the National Executive and the Parliamentary Labour Party, prior to every General Election, to define the principal issues for that Election which in their judgment should be made the Special Party Programme for that particular Election Campaign, which shall be issued as a manifesto by the Executive to all constituencies where a Labour candidate is standing.

(*c*) It shall be the duty of every Parliamentary representative of the Party to be guided by the decision of the meetings of such Parliamentary representatives, with a view to giving effect to the decisions of the Party Conference as to the General Programme of the Party.

5.—THE PARTY CONFERENCE.

1. The work of the Party shall be under the direction and control of the Party Conference, which shall itself be subject to the Constitution and Standing Orders of the Party. The Party Conference shall meet regularly once in each year, and also at such other times as it may be convened by the National Executive.

2. The Party Conference shall be constituted as follows:—

(*a*) Trade Unions and other societies affiliated to the Party may send one delegate for each thousand members on which fees are paid.

(*b*) Local Labour Party delegates may be either men or women resident or having a place of business in the constituency they represent, and shall be appointed as follows:—

In Borough and County Constituencies returning one Member to Parliament, the Local Labour Party may appoint one delegate.

In undivided Boroughs returning two Members, two delegates may be appointed.

In divided Boroughs one delegate may be appointed for each separate constituency within the area. The Local Labour Party within the constituency shall nominate and the Central Labour Party of the Divided Borough shall appoint the delegates. In addition to such delegates, the Central Labour Party in each Divided Borough may appoint one delegate.

An additional woman delegate may be appointed for each constituency in which the number of affiliated and individual women members exceeds 500.

(c) Trades Councils under Section 8, clause c, shall be entitled to one delegate.

(d) The members of the National Executive, including the Treasurer, the members of the Parliamentary Labour Party, and the duly-sanctioned Parliamentary Candidates shall be *ex officio* members of the Party Conference, but shall, unless delegates, have no right to vote.

6.—THE NATIONAL EXECUTIVE.

(a) There shall be a National Executive of the Party consisting of twenty-three members (including the Treasurer) elected by the Party Conference at its regular Annual Meeting, in such proportion and under such conditions as may be set out in the Standing Orders for the time being in force, and this National Executive shall, subject to the control and directions of the Party Conference, be the Administrative Authority of the Party.

(b) The National Executive shall be responsible for the conduct of the general work of the Party. The National Executive shall take steps to ensure that the Party is represented by a properly constituted organisation in each constituency in which this is found practicable; it shall give effect to the decisions of the Party Conference; and it shall interpret the Constitution and Standing Orders and Rules of the Party in all cases of dispute subject to an appeal to the next regular Annual Meeting of the Party Conference by the organisation or person concerned.

(c) The National Executive shall confer with the Parliamentary Labour Party at the opening of each Parliamentary Session, and also at any other time when the National Executive or the Parliamentary Party may desire such conference, on any matters relating to the work and progress of the Party, or to the efforts necessary to give effect to the General Programme of the Party.

7.—PARLIAMENTARY CANDIDATURES.

(a) The National Executive shall co-operate with the Local Labour Party in any constituency with a view to nominating a Labour Candidate at any Parliamentary General or Bye-Election. Before any Parliamentary Candidate can be regarded as finally adopted for a constituency as a Candidate of the Labour Party, his candidature must be sanctioned by the National Executive.

(*b*) Candidates approved by the National Executive shall appear before their constituencies under the designation of "Labour Candidate" only. At any General Election they shall include in their Election Addresses and give prominence in their campaigns to the issues for that Election as defined by the National Executive from the General Party Programme. If they are elected they shall act in harmony with the Constitution and Standing Orders of the Party in seeking to discharge the responsibilities established by Parliamentary practice.

(*c*) Party Candidates shall receive financial assistance for election expenditure from the Party funds on the following basis:—

Borough Constituencies, £1 per 1,000 electors.

County Divisions, £1 15s. per 1,000 electors.

8.—Affiliation Fees.

1. Trade Unions, Socialist Societies, Co-operative Societies, and other organisations directly affiliated to the Party (but not being affiliated Local Labour Parties or Trades Councils) shall pay 2d. per member per annum to the Central Party Funds with a minimum of 30s.

The membership of a Trade Union for the purpose of this clause shall be those members contributing to the political fund of the Union established under the Trade Union Act, 1913.

2. The affiliation of Trades Councils will be subject to the following conditions:—

(*a*) Where Local Labour Parties and Trades Councils at present exist in the same area every effort must be made to amalgamate these bodies, retaining in one organisation the industrial and political functions, and incorporating the constitution and rules for Local Labour Parties in the rules of the amalgamated body.

(*b*) Where no Local Labour Party is in existence and the Trades Council is discharging the political functions, such Trades Council shall be eligible for affiliation as a Local Labour Party, providing that its rules and title be extended so as to include Local Labour Party functions.

(*c*) Where a Local Labour Party and a Trades Council exist in the same area, the Trades Council shall be eligible to be affiliated to the

Local Labour Party, but not to the National Party, except in such cases where the Trades Council was affiliated to the National Party prior to November 1st, 1917. In these cases the Executive Committee shall have power to continue national affiliation on such conditions as may be deemed necessary.

(*d*) Trades Councils included under Section (*c*) shall pay an annual affiliation fee of 30s.

Local Labour Parties must charge individually enrolled members, male a minimum of 1s. per annum, female 6d. per annum; and 2d. per member so collected must be remitted to the Central Office with a minimum of 30s., as the affiliation fee of such Local Labour Party.

In addition to these payments, a delegation fee of 5s. to the Party Conference or any Special Conference may be charged.

STANDING ORDERS.

1.—ANNUAL CONFERENCE.

1. The National Executive shall convene the Annual Party Conference for the month of June (but not at Whitsuntide) in each year, subject to the Constitution and the Standing Orders, and shall convene other Sessions of the Party Conference from time to time as may be required.

2. In the event of it being necessary to convene the Party Conference upon short notice, in order to deal with some sudden emergency, the Secretaries of the affiliated organisations and Local Labour Parties shall, on receiving the summons, instantly take such action as may be necessary to enable the Society or Constituency to be represented, in accordance with the rules.

3. Any Session of the Party Conference summoned with less than ten days' notice shall confine its business strictly to that relating to the emergency, which cannot without detriment to the Party be postponed.

4. Persons eligible as delegates must be paying *bona fide* members, or paid permanent officials of the organisation sending them.

5. No delegate to the Conference shall represent more than one Society.

6. Members of affiliated organisations claiming exemption from political contributions under the Trade Union Act, 1913, shall not be entitled to act as delegates.

2.—AGENDA.

1. Notice of Resolutions for the Annual Conference shall be sent to the Secretary at the Office of the Party not later than April 1st, for inclusion in the first Agenda, which shall be forthwith issued to the affiliated organisations.

2. Notice of Amendments to the Resolutions in the first Agenda, and Nominations for the Executive, Treasurer, Auditors (2), Annual Conference Arrangements Committee (5), shall be forwarded to the Secretary not later than May 16th, for inclusion in the final Agenda of the Annual Conference.

3. No business which does not arise out of the Resolutions on the Agenda shall be considered by the Party Conference, unless recommended by the Executive or the Conference Arrangements Committee.

4. When the Annual Conference has, by resolution, made a declaration of a general policy or principle, no motion having for its object the reaffirmation of such policy or principle shall appear on the Agenda for a period of three years from the time such declaration was made, except such resolutions as are, in the opinion of the Executive, of immediate importance.

3.—VOTING.

Voting at the Party Conference shall be by Cards issued as follows:—

Trade Unions and other affiliated Societies shall receive one Voting Card for each 1,000 members or fraction thereof paid for.

Trades Councils affiliated under Section 8, clause *c,* shall receive one voting card.

Every Local Labour Party shall receive one Voting Card for each delegate sent in respect of each Parliamentary Constituency within its area.

Central Labour Parties in Divided Boroughs shall receive one voting card.

4.—NATIONAL EXECUTIVE.

1. The National Executive shall be elected by the Annual Conference as a whole, and shall consist, apart from the Treasurer, of (*a*) 13

representatives of the affiliated organisations; (b) five representatives of the Local Labour Parties; and (c) four women. The Executive shall be elected by ballot vote on the card basis from three lists of nominations.

2. Each affiliated national organisation shall be entitled to nominate one candidate for List A; and two candidates if the membership exceeds 500,000. Each candidate must be a *bona-fide* member of the organisation by which he or she is nominated.

3. Each Parliamentary Constituency organisation, through its Local Labour Party or Trades Council, may nominate one candidate for List B, and the candidate so nominated must be resident or have his or her place of business within the area of the nominating Local Labour Party.

4. Each affiliated organisation shall be entitled to nominate one woman candidate for List C, and two candidates if the membership exceeds 500,000; whether such nominees are or are not members of the nominating organisation.

5. The National Executive shall elect its own Chairman and Vice-Chairman at its first meeting each year, and shall see that all its officers and members conform to the Constitution and Standing Orders of the Party. The National Executive shall present to the Annual Conference a Report covering the work and progress of the Party during its year of office, together with the Financial Statement and Accounts duly audited.

6. No member of the Parliamentary Committee of the Trades Union Congress is eligible for nomination to the National Executive.

SUGGESTIONS FOR
FURTHER READING

For a general account one should use the standard histories of the period: the somewhat out-dated but solid R. C. K. Ensor *England 1870–1914* (1936) and its successor volume, A. J. P. Taylor *English History 1914–1945* (1965); Charles Loch Mowat *Britain Between the Wars 1918–1940* (1955); and Alfred F. Havighurst *Twentieth-Century Britain* (second edition) (1966).

Students who wish to pursue Labour party history should consult Carl Brand *The British Labour Party a Short History* (1964) as well as his *British Labour's Rise to Power* (1941); Philip P. Poirier *The Advent of the British Labour Party* (1958); Henry Pelling *The Origins of the Labour Party 1880–1900* (1954); Richard W. Lyman *The First Labour Government 1924* (1957); Stephen R. Graubard *British Labour and the Russian Revolution* (1956). Two books which should be of great value when they appear will be Philip Poirier's second volume and the second volume of H. A. Clegg, Alan Fox and A. F. Thompson *A History of British Trade Unions since 1889* (1964). The first volume, very useful itself, discusses the Union movement until 1910.

Biographies and autobiographies of practically all the major figures exist, of varying value. Of particular interest are Philip Snowden *Autobiography*, two vols. (1934), J. R. Clynes *Memoirs*, two vols. (1937 & 1938), Alan Bullock *The Life and Times of Ernest Bevin*, two vols. (1960 & 1967). David Marquand is writing the definitive biography of Ramsay MacDonald. There is no biography to scale of Lloyd George: the best extant is Thomas Jones *Lloyd George* (1951). An important essay on Arthur Henderson's later role in foreign policy is by Henry Winkler in Gordon A. Craig and Felix Gilbert eds. *The Diplomats* (1953).

335